Clashing Views on

African Issues

SECOND EDITION

TAKING SIDES

Clashing Views on

African Issues

SECOND EDITION

Selected, Edited, and with Introductions by

William G. Moseley
Macalester College

Contemporary Learning Series

A Division of The McGraw-Hill Companies

For Julia, Ben, and Sophie

Photo Acknowledgment
Cover image: William G. Moseley

Cover acknowledgment
Maggie Lytle

Manufactured in the United States of America

Second Edition

123456789DOCDOC9876

Library of Congress Cataloging-in-Publication Data
Main entry under title:
Taking sides: clashing views on African issues/selected, edited, and with introductions by William G. Moseley.—2nd ed.

Includes bibliographical references and index.
I. Africa—Politics and government—1989– II. Africa—Social conditions—1989– III. Africa—Economic conditions—1989– IV. Africa—Civilization—21st century.
1. Moseley, William G. ed. 2 Series.
916

0-07-351507-8
978-0-07-351507-6
1545-5327

Printed on Recycled Paper

Preface

This volume's cover photo features a South African woman who had recently received land under that country's land reform program. When I met her two years ago, she was extremely proud to finally be a land owner. Of course, this image, and the story of the woman behind it, says a lot about Africa today. The fact that she had limited access to high-quality farmland up until this point has everything to do with the legacy of colonialism and the policies of the former apartheid regime in South Africa. It also reflects the strength, determination, ingenuity, and pride of producing food for her family and country. As is the case for women in other parts of the word, African women suffer from discrimination and inequality. Yet, despite these disadvantages, African women are actively shaping the future of their continent. They form the backbone of the rural economy in many African settings where it is estimated that they produce 70 percent of the food supply. They are also beginning to take on formal leadership roles. At the time of writing, Ellen Johnson-Sirleaf had recently been elected as the new president of Liberia. With impeccable credentials, it is now hoped that she will be the catalyst needed to rebuild her country following several years of intense civil war.

I find studying Africa so exciting and captivating in part due to the types of issues discussed above. I have been working and conducting research in Africa for over 19 years now, originally as a development professional and currently as an academic. My applied work and research have led to extended stays in several African countries (Mali, Zimbabwe, South Africa, Malawi, Niger, and Lesotho) and to travel in many others. This firsthand experience with nuts-and-bolts development issues, as well as vital research questions, has led me to care deeply about Africa as a region and to grapple intellectually with many of the issues presented in this volume.

I have been fortunate to share my fascination for the African continent with (and learn from) some incredibly bright, insightful, and engaged students. Like other academics who have been bitten by the Africa bug, it is during my Africa course each spring that I find my own and my students' enthusiasm for the subject to be most infectious. I hope this volume will serve as a useful platform for discussions in courses offered in a variety of departments dealing with contemporary African issues, including anthropology, African studies, development studies, economics, geography, history, international studies, political science, and sociology. I find that the best way to encourage students to grapple with their preconceptions about Africa is to offer readings that both support and contradict their initial leanings. Through the process of reviewing different arguments and discussing them with their classmates, individual students continually surprise me by the degree to which their positions may change during the course of a semester (far more than if I had tried to convince them of the validity of a certain perspective). Of course, there is no obvious right or wrong to many of these issues, and some of the most rewarding class discussions occur when there is no clear majority of students for one position or the other.

Changes to this edition The second edition has been extensively revised and updated. Based on the feedback of reviews of the first edition, a new section on history has been added, featuring two completely new issues: *Did the Trans-Atlantic Slave Trade Underdevelop Africa?* (Issue 2) and *Have the Contributions of Africans Been Recognized for Developing New World Agriculture?* (Issue 3). In addition to the four new selections added to address these issues, eight other selections have also been incorporated in order to update the issues or sharpen the debate. In all, 12 of the 40 selections, or 30 percent of the material, have been changed. Additional revisions include fine-tuning the questions, reordering the material in the book, and rewriting the introductions and postscripts.

A word to the instructor An *Instructor's Manual With Test Questions* (multiple choice and essay) is available through the publisher for the instructor using Taking Sides in the classroom. Also available is a general guidebook, *Using Taking Sides in the Classroom*, which offers suggestions for adapting the pro-con approach in the classroom setting. An online version of *Using Taking Sides in the Classroom* and a correspondence service for Taking Sides adopters can be found at http://www.mhcls.com/usingts/.

Taking Sides: Clashing Views on African Issues is only one title in the Taking Sides series. If you are interested in seeing the table of contents for any of the other titles, please visit the Taking Sides Web site at http://www.mhcls.com/takingsides/.

Acknowledgements I am grateful to several students at Macalester College, especially Cole Akeson, Roland McKay, and Wes Hart, who helped me with various aspects of this text. I wish to acknowledge James Burns, Judith Carney, Max Edelson, Hilary Jones, Ron Ward, and several anonymous reviewers who provided me with invaluable feedback during the first or second editions of this volume. I thank my spouse, Julia, and children, Ben and Sophie, for their shared enthusiasm for Africa. I finally wish to acknowledge the editorial staff at McGraw-Hill, especially Larry Loeppke, Susan Brusch, Jill Peter, and Jane Mohr, for their copy editing, insight, and encouragement.

William G. Moseley
Macalester College

Contents In Brief

Contents

PART 1   INTRODUCTION AND HISTORY   1

Issue 1.   Are the Experts on Africa Part of the Problem?   2

YES: **Gavin Kitching,** from "Why I Gave Up African Studies," *African Studies Review and Newsletter* (June 2000) 4

NO: **Marc Epprecht,** from "Why I Love African Studies," *African Studies Quarterly* (2003) 9

Gavin Kitching, professor of political science at the University of New South Wales, left the field of African studies because he "found it depressing." According to Kitching, Africanist scholars have failed to see Africa's own ruling elites as the principal culprits for the continent's dire predicament. He suggests that we "have to ask what it is about the history and culture of sub-Saharan Africa that has led to ... its disastrous present." Marc Epprecht, professor of history at Queens University, is more upbeat, noting a number of African countries that have made great strides. He accepts that African elites are responsible for the welfare of their populations, but also recognizes that they "are enormously, often fatally constrained by pressure from the outside." He argues that Africanist scholars have an important role to play by holding decision makers in the West accountable for policies that further marginalize Africa.

Issue 2.   Did the Trans-Atlantic Slave Trade Underdevelop Africa?   14

YES: **Paul E. Lovejoy,** from "The Impact of the Atlantic Slave Trade on Africa: A Review of the Literature," *Journal of African History* (1989) 16

NO: **John Thornton,** from *Africa and the Africans in the Making of the Atlantic World, 1400–1680* (Cambridge University Press, 1992) 25

Paul Lovejoy, professor of history at York University, argues that the trans-Atlantic slave trade significantly transformed African society. It led to an absolute loss of population on the continent and a large increase in the enslaved population that was retained in Africa. The economic advantages of exporting slaves did not offset the social and political costs of participation, there were disastrous demographic impacts, and Africa's relative position in world trade declined. Lovejoy, therefore, supports the "transformation thesis," which holds that the external slave trade dramatically reshaped slavery and society in Africa. John Thornton, professor of history at Boston University, holds a very different view. He notes that slavery was widespread and indigenous in African society. Europeans simply worked with this existing market and African merchants, who were not dominated by Europeans, responded by providing more slaves. African leaders who allowed the slave trade to continue were neither forced to do so against their will, nor did they make irrational decisions. As such, the preexisting institution of slavery in Africa is as much responsible as any external force for the development of the trans-Atlantic slave trade.

Issue 3.   Have the Contributions of Africans Been Recognized for Developing New World Agriculture?   36

YES: Duncan Clinch Heyward, from *Seed from Madagascar* (The University of North Carolina Press, 1937)   38

NO: Judith Carney, from "Agroenvironments and Slave Strategies in the Diffusion of Rice Culture to the Americas," in Karl S. Zimmerer and Thomas J. Bassett, eds., *Political Ecology: An Integrative Approach to Geography and Environment-Development Studies* (The Guilford Press, 2003)   42

Duncan Heyward, a former Carolina rice planter writing in the middle of the last century, represents the mainstream view that Europeans were primarily responsible for developing South Carolina's remarkable rice plantations in the eighteenth century. In his own accounting of the rise of rice cultivation in the Carolinas, Heyward suggests that the techniques and approaches must have been derived from those observed in China. Judith Carney, a professor of geography at UCLA, explains that slaves from rice-producing areas in West Africa have only recently been recognized for their intellectual contributions to the development of rice cultivation in the New World. Carney describes how her work, and that of others, challenged the view that slaves were mere field hands, "showing that they contributed agronomic expertise as well as skilled labor to the emergent plantation economy."

Issue 4.   Did Colonialism Distort Contemporary African Development?

YES: Marcus Colchester, from "Slave and Enclave: Towards a Political Ecology of Equatorial Africa," *The Ecologist* (September/October 1993)   56

NO: Robin M. Grier, from "Colonial Legacies and Economic Growth," *Public Choice* (March 1999)   65

Marcus Colchester, director of the Forest Peoples Programme of the World Rainforest Movement, argues that rural communities in equatorial Africa are today on the point of collapse because they have been weakened by centuries of outside intervention. In Gabon, the Congo, and the Central African Republic, an enduring colonial legacy of the French are lands and forests controlled by state institutions that operate as patron-client networks to enrich indigenous elite and outside commercial interests. Robin M. Grier, assistant professor of economics at the University of Oklahoma, contends that African colonies that were held for longer periods of time tend to have performed better, on average, after independence.

PART 2   DEVELOPMENT   71

Issue 5.   Have Structural Adjustment Policies Worked for Africa?   72

YES: Gerald Scott, from "Who Has Failed Africa? IMF Measures or the African Leadership?" *Journal of Asian and African Studies* (August 1998)   74

NO: Thandika Mkandawire, from "The Global Economic Context," in Ben Wisner, Camilla Toulmin, and Rutendo Chitiga, eds., *Towards a New Map of Africa* (Earthscan, 2005)   82

Gerald Scott, an economist at Florida State University, argues that structural adjustment programs are the most promising option for promoting economic growth in Africa. He disputes the evidence used to suggest that these programs have a deleterious effect on economic growth in Africa. Thandika Mkandawire, director of the UN Research Institute for Social Development, counters that, while African governments have reshaped domestic policies to make their economies more open, growth has faltered. Mkandawire assesses structural adjustment from a developmental perspective, judging its effects on economic development and the eradication of poverty. He suggests that structural adjustment policies designed to integrate Africa into the global economy have failed because "they have completely sidestepped the developmental needs of the continent and the strategic questions on the form of integration appropriate to addressing these needs."

Bernard Lecomte, co-founder of Six-S, and Anirudh Krishna, assistant professor of public policy studies and political science at Duke University, describe one of the most acclaimed NGO initiatives in Africa, the Six-S network in Burkina Faso, Mali and Senegal. The network supports village groups' efforts to combat drought and poverty. The goal of Six-S has been for "village groups to gain expertise and confidence and to establish themselves as viable, independent agencies for local development, with little residual support from Six-S." Giles Mohan, a lecturer in development studies at the Open University, presents a case study of NGO intervention in northern Ghana. His examination reveals that tensions exist between the northern NGO and its partners, that local NGOs create their own mini-empires of client villages, and that some NGO officers use their organizations for personal promotion.

Dorothy Logie, a general practitioner and active member of Medact, and Michael Rowson, assistant director of Medact, argue that debt is a human-rights issue because debt and related structural adjustment policies reduce the state's ability to address discrimination, vulnerability, and inequality. Debt relief, if channeled in the right direction, could help reduce poverty and promote health. Robert Snyder, an associate professor of biology at Greenville College, counters that debt cancellation will only work if the factors that created debt in the first place are addressed. He uses a case study of Rwanda to demonstrate why political and social change must occur for debt forgiveness to work.

Oliver Maponga, Economic Affairs Officer at the United Nations Economic
Commission for Africa, and Philip Maxwell, professor at the Western
Australian School of Mines at Curtin University of Technology, describe a
resurgence in the African mining industry in the 1990s after several lackluster
decades. They assert that mineral and energy mining can make a positive
contribution to economic development in Africa. Sunday Dare, a Nigerian
journalist, describes how "much sorrow has flowed" from Africa's resource
blessing. While Dare blames African leaders for corruption and resource
mismanagement, he also implicates transnational corporations (TNCs) as key
contributors to this problem. He states that TNCs have acted as economic
predators that support repressive African leaders in order to garner
uninterrupted access to resources. The result, Dare suggests, is that Africa's
"raw materials are still being depleted without general development."

Jesse Machuka, a Kenyan scientist in the department of biochemistry and
biotechnology at Kenyatta University, argues that agricultural biotechnology
will substantially increase food production by rural resource-poor farmers.
Machuka suggests that agricultural biotechnology will help address several
constraints to crop production, including pests, diseases, weeds,
environmental degradation, and soil nutrient depletion. He is particularly
concerned that biotechnology research be undertaken by Africans for
Africans. In a case study examining attempts to control the parasitic Striga
weed, Brian Halweil, a research associate at the Worldwatch Institute,
questions whether producing maize that is bio-engineered for herbicide
resistance is really the best approach in the African context. He suggests
that improved soil fertility management practices and mixed cropping are
more appropriate and accessible strategies.

Michael Mortimore, a geographer, and Mary Tiffen, a historian and socioeconomist, both with Drylands Research, investigate population and food production trajectories in Machakos, Kenya. They determine that increasing population density has a positive influence on environmental management and crop production. Furthermore, they found that food production kept up with population growth from 1930 to 1987. John Murton, with the Foreign and Commonwealth Office of the British government, uses household-level data to show that the changes in Machakos described by Mortimore and Tiffen "have been accompanied by a polarization of land holdings, differential trends in agricultural productivity, and a decline in food self-sufficiency." As such, he argues that the "Machakos experience" of population growth and positive environmental transformation is neither homogenous nor fully unproblematic.

William D. Newmark, research curator at the Utah Museum of Natural History, University of Utah, and John L. Hough, global environment facility coordinator for biodiversity and international waters for the United Nations Development Programme, acknowledge the limited success of integrated conservation and development programs to date in Africa, but see great promise for success in the future. They call for more adaptive management in which activities are monitored, evaluated, and reformulated in an interactive fashion. Roderick P. Neumann, associate professor and director of graduate studies in the department of international relations at Florida International University, argues that protected area buffer zone programs have not lived up to their initial intent of greater participation and benefit sharing. Rather, these programs duplicate more coercive forms of conservation practice associated with parks and facilitate the expansion of state authority into remote rural areas.

World Bank economists Kevin M. Cleaver and Götz A. Schreiber argue that Africa is engaged in a downward spiral of population growth, poor agricultural performance, and environmental degradation. Academic geographers Thomas J. Bassett and Koli Bi Zuéli, counter that it is dominant perceptions of environmental change, rather than concrete evidence, that lie behind the widely held belief that Africa is engaged in an "environmental crisis of staggering proportions."

PART 4 SOCIAL ISSUES 239

Fuambai Ahmadu, an anthropologist at the London School of Economics, finds it increasingly challenging to reconcile her own experiences with female initiation and circumcision and prevailing (largely negative) global discourses on these practices. Her main concern with most studies on female initiation is the insistence that the practice is necessarily harmful or that there is an urgent need to stop female genital mutilation in communities where it is done. She suggests that "the aversion of some writers to the practice of female circumcision has more to do with deeply imbedded western cultural assumptions regarding women's bodies and their sexuality than with disputable health effects of genital operations on African women." Liz Creel, senior policy analyst at the Population Reference Bureau, and her colleagues argue that female genital cutting (FGC), while it must be dealt with in a culturally sensitive manner, is a practice that is detrimental to the health of girls and women, as well as a violation of human rights in most instances. Creel et al. recommend that African governments pass anti-FGC laws, and that programs be expanded to educate communities about FGC and human rights.

Richard A. Schroeder, an associate professor of geography at Rutgers University, presents a case study of a group of female gardeners in The Gambia who, because of their growing economic clout, began to challenge male power structures. Women, who were the traditional gardeners in the community studied, came to have greater income earning capacity than men as the urban market for garden produce grew. Furthermore, women could meet their needs and wants without recourse to their husbands because of this newly found economic power. Human Rights Watch, a nonprofit organization, describes how women in Kenya have property rights unequal to those of men, and how even these limited rights are frequently violated. It is further explained how women have little awareness of their rights, that those "who try to fight back are often beaten, raped, or ostracized," and how the Kenyan government has done little to address the situation.

Akin Jimoh, program director of Development Communications, a non-governmental organization (NGO) based in Lagos, Nigeria, argues that the AIDS epidemic in Africa is linked to a number of factors, including the high cost of drugs. He describes how some of the big drug companies, in the face of international protests, begrudgingly agreed to lower the price of anti-HIV medications in Africa. "The companies, however, remain steadfast about keeping their patent rights, which would leave ultimate control over prices and availability in their hands." Siddhartha Mukherjee, a resident in internal medicine at Massachusetts General Hospital and a clinical fellow in medicine at Harvard Medical School, asserts that the availability of cheap anti-HIV drugs in Africa, without adequate health care networks to monitor their distribution and use, is dangerous. If such medications are not taken consistently and over the prescribed length of time, new strains of HIV are likely to develop more quickly that are resistant to these drugs. He states that investment in health care infrastructure must accompany any distribution of cheap anti-HIV medications.

William A. Rushing, late professor of sociology at Vanderbilt University, explains the high prevalence of HIV/AIDS in Africa in terms of how Africans express and give social meaning to sex. He argues that the confluence of a set of sex-related behavioral patterns and gender stratification explains the HIV/AIDS infection rate. According to Rushing, these behavioral patterns include polygamous marriage practices, weak conjugal bonds, the transactional nature of sexual relations, the centrality of sexual conquest to male identity, and sex-positive cultures. Joseph R. Oppong, associate professor of geography at the University of North Texas, and Ezekiel Kalipeni, associate professor of geography at the University of Illinois at Urbana-Champaign, take issue with Rushing's conclusions. They contend that his analysis is Americentric, suffers from overgeneralizations, and problematically depicts Africans as sex-positive (and by implication, promiscuous and immoral). They assert that Rushing's cultural stereotypes are far too general to provide any meaningful insight into the AIDS crisis in Africa. An understanding of historical and contemporary migration patterns, as well as associated phenomena, better explain the spread of the virus.

Michael Bratton, professor of political science at Michigan State University, and Robert Mattes, associate professor of political studies and director of the Democracy in Africa Research Unit at the University of Cape Town, find as much popular support for democracy in Zambia, South Africa, and Ghana as in other regions of the developing world, despite the fact that the citizens of these countries tend to be less satisfied with the economic performance of their elected governments. Joel D. Barkan, professor of political science at the University of Iowa and senior consultant on governance at the World Bank, takes a less sanguine view of the situation in Africa. He suggests that one can be cautiously optimistic about the situation in roughly one-third of the states on the African continent, nations he classifies as consolidated democracies and as aspiring democracies. He asserts that one must be realistic about the possibilities for the remainder of African nations, countries he classifies into three groups: stalled democracies, those that are not free, and those that are mired in civil war.

Arthur A. Goldsmith, professor of management at the University of Massachusetts in Boston, examines the relationship between the amount of development assistance given to sub-Saharan African countries in the 1990s and the evolution of their political systems. He suggests that there is a positive, but small, correlation between donor assistance and democratization during this period. He views aid as insurance to prevent countries from sliding back into one-party or military rule. Julie Hearn, with the department of politics and international relations at Lancaster University, investigates democracy assistance in South Africa. She critically examines the role assigned to civil society by donors, questioning the "emancipatory potential" of the kind of democracy being promoted.

Robert I. Rotberg, director of the Program on Intrastate Conflict and
Conflict Resolution at Harvard University's John F. Kennedy School of
Government, holds African leaders responsible for the plight of their
continent. He laments the large number corrupt African leaders, seeing
South Africa's Mandela and Botswana's Khama as notable exceptions.
According to Rotberg, the problem is that "African leaders and their
followers largely believe that the people are there to serve their rulers,
rather than the other way around." Arthur A. Goldsmith, professor of
management at the University of Massachusetts in Boston, suggests
that African leaders are not innately corrupt but are responding rationally
to incentives created by their environment. He argues that high levels of
risk encourage leaders to pursue short-term, economically destructive
policies. In countries where leaders face less risk, there is less perceived
political corruption.

Tim Docking, African Affairs Specialist at the United States Institute of
Peace, presents the reactions of policymakers and academics to a
report on UN peace operations. The group argues that the lack of
political will by Western powers is the key impediment to successful UN
peacekeeping. Furthermore, given the situation in Africa, the group
implores the United States to re-engage with the United Nations and
African affairs. William Reno, associate professor of political science at
Northwestern University, contends that no peacekeeping is better than
bad peacekeeping. In his discussion of the failed Lomé Peace Accords,
a settlement negotiated between warring parties in Sierra Leone, he
notes that "many Sierra Leoneans regarded positions taken by the UN
and foreign diplomats who stressed reconciliation as offensive." As
opposed to the more bureaucratic peacekeeping approaches taken by
the United States and the UN, he lauds the hands-on tactics of the
British.

Introduction

Understanding African Issues in Context: Global and Local Forces

William G. Moseley

People go to Africa and confirm what they already have in their heads and so they fail to see what is there in front of them.

Chinua Achebe, Nigerian Author

When the missionaries came to Africa they had the Bible and we had the land. They said "Let us pray." We closed our eyes. When we opened them we had the Bible and they had the land.

Bishop Desmond Tutu, South African spiritual leader and novelist

African issues cannot be fully appreciated without a deep knowledge of the region and a broad understanding of its connections to the rest of the world. Every place, country, and region in Africa has its own environmental conditions, cultural dynamics, politics, and history. Yet these African places do not exist in a vacuum. They almost always have a history of connections to other areas of the continent and the world. As such, serious students, scholars, and policymakers with an interest in Africa must both seek to understand the specific geographic milieu in which an issue is being debated, as well as the extent to which a local-level problem is connected to broader scale dynamics at the national, regional, or global level. The mere act of growing food crops, for example, is a deeply local process that relates to site-specific environmental conditions, agricultural practices, and cultural preferences. But what and where certain crops are grown often has been influenced by cultural exchange, colonialism, and global markets.

Scholars and policymakers seeking to understand the synergy of global and local forces that imbue most African issues often privilege one set of causes over another. This privileging of more global or local causes is often described in terms of externalist versus internalist explanations. Scholars evoking externalist (or structuralist) explanations suggest that contemporary development patterns cannot be properly understood without an understanding of historical patterns of resource extraction and political control, as well as the position of Africa within the global economic system. In particular, these explanations often look to problematic colonial legacies to elucidate contemporary economic distortions. Scholars emphasizing internalist explanations tend to look to local factors to explain an issue or problem. These local phenomena may be negative (corruption, mismanagement, incompetence, nepotism, ethnic allegiances, regional ties, obligations to the extended family and patron-client relationships) or positive (local cultural practices, indigenous knowledge, family support networks).

Externalist or structuralist critiques of internalist positions range from accusations of spatial and temporal myopia to "blaming the victim." Internalist-leaning critics suggest that the structuralists are apologists who deny Africans' "agency" (i.e., the ability to influence contemporary events) and responsibility, thereby fostering a sense of victimization, helplessness, and further mismanagement. The reality, of course, is that good scholarship must equally explore both sets of factors. In some instances, both types of explanations will be equally critical for understanding an issue; in other cases, either internal or external factors may rightly been seen to be more important.

Interpreting African Issues:
Commentators, Scholars, Policymakers

Our impressions of Africa, our understanding of African issues, and the actions organizations take on the ground and in the policy sphere vis à vis Africa are filtered and articulated by a number of key players. Most notable among these are the popular press, the academy, and policymakers.

The Popular Press

Images and descriptions in the popular press suggest that the African continent is a troubled land where corruption, ethnic warfare, poverty, hunger, environmental destruction, and pestilence prevail. Some have even suggested that Africa is a lost cause, asserting that the continent be "written off" by international development organizations. Meanwhile, commercial tour operators also hawk the region as a place of high adventure and exoticism. Even quasi-scholarly publications such *National Geographic Magazine* often promote a vision of a primitive or wild Africa. What these popular and commercial descriptions hold in common is level of superficiality and one-sidedness. Yes, bad things do happen in Africa and there is beautiful scenery to be seen, but this is only one side of a complex and highly varied picture. It is the apparent unwillingness (or laziness) of popular commentators to provide a more nuanced view of an enormous continent that is often frustrating to scholars of Africa (or Africanists).

Africa is, after all, a place of extraordinarily diverse, vibrant, and dynamic cultures. Since the early 1990s, no other continent has seen more dramatic improvements in human rights, political freedom, and economic development—from the overthrowing of apartheid in South Africa to the revitalization of economies in countries such as Ghana and Uganda. Although environmental threats are real, African societies have proven their capacity, when given a chance, to use resources sustainably. Some conservation efforts in Africa even have become models for progressive community-based resource management in Western societies. The importance of human relations, family, and good neighborliness in many African societies also stands in stark contrast to the more closed and individualistic tendencies in a number of Western settings.

The Academy

For the past century, the Western academy has been organized largely along disciplinary lines. The disciplinary approach encourages focused investigations from one perspective across a range of geographies. Area studies complements disciplinary inquiry by promoting multi-perspective investigations of focused regions. In other words, the region or area represents a different framework around which to organize knowledge. Recent world events have revealed that there is a dearth of regional experts within the academy, government, and the private sector. The ideal scholar-practitioner may therefore be someone who not only has a firm grasp of the methods and theories of a particular discipline, but who also has a broader understanding of the issues and challenges (cutting across several disciplines) facing a particular region of the world.

While a variety of disciplinary departments offer courses that deal with contemporary African issues, it is notable that there are now a number of interdisciplinary programs and departments devoted to African and Afro-American studies. In the United States, the first African studies programs were established at Northwestern University (1946) and Boston University (1953). A number of other large programs were started in the early 1960s at places like Michigan State, Wisconsin, UCLA, Indiana, and Ohio University (*African Studies and the Undergraduate Curriculum*, Patrica Alden, David Lloyd, and Ahmed Samatar (eds.), Lynne Rienner, 1994). By the mid 1990s there were approximately 330 programs of African and Afro-American studies in the United States (*Directory of African and Afro-American Studies in the United States*, African Studies Association, 1993). African studies is as or more developed at institutions in other areas of the world. While the names of these organizations are too numerous to list, there are over 1,800 academic institutions, research bodies, and international organizations involved in African studies research in all parts of the world (*International Directory of African Studies Research*, 3rd Edition, Philip Baker (ed.), Hans Zell Publishers, 1994). In the United States, over a 1300 scholars from a broad array of disciplines meet each year at the annual meeting of the African Studies Association to present their research findings and debate key African issues. African studies associations and societies also exist in a number of other countries (e.g., Australia, Canada, France, Germany, India, Japan, Netherlands, South Africa, Spain, Sweden, Switzerland, United Kingdom).

Prior to the establishment of African studies as a recognized interdisciplinary field of study, some scholars encountered resistance from quarters of the academic establishment who perceived Africa to be lacking in history or otherwise unworthy of academic investigation. African studies has grown to be a dynamic realm of inquiry that regularly contributes to the broader academic discourse. Africanist scholars have tested the validity of widely accepted notions in the African context. They also have developed new theories that have influenced thinking in other regional contexts. Those disciplines contributing to African studies may roughly be divided between the humanities (mainly history and literature), the social sciences (anthropology, archeology, education, geography, political science, sociology) and the physical sciences (physical geography, ecology, botany). In the North American context, African studies meetings tend to be dominated by the humanities and social sciences, with historians and political scientists attending in the largest numbers (perhaps due to the sheer size of their disciplines). This volume largely deals with controversial African issues in the social sciences, although some of the questions have a significant historical or environmental dimension that pulls literature from the humanities or physical sciences.

The burgeoning field of African studies has spawned a number of academic journals, examples of which include: *Africa, Africa Today, African Affairs, African Studies Review, Cahiers d'Etudes Africaines, African Geographical Review, South African Geographical Journal, Canadian Journal of African Studies, Journal of African History, Journal of Modern African Studies, Journal of Southern African Studies*, and *Review of African Political Economy*. There are also a number of more policy-related or popular media magazines that focus on Africa including, for example, *Africa Analysis, Africa Confidential, Africa Now, Afrique Express* (French), and *Jeune Afrique* (French).

Policymakers and Development Professionals

In addition to the press and the academy, the other major sphere where African issues are framed and examined is in the offices of government bureaucrats, global policymakers, and nongovernmental organizations. These include individuals within the bilateral development agencies (e.g., U.S. Agency for International Development, British Department for International Development, Cooperation Française, or Canadian International Development Agency), international financial institutions (e.g., World Bank, International Monetary Fund, World Trade Organization), UN agencies (e.g., Food and Agricultural Organization, World Health Organization), and nonprofit community (e.g., CARE, Oxfam, Save the Children). While these organizations contribute to and influence discourse, their role is slightly different than the media and the academy in that this is where rhetoric is transformed into programmatic reality.

While I present the media, the academy, and development institutions as separate spheres of debate on Africa, there is, in fact, a considerable amount of crossover in thinking, not to mention personnel, between each realm. Policymakers and development professionals do not make decisions in a vacuum, but are influenced by public opinion (shaped by the media) and the latest academic research. Academics and policymakers attempt to influence public opinion through the media (via op-eds and interviews with the press). Governments may seek to shape academic findings by funding research projects or hiring scholars as consultants. Scholars may agree to consult on development issues because they believe this is a way for them to influence decision making. There also is a certain amount of personnel exchange between the different sectors (e.g., it is to think tanks, multilateral development agencies, and universities that a number of foreign service and aid advisors flee each time the party in power changes in Washington, Ottawa, or London). Despite these exchanges, significant differences exist in tone, timeliness, depth, and emphasis in analysis, and standards of knowledge production. The distribution of power (i.e., the power to have one's ideas heard) also differs within each group.

Major Themes

If this book has one overarching theme, it is African development. I interpret development in the broadest sense of the term, going beyond conventional measures of economic progress, to embrace processes occurring at a variety of spatial and temporal scales that allow people to meet their full potential. When viewed in this manner, nearly all of the issues presented in this volume pertain in one way or another to development. In order to give the volume a more accessible format, it has been organized into five thematic categories of African issues that are most oft debated by Africanists in the academy, as well as by policymakers and media commentators. These thematic categories are: (1) history; (2) development; (3) agriculture, food, and the environment; (4) social issues; and (5) politics and conflict resolution. While I present these themes as distinct, the reader should understand that there are often a number of connections that exist between issues in different parts of the book.

History

The number of historical debates pertaining to Africa are so numerous that they easily could constitute a separate volume. There are, however, a few issues that stand out as they highlight the connections between Africa and the rest of the world, and because these questions impinge on contemporary development patterns. First, understanding the impact of the trans-Atlantic slave trade on African development patterns is critical. Was this a significant historical moment with lasting impacts or was it consistent with existing practices and effectively managed by Africans? Given that so many Africans departed to the New World, it is also crucial to understand the active role they played in shaping and developing the Americas. Finally, to what extent has colonialism shaped contemporary development patterns? Some find that this led to huge and lasting distortions in African economies, while others argue that this was beneficial for economic development.

Development

The nature of and approach to development in the African context is highly contentious. Commentators, scholars, and policymakers argue, for example, over the perceived failure of Africa to develop, the impact of the colonial experience on contemporary events, the influence of global economic structures on African development patterns, and the role of the state versus the private and nonprofit sectors in the development process.

Closely related to the externalist/internalist debate is one concerning the most appropriate approach to development in Africa. The structuralists evoke dependency theory and world systems theory to suggest that, even though the colonial era has ended, historical patterns of resource extraction persist. In many instances, African nations are supplying cheap commodities (minerals, oil, lumber, cotton, coffee, cocoa, tea, and sugar) to Europe and North America in exchange for relatively expensive manufactured goods. As such, the participation of African nations in the global economy under current conditions leads to a process of underdevelopment. The best way to avoid this trap, according to the structuralists, is to diversify the national economy by producing imported goods at home, an approach also known as import substitution.

The general failure of import substitution, and the related Third World debt crisis, led the international financial institutions (especially the World Bank and International Monetary Fund) to begin pushing for the structural adjustment of African economies beginning in the early 1980s. With the basic aim of balancing the national budget and spurring economic growth, these programs obliged African government to privatize state-owned enterprises, devalue local currencies, cut government programs, and expand exports. The uneven success and social costs of these programs have led to bitter debates in academic and policy circles. Many contend that the role of the state in the development process has been underestimated by neoclassical economists. Although contested, debt forgiveness increasingly is seen as one way to restart development and lift the burden of past indiscretions (on the part of African governments and donors).

Another key aspect of African development is the rise in the number and prominence of non-governmental organizations (NGOs) since the 1980s. Bilateral and multilateral donors increasingly bypass the African state by providing funds to NGOs for project and program implementation. NGOs (both local and international) are perceived to be more efficient and more in tune with the needs of the local population. Critics argue that NGOs can be equally autocratic, patronizing, and detached from the local population.

Finally, what is the role of mineral and energy resources in African development? This topic has become more important in recent years as the United States and China increasingly look to African nations for their energy and mineral needs (the United States because of unstable supplies in other parts of the world, and China because of its rapidly expanding economy). The notion that a rich natural resource base may play a key role in the development of some African nations is hotly contested. Critics contend that bountiful resources may actually be a "curse" because they tend to inhibit economic diversification, fall under the control of unscrupulous government officials, and attract predatory multinational corporations. Proponents of mineral and energy resource development point to the positive contributions of mining in several developed country economies.

Agriculture, Food, and the Environment

Since the global media focused attention on large-scale droughts in the early 1970s and mid 1980s, famine and environmental destruction in Africa have loomed large in the public imagination. Key debates have centered on how best to increase food production, whether or not the continent's population is growing too quickly for its agricultural base, the resolution of conflicts between local people and wildlife, and whether or not the continent is facing a deforestation crisis.

A fundamental debate persists as to whether or not famine and food insecurity in Africa is the result of underproduction or the maldistribution of food. Many development assistance programs, including the international network of crop development institutes under the aegis of the Consultative Group on International Agricultural Research (CGIAR), are predicated on the assumption that Africa's food problems will be resolved by increases in food production. Economist and Nobel laureate, Amartya Sen, has argued that famine rarely results from an absolute shortage of food, but the inability of poor households to access available supplies.

Related to the aforementioned debate is a long-standing discussion concerning the relationship between food production and population growth. The eighteenth-century parson, Thomas Malthus, asserted that human populations would inevitably grow more quickly than food production, ultimately leading to famine. Contemporary neo-Malthusians, such as Paul Ehrlich, have similarly argued that urgent measures are needed to control population in order avert disaster. Ester Boserup has countered that Malthus had it all wrong because it is population density that controls the level of food production, rather than food production quantities setting population thresholds. In recent years, some of the best case studies (both pro-Boserupian and pro-Malthusian) on the relationship between population growth and food production have come out of Africa.

The "tragedy of the commons" is another prominent paradigm that has been used to explain resource problems in Africa. According to this theory, commonly held natural resources will tend to be overexploited by individuals seeking to maximize personal gain. The solution advocated by economists is to privatize common resources, as it is believed that the private owner will more carefully husband environmental resources over the long term. The commons is actually a misnomer in the African context because many African communities effectively have managed commonly held natural resources through traditional mechanisms of control and enforcement. It is when these traditional mechanisms break down, and the commons become "open access resources" (or resources where there is no effective management authority) that problems develop. The loss of wildlife in Africa often has been described as an open access resource problem. Here it is assumed that communities bordering parks exploit wildlife because they see the state as an ineffective or illegitimate manager. Integrated conservation and development programs seek to resolve this problem by giving local people a financial stake in the conservation of these animals. Critics argue that this approach further restricts the development of these communities. Deforestation in Africa also has been characterized as an open access resource problem. Environmentalists argue that drastic measures are needed to protect the continent's dwindling forest resources from overuse by poor households. Critics suggest that the assertion of widespread deforestation is based on bad science and a historical misreading of environmental change in many instances.

Social Issues

Perhaps more than any other set of contested African issues, those pertaining to the social sphere tend to provoke deep-seated emotional responses. Different aspects of the AIDS crisis in Africa, female genital cutting, and the position of women in African societies all have attracted considerable media attention and scrutiny in recent years.

Many of these issues get at a deeper debate between those who assert there are certain universal rights and wrongs, and cultural pluralists who believe we need to evaluate practices within their own cultural context. Advocates of the universality of norms disparage defenders of certain African practices as cultural relativists. Cultural relativism is cast as problematic because it may be used as an excuse to say that anything goes. In contrast, cultural pluralists assert that there are separate and valid cultural and moral systems, which may involve social mores that are not easily reconcilable with one another. Cultural pluralists are not necessarily cultural relativists as many would argue that everything does not go, e.g., murder is wrong. The challenge for cultural pluralists is to determine if a practice violates a universal norm when it is viewed in its proper cultural context (rather than in the cultural context of another). The result of this deep philosophical divide is that we often see Western feminists pitted against multiculturalists (two groups that frequently function as intellectual allies in the North American context) over some of the issues addressed in this section of the book.

If one does want to work for change, how should this be approached? In the case of empowering women, some argue that fundamental legal changes must be made while others suggest that the creation of economic opportunities is key.

Finally, some of the debates in this section also pit political economic, or structualist, explanations against those that emphasize internal factors. As such, AIDS may be seen as a result of broader economic processes (e.g., migration) or personal failings and problematic cultural practices.

Politics, Governance, and Conflict Resolution

The terrain of politics, governance, and conflict resolution is simultaneously one of the most hopeful and distressing realms in contemporary African studies. While more contested elections have been held in the last 10 years than at any other time in the post-colonial period, the African continent also suffers from more instances of civil strife than other world regions. Key debates have focused on the success or nonsuccess of multiparty democracy in the African context, the role of foreign assistance in promoting democracy, reasons for corruption amongst African officials, and how best to resolve ethnic conflicts in African countries.

An underlying theme related to several of these questions concerns the most appropriate form of governance in the African context. Proponents of multiparty democracy assert that this form of government will promote economic growth and minimize ethnic tensions. They also believe that a healthy civil society will serve as a check on corruption and other government excesses. Increasingly, foreign assistance for a variety of projects is conditional upon certain types of democratic reform.

Other scholars and African leaders see the imposition of democracy in Africa as a form of neo-imperialism. They suggest that the problem with multiparty democracy in many African countries is that it leads to the formation of too many political parties, each with a regional or ethnic outlook, and none representing the interests of the country as a whole. Furthermore, some Afro-centrists assert that the one-party state is more consistent with traditional consensus decision making that occurs at the village level. They maintain that the process of competitive elections is a foreign notion that is divisive in the African context. They also have also argued that democracy may actually inhibit economic growth. According to this argument, the problem with democracy is that it does not allow leaders to make tough economic decisions, such as the austerity measures required under structural adjustment.

Finally, what is the role of peacekeeping forces on the continent? Some argue that international peacekeepers are critical for resolving some ethnic conflicts while others suggest that no peacekeeping is better than bad peacekeeping.

On the Internet . . .

H-Africa

H-Africa encourages discussion of Africa's history and culture. It offers a variety of listserves related to specific themes and regions of the continent. The site also allows one to search past discussions, link to other sites that deal with the continent, and examine reviews of books on the region.

http://www.h-net.org/~africa/

African Studies Association

The African Studies Association is the largest African studies organization in North America. It coordinates a meeting each year where scholarly presentation takes place, and publishes several Africa-related journals.

http://www.africanstudies.org/

Columbia University's African Studies Internet Resources

A catalog of links to African studies programs, resources by region and country, electronic journals and newspapers, and resources by topic. It also has a directory of African studies scholars.

http://www.columbia.edu/cu/lweb/indiv/africa/cuvl/

The University of Pennsylvania's African Studies Center, History Section

The history page of this Web site offers links to several other reputable sites dealing with African history and archival resources.

http://www.africa.upenn.edu/About_African/ww_hist.html

PART 1

Introduction and History

It is important for students of Africa to place the continent in its historical and global context. Sub-Saharan Africa has long-standing connections with other areas of the world. Debates rage over the nature of these connections, their persistence and impact on the future of Africa, and how African ideas influenced development in other regions of the world. Of course, the role of Africanist scholars also comes into question as our understanding of the continent cannot be separated from those who produce scholarship on the region.

- Are the Experts on Africa Part of the Problem?

- Did the Trans-Atlantic Slave Trade Underdevelop Africa?

- Have the Contributions of Africans Been Recognized for Developing New World Agriculture?

- Did Colonialism Distort Contemporary African Development?

ISSUE 1

Are the Experts on Africa Part of the Problem?

YES: Gavin Kitching, from "Why I Gave Up African Studies," *African Studies Review and Newsletter* (June 2000)

NO: Marc Epprecht, from "Why I Love African Studies," *African Studies Quarterly* (2003)

ISSUE SUMMARY

YES: Gavin Kitching, professor of political science at the University of New South Wales, left the field of African studies because he "found it depressing." According to Kitching, Africanist scholars have failed to see Africa's own ruling elites as the principal culprits for the continent's dire predicament. He suggests that we "have to ask what it is about the history and culture of sub-Saharan Africa that has led to . . . its disastrous present."

NO: Marc Epprecht, professor of history at Queens University, is more upbeat, noting a number of African countries that have made great strides. He accepts that African elites are responsible for the welfare of their populations, but also recognizes that they "are enormously, often fatally constrained by pressure from the outside." He argues that Africanist scholars have an important role to play by holding decision makers in the West accountable for policies that further marginalize Africa.

Perhaps more so than any other world region, the African continent suffers from a public relations problem. The continent is portrayed regularly in the Western media as an area plagued by wars, disease, famine, corruption, incompetence and drought. As a result, Africa is often perceived by the rest of the world as a "lost cause." Emblematic of this genre of portrayals is Robert Kaplan's 1994 article in the *Atlantic Monthly* entitled "The Coming Anarchy: How Scarcity, Crime, Overpopulation, Tribalism and Disease Are Rapidly Destroying the Social Fabric of Our Planet." Even the recent September 2005 special issue of *National Geographic Magazine* on Africa, which was devoted to overturning stereotypes about the continent, generally described the region as awash with problems stemming from overpopulation, corruption, and resource scarcity.

Many Africans and Africanist scholars are deeply disturbed by one-sided journalistic representations of the region. While admitting that Africa suffers from a number of pressing problems, they also point to several positive developments in recent years. They argue that Africa is not only a place of extraordinarily diverse, vibrant, and dynamic cultures, but that no other continent has seen more dramatic improvements in human rights, political freedom, and economic development in the last 15 years. Advances have ranged from the overthrowing of apartheid in South Africa, to the rise of multi-party democracy in Mali, to the revitalization of economies in countries such as Ghana and Uganda. In short, many Africanists assert that sweeping generalizations are made about the entire continent based on events in a few areas. These gross simplifications overshadow many of the positive developments that have occurred in recent years.

In his provocative essay, "Why I Gave Up African Studies," Gavin Kitching riled a number of Africanist scholars by suggesting that they have failed to see Africa's own ruling elites as the principal culprits for the continent's dire predicament. He suggests that we "have to ask what it is about the history and culture of sub-Saharan Africa that has led to . . . its disastrous present."

As the title of his article suggests, Gavin Kitching, author of the 1980 award-winning *Class and Economic Change in Kenya: The Making of an African Petite Bourgeoisie 1905–1970*, left the field of African studies in 1983 because he "found it depressing." Only after repeated requests from the editor of the Australian *African Studies Review and Newsletter* did he agree to write his article in 2000. Initially, a little noticed piece in an obscure journal, the article began to attract attention when it was reprinted in the online journal *Mots Pluriels*. Kitching's ideas, and reactions to them, were featured in a March 2003 edition of the *Chronicle of Higher Education* as well as a summer 2003 special issue of the *African Studies Quarterly*.

The aforementioned special issue of the *African Studies Quarterly* was guest edited by Marc Epprecht and included his retort to Kitching entitled "Why I Love African Studies." While Epprecht acknowledges that African leaders must take responsibility for their actions, he also argues that there is much beyond their control. He suggests that Africa and the West are inextricably linked, essentially experiencing two sides of the same globalization coin. As such, given that policy maneuvers and consumptive behaviors in the West are literally (and often devastatingly) felt around the world, Africanists in the global North have a critical role to play in educating their publics about these linkages and impacts.

Gavin Kitching  **YES**

Why I Gave Up African Studies

In a word, I gave up African studies because I found it depressing. But that is hardly an explanation, even if it is an emotionally precise description of what occurred. To explain my giving up African studies I have to say why I came to find the activity depressing. This requires a little history—both personal history, or autobiography, and history of Africa.

I began to be interested in Africa whilst an undergraduate student of economics and politics at Sheffield University (1965-8) and I began my doctoral work in African politics in Oxford in 1969. That means that I first entered this field of study when the hope and optimism generated by Africa's independence from colonialism was still in the air. My doctoral research was conducted in Tanzania, and that was not accidental of course. As an undergraduate I had been deeply moved and impressed by the writings of Julius Nyerere, and like many young intellectual radicals of that period I was eager to see Nyerere's experiment in a 'Third Way' African socialism at first hand. I undertook doctoral fieldwork in Arusha district, Tanzania between 1969 and 1971, undertook further field research on peasant agriculture and rural stratification in Kenya in 1972-3, and returned to East Africa at intervals between 1973 and 1983. I also conducted shorter research and consultancy visits to Ghana, Senegal and Zambia in the late 1970s and early 1980s. My last visit to Africa—to Kenya and Tanzania—occurred in 1983.

This history means that, like many other Africanist scholars of my generation, I lived and worked through the period when optimism and hope in and about Africa were replaced by pessimism and cynicism. A particular memory comes to mind. I am in a bar on the campus of the former Kwame Nkrumah university in Kumasi, Ghana in early 1980. A number of African colleagues are there too, including a lecturer from the university's Department of Law. He has had rather too much to drink. He is watching the news on the television above the bar. A news reader announces the declaration of the formal independence of Southern Rhodesia, now to be called Zimbabwe. There is the conventional film footage of these occasions—cheering crowds, brass band, new flag rising on floodlit flag pole. My colleague smiles drunkenly, murmurs "poor sods!" loud enough for all in the bar to hear, and staggers from his bar stool and out of the door. I am shocked. But, significantly perhaps (at least in retrospect) nobody in the bar, African or European, protests. And this is not an isolated occurrence. In Ghana in 1980, in Kenya and Tanzania in the late 1970s/early 1980s, it is not difficult to meet older African people who will tell one—and totally unbidden—that "we were better off when the British were here". I even hear it from middle aged men in the Murang'a district of Kenya's Central Province, men who had been Mau-Mau fighters.

Radical Perspective

Of course I had a ready-made radical perspective into which I could accommodate and by which I could explain away such uncomfortable experiences and observations—the dependency perspective. What after all was so surprising about all this? Had I not said, in my own book on Kenya, that the country was in the political grip of a dependent African 'petit-bourgeoisie' which, by its very dependent nature, was unlikely to be an effective agent of 'real' economic development in Kenya. And had not a raft of other scholars—European and African—said similar things about a raft of other newly-independent African states. So, in such circumstances, why was it at all surprising that popular disenchantment with such elites within Africa was so widespread—up to and including a retrospective nostalgia for colonialism?

Yes. But this same perspective had been predicated on the view that these 'dependent' or 'neo-colonial' governing elites were agents of 'imperialism' or of 'transnational capital' in Africa. And as the 1970s turned into the 1980s and the political fragility and economic involution of so many African states became palpable this notion itself seemed ever more questionable. As I put it in a number of public presentations in the early 1980s—"if the ruling elites of Africa are seen as managers or agents for western capitalism or imperialism, one can only say that the latter should get itself some new agents. For the ones it has seem remarkably inefficient." In other words, the decay of Africa's production structures and economic infrastructure, the continent-wide slump in investment (domestic and foreign), the endemic inflation and balance of payments problems, the sharp absolute falls in real standards of living of the mass of African people and (accompanying all this) the massive levels of governmental corruption and persistent breakdowns in civil peace and order in so many states—all this seemed hard to square with a basically functionalist perspective which had the governing elites of Africa somehow doing the bidding of international capitalism. And it was all the harder to maintain this position when so many of the official spokespeople for that capitalism (the IMF, the World Bank, corporate executives with African investments) far from endorsing the activities of their supposed 'agents' were endemically critical of the failure of African elites to provide domestic environments in which any form of capital investment could be secure and profitable.

This is not to deny, of course, that there were powerful factors beyond the activities of Africa's governing classes which also pushed Africa into political instability and economic decline from the mid-1970s onwards—everything from the oil shocks which brought an end to the post-war long boom in the world economy and led to at least the onset of Africa's debt problem, through the Cold War flooding of the continent with arms and various forms of military subversion, to the global arms trade and traders. But it is to say that such factors did not seem to account, either individually or even in conjunction, for the particularity of the African situation. For all these factors had impacted on other parts of the South or Third World too without effects as catastrophic as those to be observed in Africa. I came up with a hackneyed but useful analogy. The African ship of state was ploughing through heavy international seas, yes. But that only strengthened the need for an excellent captain and navigator at the helm and a well disciplined crew. But as it was the captain and all his officers seemed to be drunk or absent from the bridge and the crew engaged in various forms of mutiny. No wonder the ship had run aground.

So, and leaving aside hackneyed analogies, I was returned again and again to an overwhelming question, which can be phrased in various forms, but always remains essentially the same question. Why are some governing elites economically progressive and others not? Why are some ruling classes exploitative, selfish and corrupt but also genuine agents for national economic and social improvement, while others are just exploitative, selfish and corrupt? Why are some states 'developmental' and others not? Of course these issues have come to the forefront of African studies since I gave it up, even if they are dealt with in vocabularies remote from dependency theory (which was declining rapidly in popularity as I left the field). So now we hear a lot more about African 'cleptocracy' or 'modern patrimonialism', about 'rent seeking behaviour' among state elites and about 'state failure' generally in Africa and the need for market-led 'structural adjustment'. But though the question may be posed in new forms and though helpful new descriptions of African state functioning (mainly derived from the public choice paradigm) have emerged, I see no significant progress made in answering the question 'why?' Why have African governing elites been particularly prone to behaving in ways which are both economically destructive of the welfare of the people for whom they are supposedly responsible and which have led—at the extreme—to forms of state fision, (civil war etc) collapse or breakdown?

At this point I must make a confession. After over thirty years of studying this question (including the last ten years in Australia giving far greater attention to the 'developmental states' of SE Asia) my first and predominant answer to it is still that I do not really know (or not in any hard or definite sense of 'know'). I have some suspicions about where an answer might lie. The lack of economic or social 'depth' of the colonial experience over most of sub-Saharan Africa; the fragile and inexperienced stratum of educated African people which that 'shallow' experience left behind; the chronic lack of 'fit' between Africa's indigenous structures of ethnicity and the so-called 'nation-state' structures which colonialism bequeathed and which the first generation of nationalist leaders (probably very unwisely) opted to retain; the inability (probably derived from the above) of Africa's governing elites to identify themselves with, or as part of, an 'imagined community' of the nation states which they nominally superintend; their consequent failure to manifest any sense of loyalty or of a duty of care or responsibility to the people who make up these entities; their tendency to restrict such a sense of moral duty only to some particular ethnic or other sub-group of their citizens (thus increasing both economic and social polarities among citizens and the likelihood of the political fision of the state, especially in economically desperate times). I could add further suspicions to the list if asked. But none of them are certainties or anything like certainties, and again it is comparative study which muddies the water. Because, of course, you could have said all of the same things about the post-colonial elites of Indonesia or Malaysia and some of the same things about the elites of Thailand, South Korea or Taiwan. This reflection only leads me—and rather flatly—to the conclusion that it must be the concatination of these domestic elite characteristics with the particularly weak global economic situation of sub-Saharan Africa which was the fatal two-sided recipe for developmental failure. And that may be true, but, as I say, I still have no certainty that it is or about how precisely to weight the relative importance of the list of usual suspects above.

But why did all this lead me to give up African studies? Well it compounded the depression. I was depressed, that is to say, both by what was happening to African people and by my inability even to explain it adequately, let alone do anything about it. And also, I was depressed by the polarization, within the world of African studies as it was in the early 1980s, between those advocating what were called 'internalist' explanations of Africa's problems and those who continued to favour 'externalist' explanations. I was depressed because advocates of the latter view often charged advocates of the former with "blaming African people" for Africa's parlous state, a charge which seemed at once incoherent, even in its own terms (was colonialism in Africa an 'internal' or 'external' factor, for example?) and, above all, enormously hurtful. For of course the vast majority of African people are the victims, often the horrific victims, of Africa's plight, not its perpetrators in any sense, and I, at least, would never wish to deny that. But I would also wish to assert that, though the political elites of Africa change their social composition (often quite significantly and rapidly) their economically and politically destructive behaviour mostly does not change with their personnel. And that certainly suggests—at least to me—that there are broader social/cultural factors (in the mass milieu from which such elites are recruited) continually making for, and reinforcing, this behaviour. So, we do have to ask what it is about the history and culture of sub-Saharan Africa that has led (at any rate in part) to its disastrous present. But that can only be construed as "blaming African people" or, more broadly as "blaming the victim", if a guilt-ridden confusion is made between context and agency. That is, it may be in the broadest historical and cultural context of African society that we find the clue to destructive political elite behaviour. But that does not make that context an agent of that destruction. Nor (therefore) does it prevent political and moral responsibility for their actions being sheeted home to narrow and privileged sub-groups or classes of African people (and not 'African people' as a whole) classes which have been the agents—even if not the sole agents—of that destruction.

Role for Australasian Africanists

In short, and to conclude, I left African studies because what was happening to a continent and a people I had grown to love left me appalled and confused. But I also left it because I felt that the emotionally stressed and guilt-ridden debate which arose within the African studies community about the causes of Africa's decline was itself a powerful testimony to a fact even more depressing in its implications that anything that was happening in and to Africa. This fact is, to put it simply, that the most damaging legacy of colonialism and imperialism in the world has not been the global economic structures and relations it has left behind nor the patterns of modern 'neo-imperialist' economic and cultural relations of which it was the undoubted historical forerunner. Rather its most damaging legacy has been the psychological Siamese twins of endemic guilt on the European side and endemic psychological dependence on the African side, legacies which make truth telling hard and the adult taking of responsibility even harder. Imperialism fucked up the heads of so many people whom it touched—both colonialists and colonized (Frantz Fanon was absolutely and deeply right about that) and until that—ultimately depressing—legacy of its existence is finally killed, neither Africa nor African studies will be able to make real progress. It was that conclusion which led me—very sadly—to leave both behind.

NO ↰

Marc Epprecht

Why I Love African Studies

There is much to be frustrated, heartbroken, and angry about in recent African history. The fact that scholars have sometimes been complicit by legitimizing abusive and corrupt elites on the continent is an undeniable part of this history that needs to be explored. Yet to compare the present unfavourably to the late colonial era in general terms based on select anecdotes is deeply misleading. For example, the United Nations Development Program has comparative statistics on the Human Development Index for 37 Africa countries south of the Sahara going back to 1975 (that is, a point just before the oil shocks started to whittle away the gains of the 1960s). They show slow but more or less steady improvement up to the year 2000 in all but one nation (Zambia). Other UN sources indicate improvements in child mortality rates, life expectancy and access to improved water supplies over 1960 even in some of the most ill-governed countries. In Sierra Leone life expectancy is now 39 years, the lowest in the world, to be sure, but it was only 32 years when the British took leave. In the meantime, people in Africa's most populous country (Nigeria) could expect to live an additional 14 years (or over a third) longer in 2000 compared to 1960. Continent-wide, smallpox has been eradicated, river blindness and polio are on the way out, and vaccines for malaria and HIV are in the pipeline. Fertility rates have declined, in part due to dramatic increases in the use of contraceptives but also in part due to gender and development efforts that have improved women's legal rights and female literacy.

Noting these achievements does not detract from the fact that some countries have experienced serious setbacks. There will almost certainly be further declines in life expectancy and other social indicators in the worst hit countries in the near future. Nonetheless, to paint a uniformly bleak picture or to fetishize disaster is to deny real gains in key areas of health, literacy, and even infrastructure. Consider as well some remarkable, peaceful transitions from dictatorship or oligarchy to democratic, constitutional rule—Mali, Senegal, South Africa, Mozambique, Nigeria, Uganda, Kenya, and more. These transitions are incomplete. That they are ongoing, however, is testified by the emergence of a vibrant civil society that includes outspoken feminist associations, gay and ethnic minority rights movements, and a relatively free (indeed, often startlingly bold by lame-stream North American standards) press. One can debate the merits and meaning of these successes, but simply to dismiss or to deny them in sweeping generalizations is hugely unfair. There is evidence to support the belief that hard work and good sense and close collaboration with African colleagues can make a difference for the better.

From *African Studies Quarterly*, vol. 7, no. 2 & 3, 2003. Copyright © 2003 by African Studies Quarterly. Reprinted by permission.

Dr. Kitching's observation of paralysis in African Studies also does not describe the situation as I have experienced it over the past decade or so. In my experience, Africanist academic journals are full of fascinating, sensitive, pertinent, new research. The conferences I attend are lively, colleagues are often highly politically motivated, and stodgy disciplinary and ivory tower boundaries are being torn down. Some of this new research is noticeably better than two or three decades ago, aware, for example, that women and children actually exist and that the environment, gender, and sexuality are important historical issues. In part, the richness of the new scholarship reflects the fact that there are now more Africans participating who forthrightly contest Western Africanists' intellectual hubris (or simply, pointedly ignore it in favour of more pressing concerns).

In common with many Afro-pessimists, Dr. Kitching also errs in presenting a falsely undifferentiated Africa to compare unfavourably to a similarly implicit unity in Asia. Aside from the terrible violence and exploitation that the so-called successes in Asia entailed, they surely owe at least as much to American geo-political obsessions as they do to the probity of their elites. Why then compare apples and oranges?

Speaking of which, who are these "elites" we should be excoriating? Was (British-military-educated) Idi Amin an elite? Can US-educated Kwame Nkrumah and US/Scot-trained Hastings Banda be lumped together with Samuel Doe and Amilcar Cabral? And while it is true that uber-thug Charles Taylor spent time in prison (in Boston) can we legitimately analyze his "elite-ness" as somehow analogous with that of fellow prison-alumnus, Nelson Mandela?

Another misleading analytic device common to Afro-pessimism is the construction of an implacable hostility between external and internal causes for Africa's problems. Having erected this false dichotomy, they then tend decisively to cast their vote in favour of the internalists. Yet Africanist scholars today normally see multiple, often rival external factors (governments, corporations, IFIs, NGOs, MNCs, and so on) interacting with multiple internal factors (class, gender, ethnicity, the physical environment, and so on) in dialectical fashion in differing contexts that change over time. They accept that African elites are responsible for the welfare of the population as a whole (and that more are acknowledging this now by allowing democratic elections and critical media than ever in the past). But they also recognize that African elites are enormously, often fatally constrained by pressure from outside. To suggest otherwise is self-flattering and self-deceiving to the main sources of that pressure in the West.

Tacitly exonerating the West for its role in African frustration is one thing. But Afro-pessimism is even more worrisome when it suggests abandoning African friends and colleagues who seek our help in their efforts to build a better society. They do not seek that help out of dependency on our brilliant ideas or our guilt to milk. Rather, Africans mostly welcome us as allies (indeed are remarkably patient with us) in part because of our ability to bear witness about Africa to students in the West, to politicians in the West, and to media in the West. This is potentially useful to their struggles. Indeed, Africans have ample reason to believe that without us to hold decision-makers in the West accountable for policies and interventions that further marginalize

Africa, their struggles may simply disappear from the international political agenda or be betrayed by opportunistic politics in the West.

Here is just one recent example: many Americans might be gulled into believing that African struggles against HIV/AIDS are well-served by President George W. Bush's recent promise of $15 billion toward their cause. In fact, as South Africa's Treatment Action Campaign has eloquently explained, Bush's "help" may significantly undermine their efforts. By amplifying TAC's voice closer to the political centre of the world capitalist system, Africanists in the West can play a role in alerting concerned voters of this extremely dangerous turn. Perhaps that will motivate some to put their personal energy into throwing the rascals responsible for it out of office next time around (I call this Florida-optimism).

Let me conclude by recalling an astute observation made by a grumpy old white man long before African Studies even existed. Marx noted that the higher and middle rungs of society propagate and eagerly consume an "inversion" of reality that obscures from them an honest understanding of the state of the world. This inversion justifies their continued privilege at the expense of the working class. A clear perception of the violence inherent in capitalism can thus only come from the working class experience, a concept elaborated by Antonio Gramsci, by Walter Rodney and other African or Africa-based Africanists in the 1960s, by feminist standpoint theory in the 1970s and 80s, and by variations of subaltern and queer theory since the 1990s.

Building from this insight (that is, that people in much of Africa are struggling against levels of violence and degradation whose ultimate provenance is obscured by bourgeois inversions), we can appreciate African Studies for the window it opens to the world, and to ourselves. Drought has hit southern Africa hard this year, to give one example. Shall we merely point the finger at African peasants or at leaders like Robert Mugabe who have unquestionably exacerbated the famine that has ensued? Or shall we reflect on who is raising the surface temperature of the South Pacific and changing global climate patterns? If we do the latter, Africans' disproportionate suffering of some of the consequences of global climate change reveals to us the painful inequity of the global capitalist system. People in the West consume a hundred or more times the energy that an African does on average and that, by any objective standard of need, people in the West require for a healthy and happy life. Famine in Africa (aside from its intrinsic tragedy and the spur it provides to humanitarian generosity) can thus make us wonder why our environmental footprint in North America is so vastly, destructively inflated.

In other words, looking at the world through African eyes or through empirical data honestly gathered on the developmental trenches in Africa can provide us with lessons about ourselves here in the West, and about the real as opposed to idealized nature of globalization. We urgently need to learn these lessons. If, in the process of learning, Africanists can contribute to Africans' own efforts to turn things around, all the better. And that is why I love African Studies.

POSTSCRIPT

Are the Experts on Africa Part of the Problem?

In his selection, Kitching touches on a long-running debate within African studies between "internalist" and "externalist" explanations of Africa's problems. The internalist arguments tend to focus on factors within Africa (e.g., poor leadership, corruption, immorality) to explain developmental difficulties, whereas externalist explanations emphasize exogenous factors such as the lingering effects of colonialism or globalization.

Internalist explanations date to the colonial era, but include a number of contemporary works as well, such as Ayittey's *Africa in Chaos* (St. Martin's Press, 1998). The primary criticism of these works is that they overlook deep and long-standing connections between Africa and the global economy, connections that may have a profound impact on political leadership and resource flows within African countries.

Externalist explanations have often relied on dependency theory and world systems theory to situate constraints on African development. Andre Gunder Frank is credited with the development of dependency theory, a Marxist or structuralist inspired framework that conceptualizes elites in many developing countries as pawns of capitalists in the industrialized world. See his book entitled *Capitalism and Underdevelopment in Latin America* (Monthly Review Press, 1967). Immanuel Wallerstein's related world systems theory places dependency theory in a broader spatial context by conceptualizing developing, or peripheral, nations as hinterlands supplying raw materials to industrialized, or core, nations. See his book entitled *The Modern World System* (Academic Press, 1974). What both of these theories do is place Africa in a broader global context in which African elites, and African economies more generally, are not serving the needs of their own peoples, but rather the demands of industrialized nations. Examples of scholarly works from the externalist camp include Terence Ranger's *Peasant Consciousness and Guerilla War in Zimbabwe* (University of California Press, 1985) and Allen Isaacman's *Cotton is the Mother of Poverty: Peasants, Work, and Rural Struggle in Colonial Mozambique, 1931–61* (Heinemann, 1996).

One problem with the externalist argument is that it may deny ordinary Africans "agency," that is, a recognition that local people have the ability to influence events in spite of external influences. In a 2001 article in the *African Geographical Review*, entitled "On the Politics of the Mirror: Geography and Afro-Pessimism," Jeff Popke argued that "Africans are not simply passive victims of the capricious whims of despotic leaders," but resist in obvious and not so obvious ways.

Even if one agrees with Kitching that the culpability of African elites for the political and economic impoverishment of the continent has received less than desired attention, it may be a stretch to go from this assessment to argue that one should abandon a scholarly interest in Africa out of frustration. As an anonymous writer noted in an April 2003 online discussion about the Kitching's article, "Kitching may be linking a complex personal decision to an indictment of a whole community of scholars. Kitching tends to think that Africanists should double as political activists or self-consciously imbue their scholarship with instrumentalist or presentist agendas and missions. Some scholars may in fact do that due to the nature of their discipline and the audience of their work, but many Africanists are, and will remain, scholars working hard to explain rather than transform Africa."

ISSUE 2

Did the Trans-Atlantic Slave Trade Underdevelop Africa?

YES: Paul E. Lovejoy, from "The Impact of the Atlantic Slave Trade on Africa: A Review of the Literature," *Journal of African History* (1989)

NO: John Thornton, from *Africa and the Africans in the Making of the Atlantic World, 1400–1680* (Cambridge University Press, 1992)

ISSUE OVERVIEW

YES: Paul Lovejoy, professor of history at York University, argues that the trans-Atlantic slave trade significantly transformed African society. It led to an absolute loss of population on the continent and a large increase in the enslaved population that was retained in Africa. The economic advantages of exporting slaves did not offset the social and political costs of participation, there were disastrous demographic impacts, and Africa's relative position in world trade declined. Lovejoy, therefore, supports the "transformation thesis," which holds that the external slave trade dramatically reshaped slavery and society in Africa.

NO: John Thornton, professor of history at Boston University, holds a very different view. He notes that slavery was widespread and indigenous in African society. Europeans simply worked with this existing market and African merchants, who were not dominated by Europeans, responded by providing more slaves. African leaders who allowed the slave trade to continue were neither forced to do so against their will, nor did they make irrational decisions. As such, the preexisting institution of slavery in Africa is as much responsible as any external force for the development of the trans-Atlantic slave trade.

The debate about the impact of the trans-Atlantic slave trade on Africa, and related discussions concerning the role that African elites played in this process, as well as the nature of African slavery before the arrival of Europeans, dates back to at least the time period leading up to the abolition of the slave trade within the British Empire in 1807. During this time frame, some were arguing that the majority of Africans were already slaves in Africa, and consequently their situation would not be improved by ending the trans-Atlantic slave trade.

Apologists seeking to justify slavery in the American South also pointed to the existence of slavery in Africa and the role of African elites in the trans-

Atlantic trade. Many academics (who would not have considered themselves apologists) writing in the 1950s and 1960s also made similar observations. For examples of this scholarship, see Daniel Mannix and Malcolm Cowley's *Black Cargoes, A History of the Atlantic Slave Trade* (Viking Press, 1963) or John Fage's *Introduction to the History of West Africa* (Cambridge University Press, 1961). Walter Rodney is probably the scholar most widely known for challenging these views about the nature of slavery in Africa prior to the arrival of Europeans. For an example of Rodney's writing in this vein, see his 1966 article in the *Journal of African History* entitled "African Slavery and Other Forms of Social Oppression on the Upper Guinea Coast in the Context of the Atlantic Slave Trade." In this article, Rodney essentially argued that the institution of slavery in Africa was really quite different from, and a more benign form of, what came to be practiced in the Americas. Furthermore, the trans-Atlantic slave trade left deep and lasting scars on societies in Africa.

Paul Lovejoy, professor of history at York University, is writing from a similar perspective as that described for Walter Rodney above. He argues that the trans-Atlantic slave trade significantly transformed African society. It led to an absolute loss of population on the continent and a large increase in the enslaved population that was retained in Africa. The economic advantages of exporting slaves did not offset the social and political costs of participation, there were disastrous demographic impacts, and Africa's relative position in world trade declined. Lovejoy, therefore, supports the "transformation thesis," which holds that the external slave trade dramatically reshaped slavery and society in Africa.

The contrarian view in this issue, presented by John Thornton, professor of history at Boston University, was written in the early 1990s when Walter Rodney and Paul Lovejoy's views, and related structuralist scholarship, were more dominant. He notes that slavery was widespread and indigenous in African society. Most importantly for the time period when he was writing, he argues that African elites had considerable agency (or power) in determining the shape and character of the trans-Atlantic slave trade. He asserts that Europeans worked with existing African slave markets and that African merchants, who were not dominated by Europeans, responded by providing more slaves. African leaders who allowed the slave trade to continue were neither forced to do so against their will, nor did they make irrational decisions. As such, the preexisting institution of slavery in Africa is as much responsible as any external force for the development of the trans-Atlantic slave trade. While Thornton's views are still hotly contested, he did successfully tap into a broader theme in post-structualist literature on Africa, that is the notion that Africans were not helpless pawns in a world dominated by Europeans, but active and influential participants.

The debate about the impact of trans-Atlantic slavery on Africa, and the role of Africans in this process, was most recently, and publicly, reignited by African American scholar Henry Louis Gates in his 1999 PBS series entitled *The Wonders of the African World*. In the second episode of this series he suggested that contemporary Africans bear a collective guilt for what he referred to as "the black-on-black Holocaust" that occurred during the era of the trans-Atlantic slave trade. The then president of the African Studies Association, Lansiné Kaba, responded to Gates in a November 2000 address that subsequently was published in the April 2001 issue of the *African Studies Review* as "The Atlantic Slave Trade Was Not a 'Black-on-Black Holocaust.'"

Paul E. Lovejoy  **YES**

The Impact of the Atlantic Slave Trade on Africa: A Review of the Literature

African History and the Atlantic Slave Trade

The significance of the Atlantic slave trade for African history has been the subject of considerable discussion among historians and merits attempts from time to time to review the literature. The present such attempt addresses several, but not all, the key issues that have emerged in recent years. These are, in order of discussion here: What was the volume of the Atlantic slave trade? More specifically, what were the demographic trends of the trade with respect to regional origins, ethnicity, gender and age? Finally, what was the impact of the slave trade on Africa? In brief, what is the state of the debate over the slave trade?

My own position in the debate is clear: the European slave trade across the Atlantic marked a radical break in the history of Africa, most especially because it was a major influence in transforming African society.

> The history of slavery involved the interaction between enslavement, the slave trade, and the domestic use of slaves within Africa. An examination of this interaction demonstrates the emergence of a system of slavery that was basic to the political economy of many parts of the continent. This system expanded until the last decades of the nineteenth century. The process of enslavement increased; the trade grew in response to new and larger markets, and the use of slaves in Africa became more common. Related to the articulation of this system, with its structural links to other parts of the world, was the consolidation within Africa of a political and social structure that relied extensively on slavery.

The transformation thesis identifies slavery as a central feature of African history over the past millennium. The Atlantic trade was only one, although a major, influence on the transformation of society. The Muslim slave trade was also important, and other internal African developments strongly influenced social change as well. According to this interpretation, the task of the historian is to weigh the relative importance of the various factors that incorporated Africa into an "international system of slavery" that included Africa, the Americas, western Europe and the Islamic world.

From *Journal of American History*, vol. 30, 1989, pp. 365-367, 386-393. Copyright © 1989 by Organization of American Historians. Reprinted by permission.

David Eltis has challenged this interpretation. On the basis of his study of the nineteenth-century Atlantic trade and an analysis of the value of the Atlantic trade between the 1680s and 1860s, Eltis has concluded that neither the scale nor the value of the Atlantic trade was sufficiently large to have had more than a marginal influence on the course of African history. According to Eltis,

> The slave trade for most regions and most periods was not a critically important influence over the course of African history. At the very least, those who would place the slave trade as central to West African and west-central African history should be able to point to stronger common threads, if not themes, across African regions than have so far come to light.

With respect to slavery, he claims that "whatever the origins or nature of structural changes in African slavery, it is unlikely that external influences could have been very great."

The contribution which Eltis makes is two-fold, it seems to me. First, he brings more precision to an analysis of the volume and direction of the Atlantic trade in the nineteenth century. His study of nutritional trends, age and gender, and mortality are particularly significant. Secondly, he has articulated a model of economic development for the pre-colonial era that must be taken seriously, although I disagree with his conclusions. Did exports determine the extent of economic change, as measured by standard economic indicators? He concludes that an export-led model of economic development has little to offer in interpreting African history. Climate and human genius, according to Eltis, were far more important than the export sector.

Eltis bases his startling conclusions on an analysis of the relative importance of the Atlantic trade on Africa, as determined on a *per capita* basis. In a study undertaken jointly with Lawrence C. Jennings, it is claimed that the annual average *per capita* trade of those parts of Africa involved in the Atlantic slave trade was significantly less than in other parts of the Atlantic basin and that the African share in world trade declined in relative terms from the 1680s to the 1860s. They conclude that neither the absolute nor the relative value of Atlantic trade was very great; in general, foreign trade had only a weak influence on African economies. According to Eltis,

> . . . on the assumption that the improbably low figure of 15 million people lived in West Africa [in the 1780s] at subsistence levels, then imports from Atlantic trade may be taken at about 9 per cent of West African incomes in the 1780s. With assumptions that are more in accord with reality (i.e. a population of 25 million or more and domestic production in excess of subsistence), then imports decline in importance to well below 5 per cent. For other decades in the century when both slave prices and exports were lower, imports would have been much less significant. For west-central Africa, population densities were much lower but import/income ratios could not have been much greater.

Indeed, "The majority of Africans . . . would have been about as well off, and would have been performing the same tasks in the same socioeconomic environment, if there had been no trading contact" with Europe. Eltis even advances the astonishing conclusion for Asante that ". . . the ratio of the level of exports, either before or after 1807, to any plausible population estimates of Asante suggests that the slave trade can never have been important."

The rise of commodity exports in the nineteenth century had virtually no impact on Africa either. According to Eltis,

> . . . the slave and commodity trades together formed such a small percentage of total African economic activity that either could expand without there being any impact on the growth path of the other. . . . [I]n the mid-nineteenth century neither the slave nor the commodity traders were large enough to have to face the problem of inelastic supplies of the factors of production.

In short, neither the Atlantic slave trade nor its suppression had much influence on African history.

The following review of the recent literature on the Atlantic slave trade provides a context in which to assess the revisionist interpretation of Eltis (and Jennings). I begin with the new studies on the volume of the slave trade, in which a consensus seems to have emerged. I then consider the analytical refinements in the regional and ethnic origins of the exported slave population. The demographic data allow a closer examination of the gender and age profile of the trade, which is the subject of the next section of this article. Finally, I return to an assessment of the arguments of Eltis, particularly with regard to the demographic impact of the trade on Africa. A number of important themes are not considered, including the economic significance of slavery in Africa and the importance of imported commodities on African society and economy. Nonetheless, I believe that I can demonstrate that Eltis' provocative conclusions are seriously flawed. . . .

Impact of the Atlantic Slave Trade on Africa

The discussion of the volume of the trade, the regional and ethnic origins of the exported population, and the sex and age profiles of slaves should indicate that much of Eltis' revisionist interpretation cannot be accepted. Otherwise, these factors would not matter to African history, although they are crucial to the history of slavery in the Americas. While the slight modifications in the volume and direction of the Atlantic slave trade do not affect the argument of Eltis (and Jennings), the issues remain: did the slave trade have a dramatic impact on exporting regions? Did the suppression of the Atlantic trade in the nineteenth century have a significant effect on the course of slavery? My informed opinion is that both the trade and it suppression were major factors in African history, and to show this I will examine, in order, the following issues: (1) the economic impact of the trade; (2) its demographic implications; and (3) the incidence of slavery in Africa. There are certainly other issues, but these will have to suffice.

One of the principal conclusions of Eltis and Jennings seems likely but only modifies my analysis: Africa's share of world trade from the late seventeenth until the mid-nineteenth century was relatively small in comparison with other parts of the Atlantic world, and Africa's share of that trade declined in relative terms during the period of the slave trade. Eltis and Jennings use an estimate of £0.8–£1.1 for *per capita* incomes in western Africa for the 1780s. They calculate that the export trade amounted to £0.1 per person each year. The proportion of exports to total income certainly appears to be very low by comparison with other parts of the Atlantic basin, although the room for error in measuring *per capita* income and the value of the export trade are enormous.

This observation on the value of the export trade can be accepted, but the implications that Eltis and Jennings draw from it cannot. The ratio of the value of the external trade to *per capita* income is not an accurate indicator of the impact of the slave trade on Africa. *Per capita* income in western Africa was certainly very low by the standards of other parts of the Atlantic basin. Africa was very poor. Almost any incremental increase over subsistence would have had a disproportionate impact on the economy. Eltis and Jennings quantify the relative poverty of Africa, but they are wrong to conclude that the lack of prosperity was an accurate gauge of the degree of isolation from the impact of the slave trade.

The simulation model developed by Patrick Manning provides one way to establish that the slave trade had a significant, indeed devastating, impact on Africa. Manning's model is a statistical means of measuring demographic change under conditions of enslavement, slave trade and slave exports. His analysis is based on the demography of the Atlantic slave trade and certain broad assumptions about demographic change that establish the parameters of the historical possibilities. Manning estimates that the population of those areas of West and west-central Africa that provided slaves for export was in the order of 22–25 million in the early eighteenth century. He projects a growth rate for that population during the eighteenth and early nineteenth centuries of 0–5 per cent, which he considers the maximum possibility. His simulation "model suggests that no growth rate of less than one per cent could have counterbalanced the loss of slaves in the late eighteenth-century." He uses a counterfactual argument to make the same point: "With a growth rate of 0.5%, the 1700 populations . . . [of] 22 to 25 million would have led to 1850 populations of from 46 million to 53 million, more than double the actual 1850 population." Manning concludes that "the simulation of demographic impact of the Atlantic slave trade provides support for the hypothesis of African population decline through the agency of the slave trade."

Furthermore, the simulation model suggests that the incidence of slavery increased in Africa. According to Manning, "As an accompaniment to the estimated nine million slaves landed in the New World [between 1700 and 1850] . . ., some twenty-one million persons were captured in Africa, seven million of whom were brought into domestic slavery, and five million of whom suffered death within a year of capture." As the discussion of the sex profile of the export trade makes clear, more women were retained in Africa than men. Not only did the slave population increase, therefore, but the incidence of polygyny increased as well. Indeed, the two phenomena were closely related.

By 1770 the Atlantic trade resulted in a slave population in the Americas of approximately 2,340,000. Manning's simulation suggests that the slave population in West and west-central Africa could not have been much different. It is safe to say that the slave population was at least 10 per cent of the total population of 22–25 million and that the proportion of slaves was rising. Manning concludes that there were 3 million slaves in those parts of Africa that serviced the Atlantic trade at the turn of the nineteenth century, virtually the same number as in the Americas.

The dramatic growth in the African slave population is the transformation that I highlighted initially in 1979 and more fully in 1983. The transformation was the result of a dialectical relationship between slavery in the Americas and the enslavement, trade and use of slaves in Africa. The production of slaves for the Americas also produced slaves for Africa. It is difficult to prove that the Atlantic slave trade *caused* the transformation of slavery in Africa, but it is likely. The simulation model, as well as the thesis that I advanced in *Transformations in Slavery*, consider that enslavement, trade and the use of slaves were interrelated, across the Atlantic and across the Sahara. African, European, and Muslim merchants wanted slaves, and African, European and Muslim slave-owners used slaves. The low value of exports and imports apparently confused Eltis and Jennings so that they did not perceive the importance of this interrelationship, but an examination of any part of Africa that was a supplier of the export trade reveals the dialectic.

Miller's study of Angola provides the most dramatic example of impact of the slave trade on a region in Africa. As the export data make clear, approximately 40 per cent of all slaves in the Americas came from west-central Africa, and Miller estimates that deaths in Africa related to capture and enslavement roughly equalled the number of slaves exported, that is 50,000–60,000 per year in the last half of the eighteenth century. In addition, "fully as many more people [were] seized as slaves but left to reside in other parts of western central Africa." Total population displacement would have been in the order of 100,000–120,000 per year. Admittedly, Miller paints this as a worst-possible scenario, but even if demographic change was less severe it must have been dramatic. No one has argued as much, but it may be that matrilineality and the export trade were interrelated. They certainly reinforced each other.

Miller's analysis confirms the gender and age structure of the trade. In pursuing a discovery made earlier by John Thornton, Miller shows that the sex ratio of the population in those areas most heavily involved in the export trade was strongly skewed towards women and girls. Polygyny was a central institution of wealth and political power, and slaves (females) were most heavily concentrated around the principal courts of the region. Miller refers to the centralization that was associated with the slave trade as the "great transformation," which is solace to the theorist. On the basis of Miller's analysis, it is impossible to conclude that the slave trade had a marginal impact on west-central Africa.

Eltis is on shaky ground in suggesting that the suppression of the slave trade was not a decisive event for Africa. According to his interpretation, the increased incidence of slavery in the nineteenth century was unconnected with the collapse of the Atlantic trade. Instead, increased demand for slaves arose from "rejuvenated Islam" and late in the century from European demand for primary products from Africa. Indeed there was a dramatic increase in slavery as a result of the *jihads* and Muslim commercial expansion in East Africa. Although Eltis does not explicitly argue the point, his proposed revision is one of timing and concentration, not of substance, and he presents no new data. I remain unconvinced. Certainly there was an expansion in production, based on slave labour, late in the nineteenth century, but that development is also part of the transformation thesis.

Eltis disputes the thesis that the slaving frontier continued to move inland during the early nineteenth century and that the number of slaves in Africa increased dramatically in these decades. He bases this conclusion on an analysis of slave prices:

> . . . because the price of all slaves declined, it seems clear that although domestic [African] demand increased, it did not increase sufficiently to offset the decline in trans-atlantic demand. As a consequence, the number of slaves traded as well as the price of those slaves declined during the century . . .; accordingly, suppression must have meant some reduction in the enslavement of Africans.

Eltis is correct that the price of slaves dropped between the 1790s and the 1820s and continued at a depressed level for most of the continent for the rest of the century. Slaves were cheap, and in real terms prices may have continued to fall in many of the major slave markets, but this does not mean that enslavement decreased in intensity. The cheapness of slaves reflects two factors, the generally low prices of basic commodities in Africa and the glut of the slave market.

Before the suppression of the trans-Atlantic trade, according to Eltis, the demand for slaves was divided into two sectors: one within Africa and the second in the Americas. (In fact, there was a third sector—the external Muslim market.) The collapse of American demand inevitably depressed prices in Africa, He concludes that the African market did not increase sufficiently to offset the loss of American sales; according to Eltis demand and supply declined, although he only provides slave prices as evidence. Prices did not rebound after the decline of the 1790–1820 period, it is true, but the reason was a combination of factors. Indeed Eltis shows that American demand did not decline, in the aggregate, in this period but regained its former heights. Decline only began in the 1850s, well after the period that is crucial to his argument.

Demand is an expression of price, so if prices were generally low, then demand might appear to have been depressed. In fact, the contrary could have been true, if more were known about the price structure of African economies. African demand for slaves was determined by the value of what slaves could produce, and this marginal revenue product was primarily a function of the value of food consumption, housing costs, social require-ments, taxation and similar expenditures that were not much affected by international markets. Any qualitative assessment of the eighteenth and nine-teenth centuries would judge Africa to have been comparatively poor, as the ratio of exports to *per capita* income reveals. Prices in general were low, and the price structure would have influenced the cost of slaves accordingly.

Eltis and Jennings, in concentrating on export-led economic develop-ment, have raised an important consideration: more needs to be known about internal African price structures. Until such information is available, however, it is hard to justify their conclusions, and there is sufficient evi-dence available to argue the contrary.

Eltis' conclusion that enslavement declined in the early nineteenth cen-tury contradicts the research of most Africanist historians who have written on the period. In almost every part of Africa for most of the century, enslave-ment was rampant. Slaves were generated on a scale previously unknown, as can be attested by the following examples: the wars of the *mfecane* in south-ern and central Africa, the activities of Arabs, Swahili, Yao, Nyamwezi, Chikunda and others in eastern and south-eastern Africa, and the raiding of Muslim slavers in the southern Sudan and north-central Africa, None of these cases have much, if anything, to do with the suppression of the Atlantic slave trade, and hence could be dismissed by those who favour the Eltis thesis. But what about the phenomenal levels of enslavement during the *jihads,* often in areas that once did or could have fed the Atlantic trade? How are the collapse of the Lunda states and the havoc of enslavement instigated by the Cokwe to be explained? Can the insecurity of Igbo country in the nineteenth century and the enslavement resulting during the Yoruba wars be easily dismissed? The combined impact of these phenomena was to maintain a glutted market and hence a depressed price for slaves almost everywhere. The "transforma-tion thesis" holds that the external slave trade, particularly the trans-Atlantic sector but also the Islamic market, shaped slavery and society in Africa, and that internal factors intensified slavery as the external trade contracted.

The enslavement of people and the growth of the slave population in Africa continued apace for the whole of the nineteenth century, despite local variations. As yet there are few estimates of the scale of the African slave pop-ulation, but some insights can be gained by a comparison of certain parts of West Africa in *c.* 1900 with the Americas on the eve of emancipation there.

The slave population of the Americas rose from 2,340,000 in *c.* 1770 and peaked at 2,968,000 by the end of the century. The revolt of St Domingue reduced this total considerably; St Domingue had a slave population of 480,000 in 1791. The independence of mainland Spanish America after *c.* 1820, with its slave population of a couple hundred thousand, and the eman-cipation of 674,000 British slaves in 1834 reduced the total further, but the number of slaves continued to expand in the Spanish Caribbean, the U.S.A. and Brazil, reaching a peak just before the emancipation of U.S.A. slaves in the early 1860s. In 1860, there were almost 4 million slaves in the U.S.A. and another 1.5–1.8 million slaves in Brazil and the Spanish Caribbean, for an estimated total of 5.5–5.8 million slaves. With the freeing of slaves in the U.S.A., the slave population declined considerably to a level well below two million. Puerto Rico had 47,000 slaves in 1867; Cuba 288,000 slaves in 1871, and Brazil 1,511,000 slaves in 1872. With the final emancipation of slaves in Cuba in 1880 and Brazil in 1888, slavery came to an end in the Americas.

We may compare the American figures with those of the Western Sudan that have been assembled by Martin Klein. Various estimates between 1905 and 1913 put the slave population of Haut-Sénégal-Niger at about 702,000, or 18 per cent of the total population of 3,942,000. The slave population of French Guinea was 490,000, or 34.6 per cent of the total population (1,418,000). For the French Sudan as a whole, there were approximately 1,192,000 slaves in a total population of 5,134,000, but these estimates were made *after* the slave exodus that occurred during and immediately after the French conquest. That exodus reached a climax in 1905-06, by which time hundreds of thousands of slaves had fled. Before the exodus, the slave population was probably in the order of 1.5–2 million.

The extent of slavery in the Sokoto Caliphate was comparable. J. S. Hogendorn and I have calculated that the number of slaves in the Caliphate probably represented one-quarter of the total population of 10 million in 1900. Both the percentage of slaves and the scale of the population are intended as conservative estimates. While there is a slight overlap between Klein's figures and our own, these are not significant. Eight of the thirty emirates in the Caliphate came under French rule, but only two are included in Klein's sample, and they were both small emirates. Whether Hogendorn's and my figures are accepted or not, there can be little doubt that the Sokoto Caliphate may well have been the second or third largest slave society in modern history. Only the United States in 1860 (and maybe Brazil as well) had more slaves than the Caliphate did in 1900.

About a decade after the final emancipation of slaves in the Americas, there were at least twice as many slaves in Islamic West Africa as there had been in Brazil and Cuba in 1870 and at least as many as in the U.S.A. at the start of its Civil War. These comparisons are striking evidence that slavery in Africa has to be taken seriously by historians of both Africa and the Americas. As should be obvious, no attempt is made here to estimate the slave populations of other parts of Africa, particularly areas that fed the Atlantic slave trade, but it is known that the percentage of slaves in Asante, the Yoruba states, the Igbo country and elsewhere was high.

Conclusion

The economic costs of the slave trade in African economies and societies were severe, despite Eltis' interpretation to the contrary. First, the low *per capita* income from the trade indicates that the economic advantages of exporting slaves were nowhere near large enough to offset the social and political costs of participation. Secondly, the size of the trade, including enslavement, related deaths, social dislocation and exports, was sufficient to have had a disastrous demographic impact. Thirdly, because the rise of produce exports started at such a low base and at a time when slave exports were becoming less important, western Africa suffered a relative decline in its position in world trade.

There were other heavy costs which Eltis has failed to appreciate. It is possible to calculate the gross barter terms of trade and *per capita* income from the slave trade and compare western Africa with other parts of the world. But it is difficult to assess the full costs of "producing" slaves because of the nature of enslavement. In an economic sense, as Robert Paul Thomas and Richard Bean have demonstrated, slaves were a "free good," like fish, as far as those doing the enslaving were concerned. There were costs associated with "production," but the real cost in human terms included the loss of life from enslavement, subsequent famines and disease. Furthermore, the destruction of property during wars and raids also represented a loss. Manning's simulation model has attempted to account for some of these costs, although it will never be possible to do the kind of analysis that is possible in measuring the volume and direction of the trans-Atlantic trade itself. Miller has come closest to demonstrating the effects of this impact on a particular region, but his analysis, too, is based on a considerable degree of conjecture.

When the indirect costs of enslavement and trading are taken into consideration, the insights of Eltis and Jennings take on a new meaning. Rather than demonstrating that the Atlantic slave trade had virtually no impact on western Africa, it can be concluded that the impact was in fact strongly negative, although profound.

NO ⬅

John Thornton

Slavery and African Social Structure

If Africans were experienced traders and were not somehow dominated by European merchants due to European market control or some superiority in manufacturing or trading techniques, then we can say confidently that Africa's commercial relationship with Europe was not unlike international trade anywhere in the world of the period. But historians have balked at this conclusion because they believe that the slave trade, which was an important branch of Afro-European commerce from the beginning, should not be viewed as a simple commodity exchange. After all, slaves are also a source of labor, and at least to some extent, removal from Africa represented a major loss to Africa. The sale of slaves must therefore have been harmful to Africa, and African decisions to sell must have been forced or involuntary for one or more reasons.

The idea of the slave trade as a harmful commerce is especially supported by the work of historical demographers. Most who have studied the question of the demographic consequences of the trade have reached broad agreement that the trade was demographically damaging from fairly early period, especially when examined from a local or regional (as opposed to a continental) perspective. In addition to the net demographic drain, which began early in some areas (like Angola), the loss of adult males had potentially damaging impacts on sex ratios, dependency rates, and perhaps the sexual division of labor.

In addition to these demographic effects, historians interested in social and political history have followed Walter Rodney in arguing that the slave trade caused social disruption (such as increasing warfare and related military damage), adversely altered judicial systems, or increased inequality. Moreover, Rodney argued that the slave trade increased the numbers of slaves being held in Africa and intensified their exploitation, a position that Paul Lovejoy, its most recent advocate, calls the "transformation thesis." Because of this perception of a widespread negative impact, many scholars have argued that the slave trade, if not other forms of commerce, must have been forced on unwilling African participants, perhaps through the type of commercial inequities that we have already discussed or perhaps through some sort of military pressure (to be discussed in a subsequent chapter).

When Rodney presented his conclusions on the negative impact and hence special status of the slave trade as a branch of trade, it was quickly contested by J. D. Fage, and more recently, the transformation thesis has been attacked by David Eltis. As these scholars see it, slavery was widespread and indigenous in African society, as was, naturally enough, a commerce in slaves. Europeans simply tapped this existing market, and Africans responded to the increased demand over the centuries by providing more slaves. The demographic impact, although important, was local and difficult to disentangle from losses due to internal wars and slave trading on the domestic African market. In any case, the decision makers who allowed the trade to continue, whether merchants or political leaders, did not personally suffer the larger-scale losses and were able to maintain their operations. Consequently, one need not accept that they were forced into participation against their will or made decisions irrationally.

The evidence for the period before 1680 generally supports this second position. Slavery was widespread in Africa, and its growth and development were largely independent of the Atlantic trade, except that insofar as the Atlantic commerce stimulated internal commerce and development it also led to more widespread holding of slaves. The Atlantic slave trade was the outgrowth of this internal slavery. Its demographic impact, however, even in the early stages was significant, but the people adversely affected by this impact were not the ones making the decisions about participation.

In order to understand this position it is critical to correctly comprehend the place of the institution of slavery in Africa and furthermore to understand why the structure of African societies gave slavery a different meaning than it had in Europe or the colonial Americas. The same analysis explains the reasons for slavery's extension (if indeed it was extended) during the period of the Atlantic trade and its correlation with commercial and economic growth.

Thus, as we will see in this chapter and the next, the slave trade (and the Atlantic trade in general) should not be seen as an "impact" brought in from outside and functioning as some sort of autonomous factor in African history. Instead, it grew out of and was rationalized by the African societies who participated in it and had complete control over it until the slaves were loaded onto European ships for transfer to Atlantic societies.

The reason that slavery was widespread in Africa was not, as some have asserted, because Africa was an economically underdeveloped region in which forced labor had not yet been replaced by free labor. Instead, slavery was rooted in deep-seated legal and institutional structures of African societies, and it functioned quite differently from the way it functioned in European societies.

Slavery was widespread in Atlantic Africa because slaves were the only form of private, revenue-producing property recognized in African law. By contrast, in European legal systems, land was the primary form of private, revenue-producing property, and slavery was relatively minor. Indeed, ownership of land was usually a precondition in Europe to making productive use of slaves, at least in agriculture. Because of this legal feature, slavery was in many ways the functional equivalent of the landlord–tenant relationship in Europe and was perhaps as widespread.

Thus, it was the absence of landed private property—or, to be more precise, it was the corporate ownership of land—that made slavery so pervasive an aspect of African society. Anthropologists have noted this feature among modern Africans, or those living in the so-called ethnographic present or traditional societies. Anthropologists have regarded the absence of private or personal ownership of landed property as unusual, because it departs from the European pattern and from the home cultural experience of most anthropological observers, and has therefore seemed to require an explanation. . . .

At first glance, this corporatist social structure seems to allow no one to acquire sources of income beyond what they could produce by their own labor or trade if they were not granted a revenue assignment by the state. Modern commentators on Africa have occasionally noted this, and precolonial African societies have sometimes been characterized as unprogressive because the overdeveloped role of the state inhibited private initiative by limiting secure wealth. In particular, these commentators believed that the absence of any form of private wealth other than through the state greatly inhibited the growth of capitalism and, ultimately, progress in Africa.

It is precisely here, however, that slavery is so important in Africa, and why it played such a large role there. If Africans did not have private ownership of one factor of production (land), they could still own another, labor (the third factor, capital, was relatively unimportant before the Industrial Revolution). Private ownership of labor therefore provided the African entrepreneur with secure and reproducing wealth. This ownership or control over labor might be developed through the lineage, where junior members were subordinate to the senior members, though this is less visible in older documentation.

Another important institution of dependency was marriage, where wives were generally subordinate to their husbands. Sometimes women might be used on a large scale as a labor force. For example, in Warri, Bonaventura da Firenze noted in 1656 that the ruler had a substantial harem of wives who produced cloth for sale. Similarly, the king of Whydah's wives, reputed to number over a thousand, were employed constantly in making a special cloth that was exported. Such examples give weight to the often-repeated assertion that African wealth was measured in wives, in the sense both that polygamy was indicative of prestige and that such wives were often labor forces.

Of course, the concept of ownership of labor also constituted slavery, and slavery was possibly the most important avenue for private, reproducing wealth available to Africans. Therefore, it is hardly surprising that it should be so widespread and, moreover, be a good indicator of the most dynamic segments of African society, where private initiate was operating most freely.

The significance of African slavery can be understood by comparing it briefly with slavery in Europe. Both societies possessed the institution, and both tended to define slaves in the same way—as subordinate family members, in some ways equivalent to permanent children. This is precisely how slaves are dealt with in *Siete partidas,* following a precedent that goes all the way back to Aristotle, if not before. Modern research clearly reveals that this is also how Africans defined slavery in the late precolonial and early colonial period.

Seventeenth-century African data do not deal with the legal technicalities, though we have little reason to believe that they differed from those uncovered by modern anthropological research. For Kongo, where the remarkable documentation allows glimpses of the underlying ideology, the term for a slave, *nleke,* was the same as for a child, suggesting the family idiom prevailed there.

Where the differences can be found is not in the legal technicalities but in the way slaves were used. In theory, there have been no differences in this respect either, but in practice, African slaves served in a much wider variety of ways than did European or Euro-American slaves. In Europe, if people acquired some wealth that they wished to invest in secure, reproducing form, they were likely to buy land. Of course, land did not produce wealth by itself, but usually the land was let out to tenants in exchange for rents or was worked under the owner's supervision by hired workers. In neither case would such people have to have recourse to slaves to acquire a work force.

From what we know of slave labor in Europe in this period, it would appear that they were employed in work for which no hired worker or tenant could be found or at least was willing to undertake the work under the conditions that the landowner wished. As we shall see, this lay behind most of the employment of slaves in the New World as well. Consequently, slaves typically had difficult, demanding, and degrading work, and they were often mistreated by exploitative masters who were anxious to maximize profits. Even in the case of slaves with apparently good jobs, such as domestic servants, often the institution allowed highly talented or unusual persons to be retained at a lower cost than free people of similar qualifications.

This was not necessarily the case in Africa, however. People wishing to invest wealth in reproducing form could not buy land, for there was no landed property. Hence, their only recourse was to purchase slaves, which as their personal property could be inherited and could generate wealth for them. They would have no trouble in obtaining land to put these slaves into agricultural production, for African law made land available to whoever would cultivate it, free or slave, as long as no previous cultivator was actively using it.

Consequently, African slaves were often treated no differently from peasant cultivators, as indeed they were the functional equivalent of free tenants and hired workers in Europe. This situation, the result of the institutional differences between Europe and Africa, has given rise to the idea that African slaves were well treated, or at least better treated than European slaves. Giacinto Brugiotti da Vetralla described slaves in central Africa as "slaves in name only" by virtue of their relative freedom and the wide variety of employments to which they were put. Likewise, as we shall see, slaves were often employed as administrators, soldiers, and even royal advisors, thus enjoying great freedom of movement and elite life-styles.

This did not mean, of course, that slaves never received the same sort of difficult, dangerous, or degrading work that slaves in Europe might have done, although in Africa often such work might just as easily have been done by free people doing labor service for the state. In any case, Valentim Fernandes's description of slave labor in Senegambia around 1500, one of the few explicit texts on the nature of slave labor, shows that slaves working in agricultural production worked one day a week for their own account and the rest for their master, a work regime that was identical for slaves serving in Portuguese sugar mills on the island colony of São Tomé in the same period. Slaves employed in mining in Africa may have suffered under conditions similar to those of slaves in European mining operations, though the evidence is less certain.

On the whole, however, African slavery need not have been degrading or the labor performed by slaves done under any more coercion (or involving any more resistance) than that of free laborers or tenants in Europe. Therefore, the idea that African dependence on slave labor led to the development of a reluctant work force or inhibited innovation is probably overdone.

For Europe and the European colonies in America, the distinction between the productivity of slave and free labor may have validity (though even there it is a matter of intense debate); in Africa the distinction is probably less applicable. The exact nature of the labor regime, rather than the legal status of the workers, is more relevant to a description of African economic history, and in this instance, different legal structures led Africans and Europeans to develop the institution of slavery in substantially different ways. Consequently, the conventional wisdom concerning slavery developed from the study of European or colonial American societies with landed private property simply cannot apply in Africa.

African slaves were typically used in two different ways. First of all, slaves became the preeminent form of private investment and the manifestation of private wealth—a secure form of reproducing wealth equivalent to landowning in Europe. Second, slaves were used by state officials as a dependent and loyal group, both for the production of revenue and for performing administrative and military service in the struggle between kinds or executives who wished to centralize their states and other elite parties who sought to control royal absolutism.

The private employment of slaves as heritable, wealth-producing dependents was perhaps the most striking African use. Dapper, in describing private wealth in Kongo, noted that although the households of the nobility were not wealthy in ready cash, nor did they possess much in the way of luxury goods, they were wealthy in slaves. This, he believed, was the main form of wealth in central Africa.

Likewise, slaves represented the way to achieve wealth for ambitious commoners in the Gold Coast states, and the state did attempt to regulate their acquisition. According to de Marees, a commoner who had become wealthy through trade might be able to attain noble status by sponsoring an expensive ceremony in which nobility was conferred upon him. Although the ceremony was ruinously expensive, the noble-to-be was willing to undertake it because it allowed him to acquire slaves, which, as Dapper noted a few years later, would make it possible for him to recover the expenses of the ceremony, for "as soon as he gets some goods he bestows them on slaves, for that is what their wealth consists of."

Recently, several historians have followed the careers of some prominent Gold Coast merchants who rose from relative obscurity to become great economic and political actors on the coast, using documentation from the records of the Dutch, English, and Danish commercial houses. In all these accounts, the acquisition of slaves to carry goods, cultivate lands, protect the household, and assist in trading figures prominently as an essential step. Indeed, the careers can in some ways be seen as parallel to that of the European commoners who invested first in land and then in titles of nobility, though in Africa, of course, the investment was in slaves and then in nobility.

Slaves as reproducing wealth figured prominently among the Julas and other Moslem commercial groups of the western Sudan and Senegambia. Richard Jobson, the English gold trader who spent considerable time traveling up the Gambia deep into the Sudan in the 1620s, noted that the Julas ("Juliettos") had constructed a chain of villages worked by their slaves, who provided them with provisions and served as carriers on their commercial expeditions. The heads of these villages acquired special rights (in some ways equivalent to those of nobility) from the rulers of the state in which they settled. Philip Curtin's detailed study of the Julas and other Moslem commercial groups in the late seventeenth and early eighteenth centuries emphasizes their extent and organization. Yves Person, focusing on a later period, compared them to the French bourgeoisie rising from common to noble status or seizing power if thwarted: hence he compared a series of "Dyula Revolutions" from the late eighteenth century onward to the French Revolution.

Thus, in Africa the development of commerce and the social mobility based on commerce was intimately linked to the growth of slavery, for slaves in villages performing agricultural work or carrying goods in caravans or working in mines under private supervision were essential to private commercial development.

This last point is significant to consider in transformation thesis. Both Rodney and Lovejoy, advocates of the idea that the development of the Atlantic slave trade extended slavery and resulted in larger numbers of people being enslaved and being worse treated, see this as a direct external input, foreign to African political economy. Yet, the development and extension of slavery, if it did take place (and this point is never proved by either author), might just as well be seen as the result of economic growth in Africa, perhaps stimulated by commercial opportunities from overseas, perhaps by a growing domestic economy. Even the increased incidence of maltreatment (another point that is completely without proof) may indicate only more aggressive use of the labor force by entrepreneurs, just as the European work force faced increased exploitation during the early stages of the Industrial Revolution.

The use of slaves by private people to increase and maintain their wealth was just one of the ways in which slaves were utilized in African societies. Another one, almost of equal importance, was their use by the political elite to increase their power. Slaves employed by the political elite might be use as a form of wealth-generating property, just as they were in private hands, or they might be used to created dependent administrations or armies. In this latter capacity, Africa created many wealthy and powerful slaves.

Most large African states were collections of smaller ones that had been joined through alliance and conquest, and typically the rulers of these smaller constituent states continued to exercise local authority, and the ruler of the large state found his power checked by them. Developing private resources that would answer only to themselves was an important way in which African rulers could overcome such checks and create hierarchical authority centered on their own thrones. Slaves, who could be the private property of a king or his family or might also be the property of the state, were an ideal form of loyal workers, soldiers, and retainers.

The powerful Sudanese empires relied heavily on slave armies and slave administrators to keep a fractious and locally ascendant nobility in check. These nobles were often descendants of the rulers of the constituent smaller states; this was probably the status of the territorial rulers of Mali in al-'Umaris's fourteenth-century description. These constituent states were called *civitas* by Antonio Malafante, Genonese traveler who left a description of the empire of Songhay and its neighbors in 1477, a term that implies both subordination and self-government in Latin. An anonymous description of the "Empire of Great Fulo" written about 1600 states that it dominated the whole Senegal valley and was composed of some twenty smaller units. In accounts of the western provinces of Mali during the late fifteenth and early sixteenth centuries, Portuguese travelers describe local "kings" (heads of constituent states) as virtually sovereign in their local rights and government, yet simultaneously describe Mali as a powerful overlord. These descriptions and later ones of Mali and Kaabu, a state that based its authority on being a province of Mali, all reveal apparent local sovereignty coexisting with the apparently strong rights of the overlord, who at least extracted tribute and obedience and might even intervene in local affairs.

One can observe the same with regard to a somewhat shadowy kingdom of "Kquoja" that dominated Sierra Leone from a capital near Cape Mount in the late sixteenth and early seventeenth centuries. Although Alvares de Almada noted that the Kquoja kings collected regular tribute and taxes from local rulers, historians have generally not seen it as a unitary state.

In some cases, perhaps including both Kaabu and sixteenth-century Mali, the strength of local states did cut in on revenue and authority exercised by their overlords, but slaves often offered a way around this Alvise da Mosto's description of Jolof in the mid-fifteenth century provides a good example. Here, according to da Mosto, the king was beholden to three or four other powerful nobles, each of whom controlled a region (clearly the constituent states), gave him revenue when they chose, and moreover exercised the right to elect him. But the king was able to obtain revenue of his own by distributing slaves in villages to each of his several wives; this income belonged to him. Not only did this give him independent support, but it allowed him to develop a large retinue of dependents who carried out his administrative tasks, numbering some 200 people in all. Unfortunately, the fact that at least one of his subordinates, "Budomel" (title of the ruler of Kajorr [Kayor]), was doing the same thing at the local level may well have ultimately limited his capacity to develop more central power.

Sixteenth- and seventeenth-century evidence from the *Tarikh al-Fettash*, a locally composed source on Songhay, shows quite clearly how the development of an army and administration of slaves helped that empire to become centralized. Tymowski has analyzed this text and showed that rice plantations worked by slaves, as well as villages of slaves settled throughout the country, supported an army of slaves and a bureaucracy of slaves through which the emperors conducted their business, neglecting whatever obligations they may have had to the local nobles.

Slavery probably also aided centralizing monarchs in central Africa as well as West Africa. Kongo seems to have originally been a federation of states, at least as sixteenth- and seventeenth-century tradition and law described it. The original kings of the federation owed their election to the votes of several electors, who were the heads of the member states. But collecting slaves into a central place gave the Kongo kings great power—the capital city of Mbanza Kongo and its surrounding area formed a great agricultural center already in 1491, and probably had ten times the population density of rural areas a century later. The slaves, many of whom occupied estates around the capital, provided Kongo with both the wealth and the demographic resources to centralize. As early as 1526, documents from Kongo show that the provinces (constituent states) were in the hands of royally appointed people (mostly kinsmen), and by the mid-seventeenth century local power and election were regarded more as a curse than a blessing.

Slavery played a role in the centralization of nearby Ndongo as well. Like Kongo, Ndongo rulers may have benefited from the concentration of slaves in their capital—for Kabasa, Ndongo's capital, was also described as a large town in a densely populated area. In addition, the ruler had villages of slaves who paid revenue to him scattered around in his domain. These villages were called *kijiko* (which actually means "slave" in Kimbundu), which a document of 1612 rendered as "populated places whose residents are slaves of the said king." Perhaps more significant in Ndongo, however, was the use that the kings made of slaves as administrators, for the ruler had officials, the *tendala* and the *ngolambole* (judicial and military officials, respectively), who supervised subordinates and collected tax and tribute from his slaves.

We have already seen that African rulers were sometimes limited in the amount of absolute power they could exercise. Some societies had rules of election that allowed officials to choose a weak ruler. In some of the smaller states, the use of slaves may have helped rulers develop more autocratic systems of government. In dealing with the states of the eastern Gold Coast, for example, Dapper noted that they were all quite strongly centralized and, moreover, had an abundance of slaves. Similarly, Alvaro Velho noted that among the smaller states of Sierra Leone, the income that rulers obtained from their slaves was their only steady source of income.

Thus slaves could be found in all parts of Atlantic Africa, performing all sorts of duties. When Europeans came to Africa and offered to buy slaves, it is hardly surprising that they were almost immediately accepted. Not only were slaves found widely in Africa, but the area had a well-developed slave trade, as evidenced by the numbers of slaves in private hands. Anyone who had the wherewithal could obtain slaves from the domestic market, though sometimes it required royal or state permission, as in the Gold Coast. Europeans could tap this market just as any African could.

Moreover, the most likely owners of slaves—wealthy merchants and state officials or rulers—were exactly the people with whom European traders came into contact. Because merchants selling gold, ivory products, mats, copper bracelets, pepper, or any other trade commodity in Africa would also be interested in the buying and selling of slaves, European merchants could readily find sources. This was not so much because Africans were inveterate slave dealers, as it was because the legal basis for wealth in Africa lay in the idea of transferring ownership of people. This legal structure made slavery and slave marketing widespread and created secondary legal mechanisms for securing and regulating the sale of slaves, which Europeans could use as well as Africans.

The significance of African slavery in the development of the slave trade can be clearly seen in the remarkable speed with which the continent began exporting slaves. As soon as the Portuguese had reached the Senegal region and abandoned their early strategy of raiding for commerce 700–1,000 slaves were exported per year, first with caravans bound for the Sahara (after 1448). After Diogo Gomes's diplomatic mission to the West African rulers in 1456, which opened markets north of the Gambia, exports took a dramatic turn upword, reaching as many as 1,200–2,500 slaves per year by the end of the century.

Thus, from 1450 onward, even before their ships actually reached the Senegal River, Portuguese merchants were buying slaves from northward-bound caravans from the post at Arguim, tapping a long-standing trans-Sahara trade. It is not surprising that Avelino Teixeira da Mota has been able to document the diversion of the Saharan slave trade from North Africa to the Atlantic coast in the same period. The reason that such dramatic numbers were reached immediately may indicate nothing more, therefore, than that a preexisting engagement with foreign markets was transferred to Atlantic ones. Most of the early European slave trading with West Africa, even that with such relatively remote regions as Benin and the Niger delta, known in the sixteenth century as the "River of Slaves," was simply an internal trade diverted to the Atlantic. Pacheco Pereira mentioned that the country of "Opuu," probably the Jukun kingdom on the Benue River, was a major source or slaves for the region.

The slave trade of the Benin coast shows another interesting aspect of African slavery and the export slave trade. The Saharan trade was mainly an export trade, but it also involved some internal trade. This is demonstrated by the fact that the Portuguese resold a large number of the Benin coast slaves to the Gold Coast. We know that such slaves were not simply used in the coastal mines (though we can be sure that many were) because the king of Portugal ordered this trade to cease (unsuccessfully, as it turns out) to prevent them from being sold to Moslems. These Moslems had to be northern

Jula merchants who also visited the coastal goldfields, and thus these slaves may well have been employed in goldfields located quite far in the interior.

That existing internal use and commerce in slaves lay behind the export trade is even more strongly suggested by the trade of central Africa. Unlike the West African trade, which drew on an ancient slave trade with North Africa and might thus have already been affected by external contacts, the central African region had no such external links. Nevertheless, the king of Portugal regarded Kongo as sufficiently important a potential exporter of slaves that he granted settlers in São Tomé privileges to engage in the slave trade in 1493, just a few years after the development of official trade there. Kongo indeed became an important source of slaves for the Tomistas by 1502. Unfortunately we possess no early statistics for the volume of this trade, but Valentim Fernandes noted that around 1507, in addition to some 2,000 slaves working on sugar plantations, the island held 5,000–6,000 slaves awaiting reexport. Presumably these slaves were recent imports who had probably arrived within the last year, and certainly half, but probably the majority, originated in central Africa. When the books of the royal factor on the island were inspected by Bernardo da Segura in 1516, they showed annual imports, mostly from Kongo, of nearly 4,500 slaves.

Slaves from central Africa were so numerous that they soon exceeded the capacity of São Tomé and the Mina trade to absorb them, and so they began the long journey to European markets. Although most of the slaves available in the port towns of Lisbon, Balencia, and Seville in the 1470s and 1480s came from western West Africa, Jolof in particular, by 1512 "Manicongos" were arriving in Seville, and Portuguese reports of 1513 mention a whole ship from Kongo making delivery in Europe.

Thus, at some point, probably with twenty years of first contact, central Africa was able to supply exports of slaves equal to the entire exports of West Africa. Clearly this sort of volume could not simply have been the occasional export of odd misfits. Nor have we any reason to believe that the Portuguese were able to either acquire the slaves themselves (except as clients of the Kongo kings) or force the Kongo to obtain the export slaves against their will. Instead, the growth of Kongo's trade had to draw on a well-developed system of slavery, slave marketing, and slave delivery that preexisted any European contact.

We must therefore conclude that the Atlantic slave trade and African participation in it had solid origins in African societies and legal systems. The institution of slavery was widespread in Africa and accepted in all the exporting regions, and the capture, purchase, transport, and sale of slaves was a regular feature of African society. This preexisting social arrangement was thus as much responsible as any external force for the development of the Atlantic slave trade.

POSTSCRIPT

Did the Trans-Atlantic Slave Trade Underdevelop Africa?

Today, John Thornton is not alone in his assertion that African elites had considerable influence on the continent's relationship with Europeans during the slave trading era. David Eltis (see *The Rise of African Slavery in the Americas*, Cambridge University Press, 2000) and Herbert Klein (see *The Atlantic Slave Trade*, Cambridge University Press, 1999) also have arrived at similar conclusions. Nonetheless, John Thornton's views remain quite controversial. While few question his motives or quality of his scholarship, many disagree with his conclusions. It is significant that Thornton ends his analysis before the advent of the eighteenth century at which point important changes in global trade and technology drastically transform the relationship between Africa and Europe. As Patrick Manning notes in a 1993 review of Thorton's book in the *American Historical Review*, "I question whether African institutions of slavery, and especially of enslavement, could have been as extensive in the in the sixteenth century, when some five thousand slaves were exported annually, as in the eighteenth century, when ten times that many slaves left Africa each year."

Thornton's text, while controversial, has become a departure point for new scholars who have been inspired to put his assertions to the test. One example of this is Walter Hawthorne's book *Planting Rice and Harvesting Slaves: Transformations Along the Guinea-Bissau Coast, 1400-1900* (Heinemann, 2003). Here, Hawthorne examines the Balanta of the Upper Guinea Coast and demonstrates that those living outside of more centralized African states were not mere victims of enslavement. In response to outside pressure, the Balanta developed a new rice production system and often found ways to produce slaves themselves.

A final point worth touching on is Thornton's argument that slavery developed in Africa prior to European arrival because African institutions did not permit private ownership of land, but did permit ownership of labor. It is true that labor has generally been a relatively scarce factor in African farming systems and control of labor certainly would have been a key factor in amassing wealth. Labor control in this context, however, does not necessarily correlate to the type of slavery that evolved alongside capitalism in the Atlantic world. For a good discussion of the latter phenomenon, see Eric Williams' *Capitalism and Slavery* (The University of North Carolina Press, 1994).

For an example of Paul Lovejoy's more recent work on this issue, see his book *Transformations in Slavery: A History of Slavery in Africa* (Cambridge University Press, 2000). While he makes many of the same arguments that he made in his selection for this issue, his argument is bolstered by new evidence on the numbers of slaves traded.

ISSUE 3

Have the Contributions of Africans Been Recognized for Developing New World Agriculture?

YES: Duncan Clinch Heyward, from *Seed from Madagascar* (University of North Carolina Press, 1937)

NO: Judith Carney, from "Agroenvironments and Slave Strategies in the Diffusion of Rice Culture to the Americas," in Karl S. Zimmerer and Thomas J. Bassett, eds., *Political Ecology: An Integrative Approach to Geography and Environment-Development Studies* (Guilford Press, 2003)

ISSUE OVERVIEW

YES: Duncan Heyward, a former Carolina rice planter writing in the middle of the last century, represents the mainstream view that Europeans were primarily responsible for developing South Carolina's remarkable rice plantations in the eighteenth century. In his own accounting of the rise of rice cultivation in the Carolinas, Duncan suggests that the techniques and approaches must have been derived from those observed in China.

NO: Judith Carney, a professor of geography at UCLA, explains that slaves from rice-producing areas in West Africa have only recently been recognized for their intellectual contributions to the development of rice cultivation in the New World. Carney describes how her work, and that of others, challenged the view that slaves were mere field hands, "showing that they contributed agronomic expertise as well as skilled labor to the emergent plantation economy."

$\mathbf{A}$s Judith Carney describes in her selection for this issue, it had long been thought that African slaves contributed little more than labor to the New World's burgeoning plantation economies of the seventeenth, eighteenth and nineteenth centuries. But the pioneering work of Wood (*Black Majority: Negroes in Colonial South Carolina from 1670 through the Stone Rebellion,* Knopf, 1974), Littlefield (*Rice and Slaves: Ethnicity and the Slave Trade in Colo-*

nial South Carolina, Louisiana State University Press, 1981) and Carney (*Black Rice: The African Origins of Rice Cultivation in the Americas*, Harvard University Press, 2001) demonstrated Africans' knowledge of rice production was critical to the success of New World agriculture.

The aforementioned studies also form part of a growing literature on the Atlantic World, a global region centered on the Atlantic basin. Scholars working in this context often focus on the Atlantic Ocean as a conduit for the transmission of people and ideas. Other than the titles just mentioned, other examples of scholarship in this arena include: H. Taylor's *Circling Dixie: Contemporary Southern Culture Through a Transatlantic Lens* (Rutgers University Press, 2001) and Carney and Voeks' 2003 article in *Progress in Human Geography*, entitled "Landscape Legacies of the African Diaspora in Brazil."

In this issue, Judith Carney, a professor of geography at UCLA, explains that slaves from rice-producing areas in West Africa have only recently been recognized for their intellectual contributions to the development of rice cultivation in the New World. Carney describes how her work, and that of others, challenged the view that slaves were mere field hands, "showing that they contributed agronomic expertise as well as skilled labor to the emergent plantation economy."

Carney largely was reacting to an older body of literature that celebrated the contributions of southern planters in establishing successful rice plantations in the Carolinas in the eighteenth century. The selection by Duncan Heyward, a former Carolina rice planter writing in the middle of the last century, is an example of one such tract. According to Heyward, British functionaries identified rice as a suitable crop for the Carolinas and had rice seed sent to the colony. Heyward further suggested that the techniques and approaches for such cultivation must have been observed in China and brought to the Carolinas via European settlers. Those familiar with the Reconstruction and post-Reconstruction periods in U.S. history would not be errant in associating the work of Heyward and others with a larger body of Southern scholarship that tended to glorify the antebellum period. Very interestingly, however, there are a few cases of more contemporary works that highlight the contributions of Southern rice planters. One recent example is Richard Schulze's *Carolina Gold Rice: The Ebb and Flow History of a Low-country Cash Crop* (History Press, 2005). The author is the descendant of a former rice plantation owner and is reviving Carolina Gold rice as an heirloom variety.

Duncan Clinch Heyward ➡ **YES**

Carolina Gold Rice

Often during my years as a planter, when the rice industry on our South Atlantic coast was rapidly being abandoned, I have sat under a great cypress, growing on my river bank, and, looking across the broad expanse of my rice fields, have thought of their strange and remarkable history. There would come to my mind the great and fundamental changes, racial and social as well as economic, which have taken place in a short space of time. And I have wished that the old tree above me could tell the tragic story of those fields, recounting events of which it had been a silent witness.

If the tree could only have spoken, I know its story would have begun at a time when the swamp, on whose edge it grew, was the favorite hunting ground of the red man. It would then have told of the coming of the white man, who drove the red man far away and took from him his lands. Next it would have told how the black man came, brought from far across the sea, how he felled the trees in the swamps and cleared them of their dense undergrowth, letting the sunshine in; then, how he drained the lowlands and grew crops of golden grain; and finally it would have told of the emancipation of the black man, who, after years of servitude, worked on faithfully as a freedman.

The rest of the story of my rice fields would for me have needed no telling. It would have dealt with the years when the white man was compelled, by conditions beyond his control, to give up planting, and the black man moved away seeking employment elsewhere, leaving fertile lands, the only naturally irrigated ones in this country, to revert to their former state.

The story of our former rice fields begins more than two centuries ago.

Carolina Gold rice, world renowned because of its superior quality as compared with all other varieties of rice throughout the world, was grown from seed brought to the province of Carolina about the year 1685. This rice had been raised in Madagascar, and a brigantine sailing from that distant island happened, in distress, to put into the port of Charles Town. While his vessel was being repaired, its captain, John Thurber, made the acquaintance of some of the leading citizens of that town. Among them was Dr. Henry Woodward, probably its best known citizen, for he had the distinction of being the first English settler in the province. He had accompanied Sandford on his first exploring expedition and had volunteered to remain alone at Port Royal in order that he might study the language of the Indians and familiarize himself with the country, in the interests of the Lords Proprietors.

To Woodward Captain Thurber gave a small quantity of rice—less, we are told, than a bushel—which happened to be on his ship. "The gentleman of the name of Woodward," to quote the earliest account of this occurrence, "himself planted some of it, and gave some to a few of his friends to plant."

Thus it came about that I, on the distaff side a descendant of Dr. Woodward, seem to have been destined to spend the best years of my life in seeking to revive an industry in the pursuit of which four generations of my family had been successful.

Three states bordering on the South Atlantic, North Carolina, South Carolina, and Georgia, are the only states in this country where for upwards of two centuries rice was grown. Nearly all of it, however, was produced in South Carolina and Georgia, partly because of a slightly warmer climate, but mainly because of the numerous tidal rivers which flow through these states and empty into the ocean. Along the Cape Fear River in North Carolina, it must be admitted, the finest quality of rice was grown, and for many years seed raised there was sold to the planters farther south, in order to preserve the quality of their rice.

The principal rivers in South Carolina, along which rice was planted, were the Waccamaw, the PeeDee, the Santee, the Cooper, the Edisto, and the Combahee. There were also many large rice plantations on the Savannah River, which separates South Carolina and Georgia. Farther south in Georgia were the Ogeechee, the Altamaha, and the Satilla rivers, the last near the Florida line. Some of these rivers are long, having their sources in the mountains, while others are much shorter. All of them are affected for a number of miles by the rise and fall of the tide, the result being that the fresh water they contain is backed up in the rivers and then drawn down again as the water in the ocean rises and falls. Great salt-water marshes lie on either side of the rivers as they approach the ocean, while higher up they were originally bordered by dense cypress, gum, and cedar swamps where the water was fresh, though rising and falling with the tide. It was in these fresh-water swamps that rice was successfully grown for the longest period of years.

As early as August 31, 1663, Lord Albemarle, one of the Lords Proprietors, wrote to the Governor of the Barbadoes, advising the planters there to settle in the proposed province of Carolina. Among the inducements offered he suggested the growing of rice. In his letter he said, "The commodyties I meane are wine, oyle, reasons, currents, rice, silk, etc" Of these, rice alone was destined to be successfully produced over a long period of years.

The plans of the Lords Proprietors regarding the growing of rice in the new province took practical shape in 1672, for in that year they had a barrel of rice sent to Charles Town in a vessel named the "William and Ralph"; and one must assume that this rice was intended for seed. By 1690 some headway had been made in the growing of rice, for the leading men of the province petitioned Governor Sothell to arrange with the Lords Proprietors that the people be allowed to "pay their quit rents in the most valuable and merchantable produce of their land," among which they included rice. These products, they reported, were "naturally produced here."

Also during this period the General Assembly of the province had ratified acts to protect those who should perfect labor-saving machinery for the purpose of husking and cleaning rice. A few years later the Assembly protested against an export duty on rice. How different was this attitude of the early rice planters from that of the planters of my day! We wanted an import duty. Though Southerners, we favored a tariff on rice, for we sorely needed protection. However, we never went so far as to claim that ours was an "infant industry."

By the year 1700 there was being produced in the province more rice "than we had ships to transport," according to the Governor and Council. Edward Randolph, collector of customs for the Southern department of North America that year, wrote: "They have now found out the true way of raising and husking rice. There has been above three hundred tons shipped this year to England besides about thirty tons to the Islands." This progress must have caused the Lords Proprietors to be exceedingly optimistic as to the future of rice cultivation in Carolina, for they congratulated themselves upon "what a staple the province of Carolina may be capable of furnishing Europe withall," and added that "the grocers do assure us it's better than any foreign rice by at least 8s the hundred weight."

At any rate, for the praise so soon bestowed by the grocers of London on the quality of the rice exported from the province of Carolina, and for the demand from abroad for this variety of rice, and also for the success which for upwards of two centuries attended the growing of rice in South Carolina and Georgia, we are principally indebted to Captain Thurber. Had it not been for him, the once celebrated Carolina Gold rice probably would never have been planted in America.

Another variety of rice later planted in South Carolina was known as Carolina White rice. This rice made a beautiful sample when prepared for market, and could scarcely be distinguished from the Gold rice, but its tendency to shatter when being harvested, if slightly over-ripe, caused it to be planted only to a limited extent.

It has never been known definitely from what country this Carolina White rice was first imported, but many of our rice planters believed it had been brought from China, where for unnumbered centuries rice has been grown and where there are today numerous varieties. Were I to hazard a guess as to who was responsible for bringing this white rice to the province, I should name Robert Rowand, born in Glasgow in 1738, who, when a boy, came to Charles Town. He later purchased an inland swamp plantation, on Rantowles Creek, about twenty-five miles southwest of Charles Town. He must have succeeded as a planter, for seemingly he was a man of means and traveled extensively. There is every reason to believe that he visited China, and that, while there, he had certain attractive pictures painted, illustrating the way the Chinese planted rice in those days, and showing the implements used in the process.

A few years ago in the town of Summerville, South Carolina, at the home of a friend, the late Mr. S. Lewis Simons, I saw these pictures. (They have since been destroyed by fire.) There were quite a number of them, and I am sure there are no others like them anywhere in this country. In size, they were about eighteen by fourteen inches, exceedingly well executed in bright water colors. They showed in great detail the growing of rice in China, from the preparation of the ground to the gathering and pounding of the grain. The pictures were evidently painted by a Chinese artist. The figures of men and women, the landscape, with its green trees here and there, blue mountains and hills rising out of the level plains intersected by canals, were entirely Oriental. On the front of the cover was written, "Painted in China prior to the Revolutionary War for one of the first South Carolina Rice Planters, Illustrating the Chinese Method of Cultivating Rice." The rice planter referred to was undoubtedly Robert Rowand, and the pictures had come into the possession of Mr. Simons through his wife, a Miss Mayrant, the Mayrant family having been rice planters for several generations, Mrs. Simons was a lineal descendant of Robert Rowand on her maternal side through the Drayton family.

The first of these Chinese pictures shows the plowing and harrowing of the soil of the seed-beds, both processes being done under water, the Chinaman and his black "water buffalo" nearly up to their knees, and the latter looking as if he did not trust his footing and was anxious to turn back. Then follows the sowing of the seed broadcast on the water, the transplanting of the rice by hand in the fields, the cultivating of the growing crop, the harvesting, until finally the rice is carried to the barnyard, where it is threshed and pounded. Anyone at all familiar with the methods used by the early planters in South Carolina cannot fail to be struck by their similarity to the methods shown in the old Chinese pictures, and especially is this true of the implements used. With the exception of sowing the rice in the water and transplanting it, nearly every picture recalled our system of planting. Many of the implements were almost identical with ours. There were the flail-sticks, being used in exactly the same way; the sickle, only a little straighter than ours, with which the rice was cut; the mortar and pestle and hand-fans; the "boards," as the Negroes used to call them, with which, indoors on a floor, the rice was pushed from place to place; and also the baskets in which the rice was carried.

These paintings of Robert Rowand's convinced me that our early methods of rice culture were adopted largely from the Chinese. For if, instead of the Chinese settings of the pictures, if in the place of the men with queues and black slanting eyes, dressed in bright-colored costumes, there could have been substituted the scenery of our rice fields and the Low Country Negroes at work, I could readily have believed the scenes were laid in our Black Border instead of in that far Eastern land.

Agroenvironments and Slave Strategies in the Diffusion of Rice Culture to the Americas

By the mid-1700s a distinct cultivation system, based on rice, shouldered the American and African Atlantic. One locus of rice cultivation extended inland from West Africas Upper Guinea Coast, another flourished along the coastal plain of South Carolina and Georgia, and a third developed in the corridor between Brazil's Northeast and the eastern Amazon region (Figure 1). This tidal rice cultivation system depended upon enslaved African labor. In West Africa farmers planted rice as a subsistence crop on small holdings, with surpluses occasionally marketed, while in South Carolina, Georgia, and Brazil, cultivation depended on a plantation system and West African slaves to produce a crop destined for international markets.

While rice cultivation continues in West Africa today, its demise in South Carolina and Georgia swiftly followed the abolition of slavery. Brazils experiment in tidal rice cultivation, modeled after that of Carolina, did not withstand its competition in the 19th century. Yet the U.S. South's most lucrative plantation economy continued to inspire nostalgia well into the 20th century when the crop and the princely fortunes it delivered remained no more than a vestige of the coastal landscape. Numerous commentaries documented the lifeways of European American planters, their achievements, and their ingenuity in shaping a profitable landscape from malarial swamps. These accounts have never presented African Americans as having contributed anything but their unskilled labor. The planter-biased rendition of the origins of American rice cultivation prevailed until 1974 when the historian Peter Wood carefully examined the role of slaves in the Carolina plantation system during the colonial period. His scholarship recast the prevalent view of slaves as mere field hands to one that showed that they contributed agronomic expertise as well as skilled labor to the emergent plantation economy. Littlefield built upon Wood's path-breaking thesis by discussing the antiquity of African rice-farming practices and by revealing that more than 40% of South Carolina's slaves during the colonial period originated in West Africa's rice cultivation zone.

From LANDSCAPES OF TECHNOLOGY TRANSFER: RICE CULTIVATION AND AFRICAN CONTINUITIES IN TECHNOLOGY AND CULTURE, Zimmerman and Bassett, eds., vol. 31, no. 1, 1998, pp. 5-35. Copyright © 1989 by Guilford Press. Reprinted by permission.

Figure 1

Rice cultivation along the Atlantic Basin, 1760–1860.

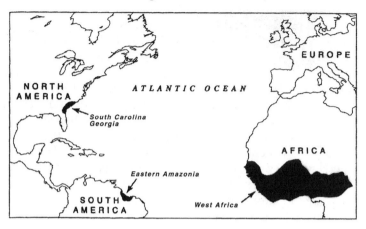

While this research has resulted in a revised view of the rice plantation economy as a fusion of both European and African cultures, the agency of African slaves in its evolution is still debated. Current formulations question whether planters recruited slaves from West Africa's rice coast to help them develop a crop whose potential they independently discovered, or whether African-born slaves initiated rice planting in South Carolina by teaching planters to grow a preferred food crop. The absence of archival materials that would document a tutorial role for African slaves is not surprising given the paucity of records available in general for the early colonial period, and because racism over time institutionalized white denial of the intellectual capacity of bondsmen. An understanding of the potential role of slaves demands other forms of historical enquiry.

This study is situated in a growing trend in scholarship that integrates detailed ethnographic and ecological investigation, particularly of agroenvironments, with social and environmental history. Such an integration invites the use of multiple and diverse tools, including analysis of archival materials and historical documents (e.g., travelers' narratives, colonial accounts, maps), oral histories, agroecological methods, and ethnographic inquiry. The following discussion of West African rice-farming technology and culture is complemented by extensive field-work conducted on rice systems in Senegambia by the author, by Olga R Linares in Senegal, and by Paul Richards in Sierra Leone. Similarities between today's West African rice culture and that of the antebellum U.S. South do not prove in themselves the case for rice technology transfer by African slaves. Field-based geographical studies, however, can substantiate and elaborate upon often-sparse observations in the archival record; provide theoretical frameworks, inspired by political ecology, for understanding past human–environment relations; and produce a richer portrait of past landscapes.

This [selection] combines geographical and historical perspectives to examine the likely contributions of African-born slaves to the colonial rice economy. The approach identifies and describes the principal West African microenvironments planted to rice in the first section as the basis for examining, in the one following, the systems that emerged in South Carolina during the colonial period. While archival documentation, albeit fragmentary, exists on rice systems in West Africa from the 14th century, the discussion in the first section of these systems and their underlying soil and water management principles is based on modern field studies. Focus then shifts to the history of rice cultivation in South Carolina, especially during the hundred years from 1670 to 1770, which is crucial since it spans the initial settlement by planters and slaves as well as the expansion of tidal (tidewater) rice cultivation into Georgia. In emphasizing the complex nexus that links culture, technology, and the environment, attention is directed to the indigenous knowledge systems formed in West Africa by ethnic groups speaking Mande and West Atlantic languages. Across the Middle Passage of slavery they brought their expertise with them, and then established rice as a favored dietary staple in the Americas. This knowledge system, moreover, enabled enslaved rice growers to negotiate and alter, to some extent, the terms of their bondage. The concluding section raises several questions about the issue of technology development and transfer, suggests a lingering Eurocentric bias in historical reconstructions of the agricultural development of the Americas, and discusses the scholarly implications of this research.

The Agronomic and Technological Basis of West African Rice Systems

Some 4,000 years ago, West Africans domesticated rice along the floodplain and inland delta of the upper and middle Niger River in Mali. The species of rice originally planted in this primary center of domestication, *Oryza glaberrima,* differs from Asian rice, *Orvza sativa.* While both species are currently planted in West Africa, the indigenous African center extends along the coast from Senegal to Côte d'Ivoire and into the Sahelian interior along riverbanks, inland swamps, and lake margins. Within this diverse geographic and climatic setting two secondary centers of *glaberrima* domestication emerged: one, on floodplains of the Gambia River and its tributaries; and another, farther south in the forested Guinea highlands where rainfall reaches 2,000 millimeters/year. By the end of the 17th century rice had crossed the Atlantic Basin to the United States, appearing first as a rainfed crop in South Carolina before diffusing along river floodplains and into Georgia from the 1750s.

Many similarities characterized rice production on both sides of the Atlantic Basin. In both West Africa and South Carolina the most productive system developed along floodplains. Precipitation in each region follows a marked seasonal pattern, with rains generally occurring during the months from May/June to September/October. Rice cultivation flourished in South Carolina and Georgia under annual precipitation averages of 1,200–1,400 millimeters, a figure that represents the midrange of a more diverse rainfall pattern influencing West African rice cultivation, where precipitation increases dramatically over short distances from north to south. Accordingly, in the Malian primary center and the Gambian secondary center of rice domestication semi-arid (900 millimeters/year) conditions prevail, while southward in Guinea-Bissau and Sierra Leone precipitation exceeds 1,500 millimeters per annum.

The topography of the rice-growing region on both sides of the Atlantic presents a similar visual field. Coastlines are irregularly shaped and formed from alluvial deposits that also create estuarine islands. Tidal regimes on the American coast differ somewhat from those of Africa. The steep descent from the piedmont in South Carolina and Georgia delivers freshwater tidal flows to floodplains just 10 miles from the Atlantic coast. But the less pronounced gradient of rivers in West Africa's rice region means that freshwater tides meet marine water much farther upstream from the coast; on the Gambia River, salinity permanently affects the lower 80 kilometers but intrudes seasonally more than 200 kilometers upstream. Rice cultivation is adapted to the annual retreat and advance of the saline corridor. Even coastal estuaries inundated by ocean tides served as a basis for West African rice experimentation. South of the Gambia River, where precipitation exceeds 1,500 millimeters/year, West Africans learned to plant rice in marine estuaries, by enclosing plots and allowing rainfall to flush out accumulated salts. Water saturation is the key to planting such soils, as it prevents oxidization to an acidic condition that would preclude further cultivation. An elaborate network of embankments provides a barrier to seawater intrusion, while dikes, canals, and sluice gates enable field drainage of rainwater used for desalination. . . .

African Rice and American Continuities

By 1860, rice cultivation extended over 100,000 acres along the Eastern Seaboard from North Carolina's Cape Fear River to Florida's St. John's River, and inland for some 35 miles along tidal waterways. The initial stage of the rice plantation economy dated to the first hundred years of South Carolina's settlement (1670–1770) and, especially, the decades prior to the 1739 Stono slave rebellion. Rice cultivation systems analogous to those in West Africa, as well as identical principles and devices for water control and milling, were already evident in this period. Dramatic increases in slave imports during the 18th century facilitated the evolution of the Carolina rice plantation economy. Technology development unfolded in tandem with the appearance of the task labor system that regulated work on coastal rice plantations. As the crop grew in economic importance, agro-environments favored for colonial rice production shifted from uplands to inland swamps and, from the 1730s, to the tidal (tidewater) cultivation system that led Carolina rice to global prominence.

This section presents an overview of the historical and geographical circumstances under which rice became a plantation crop in South Carolina. The technical changes marking the evolution of the colonial rice economy illuminate three issues that bear on comparative studies of technology and culture: first, the need to examine the technical components of production as parts of integrated systems of knowledge and not merely as isolated elements; second, the significance of cultural funds of knowledge for technology transfer; and third, in situations of unequal power relations, the extent to which claims for technological ingenuity can rest on cultural dispossession and appropriation of knowledge.

Slaves accompanied the first settlers to South Carolina in 1670; within 2 years they formed one-fourth of the colony's population; and as early as 1708 they outnumbered whites in the colony. Rice cultivation appears early in the colonial record, with planting already underway in the 1690s. By 1695 South Carolina recorded its first shipment of rice: one and one-quarter barrels to Jamaica. In 1699 exports reached 330 tons, and by the 1720s rice had emerged as the leading trade item. Years later, in 1748, South Carolina governor James Glen drew attention to the significance of rice experimentation during the 1690s for development of the colony's economy.

By the 1740s, documents firmly establish the presence of the upland, inland swamp, and tidal floodplain production systems. But rice cultivation in these areas is implied even earlier in the comments of one plantation manager, John Stewart, who claimed in the 1690s to have successfully sown rice in 22 different locations. One major point distinguished patterns of land use in West African and South Carolinian rice systems. In West Africa, subsistence security shaped the crop's production, thereby favoring cultivation in numerous microenvironments along a landscape gradient. Rice cultivation in colonial Carolina began as a subsistence crop, planted similarly in diverse environments, but as it became a plantation crop emphasis shifted to specific agroenvironments along the landscape continuum—from rainfed, to inland swamp, to tidal production—to maximize yields and returns on capital and labor.

Upland rice production received initial attention because it complemented the early colony's economic emphasis on stock raising and extraction of forest products. Slave labor buttressed this agropastoral system, which involved clearing forests, producing naval stores (pine pitch, tar, and resin), cattle herding, and subsistence farming. Export of salted beef, deerskins, and naval stores in turn generated capital to purchase additional slaves. The number of enslaved Africans imported to the colony dramatically increased from 3,000 in 1703 to nearly 12,000 by 1720, which enabled a shift in rice cultivation to the more productive inland swamp system.

The higher yielding inland swamp system initiated the first attempts at water control in Carolina's rice fields. After clearing swamp forests, slaves developed the network of berms and sluices necessary for converting plots into reservoirs. Like its counterpart in West Africa, the inland swamp system impounded water from rainfall, subterranean springs, high water tables, or creeks to saturate the soil. The objective was to drown unwanted weeds and thereby reduce the labor spent on weeding, as in West Africa. West African principles also guided the cultivation of rice in coastal marshes. Rice was grown in saltwater marshes near the terminus of freshwater streams in soils influenced by the Atlantic Ocean. The conversion of a saline marsh to a rice field depended upon soil desalination, a process not as easily achieved with South Carolina's annual precipitation regime (1,100–1,200 millimeters), which is lower than the average 1,500 millimeters per year that regulate the West African mangrove system. However, by diverting an adjoining freshwater creek or stream, salts could be rinsed from the field. The principle of canalizing water for controlled flooding also extended to other settings, such as in places where subterranean springs flowed near the soil surface. Detailed knowledge of landscape topography and hydrological conditions thus enabled the proliferation of rice growing in diverse inland swamp microenvironments.

During the 18th century rice cultivation in such areas innovated to more elaborate systems of sluices that released reserve water on demand for controlled flooding at critical stages of the cropping cycle. This inland swamp system flourished where the landscape gradient sloped from rainfed farming to the inner edge of a tidal swamp. Enclosure of a swamp with earthen embankments created a reservoir for storing rainwater, the system's principal source of irrigation. The reservoir fed water, through a sluice gate and canal, by gravity flow to the inland rice field, while a drainage canal and sluice placed at the lower end of the rice field emptied excess water into a nearby stream, creek, or river. Whereas the principle of constructing a reservoir for controlled field flooding is identical to the West African mangrove rice system, the innovative changes that subsequently developed may well provide an instance of what geographer Paul Richards calls "agrarian creolization." The term refers to the convergence of different knowledge systems and their recombination into new hybridized forms, spearheading the process of innovation.

By the mid-18th century the emphasis on rice had shifted from inland swamps to tidal river floodplains, first in South Carolina, and subsequently in Georgia. The swelling number of slaves directly entering South Carolina from West Africa between the 1730s and the 1770s proved crucial in this spatial relocation of the rice economy. Some 35,000 slaves were imported into the colony during the first half of the century and over 58,000 between 1750 and 1775, making South Carolina the largest importer of enslaved Africans on the North American mainland between 1706 and 1775. The share of slaves brought directly from the West African rice coast grew during these crucial decades of tidewater rice development from 12% (1730s) to 54% (1749–1765), and then to 64% (1769–1774) (Richardson, 1991). This pattern is illuminated in a typical handbill from the colonial period, which announces the sale in Charlestown (Charleston) on July 24, 1769 of enslaved men, women, and children from Sierra Leone.

Tidewater cultivation occurred on floodplains along tidal rivers where, similar to its mangrove rice counterpart in West Africa, the diurnal variation in sea level facilitated field flooding and drainage. Preparation of a tidal floodplain for rice cultivation followed principles already outlined for the mangrove rice system. The rice field was embanked at sufficient height to prevent tidal spillover, while the earth removed in the process created adjacent canals. Sluices built into the embankment and field sections operated as valves for flooding and drainage. The next step involved dividing the area into plots (in South Carolina these were termed "quarter sections," of some 10–30 acres), with river water delivered through secondary ditches. This elaborate system of water control enabled the adjustment of land units to labor demands and allowed slaves to directly sow rice along the floodplain. Then the rice was planted directly in the floodplain, as it is in African floodplain cultivation.

Tidewater cultivation required considerable landscape modification and ever-greater numbers of enslaved laborers than rain-fed and inland swamp cultivation. Leland Ferguson, a historical archaeologist, vividly captures the staggering human effort involved in transforming Carolina's tidal swamps to rice fields:

> These fields are surrounded by more than a mile of earthen dikes or "banks" as they were called. Built by slaves, these banks . . . were taller than a person and up to 15 feet wide. By the turn of the eighteenth century, rice banks on the 12½ mile stretch of the East Branch of Cooper River measured more than 55 miles long and contained more than 6.4 million cubic feet of earth." By 1850, aided only by hand-held tools, slaves in the Carolina rice zone had built earthworks "nearly three times the volume of Cheops, the world s largest pyramid."

While such landscape change placed considerable demands on slave labor for construction and maintenance, it reduced the need for manual weeding, one of the most labor-intensive tasks in rice production. The systematic lifting and lowering of water was achieved by sluices, known as "trunks," located in the embankment and secondary dikes; by the late colonial period these devices had evolved into hanging floodgates. With full control of an adjacent tidal river, the rice field could be flooded on demand for irrigation and weeding and to renew the soil annually with alluvial deposits. Because of this increasing reliance on water control technology, in tidal cultivation one slave could manage 5 acres of rice, as opposed to just 2 acres in the inland rice system.

The history of the term "trunk" for sluice gate in Carolina also suggests evidence for technology transfer from the West African rice coast. While the hanging gate technology likely provides another example of agrarian creolization, its name refers to an earlier device. Even when the hanging gate replaced earlier forms, Carolina planters continued to call sluice gates "trunks." In the 1930s planter descendant David Doar stumbled upon the terms origin: the earliest sluice gates were formed from hollowed-out cypress trunks. The original Carolina sluice system looked and functioned exactly like its African counterpart. Reference to them as "trunks" throughout the antebellum period suggests that the technological expertise of Africans again proved significant in Carolina rice history.

Tidewater rice cultivation led South Carolina to global economic prominence in the 18th century. It was made possible by the expertise of enslaved Africans in cultivating as well as processing the crop. Their experience with planting a whole range of interconnected environments along a landscape gradient likely permitted the sequence of adaptations that marked the growth of the South Carolina rice industry.

African contributions to Carolina rice history were not limited to cultivation practices. They also extended to the method by which the grain was processed for consumption. Until suitable mechanical mills were developed around the time of the American Revolution, the entire export crop was milled by hand, in the traditional method long used by African women, with a mortar and pestle. Even the fanner baskets used to winnow rice on Carolina and Georgia plantations display a likely African origin, as anthropologist Dale Rosengarten suggests. She links the coiled-basket-weaving tradition in fanner baskets to the Senegambian rice region, as it did not exist among Native Americans of the Southeast region.

Enslaved Africans thus contributed significantly more than physical labor to colonial rice production. They provided the critical expertise in establishing rice cultivation in South Carolina, even though accounts by planters and their descendants have long claimed for their forebears the ingenuity in developing the system. Planter accounts, however, fail to explain how they learned to transform wetland landscapes by careful observance of tidal dynamics, soils, microenvironments, and water regimes. Such systems of planting cereals in standing water did not exist in England at the time, yet surfaced within two decades of Carolina's settlement. Wetland rice represents a far more complex farming system than the rainfall cultivation practiced by the English. Enslaved Africans from the African rice region were thus the only settlers present in the Carolina colony who possessed this knowledge system.

The delayed recognition of this significant contribution to the history of the Americas stems, in part, from the way that rice has been examined by scholars. By emphasizing rice as a cereal, as a grain consumed and traded internationally, studies have failed to place it within its proper agroecological context for studies of diffusion and technology transfer. An examination of rice as a landscape of microenvironments brings into focus the underlying soil and water management regimes that inform its cultivation as well as its cultural origins. Recovery of the African contribution to American rice history also involves considering consumption as well as production, processing as well as cultivation, and the types of labor and knowledge that mediated the spatial movement of rice from field to kitchen. This requires sensitivity to ecological as well as gendered forms of knowledge in technology transfer.

While this overview of rice beginnings in South Carolina argues that planters reaped the benefits of a rice-farming system perfected by West Africans over millennia, an important question remains. Why would enslaved West Africans transfer a sophisticated rice system to plantation owners when the result spelled endless and often lethal toil in malarial swamps?

The answer is perhaps revealed in the appearance by 1712 of the task labor system that characterized coastal rice plantations. It was distinguished from the more pervasive "gang" form of work typifying plantation slavery. In the gang system, "the laborer was compelled to work the entire day", while "under the task system the slave was assigned a certain amount of work for the day, and after completing the task he could use his time as he pleased." Without underestimating the real toil involved in the two systems, the task system did set normative limits to daily work demands. Such seemingly minor differences between the two systems could deliver tangible improvements in slave nutrition and health, as Johan Bolzius implied in 1751 with his observation: "If the Negroes are Skilful and industrious, they plant something for themselves after the day's work."

The task labor system appeared at the crucial juncture of the evolution of rice as a plantation crop in the Carolina colony and the shift to the more productive, but labor-demanding, inland swamp system. A similar system of limiting demands placed on enslaved labor was already in existence along Africa's Rice Coast. The appearance of the task labor system in Carolina's fledgling rice economy may well represent the outcome of negotiation and struggle between master and slave over knowledge of rice culture and the labor process to implement it. In providing crucial technological acumen, slaves perhaps discovered a mechanism to negotiate improved conditions of bondage. But by the 19th century such gains had eroded, as the frontier for slave escape closed and slavery appeared to be a permanent feature of Southern agriculture. The task labor system became little different than the gang form of slavery.

Conclusion

"What skill they displayed and engineering ability they showed when they laid out these thousands of fields and tens of thousands of banks and ditches in order to suit their purpose and attain their ends! As one views this vast hydraulic work, he is amazed to learn that all of this was accomplished in face of seemingly insuperable difficulties by every-day planters who had as tools only the axe, the spade, and the hoe, in the hands of intractable negro men and women, but lately brought from the jungles of Africa." In 1936, when David Doar, descendant of Carolina planters, echoed the prevailing view that slaves contributed little besides labor to the evolution of the South Carolina rice economy, no historical research suggested otherwise. While recent research challenges such unquestioned assumptions, a bias nonetheless endures against considering West Africans as the originators of rice culture in the Americas.

Even authoritative texts on rice cultivation, such as that of D. H. Grist, express such a bias. In reference to a type of paddy rice cultivation found in British Guiana (now Guyana) and the neighboring former Dutch colony of Surinam, Grist describes the "empoldering" technique as "a method of restricting floods and thus securing adjacent areas from submergence." While this technique is strikingly similar to that employed in mangrove rice production along the West African rice coast, he attributes the system to 18th-century Dutch colonizers. In that era, however, Surinam possessed one of the highest ratios of Africans to Europeans of any New World plantation society (65:1 in Surinam compared to Jamaica's 10:1).

More recent work in Brazilian rice history repeats this perspective. Even though rice was not grown in Portugal during the colonization of the Americas, Pereira attributes its 16th-century introduction in Brazil's eastern Amazon and Northeast to migrants from the Azores and Portugal. There is no discussion of how the African mortar and pestle (a device not used in Portugal) came to be the sole technology for milling rice in Brazil until the mid-18th century, when it was replaced by water mills that successfully removed the hulls without grain breakage. Nor is there any acknowledgment of the possibility that rice culture became established in Brazil, as in South Carolina, because African rice routinely provisioned slave ships, providing the enslaved an opportunity to grow their food staple for subsistence.

Evidence from the American and African Atlantic thus suggests that slaves from West Africa's indigenous rice area established rice culture. A crop initially planted for subsistence became, in 18th-century South Carolina, the first cereal globally traded as a plantation export crop. This complex indigenous knowledge system guided the transformation of Carolina's swamps while serving as a source of technological innovation in rice culture, captured in the notion of agrarian creolization. These achievements in tidal rice diffused southward in the 18th century along rivers in Georgia and Florida, and, from midcentury, overseas to similar environments in Brazils Northeast and eastern Amazon regions. While rice systems of the Americas would eventually bear the imprimatur of both African and European influences, its appearance initially is linked to a knowledge system developed in West Africa and carried across the Middle Passage by slavery's victims.

Thus, as Europeans and Africans faced each other in a new territory under dramatically altered and unequal power relations, the enslaved established a subsistence crop long valued in West Africa. With the abolition of slavery, rice history led to cultural dispossession and appropriation by descendants of slave owners who credited the beginnings of rice farming to European ingenuity and presumed mastery of technology. A careful reading of the archival and historical record—one attuned to agroenvironments, power relations, ecological principles, and social history—reveals a dramatically different narrative.

The ending of this story is not yet settled: this cross-cultural, social-environmental history of transatlantic rice culture also cuts across current political and cultural debates. In the U.S. South, historical preservation of antebellum landscapes is charged with the controversy of memory politics. While many descendants of white planters view preservation of plantation landscapes as a source of pride, many African Americans perceive these as sites of toil, terror, and shame. This discussion of rice technology transfer demonstrates that despite the brutality of bondage, African slaves were active and ingenious shapers of antebellum agroenvironments rather than mere physical laborers. Historical preservation and ecological restoration efforts in the South should acknowledge the rich hybrid nature of these cultural land-scapes in a way similar to that currently underway in the reconsideration of southern family histories by black and white descendants of slave owners.

This study also has implications for the hotly debated issue of intellec-tual property rights over agricultural seeds. Today, cultivars and their germ plasm are increasingly engineered, patented, and privatized. This market logic reduces seeds to their mere biology. As this investigation of rice cultiva-tion on the Atlantic Rim implies, however, seeds cannot be so easily sepa-rated from their political and social context. The introduction of African rice in the New World was not simply the movement of seeds from one environ-ment to another, but rather the transfer and transformation of a *rice culture,* with attendant continuities and changes in technology, labor organization, social structures, and cultural meanings.

POSTSCRIPT

Have the Contributions of Africans Been Recognized for Developing New World Agriculture?

Despite the wide acceptance of Carney's scholarship, certain aspects of her work have been critiqued. In a review of Carney's book on this subject, *Black Rice* (summarized in Carney's selection in this issue), in a 2002 issue of the *William and Mary Quarterly*, Philip Morgan raises several questions about her treatment of the slave trade. He disputes her claim that Carolina planters imported a greater percentage of female slaves than did Caribbean planters. He questions whether Carolina planters paid more for female slaves than other New World slave markets (but cannot prove otherwise). He also questions whether South Carolineans were sourcing relatively more slaves from rice-producing areas in West Africa at critical junctures in the development of the rice economy. New scholarship by Max Edelson (see *Plantation Enterprise in Colonial South Carolina*, Harvard University Press, 2006) also suggests that European colonists played a much larger role in the development of a Carolina rice economy than Carney admits.

Another question to ponder, and this is raised by Carney in her selection, is why Africans would have been willing to share their rice-growing expertise with their white oppressors. Carney's answer is that they used this knowledge to bargain for a "task labor system" rather than the more oppressive "gang system," which forced slaves to work the entire day. Under the task system, a slave could use his or her time for their own activities after completing a certain quantity of work. As Carney notes, this negotiated approach was eventually lost in the nineteenth century.

A final issue to consider is the somewhat subjective nature of regions as units of analysis. What the burgeoning scholarship on the Atlantic World demonstrates is that historical transfers of peoples and ideas may bind together the two areas (i.e., the Atlantic sides of the Americas and Africa) that traditionally have been studied separately. Furthermore, it is important to note that Carney was originally trained as an Africanist and undertook most of her scholarship in West Africa. What Carney's scholarship demonstrates is that she was able to use her deep understanding of the African context to shed light on the situation in the Americas. For more reflections on comparative regional studies, see William Moseley's May 2005 article in the *Southeastern Geographer* entitled "Regional Geographies of the U.S. Southeast and Sub-Saharan Africa: The Potential for Comparative Insights."

ISSUE 4

Did Colonialism Distort Contemporary African Development?

YES: Marcus Colchester, from "Slave and Enclave: Towards a Political Ecology of Equatorial Africa," *The Ecologist* (September/October 1993)

NO: Robin M. Grier, from "Colonial Legacies and Economic Growth," *Public Choice* (March 1999)

ISSUE SUMMARY

YES: Marcus Colchester, director of the Forest Peoples Programme of the World Rainforest Movement, argues that rural communities in equatorial Africa are today on the point of collapse because they have been weakened by centuries of outside intervention. In Gabon, the Congo, and the Central African Republic, an enduring colonial legacy of the French are lands and forests controlled by state institutions that operate as patron-client networks to enrich indigenous elite and outside commercial interests.

NO: Robin M. Grier, assistant professor of economics at the University of Oklahoma, contends that African colonies that were held for longer periods of time tend to have performed better, on average, after independence.

The degree to which the colonial experience has impacted contemporary patterns of development in Africa is a major issue of discussion. Prior to 1880 roughly 90 percent of sub-Saharan Africa was still ruled by Africans. Of course slavery had had a profound impact on the continent, but the European presence in Africa was limited largely to coastal enclaves before this time. At the famous Berlin Conference of 1884–1885 (at which Africans were not represented), the European powers established ground rules to divide up the continent. Two decades later the only uncolonized states were Ethiopia and Liberia. The principal colonial powers in Africa were Great Britain and France, followed by Portugal, Belgium, Germany, and Spain. Italy would also control some African countries in the late colonial period.

What were the objectives of European colonial endeavors in Africa? Of course the colonizers themselves suggested, or rationalized, that they were agents of progress who had a civilizing influence on the African people. The reality, widely accepted by scholars today, is that African lands and peoples were colonized to provide key raw materials for the European powers. While accepting resource extraction as the principal goal of colonialism, some scholars assert that the experience had some positive benefits, namely the development of infrastructure (roads, railroads, etc.) and educational and medical systems that benefit the African peoples today. Others suggest that the influence of colonialism has been overblown, and that African leaders merely use the colonial experience as a scapegoat for their own mismanagement of African affairs.

Those who suggest that colonialism has had an enduring negative influence on Africa point out that the infrastructure, as well as the educational systems left behind, nonsensical national borders, and the political legacy of colonial governance, all serve to distort, rather than to facilitate, contemporary economic and political development. For example, the roads and railways built during the colonial era often extend from the capital or port city to interior regions rich in resources, rather than connecting a country in a fashion that would promote national unity. Educational systems emphasized rote learning as they were developed to train low-level civil servants, rather than managers and directors. Enduring and nonsensical national borders have compromised the economic viability of many African nations (there are a large number of landlocked countries in Africa) and aggravated ethnic tensions (because they often do not respect ethnic boundaries). Finally, colonial governance was anything but democratic.

In the following selections, Marcus Colchester and Robin M. Grier present contrasting views on the enduring legacy of colonialism in Africa. Colchester examines contemporary patterns of resource extraction in equatorial Africa and draws a link between these and colonial practices. In Gabon, the Congo, and the Central African Republic, an enduring colonial legacy of the French are lands and forests controlled by state institutions that operate as patron-client networks to enrich indigenous elite and outside commercial interests. In many ways, Colchester is suggesting that colonial patterns of resource extraction never really ended; we simply have gone from overt colonial control to neocolonial regimes of extraction in the postindependence era. In contrast, Grier argues that on average, African colonies that were held for longer periods of time tend to perform better after independence. Furthermore, she asserts that the level of education at the time of independence helps explain the development gap between former British and French colonies in Africa.

Marcus Colchester

YES

Slave and Enclave: Towards a Political Ecology of Equatorial Africa

The three countries of Equatorial Africa—Gabon, the Congo and the Central African Republic (CAR)—are among the most urbanized in Africa, largely as a result of the resettling of rural communities in colonial times. Of a total population of five million, only some 40 per cent live in rural areas, comprising about one hundred, linguistically closely-related peoples who are described in Western anthropology as the "Western Bantu", as well as some 120,000 "pygmies". Those remaining in the forests are reliant on self-provisioning economies, based on shifting cultivation, treecropping, hunting and fishing.

Some 47 million hectares of closed tropical forests in the three countries, combined with those of neighbouring Angola, Cameroon, Zaire and Equatorial Guinea, make up the second largest area of closed tropical forests in the world after Amazonia. These forests are some of the most diverse in Africa, and contain an abundance of wildlife, including forest elephants, lowland gorillas, various kinds of chimpanzees, forest antelopes and a wide variety of birds.

The social and political structures of Equatorial Africa have been markedly transformed by the European slave trade, the French colonial era and by the subsequent interventions of commercial interests and the new African states. Despite the current political liberalization taking place in Gabon, the Congo and the Central African Republic after three decades of single party politics, the forests and the peoples who rely on them are still being sidelined.

The Slave Trade

Long before Bantu society came into contact with colonial Europeans, its egalitarian traditions—a reflection of mobile, decentralized settlements which included an unease towards the accretion of power—had been progressively overlain during several centuries by more hierarchical forms of social organization, resulting from warfare and competition for land. This process had gradually reduced the accountability of leaders to their people with disastrous social and, later, ecological consequences. The European slave trade, however, is the most obvious example of this phenomenon, during which several millions of Africans died and millions more were transported overseas. The Portuguese began the trade in slaves on the coasts of Equatorial Africa around 1580, but it only became vigorous after about 1640. The European slavers themselves, however, were minimally engaged in raiding, never going far inland. Capture was carried out by Africans which not only intensified raiding and war between local African communities but also transformed previous systems of bondage and servile working conditions into those of absolute slavery.

This meant that slaving had a profound impact not only on those communities whose members were captured but also on those engaged in the trade. To gain control of the trading network, dispersed and differentiated social groups merged their numbers and identities to increase their power and domain. These groups were dominated by "trading firms" often comprising a chief and his sons. The increasing importance of inheritable wealth, capital accumulation and the corresponding need to resist redistributive customs led many matrilineal societies of the middle Congo to become patrilineal. Trading firms swelled their numbers by recruiting male and female slaves as labour and as wives to produce pliable heirs devoid of inheritance rights through the maternal line.

Colonial Repression and Resistance

Direct colonial rule of Equatorial Africa by the French from the 1880s onwards further exacerbated the tendency towards more hierarchical forms of social organization. As the French government was unable and unwilling to administer directly the vast area of more than 700,000 square kilometres, it allocated 80 per cent of the region to some 40 companies.

Within these vast concessions—the area controlled by the Compagnie Française du Haut Congo encompassed 3.6 million hectares—the companies had almost sovereign control including the right to their own police force and legislation, slavery, violence, killing and inhuman punishment were widely documented. Their express aim was to extract the natural resources—chiefly wild rubber, timber, ivory, and later coffee, cocoa and palm oil—as cheaply and as quickly as possible.

Labour shortages, rather than shortages of land, were the main constraint of these enclave economies. To extract labour for the concession areas, plantations, road-building, portage and, in the 1920s and 1930s, for building the Congo-Ocean railroad, "man hunts" became fundamental to the colonial economy. The military was used to support concessionaires who had insufficient labour. In the rubber regions of Ubangi (now the Central African Republic), for example, villagers who did not manage to flee from the troops sent in to ensure their "participation" were tied together and brought naked to the forests to tap the rubber vines. They lived in the open and ate whatever they could find. A French missionary who witnessed the scene wrote: "The population was reduced to the darkest misery . . . never had they lived through such times, not even in the worst days of the Arab [slaving] invasions."

The colonial authorities also introduced various taxes and levies to oblige local peoples to enter the cash economy; in practice, this meant to work for the concessionaires. Along the coasts, logging rapidly replaced the trade in non-timber products, becoming the foundation for the political economy of the region. The extraction was carried out with axes and hand-saws, the huge logs being dragged by hand to the rivers and floated out to waiting trading ships. By the 1930s, an estimated third to one half of men from the interior villages of what is now Gabon had been brought down to the logging camps on the coast, where they worked for minimal wages and in appalling conditions for months at a time. Disease was rife, alcoholism rampant and thousands died. Meanwhile, the workload of the women and children who remained in the villages increased correspondingly and their health too was undermined by the numerous diseases—influenza, yellow fever, sleeping sickness and venereal infections—which returning labourers brought back.

The conscience of the colonial authorities was obviously pricked by the all too evident degradation and exploitation of the local people. As Governor General Reste noted in 1937:

> "The logging camps are great devourers of men . . . Everything has been subordinated to the exploitation of the forest. The forests have sterilized Gabon, smacking down the men and taking off the women. This is the image of Gabon: a land without roads, without social programmes, without economic organization, the exploitation of forests having sapped all the living force from the country . . . There is not a single indigenous teacher, doctor or vet, agricultural officer or public works agent."

Those making the profits—some two billion francs between 1927 and 1938—were a few French companies in whose hands the logging concessions were concentrated. By 1939, of the one million hectares of Gabon under concessions, 66 per cent was controlled by just seven companies with only some 84 others controlling the rest. These companies were to play a key role in the transition to Independence.

Resistance, however, was widespread throughout French Equatorial Africa; villages flared up against demands to yield labour and forest products to the concessionaires and taxation to the French administration. The result was a protracted and brutal war in which the colonial regime sought to bring the whole interior of the colony under its control to facilitate its commercial exploitation. The taking of hostages, including women and children, pillage, arbitrary imprisonment, executions and massacres, the torching of settlements and the sacking of whole communities were commonplace. By the 1930s, when the last areas of resistance were being quashed in what is now the west of the Central African Republic, the French were using planes to spot villagers hiding out in the forests before sending in the army to bring them out.

Regroupement des Villages

Resettlement of dispersed and shifting African communities into larger, permanent villages on roads and portage trails became a central plank of French administrative policy throughout its colony. One of the main aims of this *regroupement des villages* was to control the local people—to oblige them to render tax and labour and to prevent further rebellions.

Regroupement had devastating impacts on the local peoples. One missionary reported to André Gide that the local people:

> "prefer anything, even death to portage . . . Dispersion of the tribes has been going on for more than a year. Villages are breaking up, families are scattering, everyone abandons his tribes, village, family and plot to live in the bush like wild animals to escape being recruited. No more cultivation, no more food . . . "

In the early days of colonial rule, it was carried out with little if any consideration of customary land rights, causing conflicts over land between different social groups. Traditional institutions, residence patterns and ties with the land were overturned while overcrowding in the new villages led to declining standards of nutrition and exposed people to epidemics. Sleeping sickness increased throughout the region in the first half of the 20th century, causing a massive decline in population.

Even after Independence in 1960, Gabon and the Congo pursued the policy right into the 1970s. As a regional *préfèt* noted in Gabon in 1963:

> "We have had enough of these isolated hamlets, which, being so numerous and of eccentric location, lost in the vastness of the Gabonese forest, have never allowed the Gabonese government to have control of their populations or permanent contact with them and have thereby prevented an improvement of their standard of living."

Convinced that "no family head can cut himself off from the duty to modernize", the post-colonial government continued to tear villages away from their crops without any compensation, overturning residence patterns that reflected local ways of life and throwing into disarray, at least temporarily, traditional systems for allocating rights to land. In some respects, *regroupement* under the independent administration was more onerous than in the colonial era: houses in the new settlements had to be laid out in regular rows with defined sizes of houseplots and pathways.

The Indigenous Elite

The striking continuity between the colonial and independence policies was assured by an élite of French-educated Africans. Under French law, most Africans were subject to the *indigenat*, a set of laws which ascribed an inferior status to local people: "persons under the *indigenat* were subject to penalties and taxation without the legal protection afforded 'citizens'". However, a small number of Frenchified indigenous people were considered as *évolué* and thus accorded "citizen" status, becoming a local "élite attuned to the French presence and subservient to its interests".

Cooption of the indigenous leadership extended down to the community level through a hierarchy of *chefs du canton* and *chefs du village*, chosen to act as intermediaries between the villagers and the authorities. Dependent on the colonial administration for their positions and often resented and even secretly ridiculed by the villagers themselves, these leaders became ready tools in the colonialists' hands and assisted with the unjust exploitation in the concessions. Favoured ethnic groups emerged, considered to be more "evolved" and less "backward"; groups which had been intermediaries in pre-colonial trade now became an important support base for the administration. This structure and practice still persist; local leaders and chiefs, and favoured ethnic groups, continue to owe their primary allegiance to the urban élites and to the administration, not to the villagers or to the remoter, more traditional, rural communities.

Independence: *Plus Ça Change . . .*

After Independence from France in 1960, French Equatorial Africa was divided into the three countries of Gabon, the Congo and the Central African Republic, a division based on the previous colonial administrative divisions. The crucial concern of the departing colonial power was to ensure that the new "independent" governments supported French interests; President de Gaulle warned African states that "France would intervene if it considered its interests in jeopardy." In both Gabon and the Congo, France's principal aim was to guarantee that French logging companies were assured continued access to the forests. Maintaining access to strategic minerals, notably manganese and uranium, the latter being of critical importance to France's civil and military nuclear programme, was also central to French policy. In the Central African Republic, France's main preoccupation was to protect its cotton, coffee and diamond interests.

Gabon

French interests were decisive in selecting the future leadership in Gabon after Independence; French logging interests poured funds into the successful election campaign of Leon Mba, an *évolué* from the coastal region. After Mba's accession to power, the press was suppressed, political demonstrations banned, freedom of expression curtailed, other political parties gradually excluded from power and the Constitution changed along French lines to vest power in the Presidency, a post that Mba assumed himself. However, when Mba dissolved the National Assembly in January 1964 to institute one-party rule, an army coup sought to oust him from power and restore parliamentary democracy.

The extent to which Mba's dictatorial regime was synonymous with "French interests" then became blatantly apparent. Within twenty-four hours of the coup, French paratroops flew in to restore Mba to power. After a few days of fighting, the coup was over and the opposition imprisoned, despite widespread protests and riots. The French government was unperturbed by international condemnation of the intervention; the paratroops still remain in the Camp de Gaulle on the outskirts of Gabon's capital, Libreville, to this day, where they share a hilltop with the presidential palace, an unforgettable symbol of the coincidence of interests between the French and the ruling indigenous élite.

With the establishment of a one-party state, abuse of power and office became the norm. Wealth became more concentrated in the hands of the ruling élite, and the network of patronage became further removed from the concerns of ordinary citizens. The Presidency passed smoothly from Mba to Omar Bongo, "the choice of a powerful group of Frenchmen whose influence in Gabon continued after independence." Bongo and his cronies have since amassed substantial fortunes, having "transformed Gabon into their private preserve, handsomely enriching themselves in the process". They have transferred *billions* of French francs annually to Swiss and French banks. Opponents of the regime have been arbitrarily imprisoned and tortured, among other human rights violations.

Central African Republic

Post-Independence politics in the Central African Republic were not dissimilar. After the independent-minded first President Barthelemy Boganda died in an aeroplane accident, his successor, David Dacko, received strong French support. But Dacko's repressive policies and lack of effective economic reforms made him unpopular locally; he was widely perceived as a "French puppet caring only about cultivating French interests."

When Jean-Bedel Bokassa replaced Dacko on New Year's Day 1966, it seemed that the country, which had been virtually bankrupted by Dacko's regime, might be given a chance to recover. However, Bokassa's capricious and violent rule became synonymous with the worst excesses of African dictatorship—"the systematic perversion of the state into a predatory instrument of its ruler". Massive corruption was the norm, and Bokassa himself appeared to make no distinction between the revenues to the state treasury and his personal income.

France only withdrew its support for the regime in 1979, when it was revealed that Bokassa visited prisons personally to torture and kill those who had stood up to his whims. As in Gabon, French paratroops were sent in and Dacko restored to power, to be replaced on his death in 1981 by army strongman General Andre Kolingba, the current President.

Congo

Independence in the Congo pursued a different course. Initially, the post-Independence regime was modelled in the neo-colonial mould—servile to French political and economic interests. However, "it was swiftly corroded by venality and became an embarrassment not only to its internal supporters but also to its French sponsors". After a street uprising in 1963, the regime was overthrown and a Marxist-Leninist government assumed power. The French did not intervene.

French influence within the Congo remained strong, however, and, despite the Congolese government's rhetoric to the contrary, the role of foreign capital was scarcely diminished. Although the state created marketing monopolies for agriculture and forestry, and nationalized some other sectors— including the petroleum distribution network—the timber concessions, some of the oil palm plantations and many other import-export concerns remained in foreign hands. Foreign oil companies, too, were assured a satisfactory cut.

Logging Enclave Perpetuated

In all three countries of Equatorial Africa, logging has intensified since Independence. Mechanized logging extended the area of extraction during the 1970s and 1980s, up to the remote forests of the northern Congo and the south of the CAR; the rate of extraction increased some six-fold between 1950 and 1970. The industry has remained an enclave of foreign companies who enjoy the patronage of the governing élites. In the Congo, foreign companies, or joint operations dominated by foreign capital, produce the vast bulk of the timber—nearly 80 per cent of the sawlogs, 90 per cent of the sawn wood and 92 per cent of the plywood. In common with both the Gabon and the CAR, the Congolese government "largely lacks adequate technical and economic competence to control and rationally manage its forests".

During the 1970s, logging in the Congo was widely used as a fraudulent mechanism for capital flight, through false declarations of the quantity and type of timber being exported and through transfer pricing. The government attempted to curb this by creating a state monopoly to market timber, but the inefficient and ineffective agency ran at a loss due to collusion between loggers and officials.

A leaked report, prepared for the World Bank, reveals that the logging industry in the Congo is still swindling the government of millions of dollars. Unpaid taxes, stamp duty, transport and stumpage (duty payable on each tree cut) fees are estimated to exceed US$12 million on declared production alone, while huge quantities of timber are slipping across the border illegally into neighbouring Cameroon and Central African Republic. According to the report, "almost all the companies in the forestry sector are 'outside the law'" and "forestry administration is nonexistent". As a result, "the forest is left to the mercy of the loggers who do what they like without being accountable to anyone".

Companies are taking maximum advantage of this lack of supervision. For example, the French company, Forestière Nord Congo, has exclusive rights over 10 years to log some 187,000 hectares in the north of the country. Its contract obliges the company to process 60 per cent of the logs on site and to establish a major sawmill and woodprocessing works constructed out of new, imported materials. In exchange, Forestière Nord Congo has received generous benefits—substantially reduced import duties and a five-year tax holiday on wood production, including company taxes, property tax and stumpage fees. Yet, in complete violation of the agreement, the company bought a non-functioning second-hand mill, has not processed any timber, has exported sawlogs for six years through its tax loophole, and has not paid even the tax it should have rendered. In total, Forestière Nord Congo has cost the Congo some US$2.9 million in lost revenue.

Elsewhere, the Société Congolais Bois de Ouesso (whose board includes the Congolese President himself) received foreign "aid" in the late 1980s and early 1990s to install a highly-sophisticated saw mill and veneer producing works. With technical advice from the Finnish company, Jaako Poyry Oy, the World Bank backed the project with some US$12 million. But costs soon rocketed from an estimated US$39 million to US$63 million. Further loans were incurred from several African banks, but the mill was never completed; today only a small sawmill is working. The World Bank report notes "the situation is catastrophic and no further activity within the present arrangement is possible". The company's failure is attributed "quite simply to the overvaluation of the project which has allowed some vultures to enrich themselves immeasurably at the Congo's expense."

In the Central African Republic, where concessions have been granted in 48 per cent of the "exploitable" forests, the accountability of the logging industry is more lax. Illegal cross-border logging into the forests of north Congo was observed by FAO [Food and Agriculture Organization] technicians in the mid-1970s, and smuggling of timber down the Oubangi and Congo rivers to the Congolese capital, Brazzaville, on the Zairean border was normal. Today it is common knowledge in Bangui, the capital of the Central African Republic, that nearly all the forest concessions are being illegally logged, the regulations are flouted and much of the timber is clandestinely leaving the country via new road connections with Cameroon. CAR President Kolingba himself is alleged to be closely linked to businessman M. Kamash who owns SCADS, the company which processes timber illegally slipped across the border from north Congo. In common with all the concessionaires in the country, "SCAD carries out no management and employs no foresters—they are just timber merchants who mine the forests".

Since the Gabonese forestry service is funded from the central government budget rather than through stumpage fees and other tariffs on logging itself, there are few incentives for foresters to impose the many rules and regulations to control logging, while the loggers themselves make sure the foresters are provided with suitable incentives not to apply them.

Rural Stagnation

For the rural communities of Equatorial Africa, the long history of exploitative, extractive and enclavistic development has meant marginalization and poverty. Despite the statistically high per capita incomes of Gabon and the Congo relative to other Sub-Saharan countries, the rural people are poor and getting poorer.

The explicit aim of most government efforts concerning agriculture has been to replace itinerant, family-based, labour-intensive agriculture with fixed, capital-intensive, mechanized agriculture serviced by wage labour. Heavily-subsidized agribusiness schemes to promote large-scale farming—cattle ranches, sugar plantations, battery farms of poultry, rice schemes, rubber and oil palm estates, and banana plantations—have undercut small farmers, destroying the last elements of a cohesive rural society.

A century of neglect and disruption of smallholder agriculture has had inevitable consequences. In the Central African Republic, only one per cent of the country is farmed. In Gabon, agriculture accounts for only eight per cent of the GDP [gross domestic product], occupies only 0.5 per cent of the land area and supplies only 10–15 per cent of the country's food needs, the remaining 85 per cent being imported; even traditional peasant crops such as taro, yams, mangoes, avocados and vegetables are imported from neighbouring states, particularly Cameroon.

In the Congo, agriculture yields only 5.9 per cent of GDP. Since Independence, there has been a massive migration to the cities. By 1990, 52 per cent of the total population, and 85 per cent of men aged between 25 and 29 years, lived in two cities alone, Brazzaville and Pointe Noire, although the Congo barely has any industrial base. As in colonial times, the lack of young men in the countryside means that 70 per cent of Congolese farms are managed by women. Education, preferentially given to young men, exacerbates this trend, resulting in the towns being considered the domain of men and the countryside that of women.

The marginalization of smallholder agriculture has also transformed local political institutions. Increasing mobility has weakened community ties and diminished customs which favour the redistribution of wealth and land. Echoing the political shifts which took place during the European slave trade, matrilineal groups have become more patrilineal and marriages with women classified as "slaves" (that is, without lineage and therefore without kin to make demands on agnatic inheritance) have been favoured. These internal trends have been reinforced by imposed national laws which favour cognatic succession, all tendencies which have further weakened the status and security of women.

NO

Robin M. Grier

Colonial Legacies and Economic Growth

Introduction

Development theorists have long hypothesized whether the identity of the colonial power mattered for subsequent growth and development. Many authors . . . once concluded that the colonial experience was insignificantly different under the major colonial powers. Recent research though has shown that colonialism did significantly affect development patterns. . . . In this [selection], I examine whether the duration of colonization has a significant effect on later development and growth and whether human or physical capital in place at the time of independence can help to explain why British colonies perform significantly better than French ones.

In the first empirical application of the [selection], I pool data from 63 former colonies and find that the length of colonization is positively and significantly correlated with economic growth over the 1961–1990 period. While the direction of causality is not conclusive, I find no evidence to support exploitation theory. Given that a country was colonized, since it would be impossible to test the counterfactual hypothesis, the longer it was held by the mother country, the better it did economically in the post-colonial era.

In the second empirical application, I reduce my sample to 24 countries in Africa. . . . I find that the length of colonization is still positively and significantly related to economic growth and that former British colonies still outperform their French counterparts. . . . I find that the newly independent British colonies were significantly more educated than the French ones. . . . I find that the inclusion of education at independence can explain the development gap between the former British and French colonies and the positive relationship between length of colonization and growth. . . .

Data and Variables

My empirical work addresses two questions. First, does the length of the colonization period matter for subsequent growth and development? Second, can education levels at the time of independence explain why British ex-colonies perform significantly better than their French counterparts?

In the first empirical application of the [selection], I perform a cross national study of 63 ex-colonial states and test to see whether the length of colonization is correlated with subsequent growth rates. . . . In the second empirical application, I reduce the sample to British and French Africa and test whether the duration of colonization matters for later development and whether human or physical capital levels at the time of independence can help to explain why British ex-colonies perform better on average than French ones. . . .

Econometric Results

Does the Identity of the Colonizing Power Matter for Economic Growth?

Five year averages are calculated on data from 63 countries for the years 1961–1990, resulting in 6 observations for each country and a sample size of 378 data points. . . .

Because of the vast differences in the length of colonization for different ex-colonial states, I add a variable called TIME to determine the effect of the duration of colonialism on subsequent growth, where TIME is the year of independence less the year of arrival. The most common argument against colonialism is that it exploited the native population, causing dependency and instability in the colonial states. The results . . . show that TIME is positively and significantly related to subsequent economic growth. I do not claim that longer colonization causes higher economic growth, but my findings do reject a crude form of the exploitation theory. While it is possible that countries in my sample might have had higher growth rates if they had not been subjected to colonialism, the results do show that colonies that were held for longer periods of time than other colonies have had more economic success in the post-colonial era. . . .

Does Colonialism Matter for African Development?

. . . I found that former French colonies perform significantly worse on average than British ones. It is possible that an African effect is exaggerating the development gap between the two. Because all of the French colonies were African (except Haiti, whose population is primarily African), and Africa has been characterized by poverty and underdevelopment in the last century, it may be that an African effect is biasing the earlier results. Limiting the sample to Africa also gets rid of the high-performing British outliers, like the United States and Canada, and helps to better distinguish the differences between French and British non-settlement colonies. . . .

French ex-colonies perform 1.38 percentage points worse on average than their British counterparts. That is, even when the sample is limited to Africa, the former French colonies still lag significantly behind the British ones. . . .

The results also show TIME to be positively and significantly related to economic growth, which implies that the length of colonization is positively related to growth and development. The next section, which examines the institutional legacies of colonialism, tries to determine why TIME is significantly related to growth and why the French ex-colonies perform worse than British ones, even when the sample is restricted to Africa.

The Colonial Legacy

To determine why ex-British colonies perform better than French ones, I look at the level of human and physical capital the colonizing power left at independence. . . . [E]ducation is an important component of growth and development. The British and French had contrasting philosophies of education, which translated into very different types of colonial education. The largest difference between colonial education policies is that the British made a conscious effort to avoid alienating the native culture, by teaching in the vernacular languages and training teachers from the indigenous tribes. While most of the teachers in French Africa were imported from France, the Advisory Committee on Native Education in the British Tropical African Dependencies recommended that, "Teachers for village schools should, when possible, be selected from pupils belonging to the tribe and district who are familiar with its language, tradition, and customs. . . . "

Students in British Africa were, for the most part, taught in their native language and in their tribal villages, which significantly eased the learning process. In contrast, in the French system, most students were boarded and only able to go home for the summertime vacation. Students were required to speak French, and all vernacular languages were forbidden. . . .

Conclusion

The literature on colonialism and underdevelopment is mostly theoretical and anecdotal, and has, for the most part, failed to take advantage of the more formal empirical work being done in new growth theory. This essay has tried to close that gap by presenting some empirical tests of oft-debated questions in the literature.

I find that the identity of the colonizing power has a significant and permanent effect on subsequent growth and development, which would deny the validity of a crude exploitation hypothesis. Colonies that were held for longer periods of time than other countries tend to perform better, on average, after independence. This finding holds up even when the sample is reduced to British and French Africa.

I also find that the level of education at the time of independence can help to explain much of the development gap between the former British and French colonies in Africa. Even correcting for the length of colonization, which has a positive influence on education levels and subsequent growth, I find support for a separate British effect on education. That is, the data imply that the British were more successful in educating their dependents than were the French.

POSTSCRIPT

Did Colonialism Distort Contemporary African Development?

Colchester describes a long process wherein relatively egalitarian and decentralized rural Bantu settlements in equatorial Africa were slowly transformed into more hierarchical forms of social organization. This process began with warfare and competition among Africans, was exacerbated by the slave trade and French colonial rule (for an excellent discussion of contemporary academic debates regarding the involvement of Africans in the trans-Atlantic slave trade, see Lassina Kaba's 2000 article in the *African Studies Review*, entitled "The Atlantic Slave Trade Was Not a 'Black-on-Black' Holocaust"), and continues today as the indigenous elite are more responsive to outside commercial interests than their own people. The limited accountability of leaders to their own people has led to exploitative logging with disastrous social and ecological consequences. As such, colonialism is not solely responsible for the lack of accountability among some African leaders in equatorial Africa today, but Colchester would argue that it definitely facilitated such behavior and created a set of relationships between French and African elites that persist today.

The process by which African elites were co-opted is worth highlighting. Colchester describes a Frenchified indigenous elite who were considered "advanced" enough to be granted French-citizen status. Through a process of acculturation, this elite came to share in and promote the interests of the French in their colonies. This approach, adopted by the French in their African colonies, is often referred to as the *policy of assimilation*. The policy of assimilation held out the carrot to all Africans (in French colonies) of potentially becoming French citizens. Although seemingly egalitarian on the one hand, it was a terribly ethnocentric policy on the other because it asserted that Africans only became civilized by adopting French culture. In many ways, the French policy of assimilation was an effective strategy for developing the group of "dependent elites" conceptualized by Andre Gunder Frank in his dependency theory.

The French policy of assimilation may be contrasted with the British policy of indirect rule. In nonsettler colonies such as Ghana and Nigeria, the policy of indirect rule meant that the British administered a country via its traditional leaders (up to a certain level in the colonial hierarchy). This difference in policy approaches is often used to explain why the British invested more heavily in education (because they relied on more Africans to run the colonial civil service). This is also a difference highlighted by Grier in her article for this issue. Grier further notes that the British encouraged instruction, at least at the lower grade levels, in local languages, whereas the French insisted that local people be educated in French (an approach consistent with their policy of assimilation).

Of course the French and the British were not the only colonial powers in Africa, but their approaches receive the most attention among academics because they had the largest number of colonies. For further information on the legacy of British and French colonialism, see a book chapter by the well-known Africanist Crawford Young, entitled "The Heritage of Colonialism," in John W. Harbeson and Donald Rothchild, eds., *Africa in World Politics: The African State System in Flux* (Westview Press, 2000). The Belgians and Portuguese have a reputation for having been particularly brutal colonial powers. See Adam Hochschild, *King Leopold's Ghost: A Story of Greed, Terror, and Heroism in Colonial Africa* (Houghton Mifflin, 1998) for a gripping account of conditions in the Belgian Congo, or Allen Isaacman, *Cotton Is the Mother of Poverty: Peasants, Work, and Rural Struggle in Colonial Mozambique, 1931–1961* (Heinemann, 1996), regarding the situation under the Portuguese in Mozambique.

World Bank Group for Sub-Saharan Africa

World Bank Group for Sub-Saharan Africa includes annual reports, publications, speeches, and other sources of information about issues including rural development, education, and the incorporation of indigenous knowledge into development.

```
http://web.worldbank.org/WBSITE/EXTERNAL/COUNTRIES/
AFRICAEXT/0,,menuPK:258649~pagePK:158889~piPK:146815~
theSitePK:258644,00.html
```

United Nations Development Programme

The United Nations Development Programme provides information on UN development work in Africa. A wide range of topics is covered, including poverty and globalization.

```
http://www.undp.org/dpa/publications/regions.html#Africa
```

Economic Commission for Africa

The United Nations' Economic Commission for Africa provides information on the regional integration of African economies, including information on regional economic organizations. The organization is attempting to reform and integrate African economies to improve the quality of life on the continent.

```
http://www.uneca.org/index.htm
```

United States Agency for International Development (USAID) in Africa

USAID in Africa details African development from the perspective of USAID, the bilateral development assistance arm of the U.S. government. Information is available by country, topic, or date and ranges from short articles and press releases to full publications.

```
http://www.usaid.gov/locations/sub-saharan_africa/
```

PART 2

Development

*W*hat *constitutes "development" in the African context very much remains an open question. Since the majority of African nations gained independence in the 1960s, how best to pursue this process has been an oft-debated question. The role of the state, the commercial sector, international financial institutions, and nonprofit organizations in development is highly contested. Controversies also have raged over the extent to which Africa's progress on the development front has been influenced by its position in the global economic system, debt obligations, and demographic trends.*

- Have Structural Adjustment Policies Worked for Africa?

- Are Non-Governmental Organizations (NGOs) Effective at Facilitating Community Development?

- Should Developed Countries Provide Debt Relief to the Poorest, Indebted African Nations?

- Are Abundant Mineral and Energy Resources a Catalyst for African Development?

ISSUE 5

Have Structural Adjustment Policies Worked for Africa?

YES: Gerald Scott, from "Who Has Failed Africa? IMF Measures or the African Leadership?" *Journal of Asian and African Studies* (August 1998)

NO: Thandika Mkandawire, from "The Global Economic Context," in Ben Wisner, Camilla Toulmin, and Rutendo Chitiga, eds., *Towards a New Map of Africa* (Earthscan, 2005)

ISSUE SUMMARY

YES: Gerald Scott, an economist at Florida State University, argues that structural adjustment programs are the most promising option for promoting economic growth in Africa. He disputes the evidence used to suggest that these programs have a deleterious effect on economic growth in Africa.

NO: Thandika Mkandawire, director of the UN Research Institute for Social Development, counters that, while African governments have reshaped domestic policies to make their economies more open, growth has faltered. Mkandawire assesses structural adjustment from a developmental perspective, judging its effects on economic development and the eradication of poverty. He suggests that structural adjustment policies designed to integrate Africa into the global economy have failed because "they have completely sidestepped the developmental needs of the continent and the strategic questions on the form of integration appropriate to addressing these needs."

Both the World Bank and the International Monetary Fund or IMF (along with the World Trade Organization) are sometimes referred to as Bretton Woods institutions because they (or their predecessors) were established during a conference of the major economic powers at Bretton Woods, New Hampshire, in 1944 (as the end of World War II was in sight). The World Bank, or International Bank for Reconstruction and Development (IBRD), was established to rebuild Europe and Japan in the aftermath of the war and the IMF was created to provide loans to help countries resolve short-term balance of payment problems. The IMF and the World Bank have persisted as major multilateral economic development institutions that are particularly influential in Africa. These institutions are more influential in Africa because much of the debt incurred by national governments is public rather than private (i.e., loans from bilateral or multilateral development agencies rather than loans from commercial banks). In Africa, the IMF tends to focus on lending to resolve short-term problems (e.g., controlling inflation) whereas the World Bank has a slightly longer, "developmental" view.

Following the Third World "debt crisis" of the 1970s, the World Bank and the IMF initiated a form of policy-based lending known as structural adjustment. Prior to this time, much of the lending of the World Bank, in particular, had been project- or program-based. So, for example, in the 1960s the World Bank funded a number of infrastructure projects in Africa (such as dams), slowly transitioning to more programmatic funding related to basic needs in the 1970s (such as rural health care projects). The policy-based lending that began in the 1980s was somewhat different (than traditional project or program based lending) in that loans were held out as a carrot for countries that agreed to undertake a series of policy reforms. The basic aim of structural adjustment reform was to balance state budgets and, as either a cause or effect of the first, promote economic growth. According to the World Bank, the basic way to achieve such an end was to cut government expenditures and raise revenues (but not in a way that would encumber economic growth).

Policy reforms under the structural adjustment rubric in Africa include the privatization of inefficient state-run enterprises (which, if they are inefficient enough, may be a drain on the state treasury); a reduction of staffing and programming in state agencies in order to cut costs; the devaluation of national currencies in situations where they are deemed overvalued, and a redoubling of efforts in the export sector to foster the generation of foreign exchange. Overvalued currencies are seen as problematic because they may make a country's exports artificially expensive (and may reduce export potential); and its imports artificially inexpensive (and thereby encourage the overconsumption of imported products).

As evidenced by the readings in this issue, the effectiveness and appropriateness of structural adjustment in the African context is hugely controversial. In this issue, Gerald Scott, an economist at Florida State University, argues that structural adjustment programs are the most promising option for promoting economic growth in Africa. He disputes the evidence used to suggest that structural adjustment programs have a deleterious effect on economic growth in Africa. Furthermore, he suggests that economic malaise in Africa is a result of corruption and mismanagement. In contrast, Thandika Mkandawire, director of the UN Research Institute for Social Development, finds little evidence to suggest that structural adjustment policies have been successful. After over 20 years of adjustment, he suggests that it is now widely accepted that these policies have failed to promote development. He argues that African countries now need to "bring development back in" by introducing "more explicit, more subtle and more daring policies to stimulate growth, trade, and export diversification than hitherto."

Gerald Scott **YES**

Who Has Failed Africa? IMF Measures or the African Leadership?

Introduction

Many writers have suggested that International Monetary Fund (IMF) Structural Adjustment Programs in Africa have not only damaged growth prospects for many countries, but have further worsened an already badly skewed income distribution. Some of these writers have claimed that IMF programs have ignored the domestic social and political objectives, economic priorities, and circumstances of members, in spite of commitments to do so. In a recent article, an African critic submitted that IMF measures have failed Africa. He claimed that "after adopting various structural adjustment programs, many [African] countries are actually worse off." Not unlike many, he seems to be suggesting that IMF programs have been somewhat responsible for the severe decline in economic conditions. Some critics of IMF programs have pointed out that the fact that economic conditions have deteriorated is not conclusive proof that conditions would be better without IMF programs. They do however stress that the developments associated with IMF programs have been extremely unsatisfactory. At the same time, this association does not necessarily imply that IMF programs cause economic decline in the region.

The main purpose of this [selection] is to argue that of all the feasible alternatives for solving Africa's current economic problems, IMF Programs are the most promising. The [selection] will not contend that the panacea for the seemingly unsurmountable problems rest with the IMF. However, it will argue that IMF programs are better poised to help Africa reach its economic goals, or improve economic performance. . . .

Why Has Sub-Saharan Africa (SSA) Performed So Poorly?

The problems of slow growth, high inflation, and chronic balance of payments problems continue to plague SSA well into the 1990s. In general these problems can be traced to international or domestic factors. During the last two decades a number of adverse events in the international economy have contributed to the economic decline in the region. These include oil crises, global recessions, deteriorating terms of trade, protectionism in the developed countries markets, rising real interest rates, and the lack of symmetry in adjustment to payments problems. In addition a number of adverse developments in the domestic economy have inhibited productive capacity and thwarted the attempts to initiate and sustain economic growth.

No doubt, many countries lack appreciable amounts of essential resources and adequate infrastructure for sustained growth. It is also true that growth and development in many nations have been set back by droughts, civil wars, and political disturbances. It may even be true that colonial economic structures still account for many inflexibilities that inhibit economic growth. However, many countries could significantly improve economic performance and reduce poverty significantly if they managed their economies more efficiently, controlled population growth, and abandoned those policies that are so obviously anti-developmental.

The major setback has been gross mismanagement, which has largely resulted from corruption, rather than from incompetence and absence of skilled administrators. In many nations, national resources for investment, growth and welfare have been consistently diverted into private hands and used largely for conspicuous consumption. Poor public sector management has resulted in large government budget deficits, which contribute to inflation, which in turn encourage undesirable import growth and serious balance of payments deficits. Quite simply African leaders, administrators, businesses, and political insiders have been engaged in corruption on a massive scale. The result has been almost complete destruction of the economic potential in many nations.

For the purpose of solving Africa's serious economic problems, there is need for the political will to attack the fundamental causes. If the present disquieting trends are not urgently tackled with the appropriate policies, then an even more somber future looms on the horizon for many Africans. Any package of measures should include policies designed to revitalize, expand, and transform the productive sectors into viable and self sustaining entities. In the absence of corruption public resources can be allocated efficiently to facilitate growth in the productive sectors. The microeconomic efficiency that results from efficient resource allocation, coupled with appropriate macroeconomic stabilization policies, would greatly enhance the prospects for economic growth and prosperity.

Assessing IMF Programs

Studies aimed at evaluating IMF programs in Africa conclude that the results are mixed, ranging from disappointing to marginally good. Inasmuch as it is difficult to assess the overall effect of IMF programs some studies have shown that they have been somewhat successful in terms of a number of key economic indicators. One main reason for the contention that IMF programs have been harmful is that many countries with programs have performed as badly as those without IMF programs. One must be cautious in examining the performance of key economic indicators following IMF programs because of the dynamics of the setting in which they are implemented. But let us suppose for the sake of argument that IMF programs actually result in deteriorating economic conditions immediately following the program. For example, suppose economic growth declines as a result of the program. Even though economic growth is perhaps the most important objective of national development policy, it is still reasonable to consider a program successful if it laid down the basis for future realization of economic growth, within some reasonable time period. In other words if it established the economic structure that promotes and facilitates long term growth, then it can still be regarded as successful. In addition it is possible that even though conditions did not improve, the program may have prevented economic conditions from deteriorating even more. It is not possible to subject IMF programs to controlled experiments. However, it seems more reasonable to argue that without IMF programs, in many countries, conditions would have been much worse, than one would argue that IMF programs cause conditions to worsen.

It has somewhat been fashionable, especially amongst those with very limited knowledge of the various economic rational behind IMF recommendations, to reject those recommendations without presenting a feasible alternative. Many object to the IMF and some regard it not only as a representation of western economic interest, but as too uncompromising and arrogant in its relationship with nations in crisis. The indications are that IMF is usually anxious to intervene even before conditions deteriorate into a crisis. But like any prudent banker it has to be concerned about repayment prospect, which is essential for its very own survival and continuous provision of its service to other deserving members.

Why IMF Programs May Be the Answer for Africa

IMF programs in the 1990s should have a major attraction for Africans genuinely concerned with the welfare of the people for a number of reasons. First, the programs are no doubt based on sound theory, always a useful guideline for policy-formulation.

The peculiar social, political and economic circumstances of African nations and the inability or refusal of the IMF to take them into account in the design and implementing of programs have been cited as reasons why IMF programs have "failed" in Africa, or are doomed to fail. On the contrary, these particular African circumstances are in fact another good reason why IMF programs may be the right answer to the problem. Because of the nature of African economic circumstances, particularly problems in economic administration, the conspicuous absence of commitment on the part of politicians and administrators to the development and welfare of the nations, the absence of institutional capacity and the weak civic consciousness, the best policy is to embrace IMF programs. IMF programs encourage the dismantling of controls and simplification of the bureaucratic process; emphasize the strengthening of institutional capacity; require public accountability and responsibility; emphasize efficiency and economic discipline; encourage private sector participation in the economy; foster coordination in economic decisions and promote macroeconomic stability; and emphasize measures designed to expand aggregate supply.

The optimal policy intervention for dealing with an inefficiency or distortion is to seek the source of the problem. IMF programs are attractive because they are designed to attack the problems at their source. In African nations there are many problems that are outside the control of the officials and administrators. However corruption is not one such problem and it need not be so pervasive and economically destructive. Although it is very important not to under-emphasize the importance of many other problems of development, corruption is an obstacle that can largely be controlled, if the top leadership is committed to that objective. It is not the same problem as say drought or poor resource endowment, or an absence of a skilled workforce, that is largely outside the control of officials.

One major attraction of IMF programs is that they tend to remove all opportunities for corruption, i.e., they seek the source of the problem. For example, the suggestion that controls should be dismantled is in recognition that the reliance on physical controls for resource allocation is inferior to the market mechanism, especially in the absence of an efficient administrative machinery for the effective administration of controls. But perhaps the more relevant point is that a proliferation of controls usually lays the foundation for corruption, which has continued to destroy economic life in the region.

In reality it is not the IMF who has failed Africa, but the African leadership. The politicians and public sector officials have conspired with private businessmen and firms to adopt and implement policies that benefit themselves at the expense of national development and welfare. The inability or unwillingness of Africans to demand more accountability and responsibility from both politicians and public servants ensures that violations of the public trust are not treated as illegal, immoral, unethical or non-nationalistic actions. If the IMF has failed Africa, it has done so by failing to vigorously condemn or expose corruption or even assign it the prominent place it deserves in the design of programs.

Many who oppose IMF programs have argued that they impose severe economic harm on the deprived peoples of Africa. Whom are these deprived peoples and what is the evidence? The majority of them are rural inhabitants who have virtually been untouched by modernity. They are largely farmers, have limited participation in the modern economy, consume limited manufactured goods and have very limited access to basic social services provided by governments. In the urban areas there are Africans of diverse economic circumstances ranging from those in abject poverty and squalor, to those of enormous wealth. The urban population is usually more politically powerful and its views have been the barometer used to measure or assess the political climate. On balance IMF programs will tend to harm the urban poor given the structure of their consumption basket and their production pattern. On the other hand the rural population could benefit immensely from IMF programs for similar reasons, and the efficiency gain to the nation would more than compensate for the loss experienced by the urban population. No convincing evidence has been advanced to support the claim of impoverishment of the majority of rural African peoples.

Even though the urban poor could face the most severe hardship as a result of IMF programs, such adverse consequences could be mitigated even within the context of those same programs that supposedly impose such hardships. There is some empirical evidence that IMF reforms will improve the distribution of income and help the poor. There is also evidence that appropriate exchange rates and price incentives improve economic performance, and that private enterprises perform better than state enterprises.

What Africans need is a set of institutions that would enable them to effectively demand the very modest conditions the people deserve and subject all officials to full responsibility and accountability. Given the levels of ignorance, ethnic loyalties, poverty, disillusionment and despair, absence of strong nationalistic and patriotic attitudes, I shudder to imagine the difficulties associated with establishing such institutions. Notwithstanding, the task is possible if the leadership is committed to doing so. Based on the current structure of African institutions, and the record of policy makers, IMF programs are more likely to be effective than other possible alternatives.

Let us examine some of the recommendations and issues in IMF programs and discuss their effects on national welfare.

Devaluation

A devaluation increases the prices of traded (relative to nontraded) goods and will induce changes in production and consumption. First, as imports become more expensive less will be demanded, thereby curbing excessive import demand which is a major source of balance of payments deficits. At the same time production of import substitutes will be encouraged. Secondly, exports will become expensive so that less will be consumed locally and more will be produced. Exports will also be cheaper in foreign countries, so that more will be demanded. Foreign firms that split production into several stages will find the country attractive for their investments, and tourism will also receive a boost. The devaluation will therefore stimulate the export and import substitution sectors. The political concern usually is that the urban consumers whose purchasing power has already been eroded by inflation partly from excessive government spending, will have to pay more for basic manufactured goods, the bulk of which are imported. Not surprisingly, there is usually an anti-devaluation sentiment in the main urban areas. It is very important to emphasize that the devaluation by itself will not correct the problem of macroeconomic instability. It must be accompanied by sound fiscal management that complements rather than counteracts the effects of the devaluation. For example, if the government continues to maintain significant fiscal deficits after devaluation, then the devaluation would soon be reversed as the exchange rate becomes overvalued again. An overvalued exchange rate is subversive to long-term growth and balance of payments adjustment.

The African rural population consumes imported manufactured goods only in limited amounts, but could potentially benefit from devaluation because it will increase the price of agricultural exports. A program that prescribes a devaluation so that exchange rates are competitive, should ensure that the producers of exports are not unreasonably exploited by middlemen (including government) to the extent that they have no incentive to expand production.

A legitimate concern is that devaluation will raise the price of essential inputs and stifle the supply response as the cost of production rises. In the first place, as long as cost of production lags behind prices, producers will find it profitable to expand production. In any case the appropriate supply response could be encouraged by an appropriate production subsidy. This of course involves an additional strain on the budget, and the IMF insists on fiscal restraint as we will see shortly. Fiscal reform involves maximizing tax revenue and ensuring that it is used to maximize macroeconomic performance. This means that those who have been avoiding their tax burden, especially the self employed, must be made to meet their tax obligations, and that frivolous and wasteful expenditures must be avoided.

Government Budget Deficit

When IMF programs recommend reductions in government expenditures, the concern is not only with the adverse effects of budget deficits on inflation and the balance of payments, but also with bogus budgetary appropriations that benefit private individuals and deprive the nation of developmental resources. As a result of the pervasiveness of corruption, many governments typically appropriate funds for the salaries of nonexistent civil servants or for goods and services that are not received. Similarly it is common for governments not only to pay highly inflated prices for goods and services, some of which are totally inessential, but also for governments to receive far less than market value for goods bought by some individuals or firms. IMF prescriptions on the budget can be viewed as perhaps a subtle way of telling African leaders that from their past record they cannot be trusted to appropriate the nation's resources in the national interest. This appears paternalistic, but should be acceptable to all concerned with the welfare of the mass of African peoples.

Government budget deficits as a percentage of GDP [gross domestic product] increased sharply after independence in many countries, as the states intervened ostensibly to correct the perceived flaws of a market economy. The evidence indicates that throughout the region the states have failed to perform the role of a prudent entrepreneur, and government investments have resulted largely in considerable inefficiency. Public enterprises have been inefficiently operated, as they have largely been used as a way of providing patronage to political insiders.

Government budget deficits financed largely through money creation, have contributed to serious inflation and balance of payments problem. These deficits have not been consistent with other macroeconomic objectives of the government. The control of the deficit usually requires reducing expenditure, including the elimination of subsidies to consumption, and increasing taxes. In many African nations it is common for the government to subsidize the consumption of essential food items, gasoline, electricity, public transportation etc. The major beneficiaries are the urban population and mostly political insiders who for example obtain goods at subsidized prices and resell at black market rates. The typical rural inhabitant, because of the structure of the consumption basket does not benefit much from government subsidies.

Market Prices

IMF programs attempt to promote a strong link between work effort and reward. This involves appropriate prices of goods and services, and factors of production. Prices not only provide information to producers but serve as an incentive that facilitate efficient resource allocation. The major problem in African countries has been inadequate production. Production has been constrained by a large number of factors including inappropriate prices. In many African countries the tax system has turned the terms of trade against agriculture and has resulted in very slow or negative growth rates in this sector. Overvalued exchange rates are an implicit tax on exporters since exporters receive the official rate.

The imposition of market prices for agricultural commodities typically results in higher food prices. Rural farmers benefit as producers, but as consumers they lose. However as long as they can respond sufficiently as producers, their gains will be more than enough to compensate for their losses and the nation as a whole will benefit. The challenge of reforming prices is to ensure adequate production response, which may require other complementary policies.

The continuous proliferation of price controls will only continue to stifle production, worsen shortages, and reduce incentive for investment.

Privatization

African governments have argued that they have an obligation to provide goods and services usually provided by private enterprises in developed countries, because too often the market fails to do so. Thus they are compelled to invest in capital formation that will increase output, improve efficiency in resource allocation, and make the distribution of income more equitable. Those are desirable objectives and any government that achieves them deserves widespread commendation. Unfortunately the record of the public enterprises which are usually set up to pursue these objectives, have been very disappointing. These public enterprises have been very inefficiently administered, and have been widely used by politicians as opportunities for patronage to their supporters.

In recommending privatization of certain public enterprises, IMF programs attempt to deal with two problems. The first is micro inefficiency in the productive sector, and the second is government budget deficits that result partly from the need to subsidize inefficiently run enterprises. Private enterprises that continuously make losses go out of business, but government enterprises with similar balance sheets receive political relief. By turning over certain enterprises to private institutions, the pressure on the budget eases, and there is a greater chance of increasing efficiency in production. . . .

Conclusion

African economic problems over the last two decades, can be traced mainly to a host of international and domestic factors. Many of the international factors and some of the domestic factors such as lack of suitable resource endowment, are outside the control of the governments and administrators. However, a significant part of the problems can be traced to corruption and other forms of inefficiencies. Instead of blaming the IMF for the dismal performance in Africa, we should focus on the African leaderships and their policies. The level of their commitment and the policies they have adopted and implemented increasingly seem to confirm only their deplorable lack of compassion for fellow Africans and a callous detachment from the people's welfare. The status quo must change to prevent further erosion of the economic base on the continent.

The best foreign assistance is one that has a lasting effect; it is one that would empower Africans to fully participate in the growth process, and provide them with the irrevocable ability to effectively demand the modest living conditions that they have been unjustly deprived of by their leaders for so long.

NO ⏎   Thandika Mkandawire

The Global Economic Context

Africa illustrates, perhaps better than elsewhere, that globalization is very much a policy-driven process. While in other parts of the world it may be credible to view globalization as driven by technology and the "invisible hand" of the market, in Africa most of the features of globalization and the forces associated with it have been shaped by Bretton Woods Institutions (BWIs) and Africa's adhesion to a number of conventions such as the World Trade Organization (WTO) which have insisted on opening up markets. African governments have voluntarily, or under duress, reshaped domestic policies to make their economies more open. The issue therefore is not whether Africa is being globalized but under what conditions the process is taking place and why, despite such relatively high levels of integration into the world economy, growth has faltered.

The word that often comes to mind whenever globalization and Africa are mentioned together is "marginalization." The threat of marginalization has hung over Africa's head like the sword of Damocles and has been used in minatory fashion to prod Africans to adopt appropriate policies. In most writing globalization is portrayed as a train which African nations must choose to board or be left behind. As Stanley Fischer, the Deputy Director of the IMF, and associates put it, "globalization is proceeding apace and sub-Saharan Africa (SSA) must decide whether to open up and compete, or lag behind." *The Economist*, commenting on the fact that per capita income gap between the USA and Africa has widened, states that "it would be odd to blame globalization for holding Africa back. Africa has been left out of the global economy, partly because its governments used to prefer it that way."

Globalization, from the developmental perspective, will be judged by its effects on economic development and the eradication of poverty. Indeed, in developing countries the litmus test for any international order remains whether it facilitates economic development which entails both economic growth and structural transformation. I shall argue that in the case of Africa this promise has yet be realized. The policies designed to "integrate" Africa into the global economy have thus far failed because they have completely sidestepped the developmental needs of the continent and the strategic questions on the form of integration appropriate to addressing these needs. They consequently have not led to higher rates of growth and, their labeling notwithstanding, have not induced structural transformation. Indeed the combined effect of internal political disarray, the weakening of domestic capacities, deflationary policies and slow world economic growth have placed African economies on a "low equilibrium growth path" against which the anaemic Gross Domestic Product (GDP) growth rates of 3–4 per cent appear as "successful" performance. I will illustrate this point by looking at two channels through which the benefits of globalization are suppose to be transmitted to developing countries: trade and investment.

The [section] is divided into three sections. The first section deals with what globalization and the accompanying adjustment policies promised, what has been delivered and what has happened to African economies during the era of globalization. The second deals critically with some of the explanations for Africa's failure. And the last part advances an alternative explanation of the failure with respect to both trade and access to foreign finance.

The Promise of Globalization and Achievements

The Promise of Trade

Expanded opportunities for trade and the gains deriving from trade are probably the most enticing arguments for embracing globalization. The Structural Adjustment Programmme's (SAP's) promise was that through liberalization African economies would become more competitive. As one World Bank economist, Alexander Yeats, asserts, "If Africa is to reverse its unfavourable export trends, it must quickly adopt trade and structural adjustment policies that enhance its international competitiveness and allow African exporters to capitalize on opportunities in foreign markets." Trade liberalization would not only increase the 'traditional exports' of individual countries but would also enable them to diversify their exports to include manufactured goods assigned to them by the law of comparative advantage as spelled out and enforced by "market forces." Not only would trade offer outlets for goods from economies with limited markets but, perhaps more critically, it would also permit the importation of goods that make up an important part of investment goods (especially plant and equipment) in which technology is usually embodied.

By the end of the 1990s, and after far-reaching reforms in trade policy, little had changed. The few gains registered tended to be of a one-off character, often reflecting switches from domestic to foreign markets without much increase in overall output. Indeed some increases in exports of manufactured goods even occurred as the manufacturing sector contracted. . . .

Furthermore recent changes in Africa's exports indicate that no general increase had occurred in the number of industries in which most of the African countries have a "revealed" comparative advantage. Indeed, after decades of reforms, the most striking trend, on that has given credence to the notion of "marginalization of Africa", is the decline in the African share of global non-oil exports which is now less than one-half what it was in the early 1980s representing "a staggering annual income loss of US$68,000 million—or 21 per cent of regional CDP."

The Promise of Additional Resources

A persuasive promise made by BWIs was that adhesion to its policies would not only raise domestic investment through increased domestic saving but would relax the savings and foreign exchange constraints by allowing countries to attain higher levels of investment than would be supported by domestic savings and their own foreign exchange earnings. One central feature of adjustment policies had been financial liberalization. . . .The major thesis has been that "financial repression" (which includes control of interest rates and credit rationing by the state) has discouraged saving and led to inefficient allocation of the "loanable funds." The suggested solution then is that liberalization of markets would lead to positive real interest rates which would encourage savings. The "loanable funds" thus generated would then be efficiently distributed among projects with the highest returns through the mediation of competitive financial institutions. Significantly, in this view saving precedes investment and growth. After years of adjustment there is little discernible change in the levels of savings and investment.

Perhaps even more attractive was the promise that financial liberalization would lead to increased capital inflows and stem capital flight. Indeed, most African governments' acceptance of IMF policies has been based on precisely the claimed "catalytic effect" of agreements with IMF on the inflow of foreign capital. Governments were willing to enter the Faustain bargain of reduced national sovereignty in return for increased financial flows. Even when governments were sceptical of the developmental validity of BWIs policies, the belief that the stamp of approval of these institutions would attract foreign capital tended to dilute the scepticism.

To the surprise of the advocates of these policies and to the chagrin of African policy-makers, the response of private capital to Africa's diligent adoption of SAPs has, in the words of World Bank, "been disappointing." The market "sentiments" do not appear to have been sufficiently persuaded that the policies imposed by the BWIs have improved the attractiveness to investors. The much-touted catalytic effect of IMF conditionality has yet to assert itself. The scepticism of private investors about the BWIs stamp of approval is understandable in light of the history of non-graduation by any African country. Indeed, there is the distinct danger that, since economies under BWIs' intensive care never seem to recover, IMF presence may merely signal trouble. The BWIs seem to be unaware of the extent to which their comings and goings are a source of uncertainty among businessmen and evidence of a malaise. This said, there is, nevertheless, a trickle of foreign investment into Africa but this has not been enough to increase Africa's share in global FDI flows. The rise in foreign direct investment in the latter part of the 1990s is cited as evidence that globalization and SAPs are working (Pigato, 2000). This celebration is premature. There are a number of significant features of the financial flows to Africa that should be cause for concern over their developmental impact and sustainability.

First, there is the high country concentration of investment with much of the investment going to South Africa. Secondly, there is the sectoral concentration on mining. Little of this has gone into the manufacturing industry. As for investment in mining, it is not drawn to African countries by macro-economic policy changes, as is often suggested, but by the prospects of better world prices, changes in attitudes towards national ownership and sector-specific incentives. Third, there is the problem of the type of investment. The unintended consequence of the policies has been the attraction of the least desirable form of foreign capital. Most of the new investment has taken the form of the highly speculative portfolio investment attracted by "pull factors" that have been of a transitory nature—extremely high real domestic interest rates on Treasury Bills caused by the need to finance the budget deficit—and temporary booms in export prices which attract large export pre-financing loans. It has also been driven by acquisitions facilitated by the increased pace of privatization to buy up existing plants that are being sold usually under 'fire sales' conditions. Such investments now account for approximately 14 per cent of Foreign Direct Investment (FDI) flows into Africa. Little has been driven by plans to set up new productive enterprises. Some of the new investment is for expansion of existing capacities, especially in industries enjoying natural monopolies (eg beverages, cement, furniture). Such expansion may have been stimulated by the spurt of growth that caused much euphoria and that is now fading away. It is widely recognized that direct investment is preferable to portfolio investment, and foreign investment in green field projects is preferable to acquisitions. The predominance of these types of capital inflows should be cause for concern. However, in their desperate efforts to attract foreign investment, African governments have simply ceased dealing with these risks or suggesting that they may have a preference for one type of foreign investment over others.

Finally, such investment is likely to taper off within a short span of time, as already seems to the case in a number of African countries. Thus, for Ghana, hailed as a "success story" by the BWIs, FDI which peaked in the mid-1980s at over US$200 million annually due mainly to privatization was rapidly reversed to produce a negative outflow. It should be noted, in passing, that rates of return of direct investments have generally been much higher in Africa than anywhere in other developing regions. This, however, has not made Africa a favourite among investors, largely because of considerations of the intangible "risk factor," nurtured by the large dose of ignorance about individual African countries. There is considerable evidence to show that Africa is systematically rated as more risky than is warranted by the underlying economic characteristics.

Capital Flight

Not only is Africa still severely rationed in financial markets, but during much of the globalization there is evidence that Africa is probably a net exporter of capital. Paul Collier and associates have suggested that in 1990, 40 per cent of privately held wealth was invested outside Africa and that in relation to the workforce, capital flight from Africa has been much higher than in other developing country groups. In a recent more systematic attempt to measure the extent of capital flight, James Boyce and Léonce Ndikumana show that for the period 1970-96 capital flight from sub-Saharan

Africa was US$193 billion, and with imputed interests the amount goes up to US$285 billion. These figures should be compared with the combined debt of these countries which stood at US$178 billion in 1996. . . .

So far financial liberalization has not done much to turn the tide. In a World Bank Study of the effects of financial liberalization in nine African countries, Devajaran et al conclude that the effects of liberalization on capital flight are "very small. . . ."

All this indicates that financial liberalization in itself may not be the panacea for reducing capital flight. Effective policy measures to reduce capital flight in the African context may need much deeper and more fundamental changes in the economic and political systems. One policy implication of both the reluctance of foreign capital to come to Africa and the huge amounts of wealth held outside Africa has been the calls for policies intended not so much to attract foreign capital but Africa's own private capital. While this is a valid option, the political economy of such attraction and the specific direct policy measures called for are rarely spelled out.

The Failed Promise of Growth

A comparison between Africa's economic performance during the period over which globalization is often said to have taken hold—the last two decades of the 20th century—and earlier periods shows clearly that thus far globalization has not produced rates of growth higher than those of the 1960s and 1970s. Per income growth was negative over the two decades, a serious indictment to those who have steered policies over the decades. This slower rate of growth is not peculiar to Africa as is suggested by some of the "Afro-pessimist" literature. During the period of globalization economic growth rates have fallen across the board for all groups of countries. The poorest group went from a per capita GDP growth rate of 1.9 per cent annually in 1960–80, to a decline of 0.5 per cent per year (1980–2000). For the middle group (which includes mostly poor countries), there was a sharp decline from an annual per capita growth rate of 3.6 per cent to just less than 1 per cent. Over a 20-year period, this represents the difference between doubling income per person, versus increasing it by just 21 per cent. The other groups also showed substantial declines in growth rates. The global decline in growth is largely due to deflationary bias in orthodox stabilization programmes imposed by International Financial Institutions (IFIs).

Explaining the Poor Performance: Has Africa Adjusted?

The poor performance of Africa with respect to the channels through which the positive effects of globalization would be gained (ie increased access to markets and finance) is now widely accepted. There are, however, disagreements over the cause of the failure. The BWIs have adhered to two explanations.

The first one is simply that African countries have rather incomprehensibly persisted with their doomed "dirigiste" ways and refused to swallow the bitter but necessary pills of adjustment. Inadequate implementation of reforms and recidivism are some of the most common themes running through the literature on African economic policy. In the 1994 report the World Bank's view was that adjustment was 'incomplete' not because of any faults in the design of the programmes but because of lack of implementation.

The second explanation was that insufficient time had elapsed to reap the gains of adjustment and, therefore, of globalization. Coming from the BWIs, this is a strange position. It was these very institutions that, in dismissing the structuralist argument on the inelasticity of the response of developing countries to economic stimuli, claimed that liberalization would elicit immediate and substantial responses and bring about "accelerated development" (the promise of the Berg Report). Indeed, in the early years, the World Bank was so certain about the response to its policies that it measured economic success by simply looking at the policy stance and assuming that this axiomatically led to growth.

Today, there is recognition that the axiomatic mapping of policies into performance was naïve and misleading. There are admissions, albeit grudging, to having underestimated the external constraints on policy and the vulnerability of African economies to them. Equally the responsiveness of the economies and the private sector has been overestimated, while the wrong sequence of policies eroded state capacities and responsibilities ("policy ownership"). However it is still insisted that the passage of time will do its job and the posture recommended to African countries has been to sit tight and wait for the outpouring of gains. There is no recognition that the accumulated effects of past policy errors may have made the implementation of "market friendly" policies in their pristine form more difficult.

By the second half of the 1990s neither of these arguments carried any weight. African countries have made far more adjustments that any other global region. Indeed the BWIs themselves began to point proudly to the success of their programmes, suggesting that enough time had transpired and a large number of African countries had perservered in their adjustment to begin to reap the fruits of the adjustment process. IMF officials talked about a "turning point" and that the positive per capita growth rates of 1995–97 (4.1 per cent) "reflected better policies in many African countries rather than favourable exogenous developments."

President of the World Bank James Wolfensohn, for example, reported in his 1997 address to the Board of Governors that there was progress in sub-Saharan Africa, "with new leadership and better economic policies." Michel Camdessus, the then Managing Director of the International Monetary Fund, at the 1996 annual meeting of the World Bank and the IMF, said, "Africa, for which so many seem to have lost hope, appears to be stirring and on the move." The two vice presidents for Africa at the World Bank, Callisto Madavo and Jean-Louis Sarbib, wrote an article, appropriately titled "Africa on the Move: Attracting Private Capital to a Changing Continent," which gave reasons for this new "cautious optimism." The then Deputy Managing Director of the International Monetary Fund, Alassane Quattara, would say the following about the good performance: "A key underlying contribution has come from progress made in macroeconomic stabilization and the introduction of sweeping structural reforms." The major World Bank report on Africa of 2000 stated "many countries have made major gains in macroeconomic stabilization, particularly since 1994" and there had been a turn around because of "ongoing structural adjustment throughout the region which has opened markets and has a major impact on productivity, exports, and investment." Even the Economic Commission for Africa (ECA), a strident critic of SAP in the past, joined the chorus.

And so by the end of the millennium, African countries had been largely adjusted. There can be no doubt that there has been a sea-change in the African policy landscape. Africa is very heavily involved in "globalization" and is very much part of the global order and much of the policy-making during the last two decades has been designed deliberately to increase Africa's participation in the global economy. In any case, more devaluations, lowering of tariffs and privatization of marketing were imposed in Africa then anywhere else. By the mid-1980s, with the exception of the franc zone countries, most SSA countries had adopted flexible exchange rates policies and there had been major real exchange rate depressions. Major reforms in marketing, including the abolition of marketing boards, had been introduced. Arguments that African countries had refused or been slow to adjust or that enough time had not transpired became less credible, especially in light to the celebratory and self-congratulatory remarks by the BWIs themselves.

However, by 1997 the growth rates had begun to falter. By 1999, in its report on global prospects and the developing countries, the World Bank made a downward revision of the 1999 growth rate "despite continued improvements in political and economic fundamentals." The report blamed the poor performance on terms of trade and the Asian crisis. In a sense we had been there before. "Success stories" have been told many times before and countries have fretted and strutted on this "success" stage only to be heard of no more. . . .

Rather than abandon the deflationary policies, supporters of adjustment have simply reframed the question to read: "Why is it that when the recommended policies are put into place (often under the guidance of—and pressure from—the International Monetary Fund and the World Bank) the hoped for results do not materialize quickly." The answer was: lack of "good Governance" and of "good Institutions." These assertions conceal a clear loss of certainty and a growing sense of intellectual disarray. This is apparent in the World Bank study, *Can Africa Claim the 21st Century?* Unlike earlier approaches, the report speaks in a much more subdued and less optimistic tone, based more on faith than analysis. There is an admission, albeit grudging, that policies of the past have not worked. The new agenda is much more eclectic and more a reflection of confusion and loss of faith than the discovery of a coherent, comprehensive policy framework. The additional set of reforms is nebulous, eclectic and largely of a more political and institutional character—good governance, participation of and consultation with civil society, democracy etc. Increasingly the World Bank's new solutions suggest that there is little to be done by way of reform on the economic front. . . .

Trade, Low Growth and Absence of Structural Change

The slow growth discussed above has also had an impact on the growth of exports and diversification by weakening the investment-export nexus crucial to the process. Here again, the orthodox view has been that increased trade or openness measured in various ways is a determinant of growth. Consequently, the major policies with respect to trade have involved trade liberalization and adjustments in exchange rates largely through devaluation.

The failure on the trade front is linked to the failure in the structural transformation of African economies so that they could produce new sets of commodities in a competitive and flexible way. Globalization in Africa has been associated with industrial stagnation and even de-industrialization. African economies were the quintessential 'late latecomers' in the process of industrialization. I have argued elsewhere that although the writing on African economies is based on the assumption that Africa had pursued import substitution for too long, the phase of import substitution was in fact extremely short—in most countries it was less than a decade. SAPs have called for policies that have prematurely exposed African industries to global competition and thus induced widespread processes of de-industrialization. African economies have somehow been out of sync with developments in other parts of the world. When most economies embarked on import substitution industrialization, financed by either borrowing or debt default, much of Africa was under colonial rule, which permitted neither protection of domestic markets nor running of deficits. And even later when much of industrialization was financed through Eurodollar loans, Africans were generally reluctant borrowers so that eventually much of their borrowing in the 1980s was not for industrialization but to finance balance-of-payments problems.

Every case of successful penetration of international markets has been preceded by a phase when import substitution industrialization was pursued. Such a phase is necessary not simply for the "infant industry" arguments that have been stated ad infinitum, but also because they provide an institutional capacity for handling entirely new set of economic activities. The phase is also necessary for sorting out some of the coordinating failures that need to be addressed before venturing into global markets. A "revisionist" view argues three main points. First, that substantial growth was achieved during the phase of import substitution industrialization; second, that even successful "export oriented economies" had to pass through this phase and maintain many features of the import substitution (IS) phase; and finally that important social gains were made.

The IS phase did lead to the initial phases of industrialization. Significantly, UNIDO notes that African countries were increasingly gaining comparative advantage in labour intensive branches, as indicated by revealed comparative advantage (RCA) but then notes:

> It is particularly alarming to note that the rank correlation of industrial branches by productivity growth over 1980-95 and RCA value in 1995 is very low. Productivity has fallen in furniture, leather, footwear, clothing, textiles, and food manufacturing. An export oriented development strategy cannot directly stimulate Total Factor Productivity (TFP). Policy must focus on increasing technological progress within the export industries—

many of which have seen very rapid progress in the application of the most modern technologies (informatics, biotechnological, etc) to their production and distribution system.

Given the conviction that import substitution in Africa was bad and had gone on for too long, there was no attempt to see how existing industries could be the basis for new initiative for export. The policy was simply to discard existing capacity on the wrong assumption that it was the specific micro-economic policies used to encourage the establishment of these industries that accounted for failure at the macro-level. The task should have been to extend and not reverse such gains by dismantling existing industrial capacity. The rates of growth of manufacturing value added (MVA) have fallen continuously from the levels in the 1970s. UNIDO estimated that MVA in sub-Saharan Africa was actually contracting at an annual average rate of 1.0 percent during 1990–97. UNIDO shows that for Africa as a whole in ten industrial branches in 38 countries labour productivity declined to an index value of 93 in 1995 (1990 = 100). Increases in productivity were registered only in tobacco, beverages and structural clay products. In many cases, an increase in productivity has been caused by a fall in employment growth (UNIDO).

The decline in total factor productivity of the economy as a whole is attributed to de-industrialization which it defines as "synonymous with productivity growth deceleration." Output per head in sub-Saharan manufacturing fell from US$7924 in 1990 to US$6762 in 1996. The structural consequence is that the share of manufacturing in GDP has fallen in two-thirds of the countries. The number of countries falling below the median has increased from 19 during 1985–90 to 31 during the 1991–98 period. While admitting such poor performance in manufacturing industry during the era of structural adjustment, supporters of SAP argue that such decline in industrialization is a temporary and welcome process of weeding out inefficient industrialization and also that insufficient time for adjustment has passed to ensure benefits from globalization through the establishment of new industries. Considering that this argument has been repeatedly deployed since 1985, Africa may have to wait for a long time before the gains from globalization materialize.

Students of historical structural changes of economies inform us that structural change is both cause and effect of economic growth. As Moshe Syrquin observes, a significant share of the measured rate of aggregate total factor productivity is owing to resource shifts from sectors with low productivity to sectors with high productivity. We have learnt from the "new trade theories" and studies on technological development how countries run the risk of being "locked" in a permanently slow-growth trajectory if they follow the dictates of static comparative advantage.

To move away from such a path, governments have introduced policies that generate externalities for a wide range of other industries and thus place the economy on more growth-inducing engagement with the rest of the world. For years, UNCTAD economists have pointed to the importance of growth for trade expansion. They have argued that it is the absence of growth, or more specifically and investment-export nexus that accounts for the failure of many countries to expand and diversify their export base. Rapid resource reallocation may not be feasible without high rates of growth and investment. The principle means for effecting export diversification is investment. Many empirical tests of "causation" have been conducted and suggest that there are good theoretical and empirical grounds for taking the reverse causation seriously as the dynamics of high growth lead to even greater human and physical investment and greater knowledge formation; which, by Verdoon's Law, leads to more productivity and therefore greater competitiveness.

Experience of successful export drives clearly shows a strong relationship between rates of structural change and rates of growth in value added in manufacturing the rates of growth of exports. Lessons from countries that have embraced trade liberalization and achieved some degree of success suggest clearly that liberalization should be in conjunction with policies that ensure that relative prices will be favourable to export industries (and not just to nontradables) and that interest rates will support investment and economic restructuring. Successful export promotion strategies have required a deliberate design of an investment–export nexus. Diversification of exports that is developmental needs to go beyond the multiplication of primary commodities and include industrial products. This requires not merely the redirection of existing industrial output to the external but the expansion of such output and investment in new activities. There is a need to design a system of incentives that favours investments that open up new possibilities or introduce new technologies to the country. In this respect infrastructure and human resource development are important preconditions for the success of pro-export policies.

The instruments used to promote investment have included not only public investment but also the provision of subsidized inputs by public enterprises, direct subsidies through tax incentives including exemptions from duties, industrial policy which, in turn, has meant selective allocation of credit and encouragement of investment by cheapening imported investment goods (often by manipulation of exchange rates in favour of the import of plant and equipment and export sector). While "diversification" has always featured in virtually all adjustment programmes, there has been no clear spelling out how this was to be achieved. In most cases, the need for diversification was overshadowed by the short-term pressures to exploit static "revealed" comparative advantage and reduce public spending. The failure to stimulate new economic activities (especially industrial ones) has meant not only sluggish growth in exports but also failure to diversify.

Under SAP all these instruments have been off limits. Evidence that more successful cases have had some kind of "industrial policy" has been dismissed on the grounds that African countries had neither the type of government nor the political acumen to prevent "capture" of these policies by rent-seekers and patron-client networks. Governments have been left with no instrument for stimulating investment and industrial development directly or for creating an environment for robust demand and profitability in which investment, or complementary public inputs such as infrastructure, research and development, education and training, could thrive. It is this passivity that has led to failure for structural transformation and the establishment of an investment-export nexus that would have led to increase and diversification of exports. . . .

Concluding Remarks

The African policy landscape has changed radically during the last two decades. Liberalization of trade, privatization and reliance on markets have replaced the widespread state controls associated with import substitution. One would expect by now to see some signs of the "accelerated development" promised by the Berg report in 1981. That adjustment has failed as a prerequisite for development, let alone as a "strategy for accelerated development," is now widely accepted. These failures can, in turn, be traced to the displacement of developmental strategic thinking by "an obsession" with stabilization—a point underscored by low levels of investment and institutional sclerosis. The key "fundamentals" that policy has sought to establish relate to these financial concerns rather than to development. The singular concentration on "opening" up the economy has undermined post-independence efforts to create, albeit lamely, internally coherent and articulated economies and an industrial structure that would be the basis for eventual diversification of Africa's export base. The excessive emphasis on servicing the external sector has diverted scarce resources and political capacities away from managing the more fundamental basis for economic development. Even the issue of "poverty" has received little attention, except perhaps when it has seemed politically expedient to be seen to be doing something to mitigate the negative effect of adjustment. SAP, owing to its deflationary bias, has placed African economies on such a low-growth trajectory, which has then conditioned the levels and types of Africa's participation in the global economy.

Over the last two decades, Africans have been faced with not merely a set of pragmatic measures but a full-blown ideological position about the role of the state, about nationalism and about equity, against which many neo-liberals, including Elliot Berg, had ranted for years. It is this ideological character of the proposals that has made them impervious to empirical evidence including the generated by the World Bank itself and it is this that has made policy dialogue virtually impossible. The insistence of "true believers" on the basic and commonsense message they carry has made dialogue impossible. The assumption that those on the other side are merely driven by self-interest and ignorance that might be remediable by "capacity building" has merely complicated matters further. Things have not been made easier by the supplicant position of African governments and their obvious failures to manage their national affairs well. These policies were presented as finite processes which would permit countries to restore growth. With this time perspective in mind, countries were persuaded to put aside long-term strategic considerations while they sorted out some short-term problems. The finite process had lasted two decades.

There are obvious gains to participation in increased exchange with the rest of the world. The bone of contention is: what specific measures should individual countries adopt in order to reap the benefits of increases exchange with other nations? With perhaps a few cases, developing countries have always sought to gain from international trade. Attempts to diversify the export base have been a key aspect of policy since independence. Import substitution was not a strategy for autarky as is often alleged but a phase in eventual export diversification. However, for years the integration of developing countries into a highly unequal economic order was considered problematic, characterized as it is by unfavourable terms of trade for primary commodities, control of major markets by gigantic conglomerates, protectionism in the markets in the developed countries together with "dumping" of highly subsidized agricultural products, volatile commodity and financial markets, asymmetries in access to technology etc. From this perspective gains from trade could only be captured by strategizing and dynamizing a country's linking up with the rest of world.

It is ironic that while analysis in the "pre-globalization" period took the impact of external factors on economic growth seriously, the era of globalization has tended to concentrate almost exclusively on internal determinants of economic performance. Today, Africa's dependence on external factors and the interference in the internal affairs of African countries by external actors are most transparent and most humiliating and yet such dependence remains untheorized. Theories that sought to relate Africa's economies to external factors have been discredited, abandoned or, at best, placed on the defensive. The focus now is almost entirely on internal determinants of economic performance—economic policies, governance, rent-seeking and ethnic diversity.

While the attention on internal affairs may have served as a useful corrective to the excessive focus on the external, it also provides a partial view of African economies and can be partly blamed for the pursuit of policies that were blind to Africa's extreme dependence and vulnerability to external conjuncture—a fact that the BWIs have learnt as exogenous factors scuttled their adjustment programmes. Indeed, unwilling to discard its essentially deflationary policies and faced with poor performance among many countries which have been "strong adjusters," the World Bank's explanations have become increasingly more structualist-deterministic and eclectic. . . .

It is now admitted that many mistakes have been made during the past two decades. When errors are admitted, the consequences of such errors are never spelled out. . . . Policy failures, especially those as comprehensive as those of SAP's can continue to have effects on the performance of the economy long after policy failures are abandoned. It may well be that the accretions of errors that are often perfunctorily admitted have created *maladjusted* economies not capable of gaining much from globalization. Both the measures of "success" used for African economies and the projections for the futures suggest that essentially the BWIs have put Africa's development on hold. This clearly suggests the extreme urgency of Africans themselves assuming the task of "bringing development back in" in their respective countries and collectively. To benefit from interacting with the rest of the world, African policy-makers will have to recognize the enormous task of correcting the maladjustment of their economies. They will have to introduce more explicit, more subtle and more daring policies to stimulate growth, trade and export diversification than hitherto.

POSTSCRIPT

Have Structural Adjustment Policies Worked for Africa?

The debate presented here may have as much to do with the authors' conceptualization of "development" as it does with the effectiveness of structural adjustment policies (which are premised on a certain vision of development) in Africa. Although both of the authors are economists, development is a vague term that has been articulated in vastly different manners.

The type of development that structural adjustment policies are designed to facilitate (and the type of development advocated by Scott in this issue) is export-led, laissez-faire economic growth. The belief (under this conceptualization of development) is that if you get the general policy environment "right," and minimize interference of the state, then capitalist actors will make efficient and rational decisions that lead to the generation of wealth that will eventually trickle down to all members of society. Furthermore, as individual nation-states exist in a global economic system, it makes sense for them to specialize in the production of goods that they can create relatively cheaply and to trade for those that others can produce more efficiently. Proponents of this view often point to the Asian Tigers (e.g., Taiwan, Singapore, South Korea) as examples of countries that successfully pursued export-led economic growth.

Other than questioning the effectiveness of structural adjustment along the narrow lines of whether or not it promotes economic growth, critics of these policies and, more broadly, development conceptualized as export-led, laissez-faire economic growth, generally raise at least three issues. First, they assert that laissez-faire economic growth often does not help the majority of the population but, rather, may serve to concentrate wealth in the hands of a few powerful individuals or entities. This is particularly problematic in the African context where large economic operators may face little to no competition. Konadu-Agyemang (in an article in a 2000 issue of the *Professional Geographer* entitled "The Best of Times and the Worst of Times"), for example, highlighted the very uneven pattern of development promoted by structural adjustment policies in Ghana, one of the World Bank's success stories. Second, critics assert that it is often problematic for African nations to engage in free trade with the rest of world because they are relegated to the production of primary commodities for which prices are low and declining. Furthermore, use of the Asian Tigers as examples of successful export led growth is disingenuous (see, for example, an article by Carmody in a 1998 issue of the *Review of African Political Economy* entitled "Constructing Alternatives to Structural Adjustment in Africa"). This, according to the critics, is because these states actively protected infant industries, and provided subsidies to promote the development of their export sectors (at least during the early years of developing this aspect of their economies), rather than pursuing a minimalistic role for the government in the economy. Finally, many of the critics would argue that an entirely different vision of development needs to be emphasized, a vision that prioritizes the fulfillment of basic human needs (e.g., adequate food, clean water, health care) and the development of human capital (via improved education). This is the perspective taken by, for example, Macleans Geo-Jaja and Garth Mangum in a 2001 article in the *Journal of Black Studies* entitled "Structural Adjustment as an Inadvertent Enemy of Human Development."

The other point worth noting is that Mkandawire is writing six or seven years after Scott, and thus has had more time to observe the effectiveness, or noneffectiveness of structural adjustment policies. In the time period between the writing of the two selections, a new hybrid approach was developed known as "structural adjustment with a human face," which is cognizant of the role of sound social services (and the development of human capital) in long-term economic development. Cynics view this change as superficial (and an approach that only was developed by the World Bank and IMF under pressure from its critics), while others see it as a real, positive development. Despite this change, Mkandawire still sees SAPs as a failure because they do not account for the inherently unfair global economic context.

ISSUE 6

Are Non-Governmental Organizations (NGOs) Effective at Facilitating Community Development?

YES: Bernard J. Lecomte and Anirudh Krishna, from "Six-S: Building Upon Traditional Social Organizations in Francophone West Africa," in Anirudh Krishna, Norman Uphoff, and Milton J. Esman, eds., *Reasons for Hope: Instructive Experiences in Rural Development* (Kumarian Press, 1997)

NO: Giles Mohan, from "The Disappointments of Civil Society: The Politics of NGO Intervention in Northern Ghana," *Political Geography* (2002)

ISSUE SUMMARY

YES: Bernard Lecomte, cofounder of Six-S, and Anirudh Krishna, assistant professor of public policy studies and political science at Duke University, describe one of the most acclaimed NGO initiatives in Africa, the Six-S network in Burkina Faso, Mali, and Senegal. The network supports village groups' efforts to combat drought and poverty. The goal of Six-S has been for "village groups to gain expertise and confidence and to establish themselves as viable, independent agencies for local development, with little residual support from Six-S."

NO: Giles Mohan, a lecturer in development studies at the Open University, presents a case study of NGO intervention in northern Ghana. His critical examination reveals that tensions exist between the northern NGO and its partners, that local NGOs create their own mini-empires of client villages, and that some NGO officers use their organizations for personal promotion.

While nongovernmental organizations (formerly known as charities) have been a long-standing fixture of the post–World War II development enterprise, these entities increasingly became important in the 1980s as bilateral donors and governmental development agencies (such as the U.S. Agency for International Development) funded them to implement local level projects in Africa. Prior to this time, bilateral donors may have used their own staff to manage projects in Africa, or they granted or loaned funds directly to African governments for the implementation of projects. NGOs, as implementing agencies, caught the fancy of donors because they were believed to be more efficient and in touch with the interests and concerns of local people. Furthermore, donors saw NGOs as a conduit for delivering assistance to the local level that bypassed African governments, which were viewed as inefficient and corrupt. More recently, NGOs have been conceptualized as a critical component of civil society in the African context. Donors increasingly view a dynamic civil society as an important check on the excesses of government.

NGOs come in all shapes and sizes. Perhaps one of the most important distinctions is between international NGOs, which are often based in North America or Europe, and national NGOs that operate in a particular African country and are staffed and directed by individuals from the nation in question. NGOs might be broken down further into those that are homegrown community organizations (frequently operating in a small area of the country) and their more professional counterparts that not only work in several regions of a country, but have paid staff (often well-educated urbanites from the capital city).

A key concern of some scholars is that NGOs may be undermining the role of the African state in some of the countries where they work (by diverting funding and power away from governmental structures). As mentioned, a key reason for the rise of NGOs is that donors sought an alternative project implementation avenue in lieu of their frustration with the inefficiency and corruption of the African state. Opponents of this approach would argue that Africa needs strong "developmental" states that will be around for the long term and effectively coordinate resources and development priorities. For an example of this perspective, see Abdi Samatar's book *An African Miracle: State and Class Leadership and Colonial Legacy in Botswana Development* (Heinemann, 1999).

In this issue, Bernard Lecomte, cofounder of Six-S, and Anirudh Krishna, former Humphrey fellow at Cornell University, describe one of the most acclaimed NGO initiatives in Africa, the Six-S network in Burkina Faso, Mali, and Senegal. Six-S was founded in 1977 by Bernard Quedrago, a teacher and school inspector from Burkina Faso, and Bernard Lecomte, a French national with considerable development experience. Both Quedrago and Lecompte were frustrated with traditional development approaches that tended to be "top-down" and emphasize projects. Six-S (which is a French acronym meaning "Making Use of the Dry Season in the Savannah and the Sahel") is an NGO created to support traditional, village-based groups, known as NAAMs, in a variety of locally inspired initiatives, from microcredit schemes to soil conservation. By all accounts, Six-S has been amazingly successful, serving several hundred thousand people organized into 30,000 groups in 150,000 villages. In contrast, Giles Mohan, a lecturer in development studies at the Open University, presents a case study of NGO intervention in northern Ghana. His case study reveals the tensions that exist between northern NGOs and their partners, the tendency of local NGOs to foster clientelistic relationships with the villages they serve, and the inclination of some local NGO officers to use their organizations for personal promotion.

Bernard J. Lecomte
and Anirudh Krishna

 **YES**

Six-S: Building Upon Traditional Social Organizations in Francophone West Africa

The Sahel region of West Africa is home to the Six-S network, a remarkable multinational organization for rural development. Established in 1977, Six-S provides support for the self-help efforts of thousands of voluntary village groups organized into unions across West Africa. By the late 1980s, the organization was serving several hundred thousand people organized into 3,000 groups, located in 1,500 villages, which were federated into seventy-five unions spread over Burkina Faso, Mali and Senegal, with additional zones created to serve enthusiastic groups in Niger, Togo, The Gambia and Guinea-Bissau.

Six-S's name—*Se Servir de la Saison Séche en Savane et au Sahel*, "Making Use of the Dry Season in the Savannah and the Sahel"—indicates its intention to support village groups, efforts to capitalize on the potential for undertaking development work during the area's long dry season, which lasts six to nine months. The largely agricultural population of the region has little work to do during this period. Through Six-S, latent human resources are harnessed to combat the poverty and drought that force many of the able-bodied, rural residents to migrate to towns in search of meager earnings during this time. These resources are used, instead, to build dams, wells and dikes, to plant vegetable gardens and trees, to construct roads and schools, and to establish savings as well as grain banks. Literacy and health care are important components of the development package, which in each case is determined by every village group for itself.

In all its activities, Six-S emphasizes the primacy of local capabilities and needs. It has a minimum number of staff who work in facilitative rather than supervisory roles; the vast majority of staff are selected by village groups from among themselves. Six-S does not assist in the formation of groups; instead it cooperates with ones that exist or spring up in villages, based on traditional patterns of local cooperation. Six-S works through unions of such groups, in Burkina Faso traditionally known as *naams*. It does not design or manage development projects on their behalf, believing that stating its own priorities will contribute to continuing dependence. Instead, Six-S seeks to strengthen local capacities by filling the gaps—with complementary resources and skills—that local residents encounter as they take on village-level development by themselves. The long-term objective is for village groups to gain expertise and confidence and to establish themselves as viable, independent agencies for local development, with little residual support from Six-S.

Ed. Krishna, Anirudh, Norman Uphoff, and Milton J. Esman, REASONS FOR HOPE: INSTRUCTIVE EXPERIENCES IN RURAL DEVELOPMENT (Bloomfield, Conn: Kumarian Press 1977) 75-90.

Two convergent streams of thinking went into the evolution of Six-S. The first came from Lédéa Bernard Ouedraogo, who was born in Burkina Faso and had worked in the rural areas there seeking especially to combat illiteracy. His ideal of developing without harming the traditional bases of social cohesion in African society resulted in Six-S becoming an authentically African experiment aimed at creating a model of social organization that is neither a carbon copy of the West, nor a return to the past.

A second set of ideas stemmed from Bernard J. Lecomte, a French national who, together with Ouedraogo and some other colleagues, founded Six-S in 1977. Lecomte's considerable prior experience with development assistance, and his disgust with its generally poor outcomes, led him to ask what could the outside world, governments or aid agencies do to support, or at least not impede, the development of local organizations. His rejection of projects as the vehicle for assistance led Lecomte to infuse the idea of "flexible funding" into the Six-S strategy.

Under the approach devised to promote local-level development, a fixed amount of funds (between one and two million dollars per year) is given over by Six-S to federations of village groups. At the general meeting of a federation, village delegates present the proposals that their village group wishes to pursue during the coming year. Except for some general restrictions set by Six-S—the same group should not get money several years in a row; money should not go to private companies or government departments; disbursements should be matched by some contributions from the recipients, including contributed labor—the federations are free to select among themselves from the lists of action proposals submitted by different village groups.

Through its arrangements with the federation committees and the simple but important restrictions it places on disbursement, Six-S insures that the people closest to and most familiar with the end-users will be allocating the money equitably. Delegates have applied a number of criteria in selecting among the action proposals before them, for instance, the number of people involved, past borrowing record, level of risks in the scheme, the feasibility of launching it quickly, whether the funds are to be in the form of grants or interest-bearing loans (in the case of economic activities), and any rate of interest to be charged. At no time does Six-S or any of its personnel intervene in the selection of proposals or in passing funds from federations to village groups; mutual trust is a basic denominator in the relationship. Vincent refers to this process as the "pedagogy of responsibilisation."

The risk—of failure, of misappropriation—inherent in advancing funds to village groups without prior approval of activities is balanced by the care taken in admitting groups to the organization. Not all groups can join Six-S, and none immediately upon request:

> The first stage . . . is to reinforce the farmers' ability to organize themselves. [Six]-S helps the groups summon up their own resources, starting with savings, which in turn leads to the trust in their own capacities . . . [it] helps the group create a network, find grassroots communicators, master elementary concepts of management, and lay the groundwork for literacy training . . . All

of these are fundamental steps without which one builds on sand. . . . Only at the second stage—once the federation has become better structured at the regional level, once the groups have demonstrated their ability to save, to manage, and to carry on a dialogues—is financial assistance offered.

Only mature groups that have proved to be responsible can avail themselves of Six-S funding, through a process whereby funds are advanced not to individual village groups but to federations, which are composed of between ten and fifty such groups. Accountability to the federation puts pressure on village groups to use the funds wisely and to repay those that are due. This is reinforced by training in account keeping for the treasurers selected by groups and federations. The first two stages in the development of a federation can take between eight and ten years, with the first (pre-project) stage itself taking up to five years in most cases. Groups are slowly nurtured to become more capable and responsible.

Success, however, has sown some seeds of failure. An excess of enthusiasm fueled by donors practically lining up to provide funding has stretched the organization out too fast. Many new groups have not taken the time they need to organize themselves and generate the collective self-discipline expected of them. Increasingly, groups have enlisted with an eye on the funding alone, which has reintroduced the element of dependency that Six-S has been trying to avoid. With donor funds diminishing in recent years, disaffection has crept into the relationship between Six-S and many of the village groups. This presents a challenge to long-term program success.

The Evolution of Six-S

This is how Lecomte remembers the beginnings of Six-S in the early days. The drought, which besieged sub-Saharan Africa in 1973, was felt as a great shock in the villages, especially among the youth. Lecomte felt that he had to do something to help people deal with this situation, but his knowledge of the African farming system at that time was more on the administrative level rather than the social. His experience with Senegalese farmers, for instance, consisted of planning and foreign aid negotiations. To reverse this situation and become more socially involved, he decided to join the Center for Economic and Social Studies in West Africa (the French abbreviation is CESAO), located in Burkina Faso. In collaboration with several other experts in planning and with the support of UNICEF, Lecomte had the opportunity to analyze the emerging gap that existed between development projects and two important social groups, women and young men. To follow up on this analysis, in 1975 he organized a conference in Accra with the support of ENDA, an African nongovernmental organization, or NGO, and with the assistance of few friends, including Lédéa Bernard Ouedraogo.

Ouedraogo's contribution was particularly valuable because of his familiarity with rural youth. He had been working as a regional inspector of rural schools, which provided three years of schooling for a small percentage of young peasants. These school programs covered his own region in Burkina Faso (Yatenga) and several other countries, including Côte d'Ivoire. Ouedraogo was not satisfied with the results of his work because education was often followed by brain drain from the rural areas. Young, educated people, especially the men, often left the villages when they completed their schooling, hoping to gain more money and happiness in the urban areas.

The results of this process disgusted him as a school inspector. In order to remedy this situation, Ouedraogo sought to implement one section of the National Educational Act, which supported the formation of post-graduation associations, called les *groupeménts post-scolaires*. His intention was that young people, after their schooling, would negotiate with their fathers to get some land which, together with some ambition, would induce them to remain in their village. Both Ouedraogo and Lecomte had lost faith in the then-prevailing methods of government-sponsored development. In contrast to Lecomte's previous experience in planning, his work at CESAO consisted mostly of interacting with both the implementers and the recipients of development projects. He saw that rural men and women regarded themselves more like plantation workers than as persons responsible for their own development. This was producing a negative reaction, especially among young farmers, who were no longer willing to obey the project monitors. Often, the farmers' only concern was to take advantage of the animals and equipment provided by the rural extension workers.

Then came the drought in 1973, and the farmers saw how little the government could do to help them cope with that disaster and that they would have to rely on their own efforts to overcome the drought. Consequently, by combining their efforts, they became more independent. "Before we were ashamed to talk about our problems with one another, but the drought has made us more united, since we recognize that we all share the same misfortune," a group of farmers told us in 1974–75. As they came to CESAO to discuss their problems, Lecomte could see the emerging conditions for the birth of autonomous grassroots organizations.

As the drought was spreading in Senegal, Mali and Upper Volta, it became necessary to combine efforts. The conference in Accra, with the theme of childhood and youth in tropical Africa, produced a report that identified the following five issues.

The first concern of the farmer associations was a desire for *more knowledge*. However, farmers strongly believed that this knowledge could be acquired only by traveling abroad. As one illiterate village woman said, "It's only in Ghana that one gets the best training." She did not refer just to academic training; short-term immigration, it was thought, would also provide the opportunity for self-development. The second concern identified was the desire for *better technology*. Farmers desired to possess some of the production tools being used in the coffee and cocoa plantations in neighboring countries, located only 1,000 to 1,500 kilometers away. There they had seen how one could use machinery and implements, which were more than anything they had ever dreamed of having in their own villages. The third concern was more radical; they desired *more authority*. The young men and the women wanted to gain the respect of their elders who held power in the villages and to participate in the decisionmaking processes. Their previous efforts to achieve a greater role for themselves had been rejected. The young men and women resented their inferior status and lack of power, yet another reason for wanting to leave the village. The fourth concern was their thirst for *experience*. This was best expressed by the young farmers' enthusiastic participation in the multiple training programs organized by CESAO. Finally, the farmers who aspired to live differently also wanted to become *autonomous*. This desire was expressed at the village level by creating numerous associations, particularly in Burkina Faso and Senegal, where people could have their own place under the sun and to try new things. Where the basis for local action was already formed, the key was to negotiate with other elements in the rural community to get them to join in.

In our report of this conference, Ouedraogo and Lecomte asked, "How can we assist sub-Saharan youth and women in carrying on self-help activities to deal with the drought?" This was the first seed sown toward the creation of Six-S. Taking actions to deal with the consequences of severe drought helped them further develop their methodology for action. During trips across the Sahel in 1976, they became aware of the multiple consequences of the drought. The dry season, traditionally the period for numerous social activities—festivals, funerals, marriages—become a dead season. Barns and granaries were empty, and two-thirds of the adult men had left to look elsewhere for work. The only adults remaining in the villages were the elders and the women with their children. This situation was resulting in social conflicts, except in few irrigated areas where some type of farming was still possible.

The main task of the farmers' associations involved finding an alternative to this scourge. As they faced the question, "Isn't there anything else to do in a village during the dry season?" they realized that market gardening (already practiced by a few farmers in irrigated areas) was a likely alternative. However, three main conditions had to be fulfilled. First, they needed to acquire adequate means of production; at a bare minimum, water supply was essential. Second, farmers needed access to, as they said, "knowledgeable" people. Third, farmers needed modest monetary support, sufficient to pay for at least thirty days of work during the dry months of December through June. Given this assurance, they could stay in the village, even if there were not sufficient stores of grain to feed the whole family.

Realizing these conditions proved to be difficult both for CESAO and the farmers' associations. It was not just a matter of implementing a given project; it was necessary to incorporate it within the existing local structures. The diverse activities of the farmers' associations covered many different areas, such as home gardens and health, and it was critical to consider every aspect of these activities—how to encourage and support them—in order to make the program sustainable. The availability of funds became a serious issue at this time, particularly because such broad projects did not easily find support from any government or private agency.

The drought made people aware that development was a challenge, not a present to be given by beneficent outsiders. They said; "Everybody must roll up his or her sleeves and get to work." Above all, the groups did not want to feel ashamed among their peers or to be seen as failures by their elders. Thus, it would be necessary to bring them assistance that could be integrated with their own efforts, that fit into their priorities, and that gave them a chance to succeed in a sustainable manner. It would be out of the question to provide one-time support to a group and then abandon it to help another. There had to be continuity as well as purpose.

Ouedraogo and Lecomte were working 400 kilometers from each other, one living in the north and the other in the south. Given all the constraints, the realization of their vision was a real challenge. About this time, they were approached by an external agency. A friend in a foreign aid organization, Swiss Cooperation, made a reconnaissance trip to West Africa after the drought to, as he put it, "find good projects," But Lecomte had become totally allergic to "projects" by this time. At the friend's suggestion, however, Lecomte and Ouedraogo tried to imagine a way of providing aid that was different from projects, and would reinforce grassroots initiatives and not make donors their patron. Why not a fund that could make loans available to these groups? Or better yet, why not form committees or associations that brought together several village groups? Actually there were already a few unions and several village groups in Burkina Faso. But with few exceptions, these dispersed groups did not know one another. Lecomte and Ouedraogo imagined an instrumentality for aid that would bring them material assistance, a little money for work if they needed it and ample opportunity for the new groups to meet.

In 1975—unlike today when local democracy and people's organizations are praised—peasants were urged to participate in organizations established by a government organization and often financed by foreign aid agencies. Any organization that showed signs of autonomy or threatened to form a peasant movement was unacceptable to governments. Even though peasant groups were necessary for indigenous development, they must be called something else. Thus the idea of a fund, in order to sound legitimate, needed a technocratic name. So they called the new association "Making Use of the Dry Season in the Savannah and the Sahel."

Before proceeding further, it was necessary to decide how the fund would be used and then to negotiate with the aid agencies. The fact that Ouedraogo and Lecomte, citizens, respectively, of Upper Volta (now Burkina Faso) and France, were backing this venture helped to get the enterprise going within two years. Thanks to a foreign grant, Ouedraogo found the time to put his thoughts together, and his appointment to a committee set up by the national governments—controlled at that time by the military—gave him the resources and the time to extend his network.

Lecomte and his wife during their three years with CESAO became acquainted with the men and women who had established groups in six West African countries and reviewed with them the least harmful methods of providing support. Then, returning to Europe in late 1976, Lecomte acquired from Swiss Cooperation a research monograph, "How to Plan External Assistance So That It Promotes Local Initiatives." Through participatory research, and with the help of officials in the foreign affairs department in Bern, he was able to lay the groundwork for financing Six-S as an international association under Swiss law, but with Sahelian peasants and cadres as a majority of its administrators.

The first funding, the equivalent of US$12,000, was provided in 1977 by a private German foundation, Misereor, whose representatives knew both Ouedraogo and Lecomte. This enabled them to begin operating in Senegal, Mali and Burkina Faso. The dry season permitted them to launch three closely related activities: exchange and training sessions; individual and, above all, collective rural works such as water, housing and roads; and land improvement, for example, controlling erosion. In the following dry seasons, a variety of production activities were made possible by the improvements achieved during the preceding years.

There were three hypotheses about the selection of groups. The first was that it was enough to observe which groups effectively used their first round of assistance and to use this experience as a basis for selecting groups that could receive larger grants and loans. The security for these loans—the second hypothesis—would not be personal property, since these young men and women had none, but their record of success with the works and improvements already achieved. The third hypothesis was that these groups which enjoyed success could be persuaded to allow new groups to come in and join their zonal committees.

Lecomte and Ouedraogo intended that resources would be available each year at the beginning of the dry season so that the groups might decide—with the funds clearly available—how to use them in the weeks and months ahead. In some cases there would be investments from which everybody would benefit because the whole working age population would remain in the village in the wake of a good harvest. In other cases, daily payments would be made for labor to those who had chosen to remain, despite the empty granaries. The plan was that this decision could be made between October 15 and November 15 of each year.

Six-S provided that the decision to take an action would be made by the groups themselves, after negotiating with fellow villagers. People's initiatives, whatever their content, were preferable to implementing courses of action with outsiders' predetermined goals. Why? Because Lecomte and Ouedraogo had observed so much pressure, narrowness and rigidity in existing foreign aid programs and the demobilizing effects of these constraints on the more vulnerable classes such as women and young people in the villages.

It was necessary to find locations where decisions could combine these two kinds of resources—the group members' own resources and the financial support from Six-S. Rejecting such decisionmaking at the level of a single village because it tends to be the center of parochialism and egoism, Six-S chose to work at the level of thirty or so villages, with 15–20,000 inhabitants spread out over distances that could be covered on foot in one day. This area was called a zone. The purpose was to facilitate contacts between a broader set of groups and to enable collective decisionmaking.

Ten or so delegates from the groups in the same zone would agree to share, at the beginning of each dry season, the external support provided by Six-S in the interest of their members. Certainly, this possibility, offering the zone committees the opportunity to decide for themselves, constituted a revolution. One local Malian civil servant exploded, "How could you trust one million CFA [equivalent to about US$5,000 at the time] to these peasants without my participation in the meeting?" The villagers replied, "How could we not appreciate the Six-S since they are the first donor that gave us confidence that we ourselves could administer their money?"

The decision not to prepare programs or projects in advance or to divide the funds arbitrarily among beneficiary groups allows Six-S to limit its number of salaried staff. In Senegal, where in 1989 there were forty-three assisted zones, there was never more than one permanent staff person, who was chosen from among the peasant *responsables*. The staff burden was a little heavier in Burkina Faso because, at the zonal level, educated peasants were rare indeed.

It was necessary to choose, from among people who had some minimum number of years of primary education, zone chiefs to guarantee the coordination of the groups' projects during the dry season. A secretariat was established in Ouahigouya, Burkina Faso, where Ouedraogo was born and lived. From 1978 to 1990 Ouedraogo and Lecomte operated in tandem. Ouedraogo assumed executive responsibility for the first three countries, then for six, while Lecomte assumed the presidency of the administrative council and handled relations with the foreign aid agencies.

Negotiations with the aid agencies proceeded step by step and turned out quite favorably. After the first grant of 5 million CFA from Misereor, we benefited from Swiss Cooperation, which provided the first three years of financing for the position of secretary-general. This permitted Ouedraogo to leave his government position and join Six-S. After 1980, a kind of consortium was formed among different donors, such as several large German and Dutch NGOs and the aid directorate of the Swiss department of foreign affairs. An even greater innovation for them was to finance a fund for which nobody knew, before each annual meeting, how much would go to each country and how it would be used. Thanks to these three-year agreements, the flow of these funds was without exception very regular, enabling activities to be undertaken at the beginning of each dry season in a number of zones—which had grown from 3 in 1978 to 110 in 1989.

Until 1990, the Six-S budget doubled almost every three years. The stability of a number of men and women—who remained in the same positions in the Six-S administrative council as well as in the aid agencies and the emergent peasant federations—has been an important factor in the management of the association. Every year the general assembly brings together various participants, Sahelian and foreign, peasants and administrators, for several days where they could decide where and how to cooperate. This has preserved a process that assures local involvement and control. After these pioneering years, Lecomte resigned as president of Six-S at the end of 1989. . . .

Selection of Activities

Six-S makes no effort to shortlist a menu of options or to suggest a list of eligible activities, unlike government-sponsored self-help programs. The activities undertaken by the different village groups thus reflect the development priorities shared by group members. Although these priorities vary among groups, a number of similar activities have been dictated by common socioeconomic conditions and concerns. To deal with the scarcity of water during the long dry season, they have dug wells and built dams. To conserve soil and moisture on their fields, they have constructed contour stone barriers, using a technique first borrowed from Oxfam-UK, then adapted to local conditions. The experience with droughts has made clear the advantages of introducing vegetable gardens and livestock raising. Such activities have been taken up jointly as well by individuals. Other groups have planted village woodlots, raised chickens and constructed schools, theaters and stores. Along with these income-generating activities, a number of social sector activities have been taken up. Groups have appointed village health agents and established rural pharmacies. School rooms have been built, and adult literacy has been taken up by most groups.

Many groups operate grain mills and have organized cereal banks. These banks buy excess grain from farmers at harvest time, store it, and resell it at cost to farmers when they run low shortly before the next harvest. Before these banks existed, farmers borrowed at usurious interest rates to buy cereal at the end of the dry season in order to feed their families, then had to sell their grain immediately after the next harvest to pay off these debts. . . .

Training

This is a central component of the support provided by Six-S to the village groups. Six-S hires "farmer technicians" each dry season and organizes work schools in which they can master specific skills for agriculture, health, well construction, maintenance of equipment or handicrafts. These people then form mobile training teams and travel to villages that request training in such skills. For example, Six-S instructional teams train women to build three-stone cooking stoves that are 35 to 70 percent more fuel-efficient than existing stoves.

In a typical training session, an instructor will demonstrate to several dozen women how to build the stove. Each woman then makes a stove herself under the instructor's supervision, breaks it up and repeats the process several times. These women return to their villages and teach their neighbors to build the stoves. Use of these stoves can save a woman up to twenty days of labor each year, which she would otherwise spend gathering wood, and it slows deforestation. Apprenticeships for gaining specialized knowledge or skills are also arranged with more experienced village groups or at a specialized institution.

In addition to gaining experience in planning and implementing specific development initiatives, generating their own funds and being assisted to learn new techniques, village groups—or some selected members—are also trained in techniques of management, especially in accountancy and record keeping. The objective is twofold: to promote transparency in all money matters ("accounts in the sunlight") and to instill within groups the management skills and accounting procedures that will later enable them to have a financial record good enough to establish creditworthiness with commercial banks and other modern financial institutions.

Each group has a person who is trained by Six-S in modern accounting, and the accounts of each union are audited annually by a professional auditor. Groups and unions whose accounts are in arrears cannot avail themselves of further funding. A Swiss-chartered accountant regularly reviews the books of Six-S, and copies of this report are freely available.

Use of Funds

Six-S recognizes that the need to repay loans helps guide a group's operations toward productive activities. The requirement of repayment also promotes social equity as it prevents a few powerful groups and individuals from appropriating a disproportionate share of funds; it also fosters solidarity within groups. Members realize that, by working together to repay loans, they will be able to avail themselves of fresh loans in the future. However, Six-S also admits that it is too much to expect that the groups can repay all of the funds they receive; they will need some grant-based assistance to meet the costs of training, community works and at least part of their operating expenditure. A mixture of grants and loans is therefore commonly found in the pattern of funds advanced to any group.

The condition that part of the funds—at least those that have been advanced for productive activities—will need to be returned, along with interest due, permits recycling of resources among groups. It is a powerful factor in knitting together the village groups in a network of mutual responsibility and assistance. An example is "son and daughter mills," a social innovation that was developed spontaneously and has now become part of the common lexicon of village groups everywhere.

There is a large demand for diesel-powered mills that can grind grain into flour. Without them, women are forced to spend long hours pounding grain by hand, often at the end of a long, tiring day. When one such mill was offered by a Western church group to a women's group in Yatenga, they were reluctant to accept it purely as a gift. They decided that each woman who used the mill would be charged a small sum. When enough money had been collected, they would buy a new mill and give it to the neighboring village. It would be a "daughter mill," since daughters marry outside the village. Later, when still more user charges had been collected, a "son mill" would be purchased to retire the original mill, which would by then have become old and worn out. Social pressure from the villages waiting for their mills keeps the process going. This innovation was further developed by other groups who decided to divide their contributions into four parts—one each for the son and daughter mills, one for the upkeep of the original mill and also an amount for assisting the helpless and the handicapped. Similar analogies are to be found for financing livestock, where the offspring are given to other groups or individuals. . . .

This unique relationship between a support agency and the grassroots, what Ouedraogo calls being "mastered by the grassroots," has rested so far on definite understandings of the obligations and responsibilities that each party has to the other. Thus, while Six-S provides flexible funding and arranges for specialized equipment and training, the groups themselves must constantly prove themselves worthy of qualifying for this support. This arrangement requires a delicate balance. Unfortunately, there are some recent indications of creeping imbalance that may erode the system of incentives, checks and balances that has been evolved as the scale of operations and their speed of expansion pick up.

NO ⮌

Giles Mohan

The Disappointments of Civil Society: The Politics of NGO Intervention in Northern Ghana

In recent years, and especially since the end of the Cold War in 1989, bilateral and multilateral donor agencies have pursued a 'New Policy Agenda' which gives renewed prominence to the roles of nongovernmental organisations (NGOs) and grassroots organisations (GROs) in poverty alleviation, social welfare and the development of "civil society" (Edwards and Hulme, 1996: 961).

Introduction

. . . [This selection] applies insights to an empirical study of state-NGO-society dynamics in northern Ghana. The study shows that strengthening civil society can create political tensions which ultimately undermine development. . . .

The Disappointments of Civil Society: Perspectives From Northern Ghana

The research upon which this section is based was enabled through contact with a UK-based NGO called Village Aid which works with partner NGOs[1] in northern Ghana, Sierra Leone, The Gambia and Cameroon. The research, undertaken within their northern Ghana programme, involved participating in programme evaluation and workshops, semi-structured interviews with their partners and reviewing project documentation. . . .

The External Determination of Local Agendas by Foreign NGOs

Within the realms of international civil society, a major line of tension exists between the northern and southern NGOs (N/SNGOs). Most donors and NNGOs work with local partner NGOs. Foreign interests may lack the local

From Giles Mohan, "The Disappointments of Civil Society: The Politics of NGO Intervention in Northern Ghana," *Political Geography*, vol. 21 (2002). Copyright © 2001 by Elsevier Science, Ltd. Reprinted by permission of Elsevier. References omitted.

knowledge or legitimacy to enter local communities so that partner NGOs are important gatekeepers in reaching the grassroots. Additionally, maintaining a fully staffed field office would be costly so that using local partners to deliver certain project elements is cheaper than using expatriates.

However, the notion of 'partnerships' is . . . a loaded process. Recent analysis (Edwards & Hulme, 1996; Bebbington & Riddell, 1997; Fowler, 1998) shows that the relations between partners is not even and that the funder tends to determine policy agendas to a far greater degree. As Nyamugasira notes, the NNGOs, despite commitments to participatory development, concentrate on ideas, networking, and education and leave the "time-bound, geographically fixed projects . . . to their Southern counterparts" (Nyamugasira, 1998: 298). While it would be tempting to place all the blame on an imperialising mission by NNGOs, the situation is far more complex. Fowler (1998) identifies various factors including paternalistic assumptions by the NNGOs, a bias towards their knowledge and procedures being superior, poor choice of field staff and a reluctance to release control of programmes that a true partnership requires. However, given the NNGOs' increasing reliance on official funding they too are pressed to show transparent success which breeds conservatism and a wariness to hand over the reins to local partners. On the SNGO side, many do lack capacity and transparency and react aggressively to any suggestions by the northern partners that this is the case. There are few transparent mechanisms for decision-making with limited methods for enshrining the principle of participation at all levels of the partnership. Partnerships are clearly suffused with political inequality which compromises the notion of an independent civil society emerging.

As donors seek out reliable and successful NGOs a market for development finance emerges where once small, agile, innovative and, at times, radical organisations quite rapidly become development 'success stories' and receive large inflows of foreign capital (Moore & Stewart, 1998). Such rapid growth is a problem for any organisation, but more importantly the funders tend to treat these organisations as infinitely flexible and capable of delivering any number of development competencies (environment, gender, water, health, etc., etc.). As a representative of NGO 'A' said "it's not easy to chew" (Interview with AS of NGO 'A', 4/2/00) implying that the organisation's 'mouth' became too full with demands from funders to deliver programmes at the grassroots. As the aid market contracts, the trend will be towards niched NGOs or larger, semi-commercial organisations which can deliver entire programmes for donors. In this sense civil society begins to massify and commodify with power increasingly concentrated in the hands of a few large organisations which may well be antithetical to a competitive and 'free' civil society.

Operationally, those NGOs receiving official aid have to be accountable to their funders which often brings conflict because the slow, flexible, culturally-specific processes do not translate easily into the fast turnaround demanded by log frame accounting techniques. On the other hand, the NGOs have a grassroots constituency, the supposed beneficiaries, who are increasingly alienated from the centres of decision-making. This double legitimacy bind leaves the NGO somewhat stranded and far away from its developmental role (Bebbington & Riddell, 1997). This is clearly demonstrated in terms of 'capacity issues' where northern partners insist on transparent accounting procedures and systematic monitoring and reporting systems (Fowler, 1998; Moore & Stewart, 1998). For some organisations this is seen as an imposition since they were established precisely to break from this bureaucratic tradition. It also runs counter to much 'participatory development' which valorises local knowledge yet the organisations impose management systems drawn from the western corporate world. For Village Aid and its partners in northern Ghana, this has produced considerable tension over the past five years which has, at times, spilled over into outright confrontation. The following extracts both use the phrase 'dictatorship' when referring to Village Aid

> But there seems to be too much dictatorship from Village Aid. Information flow is not adequate, ideas from partners are not respected or not taken (NGO 'B', 1999: 2);

> dictatorship . . . sometimes Village Aid wants to be very strict . . . as if they have no confidence in us . . . Decisions taken at the Village Aid level before coming to the agency level . . . People have not been asked to participate at the planning level (Interview with NGO 'A', 4/2/00).

From Village Aid's position these issues related to inadequate capacity and commitment to participation shown by their partners. I return to this point below as we see how the partner NGOs negotiate and manipulate their own position. . . .

The Relationships Between NGOs and Village Organisations

By and large NNGOs tend to use partners for village level activities. The underlying assumption is that the northern NGO lacks the local knowledge and connections to represent the local communities so that intermediaries are needed. It is precisely this perceived 'closeness' to local communities and understanding of their cultures that gives the SNGOs their power. In practice, this assumption is not always borne out. In many cases the local NGOs behave in equally patronising, dictatorial and bureaucratic ways towards the villages they represent. The following extracts suggest that Village Aid's partners suffer from many of the supposed problems of inflexible state bureaucrats:

> 'B' and 'A' are still adopting old-style possessive tactics towards their client villages (Smith, 1999: 8);

> They (the villages) are our people (Interview with NGO 'A', 4/2/00).

The SNGOs are taking ownership of local culture and using it as a defence mechanism. The NNGOs realised they needed to have intermediaries, ideally working in a partnership relation, but the SNGOs use this powerful position to protect their constituency of villages. They claim to represent the local communities, but have rather patronising attitudes towards them, but know they are beyond reproach. In this way civil society organisations actually impede democratisation and good governance. . . .

Another manifestation of this problem is where partner NGOs intervene between the Northern NGO and the village organisations. Again, this represents a complex politics of knowledge generation and communication. In particular 'participatory learning and action' (PLA) has become a widely used research and conscientisation procedure whereby local communities generate their own knowledge which then helps in priority setting (Chambers, 1997; Mohan, 1999, 2000). A sustained critique is given elsewhere (Mohan, 1999), but what we see is SNGOs intervening in this process and transmitting alternative interpretations of reality which the NNGO takes as authentic needs.

> Participatory Rural Appraisals are undertaken by local NGOs as a duty in order to access funding. Consequently, village communities identify needs and problems and tailor their prioritisation of them to the services which they perceive the local NGO is offering. Subsequent to this, the local NGO amends the prioritisation and, more often than not, the nature of the project itself to what they believe its northern partner will fund (Waddington, 1997: 2);

> For the most part, projects are a response to the needs of a 'B' group within a village rather than the village in general (Village Aid, 1996b: 3).

The result is that the NNGO funds acceptable priorities which may not be the genuine priorities of the villagers. To combat such problems, Village Aid have begun a programme which works within existing cultural and linguistic systems so as to avoid imposing externally-driven practices.

The Autonomy of Both Foreign and Indigenous NGOs From the State

One obvious problem associated with strengthening the NGO sector at the expense of the state is that state institutions and actors feel threatened. The good governance and social costs of adjustment initiatives came in the late 1980s and early 1990s after almost a decade of adjustment. State officials had become used to loans and aid flowing through the state so that diverting much of this lucrative source of funds was bound to excite resentment. A countervailing problem is that under the adjustment process the state had to reduce its welfare bill while austerity created such hardship that any assistance in alleviating social problems was also a vital political resource. The compromise for many states was to welcome those NGOs which had a relatively circumscribed social welfare agenda and not those which might have more transformatory political agendas.

The mechanisms for dealing with NGOs reflects these shifting and paradoxical tensions. Most common is regulation, usually taking the form of official registration (Bratton, 1989; Gary, 1996). More 'arm's length' influence can be via co-ordination through an umbrella organisation or forum which seeds debates and is selective about which NGOs are members and, therefore, privileged in terms of resources and information. More heavy-handed influence has been via co-optation where the state takes over partial functioning of NGOs via QUANGOs [quasi-autonomous nongovernment organizations]. Additionally, as the frontier between state and society has further muddled, many politicians have established their own NGOs as patronage structures for capturing foreign aid and promoting themselves in their local constituency. Finally, dissolution and harassment is the final form of state influence, especially with those NGOs taking critical views of the state. In Ghana we have seen various strategies adopted by both the state and NGOs. In this subsection I look at . . . key sites of interaction between the state and NGOs. . . .

NGOs as Patronage Structures and Party Political Vehicles

. . . [I]nsidious is the use of NGOs as vehicles for personal and party political gain by local officers. This is achieved through various mechanisms—petty corruption, largesse, interlocking political affiliations, and 'status'—and, as we have seen, the less obvious ways in which indigenous NGOs defend local culture in the face of 'outsider' intervention. In effect, some NGOs become fiefdoms for local élites to further their material and political status. As Hibou notes,

> The promotion of NGOs leads to an erosion of official administrative and institutional capacity, a reinforcement of the power of elites, particularly at the local level, or of certain factions, and sometimes stronger ethnic character in the destination of flows of finance from abroad. In many cases, these NGOs are established by politicians, at the national and local level, with a view to capturing external resources which henceforth pass through these channels on a massive scale (Hibou, 1999: 99).

Similarly, "the emergence of opportunistic organisations that call themselves NGOs but have no popular base at all. Many have been created as survival strategies for a professional middle class" (Bebbington & Riddell, 1997: 111). While 'A' and 'B' are by no means so opportunistic, both directors aspire to political power within Dagbon society. This is being pursued through various channels, one of which is the NGO. For example, the Director of 'A' is also a District Assembly member and the NGO is seen by villagers as indivisible from the former ruling party. Similarly, the Director of 'B' has been disciplined on various occasions for writing cheques without accounting for the destination of the money. His response was one of indignation in that Village Aid were behaving in a dictatorial and untrustworthy way. Recently, he was placed under investigation by the National Bureau of Investigation and the NGO's operations suspended pending the enquiry.

Decentralisation

Earlier work on local government showed that one of the key problems at the level of programme delivery is that NGOs have tended to set up parallel systems alongside a weak and under-funded local government system (Mohan, 1996b). On the other side, the decentralisation programme has been hampered by institutional dualism whereby local departments answer to central ministries and are not flexible with respect to local needs. The outcome is mutual mistrust and wasteful duplication of effort. This tendency is sufficiently widespread to exact comment from the outgoing Minister for Local Government who observed "the tendency of some of them (NGOs) to bypass laid-down structures and procedures at the district level and establish structures and programmes of their own without regards to their sustainability" (Kwamena Ahwoi reported in the Daily Graphic, 14/12/99). Within Village Aid's work similar problems occur:

> there existed a communication gap between the Project and the local extensionist in the sense that instead of communicating through District Officers the Project went straight to the local extensionist thereby marginalising the District Officers (Village Aid, 1999b: 3);

> District Agricultural Director's and District Forestry Officers appear to see themselves on the end of decentralisation policy and not a part of it (Village Aid, 1999a: 7).

As Aryeetey (Aryeetey, 1998: 308) comments "Neither the assembly members nor the technocrats in the district assemblies were seen to be in a position to make serious contributions towards strengthening consultation between the communities and the assemblies". The result is that contrary to the advocates of civil society, supporting NGOs does not lead to regularised interaction between society and state and in the process build the strength of both. In fact, it alienates the two even further and could undermine the longer term aim of building citizenship rights.

Conclusion: A Third Way for the Third World

. . . An assumption of the civil society route to development is that 'self-help' can reduce external dependency, because the local organisations more effectively 'own' the process. By multiplying the number of stakeholders it is assumed that more consensual and democratic development can be achieved which is ultimately more sustainable. In the Ghana case this clearly did not occur. While the number of development organisations mushroomed in the wake of structural adjustment and the drivers of this process championed partnership, the local 'partner' organisations and, more importantly, the rural poor were marginalised from decision-making. The paradox is that external NGOs, often heavily funded by their home governments, are charged with 'empowerment', but are so wary of upsetting their funders that they tightly circumscribe the activities on the ground and completely undermine independent development. Their partners are then trapped in an irreconcilable position of being the authentic representatives of their grassroots constituencies, but being accountable to organisations outside the locality. Squeezed in such a way they usually defer to the funder and present to them a relatively trouble-free view of local communities and their development needs, all of which further marginalises and alienates the rural poor.

The aid paradigm means that civil society organisations become more dependent on external funders as well as the market. The NGOs largely become service delivery mechanisms for pre-determined development agendas. In competing for these scarce aid resources, the NGOs position themselves strategically which creates tensions between organisations. There is nothing wrong with debate and contestation between organisations and political actors, but most of the conflict in northern Ghana was about scrapping over the spoils and not ideology. Indeed many NGOs have been set up precisely to divert aid for personal goals as opposed to responding to the needs of the poor. As the aid market has woken up to the opportunism of many so-called NGOs it has tightened up its funding criteria, which might alleviate some corrupt behaviour, but actually makes it more difficult for smaller, less professionalised organisations to succeed. It also works against the philosophy of much participatory development which seeks to valorise multiple local differences rather than impose a rigid model. This in turn undermines the democratic potential of civil society as only some interests are actively represented, whether they be ethnic, class or political party. Rather than reflecting social differences the uneven promotion of civil society covertly strengthens social divisions, promotes factionalism and deepens the marginalisation of some groups.

As we saw the real beneficiaries of strengthening civil society have been the local elites. Increasingly, we see a tier of professional NGO managers who use foreign aid and locally generated income as a means of achieving or consolidating their middle-class status. Similar processes have been observed in Britain with most social economy initiatives being "run by outsiders—professional social entrepreneurs who bring with them what amounts to an ideology of community empowerment which they can then set about enacting with local people" (Amin, Cameron & Hudson, 1999: 2041). In emphasising local knowledge, grassroots initiative, and community development this ideology of empowerment generates a discourse of discrete and bounded places amenable to a particular form of intervention that only they, albeit in partnership, can largely control. Again, the rural poor are only brought in as members of fictionalised 'communities' and are in practice denied any real voice.

In all instances the state, rather than being a detached political actor separated from society by a supposed ditch, is deeply implicated in these activities. The Ghanaian state has established its own 'non-governmental' organisations, confined registration to 'non-political' organisations, and engineered debate about the 'need' for economic liberalisation. At the local level, state agencies and NGOs are in some cases relatively separate but the civil society organisations do not channel opinion into government or scrutinise its operations, but treat it with profound mistrust and often duplicate its efforts. No synergy, in a formal sense, exists here between state and civil society. However, in more subtle ways the state and NGOs are mutually implicated. The central state in Ghana has used civil society organisations to drive local politics and actively promoted decentralisation as a means of consolidating rural support. On an even more subtle level we saw how some NGO officials purposefully misrepresent themselves to blur the boundaries between civil society and the state in an attempt to present themselves and the party in a positive light by utilising the financial resources of the NGOs. As Bebbington and Bebbington (Bebbington and Bebbington, 2001:9) comment the emphasis on society "diverts attention from the webs of relationships that link civil society organizations and the state and that may offer the prospect of changing forms of state action". I return to the possibility of changing the state below.

These developments within civil society are very much in keeping with Marx's theorisation in the 19th Century. That it is a normative concept whose realisation serves the interests of the (international) bourgeoisie. Hearn (Hearn, 1998, 2001) and Beckman (Beckman, 1993) suggest that the emphasis on civil society in Africa is central to modern imperialism in which new institutional actors are added to the array of players seeking to delegitimise the third world state and further erode what little sovereignty it has left. Hearn (Hearn, 1998: 98) comments that "In the immediate post-colonial period, the comprador class consisted of government official and private sector entrepreneurs and managers, in the 1990s it includes leaders of the voluntary sector". This neo-compradorism simultaneously fictionalises and factionalises civil society in a bold new experiment in socio-political engineering which aims to weaken the state, cheapen the cost of aid and promote market-based freedoms.

Specifically this imagining of civil society has a number of important political ramifications. First, it cheapens aid through match funding and the whole ethos of self-help. While self-help is more likely to embed ownership and inject greater relevance into projects it also serves to place the burden for poverty alleviation on the structurally poor which, in turn, leaves NGOs de facto legitimising SAPs [Structural Adjustment Programmes] by filling in the welfare delivery gap. As Hintjens (Hintjens, 1999: 386) comments "The state is no longer to be held accountable for ensuring that citizens' basic needs are met; instead private citizens, individually and collectively, are expected to provide for themselves, however poor or disadvantaged they may be". Also, as we have seen, those groups and institutions able to provide some match funding may well do so to ensure the favourable direction of aid which does not necessarily benefit the most poor and marginalised.

Second, and closely related to the first, is that 'partnership' and devolution might serve to spread the risk to 'locals'. Complex scenarios in which "social development is a matter of tidying up after the market" (Pieterse, 2001: 126) leaves development organisations in an awkward position, because there is little they can do to affect broader structures. In this sense, partnership becomes an insurance policy against lack of effectiveness. As with 'policy slippage' under SAPs, the donors can implicate the poor in the failure to achieve development which becomes a subtle form of blaming the victim. In the UK context Amin, Cameron, & Hudson (1999: 2049) observed "Very few social economy projects are underwritten by public authorities . . . (and) . . . Even less risk is borne by the private sector". Participatory development can be seen as a sensitive form of empowerment when it works or the result of grassroots incapacity when it fails.

Third, the question of risk, opens up the relationship of civil society to the market. As the Standard Chartered case in Ghana showed, the NGO effectively underwrites the risk on a multitude of small credit schemes. In this way the promotion of civil society is, as the Marxists have argued, very much about creating the conditions in which private capital and entrepreneurialism can flourish. Additionally, the NGO sector in Ghana has been at the forefront of the negotiated consensus around further liberalisation while the veneer of stable processual democracy acts as a major stimulant to inward investment from multinationals.

Finally, the emphasis on localism has a number of effects. On the one hand it factionalises and fragments political opposition. As Mamdani (1996: 300) argues "all decentralized systems of rule fragment the ruled and stabilize the rulers" so that the emphasis on atomistic civil society repeats many of the problems of governance laid down under Indirect Rule. Central regimes are often happy to promote development programmes which seek to build upon local energies because this absolves them of responsibility for welfare provision, earns political capital by being sensitive and dialogic, and disaggregates society into a series of unconnected, both spatially and politically, 'issues'. Potential alliances and solidarity against the structural forces generating poverty are undermined as civil society actors literally scrabble for the pickings of the aid regime. Where networks of local NGOs develop it is often to enhance efficiency of delivery, such as avoiding spatial overlap or sharing 'best practice', than it is to actively lobby the state or international organisations. So, localism diverts attention from the structural causes of poverty and feeds into the belief that market-based globalisation can and should be harnessed to work for the poor. . . .

Donor and NGO support for civil society, and 'localism' in general, keeps at bay debates about more fundamental structural changes to, say, unequal property rights or despotic, but economically useful, host governments. One thing that has emerged from discussions is that 'local' action must simultaneously address the non-local. As Nyamugasira (Nyamugasira, 1998: 297) observes NGOs "have come to the sad realization that although they have achieved many micro-level successes, the systems and structures that determine power and resource allocations—locally, nationally, and globally—remain largely intact". Recent efforts have begun to deal with these limitations by looking at strategies for 'scaling up' local interventions (Blackburn & Holland, 1998; Whaites, 1998). Only by linking participatory approaches to wider, and more difficult, processes of democratisation, anti-imperialism and feminism will long-term changes occur. Crucially, greater and more critical engagement with the state is required although this is incredibly difficult where states, donors and other aid organisations delimit the political space open to civil society. One route for this is more accomodatory via the recent emphasis on citizenship and rights which seeks to generate greater 'synergy' between state and society through the promotion of social capital and civic engagement. A second route is more radical and involves civil society actors opposing the dominant development discourse and challenging local, national and global structures. While the Zapatistas [Mexican rebels] have become the leitmotif [recurring theme] of this form of political action, it remains to be seen whether a new cohort of political leaders and agents emerge which actively reject the present neo-liberal consensus.

Note

1. Given the political nature of the inter-NGO relations discussed in this section, the names of these NGOs have been concealed. Village Aid works with two main SNGOs which I have re-named 'A' and 'B'.

POSTSCRIPT

Are Non-Governmental Organizations (NGOs) Effective at Facilitating Community Development?

There are a number of sub-issues that flow out of the discussion regarding the role and efficacy of the NGOs in fostering the development process in Africa, including those related to the participation of local communities in development projects, the influence of donors on NGOs, and the limitations of NGO success when broader structural problems persist. Each of these sub-issues merit further reading and discussion.

As Mohan discusses, participation has been a buzzword in NGO circles since at least the early 1990s. The emphasis on participation came about in reaction to a history of top-down development projects that left local people with little to no sense of ownership of the projects undertaken by outsiders in their communities. Besides being problematic in its own right, a lack of participation often inhibited the longer-term sustainability of programs (because local people had little interest in maintaining projects they did not initiate or request). In order to foster community participation, NGOs have employed a range of techniques (e.g., participatory action research [PAR], participatory rural appraisal [PRA], and participatory learning and action [PLA]), to facilitate community problem identification and group problem solving. For a discussion of these techniques, see numerous publications by Robert Chambers, for example, *Whose Reality Counts? Putting the First Last* (Intermediate Technology Publications, 1997). The problem, and a latent contradiction, is that communities may identify problems that many NGOs are not prepared to solve (at least in the quick and efficient manner that their funders expect). The result, as Mohan notes, is that communities often identify problems and select programmatic solutions they think an NGO can deliver. One of the great innovations of the Six-S network was its emphasis on flexible funding, an approach that allowed village-based NAAM groups to propose their own projects, which were then selected by a committee of village representatives, rather than a donor.

As NGOs increasingly receive funding from bilateral donors, there is a concern that they may become extensions of donors rather than autonomous development agents. This could mean that NGOs actually change the nature of their programming to suit the desires of donors rather than catering to the needs and wants of the communities they are serving. If, in fact, NGOs have two constituencies (donors and the communities they serve), the degree to which they are overly (and exclusively) responsive to donors may adversely influence the issue of participation discussed above. In contrast, and somewhat counterintuitively, it could be argued that overattention to donor priorities might actually increase participation in some instances if the donors themselves are insisting on participatory approaches. For further discussion of the influence of donors on NGOs, see an article by Fowler in a 1998 issue of *Development and Change* entitled "Authentic NGDO Partnerships in the New Policy Agenda for International Aid: Dead End or Light Ahead?"

Donor funding may also overwhelm the capacity of some NGOs to effectively use these funds. Lecomte and Krishna hint that this was beginning to become a problem for Six-S. There are reports that delays of reimbursements of loans are increasing. This problem may stem from the fact that the network accepted many groups without sufficiently checking their ability to save and to manage due to increasing demand for membership. Slower repayments also seem to coincide with broader economic difficulties where Six-S is operating. For this and other concerns about the Six-S network, which appears to have faltered in recent years, see Takehiko Uemura's paper entitled "Sustainable Rural Development in Western Africa: The Naam Movement and the Six-S" (SD Dimensions, FAO) or Sten Hagberg's chapter entitled "Ethnic Identification in Voluntary Associations: The Politics of Development and Culture in Burkina Faso" in *Rights and the Politics of Recognition in Africa* (Zed Books, 2004).

One of the potential limitations of NGO projects, and the project approach to development in general, is that local social change may be circumscribed by broader structural problems. As Nyamugasira is quoted as saying in the conclusion of Mohan's article "NGOs 'have come to the sad realization that although they have achieved many micro-level successes, the systems and structures that determine power and resource allocation—locally, nationally, globally—remain largely intact.'" Even more troubling is the possibility that "micro-level successes" might actually work against broader scale social change if they make people content with a bad situation, that is, have a palliative effect.

ISSUE 7

Should Developed Countries Provide Debt Relief to the Poorest, Indebted African Nations?

YES: Dorothy Logie and Michael Rowson, from "Poverty and Health: Debt Relief Could Help Achieve Human Rights Objectives," *Health and Human Rights* (1998)

NO: Robert Snyder, from "Proclaiming Jubilee—for Whom?" *Christian Century* (June 30–July 7, 1999)

ISSUE SUMMARY

YES: Dorothy Logie, a general practitioner and active member of Medact, and Michael Rowson, assistant director of Medact, argue that debt is a human-rights issue because debt and related structural adjustment policies reduce the state's ability to address discrimination, vulnerability, and inequality. Debt relief, if channeled in the right direction, could help reduce poverty and promote health.

NO: Robert Snyder, an associate professor of biology at Greenville College, counters that debt cancellation will only work if the factors that created debt in the first place are addressed. He uses a case study of Rwanda to demonstrate why political and social change must occur for debt forgiveness to work.

$\mathbf{A}$s Dorothy Logie and Michael Rowson note in their selection, 34 of the 41 most indebted nations in the world are found in Africa. Furthermore, these same authors note that 23 percent of new aid receipts in Africa are spent on debt repayment. Responsibility for the debt crisis in Africa is complex and fairly difficult to attribute to any single group of individuals or a single entity. Resolution of this problem is hugely controversial, and it has been a matter of intense debate over the past several years.

Debt has accumulated for African governments for a number of reasons. First, many African governments pursued a policy known as import substitution in the 1960s and 1970s. Rather than importing manufactured and processed goods from abroad, the idea was that African governments should foster enterprises within their own national borders in order to produce goods that would "substitute" for imports. This approach, conceptualized by the Latin American economist Raul Prebisch, was designed as an antidote to the perpetual quandary of developing countries trading inexpensive commodities for expensive manufactured goods. The problem was that these state-run enterprises were often relatively uncompetitive at best (i.e., they produced goods at a cost higher than the imported competition) or a serious drain on state resources at worst (especially if they were used as sources of patronage by the ruling elite). As a consequence, the privatization of inefficient state-run enterprises was an important aim of structural adjustment policies.

Second, while many African economies grew rapidly in the 1960s and early 1970s, this growth began to temper significantly in the late 1970s and 1980s. Part of this slowdown in growth has been attributed to a global rise in petroleum prices at the time—a problem for the majority of African nations that were (and are) petroleum importers. Even after African economies began to slow down, commercial banks and public lenders often lent to African governments based on previous levels of growth—contributing to unhealthy levels of indebtedness.

Third, the loan officers at commercial banks, and even at multilateral institutions like the World Bank, were (and are) often under a certain amount of pressure to make loans. This meant that creditors encouraged African governments, in some instances, to obtain loans they really should not have been taking. Finally, some African government officials inappropriately used borrowed monies, making it difficult to pay these loans back in a timely fashion.

The current high level of indebtedness in many African countries has led NGOs, think tanks, and religious organizations to call for debt forgiveness. Others have warned about the dangerous messages that debt forgiveness will send to future borrowers. In the following selections, Dorothy Logie and Michael Rowson contend that debt is a human-rights issue and that debt relief, if channeled correctly, can help the poorest, indebted African nations. In contrast, Robert Snyder states that the factors that created debt in the first place need to be addressed in order for debt cancellation to work.

**Dorothy Logie and
Michael Rowson**

YES

Poverty and Health: Debt Relief Could Help Achieve Human Rights Objectives

UDHR [Universal Declaration of Human Rights] Article 25

1. Everyone has the right to a standard of living adequate for the health and well-being of himself and of his family, including food, clothing, housing and medical care and necessary social services, and the right to security in the event of unemployment, sickness, disability, widowhood, old age or other lack of livelihood in circumstances beyond his control.

2. Motherhood and childhood are entitled to special care and assistance. All children, whether born in or out of wedlock, shall enjoy the same social protection.

. . . [O]n the fiftieth anniversary of the UDHR [Universal Declaration of Human Rights], human rights activists still confront the bitter reality of widespread hunger, disease and discrimination in the context of a global economy characterized by widening inequality and poverty. Although the preamble to the UDHR reaffirms the worth of each individual person and the equal rights of men and women to progress towards a better standard of living, and although the idea of freedom from poverty has been in human rights law and discourse since the adoption of the UDHR, poverty-related issues have not been given priority in the human rights agenda. This anniversary represents both an opportunity to push poverty to the front of that agenda, and to promote action that might enable its reduction.

Poverty and Ill-Health

Poverty, in both its absolute and relative forms, is the single most important driver of ill-health in the world today. This is hardly surprising. In developing countries, the pathways by which low levels of economic and social well-being affect health are easily found and are the daily reality of hundreds of millions. These pathways include: lack of access to safe water (experienced by 1.2 billion people); lack of adequate sanitation; poor housing; low income (at least 1.3 billion people live on under $US1 per day), and lack of access to

From Dorothy Logie and Michael Rowson, "Poverty and Health: Debt Relief Could Help Achieve Human Rights Objectives," *Health and Human Rights*, vol. 3, no. 2 (1998). Copyright © 1998 by The President and Fellows of Harvard College. Reprinted by permission of The François-Xavier Bagnoud Center for Health and Human Rights and The President and Fellows of Harvard College. Some references omitted.

health services (faced by 800 million people). Discrimination against women, the elderly, ethnic minorities, refugees, the disabled and other marginalized groups both causes and magnifies these problems. Many other factors, such as conflict and adverse climate changes, for example, can also contribute to poverty and ill-health. Another contributor can be the skewed spending priorities of governments which may have high levels of military expenditure or may devote most of their health budgets to secondary health care for urban citizens, at the expense of primary and preventative health services.

Human Rights Response

Faced by such diverse causes of poverty and ill-health, human rights activists obviously need to work at international, national and community levels, and both within and outside the health sector, to make their anti-poverty agenda effective and credible. . . . Here we will focus our attention at the level of the international economy.

The anniversary of the UDHR is taking place in the midst of a widespread economic crisis, which threatens to lead to a global recession. . . . For many countries, a new recession may be only the latest stage in a downward economic record—since 1980, 100 countries have experienced economic decline or stagnation, and 1.6 billion people have seen their incomes reduced. This decline has been most obvious in sub-Saharan Africa. . . .

Debt and Economic Adjustment

Today a large burden of foreign debt is carried by over 40 of the world's poorest countries. This potentially has multiple effects on their economies and acts as a significant constraint to improvements in international health. First, it undermines prospects for economic growth (and thus poverty reduction) by discouraging public and private investment; private investors, in particular, fear the higher taxes, higher inflation and currency speculation that an unsustainable debt burden can bring. Second, debt repayments siphon away precious foreign exchange needed to buy the imports essential for economic growth and the maintenance of health systems. Third, debt repayments divert money from government budgets which could be used for health, education and poverty reduction initiatives. And fourth, they use up sources of foreign exchange (other than export revenues) such as grants and loans from government and multilateral donors. For poor countries, the accumulation of a large foreign debt can thus be the prelude to a catalogue of economic disasters.

The Scale of Sub-Saharan African Debt

> *Many states in Africa lack the financial capital needed to address basic expectations and fundamental needs. This is one of the central crises in Africa today, and one that is due in large measure to the problem of African public sector debt.*[1]

In the early 1980s, the developing world as a whole faced foreign debts of around US$800 billion—the results of a decade of irresponsible actions on the part of both creditors and borrowers. Today, total debt stands at over two trillion US dollars, despite large repayments in the intervening years. Sub-Saharan Africa, containing 34 of the 41 most heavily indebted poor countries, is worst affected. Taken together, its US$230 billion debt is small compared to debt in other parts of the world, but compared to its earnings from exports or its total GDP [gross domestic product], the debt represents an overwhelming burden. More money is spent on interest payments than on health and education, and many countries are unable to afford even the most basic annual health package, estimated by the World Bank to cost around US$12 per capita. In Uganda, with one of the highest infant and maternal morality rates (and an AIDS epidemic), the government spends annually only US$2.50 per capita on health. Several other heavily-indebted countries are spending equally small amounts on health, leading to an increasing reliance on cost-recovery mechanisms (such as user charges) to cover the widening gap between health needs and budgetary capacity.

Many countries in the region are literally bankrupt, and are in the process of building up huge arrears of debts that can never be repaid. What repayment they do manage is financed by revenues from exports and other money from the domestic budget, new loans (thus incurring further debts), and grants from aid donors. It is sobering to note that in 1996, twenty-three percent of all aid given to sub-Saharan Africa was spent on debt repayments to financial institutions and governments in the North.

Structural Adjustment Policies

In return for either delaying debt repayments or lending more money, international donors such as the World Bank and IMF [International Monetary Fund] have demanded that countries undertake policy reforms, known as structural adjustment programs, aimed at reducing domestic demand by raising interest rates, devaluing currencies and reducing public expenditure. They also recommend that the state's role in public life be reduced by, for example, eliminating subsidies for food and fertilizers, relaxing foreign investment regulations, privatizing state-run industries and services, and cutting government bureaucracy (including in the health sector). . . .

Economic Crisis, Adjustment and Vulnerable Groups

Article 25 of the UDHR specifically points to mothers and children as social groups needing special attention. Today we might extend this concern to other vulnerable groups such as women, the disabled and people living with HIV/AIDS. These groups are at greater risk of suffering during economic crises for a range of reasons, most notably related to discrimination. Debt and inappropriate economic adjustment can reduce the state's capacity to intervene to correct discrimination, vulnerability and inequality, thus putting these groups at even greater disadvantage in difficult times. . . .

Due in part to the lack of funds which can result from the constraints debt and adjustment impose on social sector spending, international and national plans for improving the health of women and children remain to be fully carried out. For example, 40 African countries have prepared National Plans of Action in response to the global Plan of Action emanating from the 1990 World Summit for Children which incorporated priority health goals for children and for women. These plans include raising immunization rates, improving oral hydration, eliminating iodine and Vitamin A deficiencies and encouraging breastfeeding. But implementation has been slow or nonexistent due to lack of both money and political will.

. . . Africa is the only part of the world in which the number of children out of school is increasing. In Niger, for example, fewer than one-quarter of children attend primary school, and less than 20 percent of these are girls. Where it exists, school often means a mud hut with a leaking roof, classes of 40 or more students and a chronic lack of teaching materials. In Zambia, expenditure on primary schools is now at less than half its mid-1980s level. This is a denial of the right to education as stated in Article 26 of the UDHR and also of Article 15 of the Convention on the Rights of the Child (which has been ratified by all of the governments of Africa except Somalia).

Reproductive Health

Article 25 throws the spotlight on motherhood as a condition during which women require "special care." However, in what has been described as "the health scandal of our time," 585,000 women still die each year from pregnancy-related causes and many times that number are incapacitated as a result of child-bearing. In parts of sub-Saharan Africa maternal mortality is still rising and, a decade after the introduction of the 1987 Safe Motherhood Initiative, its implementation remains frustrated not only by lack of funds and political will but also by continuing discrimination against women.

. . . Low levels of spending on health can result in inadequate medical and physical infrastructure, maternal malnutrition, user charges, poor-quality staff training and motivation, unreliable blood supplies and lack of drugs. . . .

HIV/AIDS

AIDS has become a marker for injustice, discrimination and lack of realization of human rights. The virus thrives on poverty, social disruption, ignorance and accelerated urbanization: its spread is encouraged by lack of resources, lack of clean water, commercial sex, and rapidly declining health services. Each of these factors is potentially exacerbated when adjustment policies lead to budget cuts, unemployment, and migration. . . .

Using Debt Relief to Promote Gains in Health

After a decade of vociferous pressure from NGOs [nongovernmental organizations] and others, both creditor governments and the international financial institutions have moved to a point where they have agreed to put a mechanism into place (the Highly Indebted Poor Countries Initiative) which will cancel some low-income country debts. It is believed that by relieving a proportion of foreign debt, economic growth will be encouraged and, if the relief is deep enough, this should free resources that governments could then use to tackle some of the enormous health problems outlined above. However, the process is slow, the relief is offered to too few countries and, even where provided, the relief is often not extensive enough to make a significant impact on human development problems. Oxfam has put forward a scheme which would require countries, in return for faster and deeper debt cancellation, to use the gains from debt relief to implement national development priorities agreed to by governments, civil society, and donors. They have also shown that for some highly-indebted poor countries, debt cancellation could provide a significant portion of the external finance needed to implement the National Plans of Action agreed to after the World Summit for Children.

In the long-term, debt relief could reduce the need for countries to undertake economic adjustment—with its technical-fix approach to health as a commodity and the resulting emphasis on introducing user charges, competition, and other market mechanisms into the delivery of health care. Countries could then be free to reorient their vision of health towards universal primary health care (as contained in the Alma Ata Declaration) and to emphasize a preventative public health agenda.

The Problem of Conditionality

. . . [H]uman rights activists and health professionals might link up to ensure that debt relief does help to reduce poverty and promote health, and that it does so in a fair way. For example they might:

- work to ensure that the debt relief process is open and accountable and not dominated by the interests and agendas of creditors, but also includes the concerns of governments and civil society representatives;

- help to highlight and build upon schemes proposed by developing countries themselves—schemes that use debt relief to achieve human rights objectives. In fact, several poor countries (such as Uganda) already have human-development-oriented schemes waiting in the wings to be financed by the proceeds from debt relief;

- make sure that debt relief is not conditional on health or economic system reforms that are potentially harmful to health outcomes; and

- press for governments that have ratified human rights instruments (such as the Convention on the Rights of the Child) and the World Bank and IMF (which are components of the UN system) to modify their policies in accordance with these international obligations.

Conclusions

Debt relief is not a solution on its own, but if channeled in the right direction, and with the active involvement of civil society, it can achieve progress in reaching human development targets. There is a responsibility, and a legal obligation, for governments and international financial institutions to address the determinants of health (including income, education, safe water and food, and all human rights) in order to achieve lasting health improvement.

Human rights activists and health professionals should work toward addressing these issues by pressing for swift and generous debt relief. . . .

The fiftieth anniversary of the UDHR is a time to call again for poverty reduction and health equality to be at the center of development strategies. In the meantime, the UDHR remains a living document, a standard by which we can measure the world's imperfections and work towards righting wrongs—past, present and future. The more people—health professionals, nongovernmental organizations and activists—understand what human rights instruments have to say about poverty and health, the more these instruments can be used to lever change.

Note

2. K. Annan, from the "Report to the Security Council on the Causes of Conflict and the Promotion of Durable Peace and Sustainable Development in Africa," April 1998, quoted in Oxfam's submission to the UN Committee on the Rights of the Child, *Violating the Rights of the Child: Debt and Poverty in Africa* (Oxford: Oxfam, May 1998).

NO ↶

Robert Snyder

Proclaiming Jubilee—for Whom?

Jubilee 2000 is gaining momentum. Centers for the movement have arisen in more than 40 countries, and numerous churches and nongovernmental organizations have signed on to the campaign. The goals of this movement, which seems to have originated with the All Africa Conference of Churches and is now centered in the United Kingdom, are best summed up in the apostolic letter issued by Pope John Paul II in 1994. It states: "In the spirit of the Book of Leviticus (25:8-12), Christians will have to raise their voice on behalf of all the poor of the world, proposing the Jubilee as an appropriate time to give thought, among other things, to reducing substantially, if not canceling outright, the international debt which seriously threatens the future of many nations." . . .

The idea is appealing. After all, there is no such thing as an international bankruptcy court which allows hopelessly indebted countries to declare themselves insolvent. Countries that have no hope of ever paying off their debt languish in a state of perpetual penury. The people of these countries barely eke out a living, while the banks owned by the wealthy prosper.

The world's financial institutions have recognized that something needs to be done to change this situation. The International Monetary Fund (IMF) recently started the Heavily Indebted Poor Country (HIPC) initiative, which singles out countries undergoing extreme financial stress. On the list are many African nations, including Rwanda, Burundi, Kenya and the Democratic Republic of Congo. Each country must pass a second screening to be eligible to receive some debt relief.

The Jubilee 2000 people claim that the relief proposed by the IMF is not enough. It does indeed seem to fall far short of what is needed. However, the concept proposed by Jubilee 2000 is riddled with pitfalls; to apply it universally would be naïve.

The economies of the heavily indebted countries would clearly benefit from debt relief. In countries with benevolent governments, the citizenry on the whole would gain. However, the socioeconomic structure of some of the heavily indebted nations is such that, in the long term, debt relief might only aggravate the condition of the poor.

As a former agricultural missionary in east and central Africa, I've learned that quick fixes can sometimes become excuses for not dealing with the more painful fundamentals of international and national problems. A poorly executed act of sympathy can exacerbate the problem that it is meant to solve. Consider Rwanda.

Until 1994 Rwanda was under the rule of President Juvénal Habyari-mana. Generally, Westerners liked him. From the perspective of international agencies, he was at worst a benevolent dictator, at best a progressive peace-maker promoting development. Compared to many African countries, Rwanda experienced a time of stability and growth during Habyarimana's rule. We now realize, however, that he was a cunning power broker and, to a certain degree, a racist. He made sure that the benefits of international aid projects accrued mainly either to his extended family or to the northwestern region of Rwanda from which he came.

The people of Rwanda's southern half were well aware of this inequity. All Rwandans had to carry identity cards that showed their ethnicity. If you were Tutsi, you faced discrimination whether you were from the north or the south. Though 10 to 15 percent of the population was Tutsi, no Tutsi was allowed to hold a leadership position in government or the military. A small group of Tutsi ran profitable business enterprises, but they were well aware that the price for the freedom to carry on business was not to interfere with or criticize Habyarimana's dictatorial hold. Rwanda's leaders drained the economy into their own bank accounts, while making sure that no opponent could get enough political strength to challenge the status quo. Habyarimana mani-cured his image for Western donors, and aid dollars poured in. The government and the army put on a friendly face to those of us working in the country.

The Rwandans were not fooled by this political masquerade. They understood the rules of the game, according to the former Rwandan minister of defense, James Gasana, who escaped from Rwanda in 1993. An insightful moderate, he would probably have been killed for his political stance by the powers that eventually led to the 1994 genocide. In a paper presented at the Ecumenical Institute in Bossey, Switzerland, in 1996, Gasana stated that the Rwandan army served only one purpose: to protect the power elite. This is not unique to Rwanda. Says Steven Were Omamo of Kenya's leader: "[Daniel arap] Moi's government . . . is widely viewed as an engine of domination instead of the agent of the popular will, more interested in maintaining old forms of influence and patronage for a minority than in expanding opportunity for the majority. This, I believe, is the root of our current troubles." Wangari Maathai, the legendary leader of the Green Belt Movement in Kenya, states: "Leadership in Africa has been . . . concerned with the opportunity to control the state and all its resources. Such leadership sees the power, prestige and comfortable lifestyles that the national resources can support. It is the sort of leadership that has built armies and security networks to protect itself against its own citizens."

⋅◉⋅

In countries such as these, the army and secret service are part of the political machine. They silence their opposition and prevent any broad-based power sharing. When I lived in Rwanda, one of my employees told me that his elderly mother had tried to vote against the continuation of the Habyarimana regime and been prevented from doing so. When she then stated that an old woman with mud on her feet from the fields ought to be allowed to vote against the official who drives his Mercedes Benz to the polling booth, she was arrested.

Though it is hard to prove, it is widely accepted that some African leaders promote ethnic violence during election times or when their power is challenged. The powerful are willing to injure and kill people so that they can continue to feed unhindered on the country's resources. Mobutu Sese Seko, the former president of Zaire (now the Democratic Republic of Congo), so ferociously plundered his country's resources that at his death his estimated worth stood at between $5 billion and $10 billion. His country's national debt was $14 billion.

Even some of the church leaders in such countries become involved in power games and ethnic divisiveness instead of serving as champions of justice. They, too, may have a vested interest in maintaining the status quo. We only need to consider our own history of race relations to understand how this can happen. Sometimes the flow of international charitable aid into the church attracts self-interested people into the institution; not all church leaders are oriented to serving the people. Many courageous men and women of the church have fought for justice, but many others have manipulated the system for their own gain.

Do we need to do something to help deeply indebted countries? Absolutely. Is the industrialized world partly responsible for their plight? Absolutely. Do we want to encourage corrupt leaders by giving them money that will enable them to pretend to be benevolent lovers of the people? Absolutely not. If we are going to forgive debt, let us not fool ourselves into thinking that we can outsmart the cunning men and women who are experienced at manipulating the international community for their own benefit. These leaders who are so good at sleight of hand will empty our pockets while they throw a few crumbs to the poor, and then laugh as their own bank accounts grow.

If a country is governed by a small, corrupt power elite and the national debt is really the debt of that elite, then let them face their people without foreign aid. The international community placed strong economic sanctions on the former white South African government. Even though those sanctions also impacted the poor, no one called for their discontinuation. Everyone agreed that ending the evil of apartheid required stern measures. Why can't we see that apartheid-like policies also exist in other countries? The world has shut its eyes to the racist policies of Rwanda and Burundi. Instead of imposing sanctions, we want to forgive their debts. When Kenya's leaders stir the country's racial tensions into riots, we look the other way and then talk about forgiving the government's debts.

⋅⦿⋅

Some will accuse me of paternalism and of ignoring our own guilt. But anyone who has lived among the people of countries with corrupt regimes has seen what happens when money comes in from the outside. The Jubilee 2000 campaigners claim to be aware of dictatorial and international power cliques. They state, "Jubilee 2000 calls for co-responsibility of debtors and creditors for the debt crisis. Remission of debt should be worked out through a fair and transparent process ensuring full participation of debtors in negotiations on debt relief." But can there be such a thing as "transparent processes" in countries where spies and guns counter any threat to the status quo? Why does it take a coup d'etat to change most African governments?

We will only increase our guilt if we inhibit necessary, fundamental changes from occurring in these countries. We recognized this in dealing with the former Rhodesia and South Africa. But not with Rwanda. We seem to be blind to black-on-black racism and corruption. Only fundamental change would have prevented the genocide in Rwanda. Only fundamental change will stop the incessant coups d'etat in nations where one group after another seeks to grow fat on the country's resources.

A groundswell of opposition to corrupt leaders is rising in several African nations. The West must not provide the leaders of such nations with the means to mollify their populations temporarily while they solidify their positions of power. Where the church is in bed with the government, it should also be considered suspect. At the same time, the church in the West must educate itself about our history of foreign political manipulation focused on protecting our own self-interests. This understanding should be a prerequisite to joining campaigns like that of Jubilee 2000.

Forgiving debts is a worthwhile enterprise, consistent with biblical teachings. But the admonition to fight for the oppressed must equally be kept in mind. Forgiving a national debt and freeing the oppressed are not necessarily the same thing. In fact, they may be opposites. Let us proceed cautiously. We should not help any poor country that has a large, internally focused military or secret service. We must deal with more than the superficial issue of debt relief. The West must acknowledge its role in creating and supporting corrupt dictatorships. The economic powers need to help poor countries ruled by benevolent governments to get a sure footing in the international economic system.

Ultimately, we must realize that we in the West can not "fix" the problems of the poor countries. The people themselves must rise up and say no to their corrupt power elites. They must say no to the petty corruption that occurs at every police station and customs office. They must say no to benefiting from the ill-gotten funds of family members with access to power. They must say no to preying on ethnic groups who are outside of the power clique. They must say no to corrupt spiritual leaders. Until this is done, debt relief will provide only a temporary respite, a time when leaders can rest more peacefully in their expensive villas. It will only camouflage the slow, under-the-surface boil in countries ruled by corrupt dictators and their minions.

The church must not look to economic cures while ignoring systemic disease. We must not swing the odds against our brothers and sisters who are fighting for change. They understand the need for changed hearts. To paraphrase Bakole Wa Ilunga's book *The Paths of Liberation: A Third World Spirituality:* The path of liberation is long and winding, but it always must go through the heart of humanity.

POSTSCRIPT

Should Developed Countries Provide Debt Relief to the Poorest, Indebted African Nations?

Snyder argues that one of the main problems with debt relief is that it does not make African governments accountable to their own people. In his case study of Rwanda, he suggests that, more often than not, excessive debt exists in African countries because of corruption and mismanagement. Other arguments against debt relief tend to focus on the turmoil that debt relief would create in the international financial system. There is a fear among public and private lenders that if one country is allowed to default on its loans without serious repercussions, then there will be a raft of other countries that will quickly follow suit. Proponents of debt relief would argue that both of these perspectives ignore the role that lenders have played in exacerbating the African debt crisis.

While Logie and Rowson certainly do not agree with Snyder, it is interesting to note that the former only see debt relief as useful given certain circumstances. Similarly, Snyder seems willing to accept debt relief if certain conditions are met. In other words, both sides find debt relief useful given the right circumstances (although the conditions advocated by both sides are fairly different). According to Logie and Rowson, the debt relief process must be transparent, and not "dominated by the interests and agendas of creditors," or "conditional on health or economic system reforms that are potentially harmful to health outcomes." Snyder calls on developed countries not to provide debt relief to nations with corrupt governments, a problem he hints at as being pervasive throughout much of Africa. He fears that debt relief for such nations will only allow their corrupt leaders to remain in power longer.

One major debt relief program under way since 1996 is the World Bank and the International Monetary Fund's (IMF) Heavily Indebted Poor Countries (HIPC) initiative. This program is significant because it is the first time in the 50-year history of these institutions that some of the debt is allowed to be written off. The program also allows for debt to be reduced from bilateral donors on a block basis (rather than forcing debtor nations to negotiate individually with each creditor). The Paris Club, an informal group of bilateral creditors, helped to develop this program along with the World Bank and the IMF. Of the 42 countries eligible for HIPC debt relief, 7 African countries have qualified to date, including Benin, Burkina Faso, Mauritania, Mali, Mozambique, Tanzania, and Uganda. Since its inception, the HIPC initiative has come under heavy attack from critics because of the conditions it imposes on debtor nations wishing to receive relief. According to the World Bank (`http://www.worldbank.org/hipc/about/hipcbr/hipcbr.htm`), in order to receive relief, countries must "face an unsustainable debt burden, beyond available debt relief mechanisms", and "establish a track record of reform and sound policies through IMF and World Bank supported programs." It is the second condition in particular that has angered many debt-relief advocates.

One of the largest debt-relief groups is Jubilee Research (formerly Jubilee 2000). The Jubilee 2000 movement originated in the early 1990s with the All Africa Conference of Churches and slowly gained momentum since that time, especially in the United Kingdom. The Jubilee 2000 Petition was launched during the 1998 G8 Summit in Birmingham, England, where 70,000 people linked in a chain of arms to persuade leaders to provide debt relief to the world's poorest countries. See `http://www.jubilee2000uk.org` for more information on the Jubilee 2000 movement. The five-year anniversary of the Birmingham human chain was recently marked in June 2003, at the G8 Summit in Evian, France. Critics of the HIPC initiative continue to call for the relaxation of privatization and liberalization conditions that are linked to debt relief.

ISSUE 8

Are Abundant Mineral and Energy Resources a Catalyst for African Development?

YES: Oliver Maponga and Philip Maxwell, from "The Fall and Rise of African Mining," *Minerals and Energy* (2001)

NO: Sunday Dare, from "A Continent in Crisis: Africa and Globalization," *Dollars and Sense* (July/August 2001)

ISSUE SUMMARY

YES: Oliver Maponga, Economic Affairs Officer at the United Nations Economic Commission for Africa, and Philip Maxwell, professor at the Western Australian School of Mines at Curtin University of Technology, describe a resurgence in the African mining industry in the 1990s after several lackluster decades. They assert that mineral and energy mining can make a positive contribution to economic development in Africa.

NO: Sunday Dare, a Nigerian journalist, describes how "much sorrow has flowed" from Africa's resource blessing. While Dare blames African leaders for corruption and resource mismanagement, he also implicates transnational corporations (TNCs) as key contributors to this problem. He states that TNCs have acted as economic predators that support repressive African leaders in order to garner uninterrupted access to resources. The result, Dare suggests, is that Africa's "raw materials are still being depleted without general development."

The authors in this issue are basically wrangling over the validity of the "resource curse thesis" in contemporary Africa. This thesis posits that countries with great natural resource wealth have a tendency to grow more slowly than resource-poor countries. There are at least two types of problems (that potentially inhibit economic growth) frequently linked to resource abundance in African countries. First, is the notion that resource abundance may lead to a simplification or concentration of national economies, with increasing dependence on a single export mineral or fuel. The idea is that decision makers will tend to gravitate toward the easy money and shirk investments in other aspects of the economy. Nigeria is a potential example of this problem as productivity in a number of sectors (most notably food production and manufacturing) declined with the rise to prominence of the petroleum industry in the 1970s.

The second issue often linked to resource wealth is civil conflict. This problem may manifest itself in a couple of different ways. Rival groups may fight for control of key resources and then finance their military aggression through proceeds from the sale of these resources (such as diamond trading by rebel groups in Sierra Leone). Or, corrupt governments may sequester the proceeds from resource extraction to line their own pockets and to bankroll the suppression of opposition groups—a tactic that often leads to future opposition and unrest.

In their selection, Oliver Maponga and Philip Maxwell impugn the resource curse thesis in contemporary Africa. While acknowledging several lackluster decades in the mineral and energy sector, they describe a resurgence in the African mining industry in the 1990s. They maintain that mineral and energy extraction can make a positive contribution to economic development in Africa, ending their article on the optimistic assertion that "resource development will be seen as a blessing rather than a curse by the year 2010."

Sunday Dare counters that the resource curse thesis is alive and well in Africa. Dare blames African leaders for corruption and resource mismanagement, but he also implicates transnational corporations (TNCs) by asserting that TNCs have acted as economic predators that support repressive African leaders in order to gain access to resources.

In addition to the issues already raised, there are a few other points introduced by the authors in these texts that deserve some foregrounding. In the 1960s, when many African nations gained independence, there was a great deal of concern that transnational or multinational corporations acted as neo-imperialistic forces on the African continent. Dependency theorists suggested that major industries (including mines) either needed to be run by the government or indigenous entrepreneurs, or strictly regulated, in order to ensure that profits remained within a country's borders. This thinking led to a wave of nationalizations (or government takeovers) of foreign-owned enterprises in the 1960s and 1970s. Since the early 1980s these nationalized industries have gradually been re-privatized as part of the World Bank and International Monetary Fund's structural adjustment programs. The rationale for these privatizations is that governments are incapable of efficiently running enterprises and that foreign ownership needs to be permitted in order to encourage outside investment and technology transfer. Both of these policies, nationalization on the one hand and privatization on the other, are highly contested in the literature and, not surprisingly, appraised quite differently by the authors of the following selections.

Oliver Maponga
and Philip Maxwell

 **YES**

The Fall and Rise of African Mining

Introduction

Africa has twenty per cent of the earth's landmass and, in 2000, was home to about 800 million people. There is a highly prospective geology in much of the continent and minerals play an important role in the economic activities of many of its more than fifty sovereign nations. One reflection of this is the observation by [Graham] Davis that, in 1991, there were sixteen mineral dependent economies in Africa. They included Algeria, Angola, Botswana, Cameroon, Congo, Gabon, Guinea, Libya, Mauritania, Namibia, Niger, Nigeria, South Africa, Togo, Zaire (now the Democratic Republic of Congo) and Zambia.

Yet in a relative sense, the continent's minerals industry is still in its infancy. It has not achieved its full potential despite a long history of mining. This is in apparent contrast with the situation in Australia, Canada, the United States and Latin American nations such as Chile, where mineral discovery and exploitation has been an important source of subsequent economic development. Over the past decade there has been considerable debate about the role of natural resources in the economic development process. Authors such as Auty, Sachs and Warner and Gelb have argued that natural resources have been an economic curse for many nations. A contrary view appears in Davis.

One can classify almost every African nation as a developing economy. According to the African Development Bank, 39 African countries had GNP [gross national product] per capita levels of less than USD 1000 in 1998. The most affluent were Libya (USD 6160), Gabon (USD 4170), South Africa (USD 3310) and Botswana (USD 3070)—each major mineral producers. This compared with GNP per capita levels of USD 30600 in the United States, USD 20050 in Australia and USD 19320 in Canada in 1999.

Despite the resource curse argument, further expansion of the resources sector remains a major hope for the growth and development of many African nations. This is because of its potentially strong contribution to Gross Domestic Product [GDP] and to export income, as well as its role in generating forward and backward linkages to other parts of these economies.

From Charles Murray, "And Now for the Bad News," *Society* (November/December 1999). Copyright © 1999 by Transaction Publishers. Reprinted by permission of Transaction Publishers.

There was widespread nationalisation of minerals in Africa early in the post-independence era after 1960. In response to this foreign mineral investors showed little interest in mineral exploration or investment in most African nations during the 1970s and 1980s. This led to a loss of earlier mineral competitiveness in countries such as Zambia, Zaire, Guinea, Nigeria and Tanzania. South Africa and Botswana stood almost alone as the continent's world-class hard rock mineral producers during this time. The continent's oil and gas also struggled, particularly after 1980 when oil prices began a long period of nominal and real price decline.

Since the early 1990s the situation in Africa and elsewhere has been changing. The demise of the Soviet Union and communism, and the continuing push of global capitalism has been an important part of this story. Over the past decade, there has been a major revision of mineral policy throughout the continent to encourage foreign investment in exploration and new mineral projects. In this new area, African nations have been attracting more mineral exploration spending. This has also led to a series of new mineral projects, which are likely to boost the economic fortunes of several nations, particularly if political decision makers choose to invest taxes and royalty payments wisely. . . .

The Performance of African Economies— 1970 to 1990

An important . . . issue . . . is whether the stagnation of the resources sector in Africa adversely affected the relative performance of its mineral dependent economies. In addressing this issue it is useful initially to compare GDP growth rates in African economies with those elsewhere. . . . African economic growth between 1970 and 1979 lagged behind that in Asia and South America. Yet it was higher than in OECD [Organization for Economic Cooperation and Development] member nations. During the 1980s, the situation changed, with African economic growth comparable to that in South America, but lagging considerably behind Asia and the OECD.

When one moves to consider the performance of mineral and non-mineral economies in Africa, the results seem consistent with those put forward by Sachs and Warner. Between 1975 and 1990, the real GDP at factor cost in Africa's mineral dependent economies grew at 0.9 per cent per annum less than in the non-mineral economies. Economic growth rates in the five African fuel-exporting nations were remarkably similar to those in the eleven hard rock mineral exporting economies.

It is useful also to consider the performance of some of the related quality of life indicators used by authors such as Davis. He considered movements in indicators such as life expectancy, infant mortality, daily calorie supply, primary school enrolment and the adult literacy rate. Focusing on the fortunes of 22 mineral economies and 57 never-minerals economies in developing nations between 1970 and 1991, Davis found that more favourable movement in these measures in the mineral dependent economies.

. . . Between 1975 and 1990, the average life expectancy in Africa's mineral dependent economies increased by about 4.8 years. The fuel exporting economies experienced an increase of 6.1 years while other mineral economies rose by 3.4 years. The corresponding change in non-mineral dependent economies was 3.3 years.

Daily calorie supply, which had been at similar levels in 1975 in mineral and non-mineral economies, increased by about 100 calories more in non- mineral economies than in mineral economies. Daily calorie intakes rose 260 calories in fuel exporting nations but fell by more than fifty calories in non-fuel mineral economies. Infant mortality rates began at somewhat higher levels in the non-mineral economies than in the mineral economies in 1975. They fell by somewhat more in the non-mineral economies over the next fifteen years but still remained at higher levels in those nations.

So the findings from this analysis of quality of life variables between 1975 and 1990 are mixed. A longer time period of analysis would seem necessary to reach more definitive conclusions.

The Past Decade—Is a Renaissance Underway?

The combination of a poor investment climate, political instability and the lack of supportive infrastructure including poor geological information contributed to the decline in the minerals industry in Africa generally up until 1990. In this environment it is hardly surprising that mineral economies did not perform well. But the economic geography of the world minerals industry has been changing in recent years. A reversal of the disinvestment trend between the 1960s and the 1980s has taken place since 1990 in many developing nations. Prospective nations in Latin America, Africa and Asia have received increased exploration spending. Inflows of foreign direct investment [FDI] have also been rising. An important early indicator of a broader change has been an increase in gold production from African nations outside of South Africa. The discussion of this section considers the extent of change and some of the reasons for it. It concludes by reflecting on whether the new operating environment has had any noticeable effect on the economic welfare of mineral dependent nations.

(a) Exploration Spending and Foreign Direct Investment in Mineral Development

The Metal Economics Group, which collects key mining data from large resource sector companies, reported a significant increase in the share of exploration spending in Africa during most of the 1990s. There was an apparent increase in the region's share of exploration spending from around six per cent in 1993 to more than thirteen per cent in 1998. It fell to 11.5 percent in 1999. Exploration spending in Africa increased from USD 165 million in 1993 to USD 670 million in 1997. Between 1997 and 1999 there was a decline in mineral exploration activity throughout the world. The fall in estimated mineral exploration spending in Africa to USD 323 million in 1999 reflects this. By the late

1990s Africa had overtaken the Asia-Pacific region as the second most favoured investment destination in the developing world after Latin America. . . .

Foreign direct investment (FDI) inflows to Africa increased generally during the 1990s, compared with the 1970s and 1980s. UNCTAD [United Nations Conference on Trade and Development] estimated that FDI inflows rose from USD 2 billion in 1990 to USD 10 billion in 1998. Despite the increase in the 1990s, investments by transnational corporations into Africa represented only 1.2 percent of global FDI flows and five percent of total foreign direct investment into developing nations. Although these data refer to direct investment in all industries, the authors of the UNCTAD report acknowledge that investment in natural resources in Africa has been the main focus of foreign direct investment.

The major presence of Canadian and Australian exploration and mining companies in Africa in the 1990s reflects this change. For Canadian-based resource companies, the growth of junior exploration companies, coupled with the success of Canadian stock exchanges, provided major stimulus for overseas investment. Campbell notes that Canadian companies responded aggressively to new liberalised operating environments in Africa in the 1990s. By 1996 there were over 170 Canadian-registered companies operating on the African continent. In the early 1990s hardly any Canadian companies had operations there. Campbell attributes the overseas involvement of Canadian mining companies particularly to competitive advantages as well as to the availability of risk capital from the Vancouver Stock Exchange.

Australian-based resource companies also became active in exploration and mine development in Africa during the 1990s. In 1985, Bridge Oil was apparently the only Australian resources company with interests in Africa. By 1992 fifteen Australian companies had African interests and this had increased to seventy-five by 1997. They operated in thirty African nations. . . . Australian companies had 134 projects in thirty African nations in 1999. This compared with 88 projects in 1995. Data collected by the Minerals Council of Australia also show increased offshore exploration spending by Australian mining companies, with Africa as one of the major destinations.

One reflection of the revival of Africa as a major mineral producer is the recent growth of the gold industry outside of South Africa. Despite declining prices, the gold sector has been the largest beneficiary of the new investment boom. Output increased from 40 tonnes in 1990 to more than 140 tonnes in 1998. Successful exploration has led to significant new gold mines coming on stream in Ghana, Mali, Tanzania, Guinea and Burkina Faso.

Tanzania's first mine in more than thirty years, Golden Pride, opened in 1998. The opening of Mali's Sadiola gold mine in 1997 propelled the country to one of the top twenty gold producers in the world. Mali now ranks as Africa's fourth largest gold producer behind South Africa, Ghana and Zimbabwe. Ghana's experience since 1988 illustrates the renaissance of the region's minerals industry more than any other country. Ghana's gold output increased from 12 tonnes in 1988 to over 70 tonnes in 1998. Australian companies opened two new gold mines at Damang (Ranger Minerals) and Obotan (Resolute) in the late 1990s.

Despite these positive developments . . . between 1989 and 1998 . . . Africa lost market share for ten of the eleven minerals reported. One might explain this apparently perverse trend by arguing that the new exploration and investment is taking several years to exert its full impact. Other forces may, however, be important. Before turning to this later issue we consider further some of the positive influences.

(b) Positive Influences on the Competitiveness of African Mining

Several factors have played a role in facilitating a re-emergence of African minerals and energy. They include:

- the modernisation of mining regimes through new legislation, formal mineral policy statements and observation of international agreements;
- availability of investment insurance;
- greater political stability in several prospective nations;
- a movement of privatisation of state mining companies; and
- changed conditions in home countries which have led to international expansion.

Otto reports that "Between 1985 and 1995 over 90 nations introduced, or commenced working on, new or major revisions to mining sector legislation." African nations were well represented in this group. This has created a more favourable environment for private sector investment. Campbell recognises the importance of these reforms to inflows of Canadian investment in Africa in the mid-1990s.

During the 1990s, fiscal regimes continued to evolve as competition for shrinking investment budgets increases. Countries like Botswana, one of the continent's most stable and attractive economies, introduced a new Mines and Minerals Act in 1999. This abolished free equity for government and simplified licensing systems. The Government of Namibia enacted a new Diamond Act in 1999, while Nigeria introduced its Mining and Minerals Decree No. 34. Recent changes to fiscal regimes in Benin, Burkina Faso, Central African Republic and Cote d'Ivoire have resulted in increased investor activity. Because of these changes the highly prospective Birimian greenstone belts in West and Central Africa have become major attractions for Canadian and South African mining companies.

The efforts of the World Bank to regenerate the African minerals industry are also playing a facilitating role. This occurs particularly through the activities of three of its associated organisations, the International Development Association (IDA), the Multilateral Investment Guarantee Agency (MIGA) and the International Finance Corporation (IFC).

Through its technical assistance program, the International Development Association currently makes credit available to countries wishing to reform their minerals sector. The International Finance Corporation (IFC) provides equity finance for projects in the developing world and helps mobilise private loans for private investors in the developing world. The Multilateral Investment Guarantee Agency provides investment risk guarantees to lower the risk profile of mining projects for foreign investors. Forty-two African nations were signatories to the MIGA convention by 1999. MIGA provides insurance against transfer restrictions, expropriation (direct and creeping), war and civil disturbance and against breach of contract by governments and helps mobilise insurance. The organisation also provides a mechanism for the settlement of investment disputes. Between the commencement of its guarantee scheme in Africa in 1991 and 1999, MIGA had issued 61 guarantees. Two examples of the work of IFC and MIGA relate to loans to finance the Sadiola gold mine in Mali and the Mozal Aluminium Smelter in Mozambique.

Institutions in Britain, France, Belgium, the United States and Canada have also been active in supporting investment risk protection measures to encourage movement of their companies into Africa. Two examples of these institutions are OPIC (for U.S. companies) and the Export Development Corporation (for Canadian companies).

Despite some notable exceptions, Africa was more politically stable in the 1990s, compared with the previous 30 years. The changes in political climate in countries such as Mozambique, Angola and the Democratic Republic of Congo, together with the post-apartheid government in South Africa, created a more favourable investment climate in the minerals sector. This had a particularly favourable impact for the major South African mining companies. They followed a program of greater diversification into the rest of the continent to replace aging and costly mines at home. Relative political stability in Mozambique and Angola led to legal mining resuming in these nations. Two diamond properties in the Luo and the Catoca in the kimberlite areas of Angola came into production in 1996. The aluminium smelter in Mozambique became a viable project after the UN supervised elections in the mid-1990s. Successes of foreign mining companies in Ghana, Tanzania and Mali and Mauritania have also enhanced the region's image.

Whereas privatisation of state-owned enterprises in most developed countries began in the mid-1980s, the process started much later in developing nations. Gathering momentum after 1990, it has been an important influence in attracting foreign direct investment. There have been several different privatisation approaches. They have included change in ownership status, complete divestiture or partial divestiture. Seventy percent of total FDI inflows into Africa in 1999 were in Angola, Egypt, Nigeria, South Africa and Morocco where major privatisations had occurred. UNCTAD reports that South Africa received USD 1.4 billion of foreign direct investment between 1990 and 1998. Ghana attracted USD 769 million, Nigeria, USD 500 million, Zambia USD 420 million, and Côte d'Ivoire USD 373 million.

Changing policy and legislative frameworks in the developed mining nations have also influenced the move of foreign mining companies into Africa. Factors such as more demanding environmental legislation and native title issues at home have been particularly important in encouraging European, North American and Australian resource companies to consider moving offshore. The activities of junior exploration companies have played a key role in promoting this change. Willing to take more risks, they have often been thwarted at home because mining and exploration tenements are more difficult to obtain.

(c) Mining Sector Reform and Economic Performance

Despite the above changes, the impact of reform in mineral rich African nations did not translate into economic or quality of life gains during most of the 1990s. . . . [B]etween 1990 and 1998, GDP at factor cost in Africa's mineral dependent economies grew at an average rate of 1.7 percent per annum. It compares with a growth rate of 3.1 percent in non-mineral economies. Furthermore, . . . a reduction in life expectancy in the mineral economies from 1990 to 1998 [occurred], as opposed to an increase in the non-mineral economies. Daily calorie supply increased at a faster rate in non-mineral economies and infant mortality rates declined more quickly than in their mineral dependent counterparts. . . . [F]uel exporting mineral economies fared considerably better than the non-fuel exporting mineral economies.

It is tempting to appeal directly to the resource curse thesis to provide an explanation for these trends. It would seem premature, however, to do so for at least two reasons. Firstly, the reform and renaissance of the African minerals sector is a process from which tangible benefits may take perhaps five or ten years more to flow into expected economic gains. Without consistent and continuing investment, a minerals industry loses its competitive strength. Rebuilding this in a consistent manner will take perhaps two decades, since it requires investment in infrastructure and human capital as well as exploration and mine development. The new policy and regulatory frameworks are establishing a good foundation for this to take place but the process is far from complete. Secondly, the poor performance of quality of life indicators in the non-fuel mineral economies appears to reflect the impact of the HIV/AIDS epidemic in Southern Africa.

An associated line of empirical investigation is to review the most recent rates of economic growth—say between 1996 and 1998—in African nations. In the 16 mineral dependent economies, real GDP at factor cost grew from an estimated USD 348.5 billion to USD 365.3 billion during this time—a growth rate of 2.3 percent per annum. In the 37 non-mineral economies estimated GDP at factor cost grew from USD 143.5 billion to USD 155 billion. This was an annual growth rate of 4.1 percent per annum. It is clear that a minerals-driven recovery is not yet under way.

(d) Mineral Endowment, Labour Productivity, Comparative and Competitive Advantage

. . . Africa's mineral endowment is substantial. The continent's favourable geology and the relative lack of recent mineral exploitation means that there are many high quality and potentially profitable deposits available, other things being equal. Recent mineral sector reforms and other legislative changes have apparently "levelled the playing field" for potential African mineral producers.

Despite this, developed nations such as the United States, Canada and Australia retained their percentage shares of world mineral production during the 1990s. This followed an increase between 1980 and 1990, despite a significant decline in ore grade at operating mines. By utilising new mineral processing technologies, adopting modern mining methods and operating more efficiently in other ways (particularly through outsourcing), resource companies in these nations improved their fortunes. In recent papers on the U.S. copper industry, Aydin and Tilton and Tilton and Landsberg find that labour productivity tripled between 1975 and 1985. Between 1985 and 1995 this enabled the US industry to recover the share of world copper output lost in the preceding ten years. New technology and innovation appeared either as important or more important than mineral endowment in shaping comparative advantage in the copper industry. Australia's re-emergence in the 1980s as a major world gold producer and its holding of this position in the 1990s seem consistent with these findings.

It is useful to reflect on a model such as the Porter "diamond" in assessing the current position of the African mineral industry. The four attributes in this model that determine competitive advantage are

- factor conditions. As well as mineral endowment, these include the quality of human and knowledge resources, the availability of capital and the quality of infrastructure.
- home demand conditions and the potential for their growth,
- the presence of and development of related and supporting industries, and
- firm strategy, structure and rivalry.

"Chance" events such as major technological or input cost discontinuities, surges in world demand, shifts in world financial markets or exchange rates, political decisions by foreign governments or wars may also affect these main determinants.

The role of government policy stance is also important. As well as establishing a suitable mineral policy framework its activities in other areas such as education, taxation, environmental protection, road, rail and telecommunications have an important complementary role. These will enhance factor conditions, encourage the growth of domestic demand and promote the growth of supporting industries. If applied over an extended period of a decade or two it will set the stage for movement through the factor-driven stage of national competitive development towards the investment-driven and innovation-driven stages. It is during these stages that nations move towards the "developed economy" status. Nations such as Canada, Australia and the United States have reached the innovation-driven stages with their mineral industries and this has facilitated the broader development of the rest of their economy.

Porter notes that "to progress, the developing nations face the daunting task of upgrading all four parts of the national "diamond" sufficiently to reach the threshold necessary to compete in advanced industries." Yet successes of Japan, Korea, Taiwan and Hong Kong in the second half of the twentieth century provide important case studies of this taking place. The recent strong economic performance of China and India is also encouraging. From a mineral and energy sector perspective, the emergence of nations such as Saudi Arabia, Chile and the United Arab Emirates suggests promise. The development experiences of countries such as South Africa, Brazil and Mexico are also worthy of mention.

An important conclusion from this discussion is that new mine development (or the expansion of existing mines) requires more than a favourable mineral endowment and the delineation of viable deposits with recent mineral exploration activity. As well as a favourable policy environment, technology and management issues are an important part of mineral sector development. Strong supporting infrastructure and a capable human capital base both are necessary to reap major benefits and to retain competitiveness over longer periods of time. Political stability is essential. For new mineral development to provide a platform for economic growth and development in African nations with major mineral endowments, as it has in Canada, Australia and the United States, the process will take perhaps a generation or more. It has recently taken each of the High Performing Asian Economies (Japan, China and the Asian Tigers) two or three decades to build their human and physical capital bases to a point where they have been able to compete favourably with the developed nations.

Concluding Remarks

With high geological prospectivity in many nations a safer and more attractive investment climate, Africa has recently shown the capacity to capture a greater share of the investment budgets of global mining companies. If this is continue further, African nations must continue to change images of a continent of civil unrest, starvation, deadly diseases and economic disorder.

The [selection] has shown that in general, FDI in Africa has increased in recent years due to improved regulatory frameworks, permitting profit repatriation, tax incentives provision and trade liberalisation. Progress on modernisation is uneven on the continent but countries have generally embraced the importance of private-sector led investment growth and realised that governments have to play a regulatory role. Sustaining a long-term renaissance will depend on many factors including the pace of reform, political stability, economic growth and developments in other investment destinations such as Asia and Latin America.

Ethnic disturbances and military coups remain major challenges to political stability. Political stability is also related to good governance, low levels of corruption and transparency. Weak institutional capacity remains a major constraint in many African countries.

The success of many current projects will be critical in ensuring a sustained flow of investors to Africa. Good macro-economic performance is a key for continued inflow of foreign investment and also for local investors. The change in the policy and regulatory environment, deregulation and privatiation programs are each important areas in reversing investment trends towards Africa. Programs supported by the United Nations and the World Bank to improve the operating environment in the region also appear to have an important place in this process.

Although the recent signs appear promising, it remains too early to appraise whether the "renaissance" of the African minerals sector will provide the impetus for the large number of mineral dependent nations to move forward significantly in their development. Given the difficult experiences of many African nations in their immediate post-colonial histories, an optimistic hope is that resource development will be seen as a blessing rather than a curse by the year 2010. Perhaps by that stage, economists will be writing of an African economic miracle under way.

References

African Development Bank (2000). *African Development Report 2000.*

Auty, R. (1986). "Multinational Resource Corporations, Nationalization and Diminished Viability: Caribbean Plantations, Mines and Oilfields in the Seventies," in C. Dixon et al. (Eds), *Multinational Corporations and the Third World,* Croom Helm, London, pp. 160–187.

Auty, R. (1993). "Determinants of state mining enterprise resilience in Latin America," *Natural Resources Forum,* pp. 3–11.

Aydin, H., and J. Tilton (2000). "Mineral Endowment, Labor Productivity, and Comparative Advantage in Mining," *Resource and Energy Economics,* Vol. 22, pp. 281-293.

Blainey, G. (1993). *The Rush that Never Ended: A History of Australian Mining,* Fourth edition, Melbourne: Melbourne University Press.

British Geological Survey (2000). *World Mineral Statistics.* Keyworth: Nottingham.

Campbell, B. (1998). "Liberalisation, Deregulation, State Promoted Investment— Canadian Mining Interests in Africa," *Journal of Mineral Policy, Business and Environment,* Vol. 13, No. 4. pp. 14–34.

Crowson, P. (1998). *Minerals Handbook 1998/99,* Mining Journal Books, London.

Davis, G. (1995). "Learning to Love the Dutch Disease: Evidence from the Mineral Economies," *World Development,* Vol. 23, No. 10, pp. 1765–99.

Ericsson, M. (1991). "African Mining: Light at the End of the Tunnel," *Review of African Political Economy,* Vol. 51, pp. 96–107.

Gelb, A.H. (1988). *Oil Windfalls: Blessing or Curse?* Oxford University Press, New York.

Minmet Australia (2001). Home Page, available at www.minmet.com.au.

Minerals Council of Australia (various years): *Mineral Industry Survey,* Canberra, available at www.minerals.org.au/.

Norrie, K. and D. Owram, (1996). *A History of the Canadian Economy,* 2nd edition, Toronto: Harcourt Brace Jovanovich.

O'Brien, J. (1994). *Undoing a Myth: Chile's debt to Copper and Mining,* Ottawa: International Council on Metals and the Environment.

O'Neill, D. (1992). "Australian Miners in Africa: An Australian Perspective," *Mining Review,* Vol. 16, No. 4, pp. 34–40.

Otto, J.M. (1997). "A National Mineral Policy as a Regulatory Tool," *Resources Policy,* Vol. 23, Nos. 1/2, pp. 1–7.

Otto, J.M. (1998). "Global Changes in Mining Laws, Agreements and Tax Systems," *Resources Policy*, Vol. 23, No. 4, pp. 79–86.

Porter, M. (1990). *The Competitive Advantage of Nations*, Macmillan, Basingstoke.

Premoli, C. (1998). "Mineral Exploration in Africa: The Long View," in S. Vearcombe and S.E. Ho (Eds.), *Africa: Geology and Mineral Exploration, AIG Bulletin*, No. 25, pp. 35–46.

Radetzki, M. (1985). *State Mineral Enterprises: An Investigation into Their Impact on International Mineral Markets*, Resources for the Future, Washington, DC.

Radetzki, M. (1990). *A Guide to Primary Commodities in the World Economy*, Basil Blackwell, Oxford.

Sachs, J., and A. Warner (1995). "Natural Resource Abundance and Economic Growth," Development Discussion Paper No. 517a, Harvard Institute for International Development, Cambridge, USA.

Sinclair, W.A. (1976). *The Process of Economic Development in Australia*, Melbourne: Longman Cheshire.

Slater, C.L. (1996). "The Investment Climate for Gold Mining: Comparing Australia with the USA," *Natural Resources Forum*, Vol. 20, No. 1, pp. 37–48.

South African Chamber of Mines (1998) Available at www.bullion.org.za/.

Tilton, J. (1989). "The New View of Minerals and Economic Growth," *The Economic Record*, Vol. 65, No. 190, pp. 265–278.

Tilton, J., and H. Landsberg (1999). Innovation, Productivity Growth and the Survival of the U.S. Copper Industry, in R.D. Simpson (Ed.), *Productivity in Natural Resource Industries: Improvement through Innovation*, Resources for the Future, Washington, DC.

UNCTAD (1999). *Foreign Direct Investment in Africa: Performance and Potential*, UNCTAD/ITE/IIT/Misc. 15, United Nations, Geneva.

UNCTAD (2000). *The World Investment Report 2000: Cross-border Mergers and Acquisitions and Development*, United Nations, Geneva.

United States Geological Survey (2000). *Mineral Industry Surveys*, available at minerals.usgs.gov/minerals/pubs/commodity/mis.html, Washington, DC.

World Bank (1992). *Strategy for African Mining*, Technical Paper No. 181, Mining Unit and Energy Division, Washington, DC.

NO ⬅

Sunday Dare

A Continent in Crisis:
Africa and Globalization

From the oil fields of the Niger Delta in Nigeria, to the diamond and copper fields of Sierra Leone, Angola, and Liberia, to the rich mineral deposits of the Great Lakes region, to the mountain ranges, plains and tourist havens of the East African countries, the continent of Africa is undoubtedly blessed.

From these blessings, however, much sorrow has flowed. During the colonial era, most Africans did not benefit from the continent's resources. African economies were geared toward cultivating raw materials for export, and roads, health care, and other infrastructure were available only in areas where those materials were produced. The end of colonialism unleashed struggles for political control, social emancipation, and access to resources—struggles that, in turn, have degenerated into conflicts and internecine wars. Retarded in their development, unbridled in their lust for power, steeped in official corruption, chaotic in their political engineering, many African states are now sprinting toward total collapse.

Much of the blame for Africa's spiral of violence belongs to generations of opportunistic and venal African leaders, who have done little to develop their societies and emancipate their peoples. But the expansion of corporate dominance has accentuated the steady descent into near economic strangulation and political chaos. Many transnational corporations (TNCs) have acted as economic predators in Africa, gobbling up national resources, distorting national economic policies, exploiting and changing labor relations, committing environmental despoliation, violating sovereignties, and manipulating governments and the media. In order to ensure uninterrupted access to resources, TNCs have also supported repressive African leaders, warlords, and guerrilla fighters, thus serving as catalysts for lethal conflict and impeding prospects for development and peace.

TNCs and the African State

In the post-colonial period, many African leaders have exerted dictatorial control over their societies. Through their undemocratic policies, they have spread dissatisfaction among the people, which has manifested over time in nationalistic feelings and even popular rebellions. These political tensions, in turn, have generated fierce conflicts over resource control.

In response to these conflicts, many African governments have embraced collaboration with TNCs and other foreign investors. Lacking the technological capacity to harness massive reserves of oil, gold, diamonds, and cobalt, these leaders grant licenses to foreign corporations to operate in their domain, and then appropriate the resulting revenue to maintain themselves in power. For example, both the late General Sani Abacha of Nigeria and the late Mobutu Sese Seko of Zaire looted hundreds of millions of dollars in government funds derived from corporate revenue, stashed the money in private foreign accounts, and used it for political patronage and to silence political opponents.

In turn, these authoritarian governments have stifled economic growth. Frequent changes in leadership through *coups d'etat* have made it impracticable to implement development plans. Each new government comes in with a new set of policies that often undermines earlier progress by previous governments. Also, many African leaders have used revenue to reward political pals with bogus contracts for white-elephant projects that contribute nothing to development. In the late 1990s, for example, President Daniel Arap Moi of Kenya built an airport—which handles almost no traffic—in his own hometown of Eldoret. And of course, money used as handouts to members of the ruling elite and to fight political opposition is money *not* spent on development.

After decades of economic mismanagement and political gangsterism, most African societies are in terrible shape. African unemployment rates are at crisis levels, with over 65% of college graduates out of jobs. Because manufacturing is at a low ebb, unskilled workers suffer a similar fate. Wages are also low. According to the *United Nations Development Report*, the average unskilled worker earns about 55 cents daily, while the average white-collar employee brings home a monthly check of between $50 and $120. Many African societies are characterized by minimal opportunities for education and self-development, collapsed infrastructure, and a debilitating debt burden.

These conditions have made the continent even more susceptible to international financial control. Typically, TNCs seek out societies with low production costs, poor working conditions, and abundant and easily exploitable resources, where profits can be maximized and repatriated without legal constraints. The icing, of course, is a political leadership that is weak, corrupt, and ready to cut deals. TNCs make huge investments in countries that meet those criteria, and many African countries fit the bill.

Economic Exploitation in Africa

The sheer growth of TNCs in recent decades has had profound consequences for Africa. The average growth rate of TNCs is three times that of the most advanced industrial countries. Of the 100 biggest economies in the world, more than half are corporations. TNCs hold enormous power to transform the world political economy, and Africa's vast resources, cheap labor, huge population, and expanding markets are crucial to their plans.

The globalization optimists maintain that global capital has served as a dynamic engine of growth, opening the window for diverse opportunities in terms of goods and services, creating employment, and boosting government revenues. This has been true in a few cases. In South Africa and Nigeria, for example, gold mining and oil companies respectively have brought new technology, attracted subsidiary industries, and made it possible for indigenous personnel to acquire skills.

However, any such benefits are far outweighed by activities that deplete local resources, stifle local or indigenous industry, and subvert the fragile democratic process. Africa is still confined to the role it played in the industrial revolution(s) that preceded globalization. Its raw materials are still being depleted without generating development.

In addition, the continent's increasing dependence on imported capital and consumer goods and services has left various sectors of the domestic economy comatose. African markets are specially targeted as dumping grounds for new and second-hand goods. Because of stiff competition from these products, infant manufacturing established earlier in Africa has quickly withered away. For example, imports of used clothing from the United States are threatening to destroy Kenya's domestic textile industry.

Finally, as soon as the TNCs have African economies firmly in their grip, they deploy funds and patronage to manipulate the media and influence government policies. Governments, in turn, grant them *carte blanche* to sidestep labor and environmental laws.

Other global institutions have contributed to the deregulation of African economies. The Generalized Agreement on Tariffs and Trade, the World Trade Organization, and the International Monetary Fund (IMF) all promote increased liberalization of international trade. The IMF's structural adjustment programs (SAPs) require African states to freeze wages, devalue currency, remove public subsidies, and impose other austerity measures, which have brought about even greater unemployment and under-utilization of productive capacity. These policies have caused considerable turmoil in Africa. In the early 1980s, Uganda was rocked by weeks of demonstrations, as industrial workers and students took to the streets to denounce President Milton Obote's IMF-imposed economic program. In 1990, Matthew Kerokou of the Benin Republic in West Africa was swept out of power in a wave of anti-SAP riots.

Corporations and Lethal Conflict

At the advent of the new millennium, Africa is hurting badly. Most parts of the continent are embroiled in independence wars, ethnic conflicts, violent wars for political and resource control, and cross-border conflicts. In a recent study of armed conflicts around the world, the University of Maryland's Center for International Development and Conflict Management found that 33 countries were at high risk for instability. Of these, 20 were in Africa.

In their quest to unravel the forces generating conflict in Africa, human-rights groups are closely scrutinizing TNCs. TNCs are not always responsible for the genesis of the crisis. But some of the deadliest conflicts that litter

Africa's political landscape, at least in the last decade, can definitely be traced to the expansion and domination of TNCs.

This is especially true in extractive states where resources with global appeal, value, and markets are found. While the state's interest in generating revenue from these resources coincides with that of the TNCs, the latter's interest in maximizing profits conflicts with the welfare of the citizens. Thus, the state is caught between protecting a vital source of revenue, and defending the rights and privileges of its citizens. Too often, the state, in order to ensure an ongoing flow of revenue, sides with the TNCs against the citizens.

For example, the oil-producing Niger Delta region is perpetually at war with the government and oil corporations. For decades, successive Nigerian governments have been beholden to the TNCs that possess the technology, technical expertise, and capital to exploit the country's oil. The exploitation has resulted in serious environmental damage, developmental neglect, human-rights abuses, economic oppression, and inequitable resource allocation. These abuses, and the need for redress, are at the heart of the conflict. In recent months, calls for secession by the oil-yielding region have grown louder. As other parts of the country caught up in oil politics fight to defend their interests, the drums of war continue to beat. . . .

TNCs have played a major role in the Nigerian conflict. They gave their unalloyed support to the brutal military regimes of Generals Ibrahim Babangida and Sani Abacha. Under Abacha, Ken Saro-Wiwa and eight other activists were hanged for crusading against the government and the oil companies. Officials at Royal Dutch Shell, which dominates the lucrative Nigerian oil industry, admitted in a press statement that the company could have stopped the hangings if it had so desired. Shell executives also confessed publicly to purchasing arms for the Nigerian State Police, who have attacked community residents and picketers. Also, in 1998, oil giant Chevron used its own helicopter to carry Nigerian soldiers, who stormed Parambe, an oil-yielding community, and killed several protesters.

In Angola, meanwhile, the global trade in diamonds—widely known as "blood diamonds" or "conflict diamonds" because of their lethal consequences—has helped to perpetuate more than 20 years of civil war. With revenue from the illegal mining and sale of rough diamonds, the UNITA [Portuguese acronym for the National Union for the Total Independence of Angola] rebels, led by Jonas Savimbi, have been able to purchase and stockpile ammunition to prolong the war. Though fully aware of this, a number of corporations—such as American Mineral Fields (AMF), Oryx, and the world's leading diamond company, De Beers—continue to do business in the war-torn territory, where more than half a million citizens have been killed.

Also, Jean-Raymond Boulle, AMF's principal shareholder, is known to have invested millions of dollars in support of corrupt African governments and rebel leaders in order to secure juicy mineral contracts. The late Congolese leader Laurent Kabila used Boulle's jet and funds to prosecute his war against Mobutu of Zaire. When Kabila came to power in 1997, AMF secured exploration rights to 600 million pounds of cobalt and three billion pounds of copper, among other deals.

Similarly, the Foday Sankoh-led Revolutionary United Front (RUF) in Sierra Leone derives most of the funds it has used to unleash terror and mayhem on the country's people from the international trade in conflict diamonds. The RUF continues to fight a war that has claimed more than 80,000 lives, with no end in sight. According to the U.S. State Department, revenue from rough and uncut diamonds mined in conflict areas forms a large percentage of the commodity's over $50 billion in annual sales.

The conflicts that grip Africa can also be traced to a steady flow of arms. To safeguard their economic interests, Western corporations are procuring weapons and providing arms training in areas of conflict. Embattled African leaders, anxious to defend their own interests and protect their hold on power, readily grant contracts to private security armies run by TNCs. Since the early 1990s, the growth of the corporate private security sector in Africa has been phenomenal. TNCs have become direct parties to conflicts by recruiting or hiring private security companies to help protect their installations, operations and staff. In the process, they have connived with governments and sometimes with rebels, whichever is most expedient, thereby instigating further conflict and perpetuating civil war.

For example, in 1995, Executive Outcome (EO), a private security company, arrived in Sierra Leone. The Sierra Leonean government paid EO almost $40 million in cash, along with mining concessions, to assist in its campaign against the RUF. The peace it secured did not last; rather, the country was plunged into deeper crisis. EO was also in Angola, training the national army and helping to recapture lucrative mineral fields. In 1993, the Angolan state oil company, Sonangol, contracted with EO to provide security for its installations against UNITA attacks. The Angolan government also signed a three-year, $40 million contract with EO to supply military hardware and training.

In addition, J. & S. Franklin, a British supplier of military equipment, won a contract to train the Sierra Leonean military using the notorious U.S.-based Gurkha Security Guards. The Guards have carried out a series of military attacks in various mining areas to protect the activities of TNCs. J. & S. Franklin has also won supply contracts with several other African governments engaged in conflicts.

Clearly, where minerals abound, TNCs find the lure irresistible. They accrue substantial profits from diamonds, which are sold in wedding rings, bracelets, and necklaces all over Europe and the United Stares. TNCs also profit enormously from cobalt, a vital raw material for the manufacture of jet fighters. The unbridled lust for excessive gain has deadened the senses of corporate giants like De Beers, Royal Dutch Shell, Chevron, AMF, and others to the damaging impact of their activities.

Out of the Labyrinth

Because of the twin problems of rogue leadership and the exploitative tendencies of TNCs, Africa is caught between a rock and a hard place. As the history of conflicts in Africa shows, the extraction of mineral resources creates and reinforces government corruption, which easily begets repressive societies. As would be expected, poverty, unemployment, and insecurity spread, while social services decay. This leaves the citizens more prone to take up arms and fight in oil, diamond, and copper wars, as the conflicts in Sierra Leone, Angola, Nigeria, Sudan, Liberia, and the Great Lakes region all attest.

How can Africa wrench itself from itself and curb the rampaging TNCs? In response to corporations' bad behavior, and their brazen disregard for the political stability and economic viability of the states in which they operate, international human-rights organizations have tried to establish mechanisms of accountability.

The key, however, is action by Africans on their own behalf. Their options for ending the circle of violence and economic exploitation are few but practicable. Africa needs a new generation of leaders to define and pursue a dynamic political and economic agenda. The African states must renegotiate their terms of trade in the international marketplace. Diverse groups must achieve a sense of national pride and internal cohesiveness, in order to create an atmosphere conducive to implementing development programs. As long as the resources have not yet been depleted, there is still hope of rising again for a continent that has tarried for too long in the labyrinth.

POSTSCRIPT

Are Abundant Mineral And Energy Resources A Catalyst For African Development?

The issue of resource abundance and economic growth in Africa has received renewed attention in recent years due to at least three developments: increased interest by the United States in African energy resources leading up to and after the 2003 Iraq War, particularly brutal civil conflicts in Sierra Leone and Angola financed by the sale of mineral resources, and growing investments by South African entrepreneurs in the mining sectors of other African countries since the end of apartheid.

First, with escalating concerns about dependence on oil from the Middle East, the United States increasingly has become interested in oil exploration and oil field development in a number of African countries. In a January 13, 2003, *Los Angeles Times* article entitled "U.S. Quest for Oil in Africa Worries Analysts, Activists," Warren Vieth reports that "the Bush administration's search for more secure sources of oil is leading it to the doorsteps of some of the world's most troubled and repressive regimes: the petroleum-rich countries of West Africa." While the Bush administration states that it is committed to improving conditions in Africa, the concern among Africanist scholars and policy analysts is that production will be put ahead of balanced reform and development. The history of U.S. interaction with other oil-rich African nations does not portend well for good governance and broad-based development.

Second, in the last several years the links between brutal civil conflicts and the diamond trade in Sierra Leone and Angola have become increasing clear. This recognition led to the appellation of diamonds from these countries as blood, or conflict, diamonds. See a recent book by Greg Campbell entitled *Blood Diamonds: Tracing the Deadly Path of the World's Most Precious Stones* (Westview Press, 2002).

Finally, the mining sector in Africa has been transformed in recent years by the infusion (some would say invasion) of South African capital and expertise. This is related to the fact that South Africans were often prohibited from investing in other parts of the continent prior to the end of apartheid in 1994. Given the history of antagonism between South Africa and the frontline states, many countries are leery of a growing South African presence in their economies. Despite these concerns, some are grateful to have a new eager investor. See a February 17, 2002, *New York Times* article by Rachel Swarns entitled "Awe and Unease as South Africa Stretches Out."

On the Internet . . .

DUSHKIN ONLINE

AFROL News—Agriculture

AFROL News of the Heifer Project International provides information on agriculture from across Africa, including general agricultural trends for the continent and country-specific news.

http://www.afrol.com/Categories/Economy_Develop/
Agriculture/msindex.htm

African Conservation Foundation

The African Conservation Foundation Web site allows one to search its databases of African environmental topics by country, organization, type of information, and environmental category.

http://www.africanwebsites.net

African Data Dissemination Service

The U.S. government's African Data Dissemination Service offers a warning system for possible famine or flood conditions. It also allows one to download data, both map based and tabular, regarding crop use, hydrology, rainfall, and elevation (as well as several other datasets).

http://earlywarning.usgs.gov/adds/

United Nations Environment Programme: Regional Office for Africa

The United Nations Environment Programme: ROA provides information on UN environmental initiatives in Africa, both in restoring the natural environment and harnessing the environment for human use in an environmentally friendly way.

http://www.unep.org/ROA/

Food and Agriculture Organization of the United Nations

The Food and Agriculture Organization of the United Nations Web site contains news articles and other information about agriculture, food, and environmental issues. Contains information with both African and international emphases.

http://www.fao.org/

PART 3

Agriculture, Food, and the Environment

*W*ith more rural inhabitants as a share of total population than any other world region, questions regarding agriculture, food production, and environmental management have loomed large in debates concerning Africa. As a region rich in wildlife and natural resources, local, national, and global actors struggle over access and control of these environmental assets. Real and imagined crises also have fueled discussions over how to prevent famine and augment food production without undermining the integrity of the ecosystem.

- Will Biotech Solve Africa's Food Problems?

- Is Food Production in Africa Capable of Keeping Up With Population Growth?

- Are Integrated Conservation and Development Programs a Solution to Conflicts Between Parks and Local People?

- Is Sub-Saharan Africa Experiencing a Deforestation Crisis?

ISSUE 9

Will Biotech Solve Africa's Food Problems?

YES: Jesse Machuka, from "Agricultural Biotechnology for Africa. African Scientists and Farmers Must Feed Their Own People," *Plant Physiology* (May 2001)

NO: Brian Halweil, from "Biotech, African Corn, and the Vampire Weed," *World Watch* (September/October 2001)

ISSUE SUMMARY

YES: Jesse Machuka, a Kenyan scientist in the department of biochemistry and biotechnology at Kenyatta University, argues that agricultural biotechnology will substantially increase food production by rural resource-poor farmers. Machuka suggests that agricultural biotechnology will help address several constraints to crop production, including pests, diseases, weeds, environmental degradation and soil nutrient depletion. He is particularly concerned that biotechnology research be undertaken by Africans for Africans.

NO: In a case study examining attempts to control the parasitic *Striga* weed, Brian Halweil, a research associate at the Worldwatch Institute, questions whether maize that is bioengineered for herbicide resistance is really the best approach in the African context. He suggests that improved soil fertility management practices and mixed cropping are more appropriate and accessible strategies.

Humans have long sought to increase agricultural output through the use of improved seed. Initially this was done by repeatedly (over generations) saving seeds from plants with the most desirable characteristics. African farmers have been found to maintain and utilize an amazing number of crop varieties. Even when fields are not intercropped (i.e., several different crops planted in the same field), African farmers will often plant different varieties of the same crop in accordance with soil and moisture conditions that may vary throughout the field. Preserving the rich genetic diversity among crops at the local level in Africa has been concern of some environmentalists.

Formal plant breeding emerged at the end of the eighteenth century. Here, crops were systematically cross-fertilized in hopes of obtaining plants with a desirable mix of characteristics. A significant advance was the development of a technique known as hybridization in the early twentieth century. Normally, a plant must cross-pollinate with another. A plant that mates with itself is known as an inbred, and it usually produces offspring that perform less well than the parent. Hybridization involves cross-breeding two inbreds from desirable parentage, a technique that produces highly productive plants (Robert Tripp, *Seed Provision & Agricultural Development* (ODI, 2001)). In the 1960s, a concerted effort, known as the Green Revolution, was undertaken to boost food crop production in the developing world. The Green Revolution, involving highly productive hybridized crops in conjunction with pesticides and inorganic fertilizers, largely benefited Asia and South America because it devoted most of its attention to food crops prevalent in these regions (mainly rice, wheat and maize to a lesser extent). Africa was bypassed by the Green Revolution for the most part, with a few significant exceptions, such as maize in Zimbabwe. While the Green Revolution did boost food production, it has been criticized for not really resolving the hunger issues it was designed to address, tending to favor wealthier farmers and spawning a host of new environmental problems related to chemically intensive agriculture.

The debate over the use and proliferation of agricultural biotech in Africa evokes many of the old pro and con arguments related to the Green Revolution, not to mention a host of new issues. The key advance of biotech, over hybridization, is that plant breeders are now able to insert genes from other (unrelated) species to affect desirable characteristics in a food crop. In this issue, Jesse Machuka, a Kenyan scientist in the department of biochemistry and biotechnology at Kenyatta University, argues that agricultural biotechnology will increase food production by rural resource-poor farmers, while preserving environmental resources. For Machuka, biotech is the most promising approach for addressing a host of crop production constraints, including pests, diseases, weeds, environmental degradation, and soil nutrient depletion. He is particularly concerned that biotechnology research be undertaken by Africans for Africans. Africans, he argues, desperately want to become food self-sufficient because they are tired of accepting handouts. Brian Halweil, a research associate at the Worldwatch Institute, is concerned that most Africans cannot afford bioengineered crops and that reliance on such solutions transfers problem solving from the farmer to the labs of multinational firms. Using control of the parasitic weed *Striga* as an example, he argues that more appropriate and accessible solutions exist in many instances.

One of the fundamental questions in this debate is whether food insecurity in Africa is a question of underproduction or maldistribution. Until quite recently, there was a consensus among food security specialists that hunger was more often the result of conflict, mismanagement, or poor distribution than underproduction. This pre-existing consensus was catalyzed, in large part, by the pioneering work of the Nobel laureate economist, Amartya Sen (*Poverty and Famines* (Clarendon, 1981)), who showed how national markets could be replete with grain, yet poor households might still not have the means to access this food.

Jesse Machuka  **YES**

Agricultural Biotechnology for Africa. African Scientists and Farmers Must Feed Their Own People

Few would disagree that the many claims and counterclaims concerning what biotechnology can or cannot do to solve Africa's food insecurity problem have mainly been made by non-Africans. It is no wonder that Florence Wambugu's (1999) excellent article titled "Why Africa needs agricultural biotech" is now widely cited by those who support the view that developing countries, particularly in SubSaharan Africa (SSA), stand to gain the most from modern biotechnology applications. The article explained in a nutshell some of the potential benefits Africa stands to gain by embracing biotechnology. Although opinions differ regarding the role biotechnology can play in African development, all (hopefully!) must agree about the urgency to eradicate the perpetual cycle of hunger, malnutrition, and death in a world of plenty. It is an acknowledged fact that Africa is endowed with tremendous natural (including genetic) and human wealth that has yet to be harnessed to the benefit of its people. Sadly, some of this reservoir of resources have been disintegrating and the trend is bound to accelerate unless urgent measures are taken to stop and reverse this drift. Since farming is the most important source of income and sustenance for about three quarters of the population of SSA, there is no doubt that agricultural biotechnology (agbiotech) can make very substantial contributions toward increasing food production by rural resource-poor farmers, while preserving declining resources such as forests, soil, water, and arable land (Bunders and Broerse, 1991). However, application of modern biotechnology tools is not likely to significantly reduce the contributions that conventional disciplines such as soil science, breeding, plant health management, agronomy, agricultural economics, and social sciences make to enhance crop production.

In villages, constraints to crop production include pests, diseases, weeds, environmental degradation, soil nutrient depletion, low fertilizer inputs, inadequate food processing amenities, poor roads to markets, and general lack of information to make science-based decisions that underlie farming methodologies and systems. For some of these constraints, biotechnology is the most promising recourse to alleviate them. For example, an insect known as *Maruca* podborer is the major constraint restricting increased grain legume production in Africa, often causing up to 100% crop failure during severe attacks on important crops such as cowpea. Many decades of conventional breeding efforts have failed to control this pest. However, recent research in U.S. universities and at the International Institute of Tropical Agriculture based in Ibadan, Nigeria, shows that this pest can be controlled by applying biotechnology tools. This is just one of the myriad problems facing food production systems in Africa for which biotechnology can provide at least some solutions. Although biotechnology has potential downsides, the major "concerns" in Africa are not so much about justifying its role in agricultural production—the "why" question. It is conceivable that the millions of dollars being wasted each year by antibiotech activists elsewhere could go a long way to help build badly needed capacity for agbiotech research in Africa! The key issues revolve around questions of where, when, how, and who will do biotechnology for Africa's benefit? If we are thinking of ultimate answers, then there is probably only one answer: biotechnology for Africa should mostly be done in Africa and mostly by Africans themselves, now. And yes, this is being realistic, and it can be done, if there is consensus and goodwill.

Despite many years of agricultural and other "development" aid and promises by different agencies related to increased food security and poverty eradication, those of us who live in Africa do not have confidence that things are getting any better. Because of this history, some are either pessimistic or skeptical, but the majority remain cautious and optimistic, that modern biotechnology opens new opportunities to address constraints that have led to declining harvests in farmers' fields in the midst of an expanding population. Richard Manning (2000) makes a good point when he suggests that one way to feed the increasing world population is to help "third world scientists to feed their own people, while ensuring sensitivity to culture and environment that we missed in the first green revolution" (http:// www.mcknight.org/ crop-frontier.htm). For SSA, the pertinent question is, how does the international community of public and private institutions and donors, governments, scientists, and other actors help African scientists (and farmers!) to feed their own people? It is crucial that scientific information reaches farmers in the rural areas who have space to practice farming and that other actors such as agricultural scientists and extensionists interact with farmers to attain acceptance and use of new technologies for sustainable food production and development. In this regard, we must have it in mind that life science technologies that offer hope to farmers, such as agbiotech, belong to the farmer. We must also ensure that the technology not only reaches farmers but that they understand it and are empowered to use it. Furthermore, our starting point is not the "ignorant peasant" but the practices, techniques, experience, and knowledge of the African farmer built over the centuries (Duprez and DeLeener, 1988).

A good example of how biotechnology can reach rural farmers involves a special program by the Biotechnology Development Co-operation of the Netherlands Government, the Kenyan Ministry of Research, Science and Technology, and the small-scale farming system stakeholders. The program structure is designed to ensure that biotechnology reaches the small farmer (end-user) through a bottom-up approach steered by the Kenya Agricultural Biotechnology Platform. The composition of farmers includes male and female farmers, oxen owners, different age groups from different subvillages, etc. Projects under the Kenya Agricultural Biotechnology Platform funding bring together collaborators who include scientists from research institutions such as universities, national agricultural research centers, and farmers. A Farming Systems Research Program ensures that farmers participate in the research as partners with scientists, extensionists, and other actors and enables scientists also to utilize indigenous knowledge in research and development. This prevents "cut and paste" approaches that may be foreign market-driven and which tend to provide short-term, quick-fix solutions to unique problems faced by small-scale farmers in Africa who have developed their own unique crops, cropping, and farming systems that cannot be changed without their full and careful involvement. Since 1992, Farmers Research Groups and Farmers Extension Groups, established along the lines of Farming Systems Research Programs, have been in existence in the Lake Zone of Tanzania for purposes of farmer participatory research. This experience shows that such participatory methods increase farmers' inputs in the decision-making process as well as in the dissemination of research products through their involvement in field trials, farmers' and "on-station" field days, PRA surveys, and farmer-to-farmer diffusion of information through Village Extension Workers rather than institutional extension. Since Farmers Research Groups represent different geographic zones and hence different agro-ecological and farming systems, linkage mechanisms that bring together their experiences need to be established to allow horizontal and vertical dissemination of technologies as well as collaboration in the SSA region. Obviously, this is not the only way that research results from the laboratory reach farmers' fields, but it illustrates the fact that applied agbiotech research can similarly be targeted and tied to meet specific needs of rural farmers, both in the short- and long-term, in the face of scant resources. With African farmers and scientists working together to set the research agenda, there is hope that the research will focus on uniquely African ("orphan") crops such as millet and sorghum that are very important in marginal, famine-prone regions such as the Sahel and Horn of Africa. Root and tuber crops such as yam, sweet potato, and cassava may also begin to receive the attention they deserve.

Although Africa lags far behind other regions when it comes to public information and awareness of biotechnology issues, excellent work is being done by organizations such as the Nairobi-based African Biotechnology Stakeholders Forum and South African-based AfricaBIO to educate the general public in biotechnology. Opportunities abound for scientists in Africa to get involved in these efforts that are urgently needed if Africans are going to decide for themselves what biotechnology can do for them rather than let others decide for them, especially anti-genetically modified organism activists! There is also urgency to educate policy makers in African governments and the private sector concerning the need to support and invest in biotechnology Research and Development (R&D). At the same time, the international donor community needs to begin to trust Africans and allow them to manage their research agenda for themselves. They can take the cue from very successful initiatives undertaken by the Rockefeller Foundation in Africa. There are enough African scientists around to make a difference on farmers fields if resources are properly channeled for agricultural R&D. African scientists and science managers in government and other institutions as well as farmers, on the other hand, need to be efficient and faithful in the way they manage research programs and funds if they are going to be trusted with money by national and international donors. The current success in tissue culture-aided production and multiplication of disease-free planting materials for cassava, yam, banana, plantain, citrus, and flowers in countries such as Kenya and Ghana is attracting private sector companies who are seeing the potential to invest in successful new biotechnologies.

On November 8–11, 2000, the Strategic Alliance for Biotechnology Research in African Development (SABRAD) held a workshop in Accra, Ghana, that brought together more than 150 participants from southern, East, Central, and West Africa as well as partners from the U.S. 1890 Land Grant Universities, U.S. Department of Agriculture, Food and Agricultural Organization of the United Nations, United Nations Environment Program, International Agricultural Research Centers, other non-governmental organizations, private companies, and journalists. International Agricultural Research Centers were represented by the Mexican-based International Maize and Wheat Improvement Centre and International Institute of Tropical Agriculture. The theme of this first SABRAD Workshop was "Enabling Biotechnology for African Agriculture." Increasing education and awareness and formulation of regulatory (policy) frameworks that would allow access to modern biotechnology for R&D were identified as key priorities for enabling biotechnology for African development that targets resource-poor rural farmers. The one thing that was unique at the Accra meeting was that Africans themselves were at the center of discussions to work out plans for enabling biotechnology to take root in their respective countries. The action plans agreed upon will be implemented through networking between regions. The ultimate socioeconomic impact is food self-sufficiency and improved living conditions of resource-poor farmers who were identified as the target recipients for products generated from biotechnology applications.

We live in a world that has become an increasingly interdependent "global village" due to advances in information and transportation technology. In this global village, millions have plenty of food to throw away, while millions of others die daily because they have nothing to eat. It is not always true that those with surplus food do not care about those who die in near and far away places! In Africa itself, there are many that have plenty of food, acquired either genuinely or by stealing public wealth, and who still watch their hungry neighbors die helplessly. Although Africans are thankful for development and relief aid, they are uncomfortable about their condition of continuous dependence on handouts that come in many forms, including food and expatriate foreign aid, with no permanent solutions apparently in sight. The SABRAD initiative is one step in the right direction that deserves support from all those who want to help African scientists and farmers to feed their own people.

Literature Cited

Bunders FG, Broerse EW (1991) Appropriate Biotechnology in Small-Scale Agriculture: How to Reorient Research and Development. CAB International, Wallington, Oxon, UK

Duprez H, DeLeener P (1988) Agriculture in African Rural Communities. Macmillan and Technical Centre for Agricultural and Rural Co-operation. CTA, London

Manning R (2000) Food's Frontier: The Next Green Revolution. North Point Press, New York

Wambugu F (1999) Why Africa needs agricultural biotech. Nature **400**: 15–16

NO ⬅

Brian Halweil

Biotech, African Corn, and the Vampire Weed

A parasitic weed is sucking the life out of East African corn. One way to deal with it would be to engineer corn for herbicide resistance, so that herbicide could be sprayed on the corn to kill the parasite—even though the corn seed and the herbicide would probably be too expensive for poor farmers, the herbicide would pollute, and the weed would likely become resistant. Another way would be to improve soil health. Tough call.

I was hot on the trail of the infamous Striga weed. Though I'd never confronted a live specimen, the plant had been hounding me *in absentia*, and often in public, for several years. Again and again, in various panel discussions on biotechnology, I have listened to my debating opponents hold up Striga as proof that genetic engineering could one day eradicate hunger and poverty in the Third World. The particulars varied, of course, but I had heard the same basic Striga argument from biotech executives, from industry-funded scientists, and from the industry's advocates in academia and government.

Striga hermonthica is a member of the Scrophulariaceae family, a widespread group of about 4,000 plant species that includes a couple of "heirloom" garden favorites, foxglove and snapdragon. But it also includes several important Old World plant parasites—plants that live off other plants. S. hermonthica is one of these. It's common in East Africa, where it's called "witchweed" or in Swahili, "buda." It looks innocent enough, standing about 15 centimeters (around 6 inches) tall, and bearing little lance-shaped, pale-green leaves that make a pleasing contrast with its pink-purple flowers. But below ground, the plant is a monster. Its root-like organs, called haustoria, seek out the roots of nearby crops, then rob them of water, nutrients, and life. And those pretty flowers can set as many as 20,000 seeds per plant. The seeds are easily dispersed and can lie dormant in a range of soil conditions for decades.

In a badly infested field, Striga can destroy most of the harvest, perpetuating not only poverty and hunger, but also gender inequity, since it's usually women who must undertake the largely futile task of disentangling Striga from the crop. Throughout East Africa, Striga causes several billion dollars in losses each year.

The solution, according to the biotech advocates, is to engineer varieties of African staple crops to resist herbicides, so that farmers can spray their infested fields—and kill the Striga without killing the crop. This is an extension of agricultural biotech's dominant commercial application: the engineering of soybeans, corn, cotton, and canola by Monsanto to withstand the company's best-selling herbicide, glyphosate ("Roundup").

An anti-Striga niche would make it easier to claim the moral high ground for herbicide-tolerant crops. Such products might eventually seem as humanitarian as the industry's "golden rice"—the beta-carotene enhanced rice variety that is being developed to combat vitamin A deficiency. Beta-carotene is the precursor of vitamin A, an especially important nutrient for children. Worldwide, nearly 134 million children suffer some degree of vitamin A deficiency, a condition that can suppress immune system function, cause blindness, and in extreme cases, even kill. Little wonder that golden rice has become the emotionally compelling hook for a $50 million public relations campaign launched by the Biotechnology Trade Organization. (It's true that not everyone is sold on this idea. Some nutritionists argue that it would make more sense to help poor people grow green vegetables, which produce more beta-carotene than golden rice—along with various other nutrients completely lacking in rice, golden or otherwise.)

❧

But in any case, I decided that the time had come for me to get a first-hand sense of this expanding moral high ground. From a political point of view, the Striga issue looked especially interesting because Striga, unlike vitamin A deficiency, is almost exclusively an African problem, and Africa is ground-zero in the global food debate. Although hunger is sorely persistent throughout much of the developing world, Africa is the only region where it is actually getting worse. In Latin America and Asia, the past two decades have seen a modest decline in malnourishment among children, in terms of both the percentage of children affected and their absolute numbers. In Africa, however, the share of children who are hungry has risen from 26 to 29 percent over the past 20 years, and the absolute number of hungry children has doubled. It now stands at 38 million. That helps explain why, sooner or later, almost any major agricultural development will have to justify itself in an African context.

That, in turn, explains why I was looking at cornfields outside Maseno, Kenya last February. Maseno is a small but rapidly growing town near the Ugandan border, about 30 kilometers northeast of Lake Victoria. And from what I could see, the local harvest was going to be an uncertain affair. In some fields there seemed to be more Striga than corn, which is often called maize in Africa. Spindly corn stalks with pitiful, dried-up ears stood above a carpet of purple flowers. But in other fields, the corn looked good and there was no Striga at all. Several farmers and ag extension agents helped explain what seemed like pure chance. One of them, a farmer named Paul Okongo, put it categorically: "Striga is only a problem in overused and depleted soils."

Striga thrives where farmers have grown nothing but corn for decades, especially where fallow periods have been shortened or eliminated. (During a fallow period, land is allowed to "go wild" or soil-building fallow crops are sown. The practice helps maintain long-term productivity by reducing weed and pest infestations and by allowing soil nutrient levels to recover.) But as Kenya's population has grown, the size of the average family field has declined, and farmers have become increasingly reluctant to take land out of production. Of course, fallowing isn't the only way to renew soil; another standard approach is fertilizing. And where farmers are able to do this—whether in the form of manure or artificial fertilizer—Striga is rarely a problem. But most East African farmers can't afford commercial fertilizer. And manure is often scarce because livestock are not generally penned, where their droppings could be collected, but grazed out in the open. No fertilizer and little fallowing: the result is depleted soil, and then Striga moves in. Striga infestation, in other words, is a kind of second- order effect: it's what happens *after* soil health declines. It was obvious that a herbicide-resistant fix wasn't going to get at this problem.

It was also obvious that Paul knew what he was talking about, and I began to wonder what local expertise might have to offer in lieu of a prepackaged, imported solution. And indeed, it turns out that some African farmers have found a way to suppress Striga with a widely available, home-grown technique: planting leguminous tree crops—that is, tree species that are members of the legume family. Plants in this family often have certain microbes on their roots that can "fix" nitrogen: the microbes withdraw elemental nitrogen from tiny air pockets in the soil and bond it chemically to hydrogen, producing compounds that plants can metabolize. (Pure, elemental nitrogen is useless to plants; fixed nitrogen, on the other hand, is the principal component of fertilizer.)

These nitrogen-fixing trees are grown as a fallow crop, during the one more-or-less obligatory fallow period of the year: from February to April. This is the dry spell between the two rainy seasons—the long rains of late spring, which yield the main corn harvest in July, and the erratic, short rains of fall, which produce the smaller, January harvest. Of course, three months isn't long enough for the trees to get very big; they're usually 2 or 3 meters high when they're pulled to sow the fall corn. But that one season of tree growth can cut Striga infestations by over 90 percent. This is not just the effect of the added nitrogen. Some of the preferred tree crops are native to the region and have co-evolved with Striga; their evolutionary defenses to the parasite apparently include chemicals that they exude into the soil and that disrupt the Striga lifecycle.

Control of Striga is not the only benefit of nitrogen-fixing crops, according to Bashir Jama, a scientist with the Nairobi-based International Center for Research in Agroforestry (ICRAF), the main promoter of these "improved fallows." Where farmers can be persuaded to employ longer fallows, leguminous trees can accumulate 100 to 200 kilograms of nitrogen in 6 months to 2 years.

(The results depend on the species used, soil quality, moisture levels, and whether the fallow is taken all at once or in intermittent periods.) These fertilization rates would satisfy most U.S. and European farmers. In severely depleted soils, they generally increase corn yields two to four times—not bad for adding just one crop to the rotation.

Bashir reports other benefits as well, such as improved soil structure, better water retention, and higher levels of other nutrients besides nitrogen. The fallow crop also shades out weeds—which means fewer weed seeds to cause problems when the field goes back into production. And because it adds diversity to the agroecosystem, the fallow tends to suppress the most serious insect pests of corn as well. (Monocultures foster very high insect infestations; in more complex systems, the pests encounter more predators and less food so their populations tend to be much lower.) Fallow greens are also nutritious livestock feed; the wood is useful for fuel. A six-month tree crop fallow on as little as half a hectare can meet a family's cooking needs for an entire year.

⁓◈⁓

Another Striga control has emerged as the byproduct of an ingenious local response to the most important insect pest of corn, the stemborer. The borer is thought to chew up between 15 and 40 percent of Africa's corn harvest each year. In other corn-growing regions of the world, the borer is the target of extensive insecticide spraying. African farmers generally can't afford insecticide, but they may not need it anyway, to judge from the work of another Nairobi-based organization, the International Center for Insect Physiology and Ecology (ICIPE). ICIPE's work is founded on the idea that pest problems are caused by ecological imbalances; progress is therefore a matter of correcting the imbalances, rather than simply trying to poison the pests. "The long-term solution is generally more insect diversity, not less," says Hans Herren, ICIPE's director. This attitude helps explain why the gates at ICIPE headquarters bear a sign reading "Duduville." "Dudu" is Swahili for bug. Kenyans don't generally seem to like bugs any more than Americans do; I saw billboards throughout Kenya that read, "Raid kills dudus dead."

ICIPE scientists have developed what they call a "push-pull" strategy for dealing with the stemborer. The corn is sown with certain plants, such as molasses grass (*Melinis minutifolia*) and silver leaf desmodium (*Desmodium uncinatum*) that repel, or "push" the borer. The field perimeter is sown with other plants, such as napier grass (*Pennisetum purpureum*) and Sudan grass (*Sorghum vulgare sudanense*), that attract, or "pull" it. Most of the larvae end up trapped in the gummy substances produced by these grasses. This system can cut stemborer losses from 40 percent to below 5 percent. It also offers substantial relief from Striga, because desmodium secretes a chemical that interferes with the parasite's ability to tap into the roots of other plants. (Desmodium is a legume genus from the New World, so this mechanism is not an adaptation to Striga specifically, but perhaps the genus coevolved with a similar parasite.)

Ironically, a major U.S. foundation, which has been funding the "push-pull" research, has asked ICIPE to isolate this chemical—and the related gene. "Part of their interest is to use that gene to come up with molecular biology solutions to the Striga problem," says Zeyaur Khan, who directs work on the push-pull strategy at ICIPE. In other words, they might be interested in funding the development of a corn variety engineered to produce this substance. How would that relate to ICIPE's interest in promoting ecological balance? Presumably, it would tend to undercut it, because it would push the system back towards monoculture—and it would likely do nothing for the borer problem. The full benefits of ICIPE's system are only available if you buy in at the ecological level—not the molecular level. And of course, the ecological level is the one that's available to farmers.

$\diamond$

After several days of farm visits in western Kenya, I was beginning to get a better sense of how the biotech approach to Striga compared with the improved fallow technique. The biotech fix would be costly for the farmer, would increase chemical use, would add no other benefits to the system, and in any case, does not yet even exist. On the other hand, improved fallowing is extremely low-cost and confers all the benefits mentioned above. It's also readily accessible. In at least a rudimentary form, the technique is already being used by tens of thousands of farmers in eastern and southern Africa. Pedro Sanchez, who recently stepped down as director of ICRAF, sees improved fallowing at the early stages of an exponential growth curve similar to what happened with Green Revolution rice varieties in Asia. Sanchez envisions 50 million farmers using improved fallowing within the next five to ten years.

One of the most interesting features of the improved fallow system is that it allows for forms of R&D that farmers can do on their own. In 1997, for example, a moth infestation began to threaten a popular East African tree crop known as sesbania (*Sesbania sesban*)—until some farmers discovered that occasional rows of tephrosia trees (either *Tephrosia vogelii* or *T. candida*) would keep the pest in check. This field-level innovation is very far removed from the biotech paradigm, where innovation occurs, not on the farm, but in million-dollar laboratories, and where the principal actors are not farmers, but Ph.D. biologists and patent attorneys.

This distinction is critical, and not just for the harvest. The ability to innovate could be crucial to the future of farmers themselves. But if innovation is to contribute to the welfare of farming, it will have to extend beyond issues of yield. After all, many U.S. and European farmers have been teetering on the brink of economic extinction for years, and a substantial number have gone over it—even though they produce some of the highest yields in the world. In most developing countries, agriculture is still the predominant way of life, so the economic health of farming is a basic social issue. This is why the agricultural status quo is a dangerous absurdity. The multinational corporations that sell farmers seed and pesticide are ringing up tens of billions of dollars in sales each year; the multinationals that distribute, process, and retail the harvests are ringing up hundreds of billions. But farmers themselves are now members of the poorest—and ironically, the hungriest—occupation on Earth.

This is the problem that has come to dominate the agenda of another Kenyan NGO, the Association for Better Land Husbandry. ABLH was set up in 1994 to promote a variety of conservation farming techniques, including bio-intensive farming, a form of organic production popularized by one of organic agriculture's best-known proponents, John Jeavons of Willets, California. When I visited farmers working with ABLH in the Vihiga district of western Kenya, I instantly recognized the neatly laid out "beds" that characterize the biointensive method. In 1996, I had attended a three-day workshop taught by Jeavons, and I knew from direct experience how much effort went into those beds. They are prepared through a deep-digging technique, called "double- digging," which aerates the soil, and permits better nutrient circulation. Jeavons places tremendous emphasis on soil health. "Feed the soil, not the plants" is one of his mantras.

Biointensive farming can boost yield dramatically, and it packs a one-two punch against Striga by enriching soils, then producing a dense, diverse plant canopy that shades out most weeds. But by themselves, such improvements aren't going to bring prosperity to farmers. "Doubling maize yields and tripling kale yields doesn't make much of a difference if you can't get your product to market, or if a flood of cheap imports squashes your local market," says Jim Cheatle, founder and director of ABLH. To get at these issues, Cheatle expanded the group's agenda to include a kind of farmer empowerment. ABLH now coordinates seven farm cooperatives so that local growers can capture the marketing and distribution advantages that come with scale. (Nine more co-ops should be in operation by the end of the year.) "Instead of each of several thousand farmers buying their own delivery truck and setting up their own marketing offices," says Jane Tum, an ABLH extensionist, "the cooperative can pool its resources for a much larger delivery truck and a marketing staff." This might seem like kind of an obvious thing to do, but *any* concern with marketing is still unusual in places like Kenya. A recent survey of over 200 sustainable farming projects in the developing world found that only 12 to 15 percent had tried to improve marketing or processing.

Co-op produce is now selling in both local and national markets under the "Farmer's Own" brand name. Among the products bearing this label are Mr. Brittle, a macadamia nut energy bar, and Mchuzi Mix, a soup and sauce thickener made from locally grown beans and corn. "We're competing with the big boys," says Francisca Odundo, the marketing manager for Farmer's Own. Francisca is trying to cultivate allegiance for the new brand, which now sits on shelves alongside the Cadbury and Nestlé labels.

Farmer's Own products also bear the label, "Conservation Supreme," a quasi-organic designation that permits limited use of approved biopesticides, like the insect-killing "Bt" bacterium. The designation is a kind of marketing tool to help small-scale farmers make the transition to certified organic production. (Before it can pay off, the transition usually involves several years of uncertainty, in which both the farm and the farmer must adjust to the new regime.)

I got a sense for the tangible results of these efforts when Jane Tum took me to a farm to pick up produce for a Farmer's Own vegetable stand. The farm was run by Flora Mwoshi, a young mother of three. On the day I visited, she was harvesting bright green bell peppers. With a young child resting on her hip, Flora balanced a five-gallon plastic bucket of peppers on her head and bore it to our truck, where it was weighed. Several more buckets followed. Her six-year-old daughter, barefoot but wearing her best white dress because the family had heard that white people were coming to visit, watched in awe as her mother became the center of attention.

Jane paid the woman 600 Kenyan shillings, about $10. That doesn't sound like much, but that money went directly into her pocket—no middleman to pay, no bills for agrochemicals or expensive seeds. And many more veggies remained to be harvested. This simple transaction was the most inspiring moment of my trip. We, the "white people," hadn't arrived with some foreign technology of highly dubious potential. We were there as witnesses and—in a broad sense—colleagues. What we witnessed was a local response to a local problem. And we could see that the response worked, because the produce was beautiful, and the farmer got paid.

POSTSCRIPT

Will Biotech Solve Africa's Food Problems?

There are a number of health and environmental concerns related to the use of agricultural biotechnology in Africa. Some of these are mentioned in the selections by Machuka and Halweil, while others are not.

Perhaps one of the most controversial concerns is the apprehension about food safety. While there is considerable unease among some consumers regarding GM foods, not to mention a ban on the use and importation of GMO crops by the European Union (EU), studies definitively linking these foods to health risks are still lacking. Nonetheless, whether or not the health concerns are justifiable, EU restrictions on these crops have genuine implications for African farmers who may wish to export their crops to Europe.

Some of the most widely used GMO crops in North America are the Roundup Ready varieties of maize, soybeans, and canola (mentioned by Halweil) and Bt crops produced by the Monsanto Corporation. The Roundup Ready crops are resistant to the popular herbicide of the same name. As such, weeds may be eradicated through spraying with no negative effect on crop growth. Bt crops contain a gene from the soil bacterium *Bacillus thuringiensis* (Bt) that acts as a toxin to insects that prey on the crops. Environmental concerns related to these crops number at least two.

First, Bt and Roundup Ready crops may cross-pollinate with weeds or neighboring vegetation and thereby release herbicide resistance (in the case of the Roundup Ready varieties) or insect resistance (in the case of Bt crops) into the broader plant population. The concern in the former instance is the appearance of "super weeds" that are resistant to the Roundup herbicide. The concern in the latter case is a growing number of plants (crops and wild relatives) that have insect resistance.

Second, because the Bt in plants does not discriminate between the insects it kills, useful or benign insects (such as butterflies) may be destroyed. Furthermore, some insects may more quickly develop a resistance to Bt (a problem known as pesticide resistance) through constant exposure to the toxin and evolutionary adaptation. At the time Machuka wrote his article, there had been no documented cases of Bt or Roundup Ready genes jumping to other plants. Since 2002, both have occurred in North America. Some scientists would assert that these environmental problems are particularly problematic in the African context because they may become extremely costly to control once they are pronounced. Still others would assert that the gains in food production justify the risk of a genetic mishap.

A third issue that one may want to consider when evaluating the usefulness of GM crops in Africa is that of "terminator technology," where seeds are engineered to be useless after the first generation. This issue is more of a socioeconomic than a health or environmental concern. It has been pointed out that terminator technology is disruptive to traditional African farming systems where seeds are saved from one year's crops to be planted the following season. Some may find it problematic, even if yields are higher, that farmers would be dependent on the market for their seed supplies each year. Others suggest that this is simply part of the agricultural modernization process in Africa and that seed companies are justified in developing this technology given the large amount of R&D that went into creating the improved seeds.

It is finally worth noting that this debate took on added prominence in 2002 when some southern African countries rejected food aid containing bioengineered crops. This occurred at a time when millions of people were at risk of starvation in these countries (see Ruth Gidley, "African Crisis Fuels Debate Over Gm Food," *AlertNet*, July 19, 2002). For more general information on this debate, see three articles in the journal *Nature*, an oft-cited article by Florence Wambugu in the July 1, 1999 issue entitled "Why Africa Needs Agricultural Biotech," a piece by H. Hoag in the March 20, 2003 issue entitled "Biotech Firms Join Charities to Help Africa's Farms," and a paper by N. McDowell in the August 8, 2002 issue entitled "Africa Hungry for Conventional Food as Biotech Row Drags On."

ISSUE 10

Is Food Production in Africa Capable of Keeping Up with Population Growth?

YES: Michael Mortimore and Mary Tiffen, from "Population and Environment in Time Perspective: The Machakos Story," *People and Environment in Africa* (John Wiley & Sons, 1995)

NO: John Murton, from "Population Growth and Poverty in Machakos District, Kenya," *The Geographical Journal* (March 1999)

ISSUE SUMMARY

YES: Michael Mortimore, a geographer, and Mary Tiffen, a historian and socio-economist, both with Drylands Research, investigate population and food production trajectories in Machakos, Kenya. They determine that increasing population density has a positive influence on environmental management and crop production. Furthermore, they found that food production kept up with population growth from 1930 to 1987.

NO: John Murton, with the Foreign and Commonwealth Office of the British government, uses household-level data to show that the changes in Machakos described by Mortimore and Tiffen "have been accompanied by a polarization of land holdings, differential trends in agricultural productivity, and a decline in food self-sufficiency." As such, he argues that the "Machakos experience" of population growth and positive environmental transformation is neither homogenous nor fully unproblematic.

There is a long-standing debate about the ability of agriculture to keep up with population growth in Africa. Those who are concerned that population growth will outstrip agricultural production are often referred to as neo-Mathusians. This perspective is designated as such in deference to the eighteenth-century British clergyman, Thomas Malthus, who posited such a scenario as inevitable in his famous 1798 tract, *Essay on the Principle of Population*. The neo-Malthusians generally have dominated contemporary debates concerning global population growth and food supplies and are led by such figures as Paul Ehrlich (*The Population Bomb*, Simon and Schuster, 1968) and Lester Brown (see numerous World Watch Institute publications). The major contrarian perspective in

African studies is the Boserupian view point, named after Ester Boserup (*The Conditions of Agricultural Change,* Aldine Publishing, 1965). She established that increasing population densities may induce farmers to intensify their efforts and thereby produce food at a rate that keeps pace with population increase.

A third perspective, often referred to as the technocratic or cornucopian view, is somewhat akin to the Boserupian population thesis. This view, most commonly associated with the late Julian Simon (*The Great Breakthrough and Its Cause,* University of Michigan Press, 2000), asserts that human ingenuity will resolve resource constraints created by population growth if the free market is allowed to operate and appropriate price signals are transmitted to producers. The major difference between the Boserupian and technocratic viewpoints is that the former tends to emphasize indigenous methods of adaptation whereas the latter stresses the importance of market-led change.

To some extent, both of the perspectives in this issue are sympathetic to the Boserupian view, but they arrive at different conclusions in the final analysis. The case presented by Michael Mortimore, a geographer, and Mary Tiffen, a historian and socio-economist, about the situation in Machakos, Kenya, is probably the most well-referenced piece of analysis supporting the Boserupian thesis in African studies. Mortimore and Tiffen assert that increasing population density has had a positive influence on environmental management and crop production. Furthermore, they find that food production kept up with population growth from 1930 to 1987. The study shows that farmers were able to reverse land degradation, enhance their livestock, invest in their farms, and increase productivity despite increasing population density.

John Murton, with the British Foreign and Commonwealth, agrees with the findings of Mortimore and Tiffen in the aggregate, but then uses household survey data to demonstrate that there is a difference between the trends for wealthier households with access to nonfarm income and poorer households without access to such revenues. It is households with nonfarm income that are able to invest in the inputs needed for increasing agricultural productivity. For those households unable to make such investments, yields are declining. As such, Murton is essentially saying that increasing labor alone will only go so far in the agricultural intensification process, after which point capital expenditure on inputs is critical.

Michael Mortimore
and Mary Tiffen

➡ **YES**

Population and Environment in Time Perspective: The Machakos Story

Introduction: Linkages Between Population Growth and the Environment

The linkages between population growth and environmental degradation are controversial. The view, widely held, that rapid population growth is incompatible with sustainable management of the environment is influenced, knowingly or not, by the neo-Malthusian belief that resources are limited. According to literature prepared for the United Nations Conference on Environment and Development (the Rio Earth Summit), 'the number of people an area can support without compromising its ability to do so in the future is known as its population carrying capacity.'

In agricultural terms, each agro-ecological zone is believed to have a carrying capacity which must not be exceeded if environmental equilibrium is to be maintained. In the words of Mustapha Tolba, formerly head of the United Nations Environment Programme, 'when that number is exceeded, the whole piece of land will quickly degenerate from overgrazing or overuse by human beings. Therefore, population pressure is definitely one of the major causes of desertification and the degradation of the land'. According to such a view, degradation threatens to diminish food production, and thereby the human carrying capacity, in a cumulative downward spiral.

More sophisticated estimations of population supporting capacities take account of technological alternatives to the low-input systems that are found in much of the tropical world. A recent study shows that if technology is varied (or levels of inputs increased), the limits rise accordingly. The critical constraint, for practical purposes, is access to technology. However, poverty inhibits investment, and the poor are said to be incapable of conserving their environment: rather, 'poverty forces them to exploit their limited stocks just to survive, leading to overcropping, overgrazing, and overcutting at unsustainable rates. A vicious circle of human need, environmental damage and more poverty ensues.'

A negative view of the effects of population pressure on the environment, which has been underwritten by several UN organizations, the Rio

From Michael Mortimore and Mary Tiffen, "Population and Environment in Time Perspective: The Machakos Story," in Tony Binns, ed., *People and Environment in Africa* (John Wiley & Sons, 1995), pp. 69–70, 72, 75–78, 81–84, 86–87. Copyright © 1995 by John Wiley & Sons, Ltd. Reprinted by permission. Notes and references omitted.

Earth Summit, and influential writers carries great weight in the environmental debate. Nevertheless it is not supported by some well-documented situations in Africa.

One of these, Machakos district of Kenya, is the subject of a recent study of resource management by African smallholders. The study covered the period 1930–90, which is long enough to control for rainfall variability, and for changes in the political economy. Profiles of change were constructed for all the major environmental and social variables. The linkages in what the World Bank has called the 'population, agriculture and environment nexus' were systematically investigated. The study shows positive, not negative influences of increasing population density on both environmental conservation and productivity.

Characteristics of Machakos District, Kenya

Machakos lies in south-east Kenya. Its northernmost point is about 50 km from the capital, Nairobi, from which it stretches some 300 km southwards. Since at least the eighteenth century it has been inhabited by agropastoralists known as the Akamba, who also populated the neighbouring Kitui district. Men looked after the livestock and cleared new land, while women cultivated a small plot for food crops. . . .

Setting the Scene for an Ecological Disaster

When British rule was imposed on Kenya, the Akamba people were confined in the Ukamba Reserve by the colonial government's Scheduled Areas (White Highlands) policy. . . . It was bounded by European settlers' farms and ranches on the north and west. To the east and south were uninhabited Crown lands, on which the government allowed only grazing, by permit. Thus encircled, the Akamba grew in numbers, and in livestock, while clearing extra land for shifting cultivation of maize and other crops, and chopping down trees for fuel burning and construction of their homes. Despite their protests, the government refused to relax its policy of containment.

During the period 1930–90, the population of Machakos district grew from 238 000 to 1 393 000, and an annual rate of increase of over 3% was maintained from the 1950s until after 1989. After 1962, the Akamba were allowed to settle on the semi-arid former Crown lands, and also took over some of the Europeans' farms in government schemes. Thus the land available to them effectively doubled. However, the growth of the population reduced the amount of land available to less than a hectare per person by 1989.

This conjunction of rapid population growth with unreliable rainfall, frequent moisture stress, low soil fertility and high erodibility, suggests the likelihood, on the premises outlined above, of population-induced degradation on a grand scale. This was indeed the diagnosis offered in assessments of the reserve in the 1930s. A disastrous series of droughts (in 1929, 1933, 1934,

1935 and 1939) caused major crop failures, losses of livestock, pest outbreaks, the deterioration of vegetal cover and accelerated erosion. In 1937, Colin Maher, the government's soil conservation officer, wrote despairingly:

> The Machakos Reserve is an appalling example of a large area of land which has been subjected to uncoordinated and practically uncontrolled development by natives whose multiplication and the increase of whose stock has been permitted, free from the checks of war and largely from those of disease, under benevolent British rule.
>
> Every phase of misuse of land is vividly and poignantly displayed in this Reserve, the inhabitants of which are rapidly drifting to a state of hopeless and miserable poverty and their land to a parching desert of rocks, stones and sand.

No less than eight official visits, reports and recommendations were commissioned between 1929 and 1939, strongly reflecting an official consensus view centred on overstocking, inappropriate cultivation, and deforestation in a reserve thought already to be overpopulated in relation to its carrying capacity. Did events bear out this gloomy prognosis? . . .

A Farming Revolution

Change in Machakos was multi-faceted. Technical innovation was not restricted to soil and water conservation. . . . An inventory of production technologies in Machakos identified 76 that were either introduced from outside the district or whose use was significantly extended during the period of the study. They included 35 field and horticultural crops, 5 tillage technologies and 6 methods of soil fertility management. The technical options available to farmers were thereby extended, adding flexibility to the farming system. Such flexibility is a great advantage in a risky environment.

Making Money From Farming

In the 1930s, capital was mostly locked up in livestock, and occasional sales provided needed cash. From cultivating maize, beans and pigeon peas for subsistence, farmers have since moved into marketing crops. The most successful of these, until its price fell in the 1980s, was coffee. Some Akamba learnt to grow it while employed on European coffee farms, but in 1938 the government expressly forbade 'native' coffee growing in order to protect the European producers' interests. After the overturning of this ban in 1954, strict rules were enforced in the growing, processing and marketing of coffee. African producers successfully achieved high grades. Coffee was an attractive component of rehabilitation programmes, since it was profitable and had to be grown on terraces. Coffee output increased spectacularly in the 'boom' of the later 1970s. It generated investment funds, and supported improved living standards, in the sub-humid zone. This had spill-over effects in the drier areas, through the demand of coffee-growing farmers for agricultural labour, for food and livestock products in which they might no longer be self-sufficient, and for a whole range of consumer goods, housing improvements and services. By 1982–83 over 40% of rural incomes in Machakos district were being generated by non-farm businesses and wages.

In contrast to coffee, cotton, which is recommended for the drier areas, was not a success in the long term. Its price was only rarely high enough to compensate for its tendency to compete with the food crops for labour and capital, and the profit margins were reduced by marketing inefficiencies. Three attempts to promote cotton—in the 1930s, 1960s and 1978–84—ran into the sand. Output limped along, and in 1991 the closed ginnery at Makueni offered silent testimony of failure.

Both coffee and cotton were sold to monopsonist parastatal marketing boards and required government support in extension and supervision, and in supervising officially sponsored co-operatives for input provision, processing and grading. By contrast, expanded growing of a great variety of perennial and annual fruit and vegetables was closely linked with the growth of Kenya's canning industry, the Nairobi and Mombasa retail markets, and exports of fresh vegetables by air. Itinerant Asian buyers, firms operating contract-buying and enterprising Akamba, as individual traders or in formal co-operatives or informal groups, have all played a role. A generally high value per hectare facilitated the skilful exploitation of wet micro-environments, even in the driest areas, and the development of technologies such as micro-irrigation and the cultivation of bananas in pits. Fruit production is attractive to women farmers, as trees do not compete with food crops (for which they often have the main responsibility).

Akamba farmers have adapted rather well to the opportunities provided by the market. No amount of promotion can succeed without incentives. But given these, innovation in both production and marketing aspects is commonplace. Meanwhile, livestock sales, on which they depended for market income in the 1930s, have steadily declined.

Achieving Food Sufficiency

The staple food of the Akamba is white maize. The shortness of the two growing seasons, and the high probability of drought, call for varieties that either resist drought or escape it by maturing quickly. In the 1960s, the government's local research station began a search for drought-escaping varieties that culminated in the release of Katumani Composite B (KCB) maize in 1968.

The new maize was promoted by the extension service, and it was steadily, if unspectacularly, adopted by the farmers. Various surveys suggest that from two-thirds to three-quarters use it, but it is not known how much of the maize area is planted to it, nor what proportion of output it contributes. Of 40 farmers interviewed in five locations in 1990, only a third said they used it exclusively, and another third used it together with local and hybrid varieties.

This was no 'green revolution.' The ambivalent response has, however, an explanation. Given the unpredictable rainfall, farmers need to keep their options open. Their local varieties, though slower to mature, are more resistant to drought, and hybrids do better in wetter sites. KCB is liked because, in combination with other varieties, it strengthens this flexibility rather than undermines it. Some farmers cross-pollinate it with their local varieties, further enhancing their adaptive choice.

With and without KCB, food crop production per person kept up with population growth from 1930 to 1987 although imported foods remained necessary after a series of bad seasons. The district's dependence on imported food in the period 1974–85 was less than in 1942–62 (8 kg per person annually compared with 17), notwithstanding major droughts in both periods. Food output per person in 1984 (after three seasonal droughts) was slightly higher than in 1960–61 (after two seasons with drought, and one with floods).

Faster Tillage

In view of the reputation then enjoyed by the Akamba for resistance to change, it is surprising that the ox-plough, introduced to the district as early as 1910, had spread to about 600 (or 3%) of the district's households by the 1930s. Farmers trained their own cattle, and ploughs were cheap (about equivalent to the price of a cow in 1940); furthermore the technology was being tested and developed on nearby European farms where some Akamba worked. Ownership greatly increased the area a farmer could cultivate, and enabled him to sell maize or cotton. Its adoption called for the cessation of shifting cultivation, and facilitated the adoption of row planting and better weeding, in place of broadcasting seed.

After the Second World War, ex-soldiers who had seen ploughs in India returned with the capital to buy their own. Proceeds from trade and employment outside the district were also invested in ploughs. The government made ox-ploughs the basis of a new farming system imposed on a supervised settlement at Makueni location. The government, and traders, provided some credit. Coffee (after 1954), horticulture and cotton (in some years) generated investment funds. Adoption accelerated in the 1960s and was more or less complete by the 1980s. Surveys found 62% or more of farmers owning a plough, the remainder being too poor, or having fields too small and steep for its use.

The plough proved to be both a durable and a flexible technology. The first ones in use were adapted to opening new land, with teams of six or eight oxen. Farmers later selected a lighter, two-oxen instrument suitable for work on small, terraced, permanent fields. The Victory mouldboard plough, though much criticized on technical grounds, is used everywhere, and for several operations—primary ploughing, seed-bed preparation and inter-row weeding—and attempts to promote its replacement by a more expensive tool-bar have failed. It saves labour, and is also used by women. The 'oxenization' of Akamba agriculture was, in a measure, a triumph of capitalization in a capital-poor, risk-prone and low productive farming system.

Fertilizing the Soil

Shifting cultivation used to rely on long fallows for replenishing the soil. In the 1930s, there was very little systematic manuring. But the fertility of arable land, as measured by yields, was low. The Agricultural Department favoured farmyard manure over inorganic fertilizers. It also, unsuccessfully, promoted composting. It was not until the 1950s that manuring became widespread, in the northern sub-humid areas. By this time, arable fields were fixed, and cultivated every year. The silent spread of this practice can be judged from the fact that by the 1980s, 9 out of 10 farmers were doing it, in both wetter and drier areas. Now, most arable land is cultivated twice a year—in both rainy seasons— and composting is being adopted by small farmers with few livestock.

By contrast, the use made of inorganic fertilizers is minimal, the bulk of it on coffee. Manure is made in the *boma* (stall or pen) and supplemented with trash and waste. The amount applied depends on how many livestock there are, and how much labour and transport are available when needed. Every farmer knows that, under present technical and economic conditions, sustaining output depends on the use made of boma manure. Few can afford inorganic fertilizers in quantity.

Feeding the Livestock

At the beginning of our period (the 1930s), Akamba women cultivated food crops at home, while their men used to take the livestock away to common grazing lands for several months of the year. However, common grazing land vanished as it was transformed into new farms. After about 1960 settlement on Crown lands could no longer be restrained, and thousands of families moved into them. Each household must now keep its animals within the bounds of the family farm, or obtain permission to use another family's land, often in return for some rent or service. More than 60% of the cattle, sheep and goats are stall-fed or tethered for a part or all of the year. When in the boma, cut fodder and residues are brought to them, which requires additional labour. Fodder grass is grown on terrace banks. These changes are most advanced in the sub-humid zone. A third of the livestock are grazed all the time, mostly in the dry semi-arid zone. The effort required to maintain livestock is making grade or crossbred cattle popular (estimated to number about 9% of the total in 1983 and to have grown rapidly since), whose milk yields and value are superior to those of the native zebu, though their increased health risks call for frequent dipping.

Farming the Trees

From the 1920s, the Forest Department believed that reafforestation was necessary to arrest environmental desiccation, and supply the growing need for domestic fuel and construction timber. For several decades the department struggled, under-resourced, to reserve and replant hilltop forests. In 1984, however, estimates of household fuel requirements put the need for new plantations at 226 000 ha (15 times the area of gazetted forest reserves!). The destruction of surviving natural woodland seemed an imminent possibility.

But sites photographed in 1937 and 1991 showed little sign of woodland degradation. A fuel shortage has failed to develop on the expected scale and the district does not import wood or charcoal in significant quantities. Indeed it exports some. Part of the explanation for this expert miscalculation lay in ignoring the use made of dead wood, farm trash, branch wood from farm trees, and hedge cuttings, for domestic fires. The other part lay in failing to appreciate a major area of innovative practice: the planting, protection and systematic harvesting of trees. Forest policy in the 1980s was shifting towards farm forestry promotion, but in this it was following, not driving, farmers.

Tree densities on farmland in one location, Mbiuni, averaged over 34 per ha (14 when bananas are excluded) by 1982. Furthermore, the smaller the farm, the greater the density. The range of trees planted includes both exotic and indigenous, both fruit and timber species. Akamba women generally manage fruit trees, while the men look after the timber trees. Owners of grazing land manage the regeneration of woody vegetation, which is used for timber, fuel, browse, honey production, edible and medicinal products.

Producing More With Less

These were some of the features of a revolution in farming wrought in unpromising circumstances. What was the driving force behind these changes?

The growth of population had two important outcomes: the subdivision of a man's landholdings among all his sons, according to Akamba custom, and the increasing scarcity of land as former communal grazing and Crown land became new private farms.

As holdings shrank in size, the arable proportion rose, leaving less and less land for grazing while the cultivated area per person stagnated. [T]he percentage of arable land increased from the older settled areas to the new, and from the wetter to the drier areas.

These changes created the imperative for intensification. By intensification we mean the application of increasing amounts of labour and capital per ha to raise crop yields. Crop–livestock integration is intrinsic to this process in dryland farming systems in Africa. It was driven by the needs for draft energy on the farm, for fodder (the stalks of maize and haulms of beans, for example), for manure and milk.

Two changes—to intensive livestock feeding systems, and to permanent manured fields, often under plough cultivation—were pivotal in this transformation, whose outcome was an increasingly efficient system of nutrient cycling through plants, animals and soil. The changes could not have occurred without security of title. Akamba custom had already recognized individuals rights in land, including the right of sale, in the older settled areas by the 1930s. Security has been reinforced by statutory registration of title, a slow legal process which began in Machakos in 1968 and has still not covered all areas.

Equally important were sources of investment capital. This was not only required for terraces and ploughs. To clear and cultivate new land, build hedges or plant trees requires labour which often has to be hired, as well as tools and expertise. The off-farm incomes earned by Akamba men inside and outside the district have contributed for decades to agricultural investment. Such incomes are often high in households with small farms, and there is little evidence that investment per ha falls where farmers are poorly resourced in land.

The outcome of this process of intensification was an increase in the value of output per square kilometre (at constant prices) from 1930 to 1987. This was calculated by taking output data for the only three available years before 1974 (1930, 1957 and 1961), selecting two later years which were climatically average (1977 and 1987), and converting all the values into maize equivalent at 1957 prices. The year 1957 was an unusually good one and 1961, as already noted, unusually bad, hence the upward trend was interrupted. The trend continued despite the additions of large areas of the more arid types of land in 1962. Output per capita closely reflected this curve.

We conclude that, contrary to the expectations expressed in the 1930s, the Akamba of Machakos have put land degradation into reverse, conserved and improved their trees, invested in their farms, and sustained an improvement in overall productivity. . . .

No Miracle in Machakos?

What happened in Machakos did not contravene the laws of nature, as the Malthusian paradigm would express them, but rather grew logically from a conjunction of increasing population density, market growth and a generally supportive economic environment. The technological changes we have described, in conservation and production, cannot be adequately understood as exogenous, as mere accidents that gave breathing space on a remorseless progression towards irreversible environmental degradation and poverty. Rather, as argued long ago by Ester Boserup and more recently by Julian Simon, they were mothered by necessity. Technological change was an endogenous process, in which multiple sources and channels were employed, involving selection and adaptation by farmers.

Increasing population density is found, then, to have positive effects. The increasing scarcity (value) of land promoted investment, both in conservation and in yield-enhancing improvements. The integration of crop and livestock production improved the efficiency of nutrient cycling, and thereby the sustainability of the farming system.

The Machakos experience offers an alternative to the Malthusian models of the relations between population growth and environmental degradation. Elsewhere in Africa, there are more documented cases of positive associations, though it would be foolish to ignore the differences.

Successful intensification under rising densities has certain preconditions. These are peace and security, for trade and investment, and a marketing and tenure system in which economic benefits are shared by many, rather than monopolized by a few. Degradation may occur, as it did in Machakos, when a change from a long fallowing system is first needed, but when population densities or other conditions are not conducive. Normally, as population grows, so do the opportunities for specialization and trade. To the stick of necessity the market adds the carrot of incentives and resources for investment in new technologies.

In the past, development planners tried to transform farming systems that were seen as inefficient and technically conservative. In fact, they are changing themselves, as studying them in time perspective shows, and there is scope for supporting positive change with appropriate policies. The guiding principle must be to go with the grain of historical change. This means encouraging investment, by encouraging trade and by improving farm-gate prices (for example, by improving roads and by avoiding heavy taxation of agricultural products). There is also a need to protect investment when crises (e.g. famines) threaten to force households to sell their assets. Increasing the technical options available to local resource users in a risky environment is one of the most productive avenues to pursue, by encouraging endogenous experimentation; by increasing information through general education as well as agricultural extension, and by creating new avenues for technological development and transfer.

NO

John Murton

Population Growth and Poverty in Machakos District, Kenya

The influential book *More People Less Erosion* investigated population growth and environmental change in Machakos, Kenya. Tiffen *et al.* argued that population growth need not lead to environmental degradation, since if smallholder farmers were allowed to operate freely within competitive markets, responding profitably to new agricultural opportunities, they would logically manage their resources in a sustainable way, with a resultant benefit to society and the economy. Although environmental improvements in Machakos seem beyond dispute, Rocheleau argues that the aggregate District level data used by Tiffen *et al.* mask social and economic differentiation as a result of these changes, and that many farmers in Machakos are experiencing declining welfare amidst the improving environment.

The current paper seeks to address this debate by examining the results of a household-level village study in the old Machakos District of Kenya. The new research found that agricultural intensification has not been a homogeneous experience. Rising living standards have been experienced largely by those families who have access to non-farm (and usually urban-derived) income. This income facilitates security in agricultural crises such as drought, and enables a virtuous cycle of on-farm investment, leading to higher agricultural yields, rising incomes and higher standards of living. In contrast, families without access to such income were found to be experiencing a cycle of declining soil fertility and declining yields per head. These divergent experiences of vicious cycles and virtuous spirals were found side by side within neighbouring households in the study area. In the past it was easy for farmers to obtain non-farm income and so make social and economic progress. However, the combination of population increase, slow economic growth, and structural changes in the Kenyan economy mean that poor families are now enjoying less social mobility than they did previously.

This paper highlights how differential access to non-farm income has driven a polarization of land holdings within the village, with the result that, for poorer families at least, environmental sustainability is no longer proving to be a guarantee of livelihood sustainability under conditions of rapidly rising population.

From *The Geographical Journal*, vol. 165, no. 1, March 1999, pp. 37-45. Copyright © 1999 by Blackwell Publishing, Ltd. Reprinted by permission.

The Study and Study Site

In common with other recent work studying environmental transformation, and work in Kenya investigating agricultural change and differentiation, change in Machakos was studied by means of a longitudinal data set. The results of research into agricultural practices and land holdings conducted in Machakos in 1965 by Frederick Owako were compared to new data from the same area today. Both sets of research were conducted in Ndueni village of Mbooni location, in what is now Makueni District; Makueni District having been created when the old Machakos District was carved in two in 1993.

Owako's research formed part of a PhD thesis entitled "The Machakos Problem," and investigated the ability of local agriculture to cater for the growing number of people in the District. His work compared the state of agriculture in study villages in Mbooni, Iveti, Masii, Kangundo and Nzaui locations. He found uneven distributions of land and livestock in each of the villages, with more skewed distributions in the most densely populated areas. Owako believed that agriculture would not be able to continue to support the growing population of Machakos District, and that a landless class would evolve which supported itself through non-agricultural activities and professions.

The current research sought to investigate temporal processes of change, and was carried out between January and May 1996, involving a survey of households from Ndueni village, followed by rapid rural appraisal work conducted in Iveti, Masii and Kangundo, and archival research in Nairobi. For the purposes of comparison, fieldwork in Ndueni followed the door-to-door sampling procedure adopted by Owako, but utilized improved methods of field measurement and crop and income recording. In this way the current survey was able to conduct questionnaires in 180 households in Ndueni, with only three households refusing to answer the questionnaire. After the questionnaire a stratified sample of 56 households was revisited for more in-depth interviews regarding the results of the first phase of the study. In addition to the data collected by Owako on land and livestock holdings, the present research also elicited information on agricultural and non-farm income, as well as investigating the agricultural labour market.

The study was conducted in Ndueni village, Mbooni location, 35 kilometres from Machakos town (population 80 000) along a dirt road which is often muddy, and occasionally impassable during the rainy seasons. Nairobi is a further 60 kilometres from Machakos, and is the destination of many of the cash crops from the village. Whilst the dominant crops are mixes of maize and beans, export crops such as French beans grown in Mbooni are purchased by export companies and flown out of Nairobi International Airport. Other horticultural produce is trucked down to Nairobi and Mombasa by local traders. Coffee from the area is processed at the Kenya Planters Cooperative Union in Nairobi, as well as at independent millers in adjacent Thika District.

The study village, Ndueni, lies on the side of a highland massif which rises out of the Makueni lowlands. The bottom of the village lies near the valley floor at 1400 metres, whilst the upper parts of Ndueni reach a height of just over 1850 metres. Most of the village is thus quite cool and temperate, and similar to other high-potential areas of Machakos such as Kangundo and Iveti. Rainfall is moderate but unpredictable, with an average of 1250 millimetres a year in a bimodal pattern. The area is of a fairly high agricultural potential, lying between agro-ecological zones 2 and 3, and supporting coffee and rainfed horticulture. Despite this the most widely-grown crops are the maize, beans and peas which form the basis of most people's diets. The area also has many zero grazed dairy cows, and sends milk down to the nearby lowlands on a daily basis.

Change in Ndueni

Much of the change seen in Ndueni mirrors the development of the wider area described by Tiffen *et al.* Because of its high agricultural potential, Mbooni (of which Ndueni is a part) was the first area of Machakos or Makueni to be settled by the people of the Akamba tribe, who make up over 95 per cent of the population of the two districts. However, as land grew more scarce in Mbooni, farmers began to move to other hill areas, and thereafter down on to the less well-watered lowlands of Machakos and Makueni.

Just as in the rest of Machakos and Makueni, Ndueni village has been experiencing rapid population growth. Ndueni was first settled by six families from nearby villages in around 1840, and 161 of the 180 households in the village's survey were traced to these original pioneers. This rapid population growth has forced a decrease in the average size of landholdings in Ndueni, as the original holdings carved out by pioneers have been subdivided amongst their descendants. This decline has driven the adoption of more intensive agricultural practices as families seek to maintain agricultural livelihoods.

Crop Patterns

Table 1 shows changes in cropping patterns since Owako's survey in 1965. The main points to note are an increase in the area planted to cash crops such as coffee, and an increase in tree cover (including a big rise in the number of fruit trees, often interplanted with food crops). Other changes seen include a big decrease in the amount of grazing land as it is given over to food and cash crops, and a virtual disappearance of traditional grains such as millet and sorghum.

These aggregate changes appear similar to those described by Tiffen *et al.* However, the household-level data collected in the current survey show how only 57 per cent of farmers have been able to afford the capital necessary for investment in cash crops. In contrast, the abandoning of sorghum and millet has not necessitated capital expenditure, and has been carried out by almost

Table 1

Cropping patterns in Ndueni

Crop	% Area 1965	% Area 1996
Maize, beans, peas	63	63
Grazing and waste land[1]	18	9
Coffee	4	13
Vegetables	4	4
Root crops	2	3
Millet, sorghum	2	negligible
Tobacco	2	none recorded
Tree lots	none recorded	3
Housing	none recorded	3
Others	5	2

Note: [1]Over 4% of the village is covered by expanses of exposed granite which are of little use for either grazing or cultivation, although are used as water collectors for downhill crops.

everyone in the village. Whilst the adoption of crops such as coffee has increased the diversity and the sum of many farmers' income, the move away from traditional grains has led to a reduction in the income diversity of poorer farmers, and increased dependence on only maize and bean cultivation on the smallest farms.

Livestock

Traditionally, it was thought that cattle were kept by the Akamba for the status they conferred, and only more lately for their meat. Stock were grazed in the open and looked after by young men and boys. The period since 1965, however, has seen an almost complete transition towards the zero grazing of cattle. This has allowed the stocking density of cattle per hectare to rise at the same time as land devoted to grazing has fallen. Despite this, cattle numbers have not grown as fast as human populations and there are thus fewer cattle per household. Zero grazing has been accompanied by a widespread transition from traditional breeds to exotic dairy cattle and half breeds, as farmers seek to maximize revenue from the sales of milk, which made up 34 per cent of agricultural income in the village.

These changes are much as described by Tiffen *et al.*, but the current household-level survey shows such changes to have been accompanied by a switching of gender roles, as those aspects of livestock care traditionally associated with women such as foddering and milking have become ever more important as male roles (herding and guarding) have declined. Women have guarded their roles carefully, with the result that livestock are now almost entirely under the care of women, who consequently often control the money from dairy sales.

Terracing

Unlike much of more lowland Machakos, terracing in Mbooni was almost complete by the time of Owako's survey in 1965. As early as 1955 the Divisional Officer for Mbooni was able to report that

Bench terracing has proceeded at an ever greater pace during the year, and I believe it should be possible within only two years to ensure that all cultivation takes place on benches only.

KNA DC/MKS/3/1

The current survey is thus in many ways a study of changes occurring after the environmental transformation described by Tiffen *et al.* (1994). Despite this, terracing has continued to affect the relationship between society and its environment beyond the initial purpose of erosion control. For instance, terracing (together with the decreases in livestock holdings per family) now acts as a brake upon mechanization, and has led to a wide-scale abandonment of previously common technology such as ploughing, and a reversion to more labour intensive technologies such as hoeing. In 1965 over 25 per cent of farmers in the study area owned ploughs; in 1996 the figure was less than two per cent.

The trends outlined above show how, whilst *More People, Less Erosion* was able to overturn many received wisdoms regarding the relations between environmental degradation and population growth, household-level data have been able to reveal a more nuanced picture of change. Erosion control and agricultural intensification have not occurred simply as a result of societal processes, subsequently to exist in isolation from that society; but rather have reacted back in a dialectical way upon consequent economic and societal decisions. Such a process has been charted in sociology by Giddens and industrial geography by Massey, being only more recently applied to development studies by Leach *et al.* Landscape change is a fundamentally political process, and no assessment of environmental transformation is complete without a consideration of the accompanying economic and social change. The rest of the paper uses household-level data to describe more of the social and economic impacts of agricultural intensification.

Findings from Household-level Data Analysis

A significant polarization of wealth has occurred in the village in recent years, largely as a result of farmers' differential ability to tap into sources of urban capital.

In 1965 the poorest fifth of households owned eight per cent of the land whereas by 1996 the figure was three per cent and so the amount of land owned by poor families had decreased. In 1965 the richest quintile of farmers owned 40 per cent of the land, but the figure is now over 55 per cent, and so the amount of land owned by the rich has increased. In absolute terms this means that whilst average landholdings amongst the most landed 20 per cent are currently over 3.4 hectares, those with the smallest 20 per cent of holdings now own an average of only 0.2 hectares of land.

More uneven than the current distribution of land is the very unequal distribution of non-farm income in the village. Whereas the 20 per cent of families earning the most non-farm income controlled 67 per cent of the non-farm income of the village, earning an average of over $102 a month (US$1 = 58 Kenyan Shillings), over 30 per cent of the households in the village earn no non-farm income at all, except for the small amounts they can gain from occasional agricultural wage labour.

It is this differential access to non-farm income that has driven unfavourable changes in the distribution of land holdings and agricultural incomes. This is because land is very expensive in Ndueni and only people with non-farm income can afford to buy it. Irrigated land and land planted to coffee in the village is sold for prices in excess of $3400 per hectare, whilst other plots can expect to fetch around $1700 per hectare. By comparison, casual agricultural labour rates hover at around $0.90 a day when work is available. There is no tradition of rural money lending in Machakos in the same way as exists in parts of West Africa, and thus it is only people with access to income from non-farm employment, and more particularly, the soft loans and credit circles associated with formal sector work, that can afford to buy significant portions of land in the village.

For example, J- M- is one of the biggest landowners in the village, but has so far inherited nothing but an education from his father. He has purchased all his land from the proceeds of loans from his job as a Store Manager at the Ministry of Water in Machakos. Similarly, N- M- is a local entrepreneur who buys vegetables at the local market and then transports them down to Mombasa for sale. The profits from this trade have funded the acquisition of over 90 per cent of Nzasi's 16 hectares of land—the largest holding in the village. Thus whilst Owako thought that those taking up urban professions would be the rural poor, it appears that it is those households who have secured significant non-farm incomes who have been able to accumulate the most land in the countryside.

High earners are, therefore, climbing up the village land-holding scale from whatever position they started at because they have access to loans and credit to help them buy land. Indeed a limited reversal in the village wealth hierarchy has occurred over the last 50 years, as in the early colonial period it tended to be the sons of the poorest farmers (who had no cattle to provide a livelihood) who were the first to be sent to schools, and who then proceeded to buy land with the income from their urban jobs. For instance M-M-'s father was poor and had very little land or livestock. The clan (a form of extended family) sent M- to school, after which he secured a job driving road graders for the colonial administration. His wages enabled him to buy a lot of land before he retired.

In the past, farmers who made distress sales of land to people like M- were able, if things got too difficult in Mbooni, to migrate down to the lowlands where they could settle new land of lower agricultural potential. In this sense, many of the very poorest people from Ndueni are no longer there any more, but have been spun out of the upland system. However, such migration to escape poverty is no longer feasible for the poorest families in Mbooni, owing to the rising costs of migration and the closure of the land settlement frontier. Such people are now forced to remain in the uplands farming micro-scale holdings often less than 0.2 of a hectare.

The Productivity of Agriculture

According to the Boserup hypothesis, the decline in farm sizes occurring as a result of population growth and also, amongst the poorest families in Ndueni, owing to distress sales of land to richer farmers, should be offset by an increase in the productivity of agriculture per hectare, thereby preventing food availability decline. However, just as non-farm income has allowed farmers to invest in the quantity of land that they own, it is also becoming an increasingly necessary part of investment in the productivity of the land, with those farmers unable to purchase manure or artificial fertilizers struggling to maintain (let alone improve) the productivity of land per hectare with additional labour inputs alone. Average maize yields in Ndueni have fallen from 14.8 bags (90 kilograms per bag) per hectare in 1948 (DC/MKS/18/5) to only 12.3 bags per hectare in 1996. This decline has occurred despite the adoption of improved seed varieties and farming techniques such as planting before the rain, suggesting an inherent fall in the fertility of the soil.

Land in many parts of Mbooni has been cultivated for over 200 years. In the last 30 or so of these years, many fields have been continuously cultivated without breaks for fallow. Using the spatial analogue soil survey technique adopted by Tiffen *et al.*, a soil survey in the village showed that concentrations of soil nutrients in fields which had never received applications of manure or fertilizer were less than in non-cultivated areas or sites where such productivity investments regularly took place. Thus for poorer farmers in the village without access to livestock or non-farm income 'More People' may have meant 'Less Erosion', but it did not guarantee 'More Productivity'. The families which were found to be most able to invest in the maintenance and improvement of soil productivity were those earning significant quantities of non-farm income, with the result that those families who were most prosperous off the farm, were also likely to be the most prosperous on the farm. This can be demonstrated by looking at the maize yields achieved by farmers in Ndueni, whereby a significant positive correlation ($r = 0.155$, significant $r = 0.123$ at 0.05 uncertainty) exists between non-farm income and maize yields.

More significant is the inverse relationship between maize yields and area planted ($r = -0.284$, significant $r = 0.231$ at 0.001 uncertainty), a relationship observed elsewhere by Sen and Hill. This inverse pattern reflects the more careful and labour intensive cultivation practices of farmers with microholdings, and has presumably existed in Mbooni ever since land shortages began. However, the trend is bucked by the higher yields obtained by the farmers planting the very largest amounts of maize and using more capital inputs. The five largest planters in the village achieved average yields of over 20 bags a hectare—raising the figure for the richest quintile, and creating a reverse 'J' distribution. What this suggests is that whilst Sen's theory is correct for the majority of smallholders, there now exists a small group of very commercial farmers who through their capitalization of production have managed to raise yields above those obtained by most of their more labour intensive peers. This breakdown of the inverse relationship between yields and area as a result of new technology and capital inputs has already been noted by Rahman in Bangladesh, and Lipton and Longhurst in India.

Social and Economic Trends

As a result of shrinking holdings of land due to the population growth and economic polarization described earlier, and, as a result of the static or declining productivity of agriculture on many poorer farms with no non-farm income, over 90 per cent of families are unable to feed themselves throughout the year from the food they harvest from the fields. Fortunately around 60 per cent of households in the village can afford to plant some cash crops, and so can make up a varying proportion of this subsistence gap by selling commodities such as coffee or tomatoes. However, over 40 per cent of farmers are, for between two and ten months of the year, dependent on selling their labour to buy food. For the majority who are unable to find permanent jobs in the towns, this results in participation in rural labour markets. These labour markets exist to supply the labour required for cash crops such as coffee and French beans grown by the richer farmers. However, when agricultural wage labour is unavailable locally, poor people in Mbooni go hungry.

A recent welfare survey in Makueni by a Danish International Development Agency (DANIDA) group found that malnutrition in the district was highest in Mbooni, despite the abundant greenery and horticultural exports. Food availability in Mbooni obviously does not equate easily with food entitlements. In contrast, the dryer but more sparsely populated lowlands enjoyed greater food security. This is counter-intuitive, even to people in other parts of Machakos and Makueni. Thus when a local councillor, T- M-, made a request for food aid for Mbooni at a District council meeting he was told 'You councillor, you just keep quiet!'. T- complained about people from other areas:

> Once they see all these trees (in Ndueni) they think that we are quite alright here—but trees are never eaten. At times the experts come and they go to (the local) market and they find a lot of sukumawiki (a local vegetable), cabbages and somebody goes away thinking that everybody has (food), while others living in the same area, unless they reach deeper into their pockets cannot even afford sukumawiki for a day.

Whilst these processes do show differentiation, only more recently has such differentiation been accompanied by class formation and diminishing social mobility. Before the late 1970s it was still relatively easy for members of even the poorest families to obtain an education and subsequently secure employment. Indeed, some of the richest people in the village today are old men from what were very poor families, who were sent to school by their clans, and who then accumulated land from the proceeds of their jobs, just as in the case of M- M- described earlier. However, as a result of recent economic reforms raising the costs of education and the concomitant decline of the clan as an institution of welfare support, poorer families are increasingly unable to afford an education for their children at the same time as educational requirements for jobs have been increasing. Consequently children from poor families are finding it more difficult to escape from poverty by working in the towns in the way that their forebears did in the past, and an undeniable element of structure is building up in society.

The Growing Importance of Capital in Agricultural Innovation and Environmental Conservation

The non-farm economy of Mbooni is largely focused around remittances from migrant labour in Machakos town and Nairobi. In a similar way, many of the other examples of high population density and sustainable intensive cultivation in Africa are to be found near major urban centres such as Kano. Without the widespread availability of such urban capital agricultural intensification may take an involutory path of diminishing returns to effort. It is in this context that Haugerud acknowledges how the economic sustainability of rural Embu has only been maintained by becoming an 'outpost' of the wider Nairobi and Kenyan economy.

Agricultural intensification and conservation technology in Mbooni appear to have come in two waves, with 'second phase' technologies being increasingly dependent upon inputs of (urban derived) capital. Whilst almost everyone has adopted those first phase intensification practices that required no monetary inputs and only labour (such as terracing and mulching), second phase agricultural practices which require capital availability (such as manuring or the use of inorganic fertilizer) have been adopted only by those that can afford them. Families without access to such capital are, therefore, experiencing a detrimental and involutionary cycle of declining yields, declining soil fertility and diminishing returns to labour, as first phase conservation and productivity gains are overtaken by population growth. As one poorer respondent noted 'in the past there was a desire for more people, but now there is a fear'.

Thus Boserupian intensification on richer farms, and a form of Geertzian involution on poorer farms are seen to be proceeding side by side within the same village. At a village level, if the demands of population growth increase faster than the supply of capital to meet those demands through investments in productivity and new cash crops, then the village will tend further down the involutionary path of declining yields and returns to labour.

In such a situation, the importance of non-farm income becomes twofold. Richer farms use non-farm income to make productive investments in agriculture, and so 'straddle' the urban and rural economies. Poorer households, on the other hand, are forced to use non-farm income to make up shortfalls in food needs, after which they often have very little investible surplus to put into agricultural production. Only greater access to land or non-farm income will enable escape from this trap. By contrast, continued population growth is increasing land hunger still further, and consequently inflating the numbers of people looking for non-farm employment in a slowing Kenyan economy. More people chasing a static number of jobs will only serve to push down the value of wages in real terms, and further reduce the ability of local farmers to 'straddle' the rural and urban economies.

Conclusions—Wealth Comes From the City

Having studied in the area of the ODI project 'More People Less Erosion', this research can agree with many of the findings of the ODI project regarding the environmental effects of agricultural intensification and can also agree that it has come about as a result of people's profitable responses to market opportunities. However as a result of its focus on household-level processes, the new study is able to show that there has been a polarization of landholdings in the study village, driven largely by differential access to urban wages and capital. The application of such capital to production on the land, has resulted in those who earn the most off the land earning the most on the land as well. Recent changes have accelerated this process, and made it more difficult for the poorest farmers to enjoy upward social mobility.

Whilst these findings cannot be unproblematically extrapolated to other areas undergoing agricultural intensification, this study is not alone in observing increasing differentiation in such an area. A recent study in the Kabale region of Uganda by Lindblade *et al* also noted a polarization of wealth, as did Haugerud in Embu, Kenya. In Rwanda, André and Platteau graphically chart the role of extreme land hunger and differentiation in fuelling the recent genocide. However, what is clear in Machakos at least, is that increasing inequality has not arisen, by and large, as a result of exploitation of the poorest farmers by a local bourgeoisie within rural labour markets; as has been shown to be the case in areas of India. Rather, such agricultural labour (generated by richer farmers growing new labour-intensive crops such as coffee and French beans) creates a lifeline to poorer households in the area, enabling them to cling onto their stake in the rural economy.

Polarization, appears to have been driven by the application of, and differential access to, the 'investible surplus' from non-farm income. Whilst this is largely a function of non-farm income, it cannot be divorced entirely from the existing distribution of landholdings within the village. Farmers with the most land are likely to spend less of their income making up subsistence shortfalls, and thus will be able to utilize a greater proportion of their non-farm income to buy land and invest upon it. Obtaining non-farm income in this way helps smaller farmers to hold their economic ground in the face of increased pressures stemming from population growth. In contrast, those who fail to tap into new income streams are deriving diminishing returns from ever smaller pieces of land, lacking as they do the capital to intensify productively.

For many poorer families then, the environmental sustainability charted by Tiffen *et al.* has not been accompanied by a similar economic sustainability, with the implication that ecological and economic sustainability ought to be decoupled in the manner suggested by Mortimore and Munasinghe. Furthermore, the wealth and investment capital of many of the richer families in Ndueni has come from the city, with the implication that proponents of rural development ought to be looking to create not more rural 'Machakoses' but more urban 'Nairobies'. In the absence of greatly increased capital availability for investment in agricultural productivity, population growth will continue to drive many households in Ndueni along an involutionary spiral of poverty amidst green and terraced fields.

POSTSCRIPT

Is Food Production in Africa Capable of Keeping Up with Population Growth?

An interesting aspect of Mortimore and Tiffen's Machakos story was this rural community's ability to positively engage with the market. This is also a key point that Murton makes, as it is those households with nonfarm incomes who are most successful at agricultural intensification. This stands in contrast to a large amount of Africanist scholarship, which sees interaction with the global market as extremely problematic. Boserup herself, whose theory was described in the introduction, and whose ideas drove both of these studies, saw the market as a potential stumbling block. Her concern was that employment opportunities elsewhere would draw off enough labor that the intensification process would be derailed. This concern is not entirely unfounded in the African context where labor (often more than land) is frequently the key constraint to agricultural production. Both Mortimore and Tiffen, as well as Murton, suggest that nonfarm income seems to more than compensate for any loss of labor in Machakos. What is crucial, however, is that households are willing to continually invest in this area. In other African contexts, labor constraints and lack of investment have been much more pronounced. See, for example, Jeffrey Alwang and P.B. Siegal's article in the August 1999 issue of *World Development* entitled "Labor Shortages on Small Landholdings in Malawi: Implications for Policy Reforms."

Murton is not alone in his criticism of Mortimore and Tiffen's analysis of the Machakos situation (but his study is an ideal match for this issue as it occurred in the same locale). Diane Rocheleau was actually the first scholar to articulate (in published form) the concern that Mortimore and Tiffen did not address properly the problem of economic differentiation over time (i.e., a growing gap between the rich and poor). For an excellent, and concise, articulation of this concern, see Rocheleau's September 1995 piece in the journal *Environment* entitled "More on Machakos." The same issue of the journal also carries a response to Rocheleau by Tiffen and Mortimore. Many other scholars have also sought to critically examine the relationship between population growth and agricultural change in African situations. For example, Thomas Conelly and Miriam Chaiken, in a 2000 article in *Human Ecology* entitled "Intensive Farming, Agro-Diversity, and Food Security Under Conditions of Extreme Population Pressure in Western Kenya," study an area in Western Kenya with similarly high population densities. Despite the wide variety of sophisticated practices that maintain a high level of agro-diversity, they conclude that intense population pressure has led to smaller land holdings, poorer diet quality, and declining food security.

Two final points about Machakos case are worth considering. First, free hold tenure (or private property that may be bought and sold) now prevails in Machakos. This is not the case in many areas of Africa where only use, or usufruct, rights to land are allocated to community members (and, therefore, land may not be bought and sold). Some would view the lack of private property as a problem (because they believe this inhibits investment in land) while others would see the tradition of usufruct rights as beneficial because it may slow down the transfer of land from rich to poor households. Because there are local land and labor markets in Machakos, scholars should also consider how power differences between households might influence these economic transactions.

The second point to consider is that both authors in this issue agree that food production, on average, was able to keep up with population growth in this area. This is analogous to what is happening on the global scale over the same time frame, that is, global food production is keeping up with global population growth. The problem is that not all households are able to keep up and some may not even have the resources to buy available food on the market. This insight has important policy implications as it means that simply developing technologies to produce more food will not solve the problem for everyone (as these technologies, or the food produced, may be inaccessible to poor households). As such, finding ways for poor households to access food (through their own production or purchase) may be as or more important than simply producing more food.

For further reading on this topic, see a volume edited by Turner, Hyden and Kates (*Population Growth and Agricultural Change in Africa*, University Press of Florida, 1993) that includes case studies from around the continent; or an article by Lamdin et al. in the December 2001 issue of *Global Environmental Change* entitled "The Causes of Land-Use and Land-Cover Change: Moving Beyond the Myths." For a more Malthusian perspective, see a book by Cleaver and Schreiber entitled *Reversing the Spiral: The Population, Agriculture, and Environment Nexus in Sub-Saharan Africa* (World Bank, 1994).

ISSUE 11

Are Integrated Conservation and Development Programs a Solution to Conflicts Between Parks and Local People?

YES: William D. Newmark and John L. Hough, from "Conserving Wildlife in Africa: Integrated Conservation and Development Projects and Beyond," *BioScience* (July 2000)

NO: Roderick P. Neumann, from "Primitive Ideas: Protected Area Buffer Zones and the Politics of Land in Africa," *Development and Change* (July 1997)

ISSUE SUMMARY

YES: William D. Newmark, research curator at the Utah Museum of Natural History, University of Utah, and John L. Hough, global environment facility coordinator for biodiversity and international waters for the United Nations Development Programme, acknowledge the limited success of integrated conservation and development programs to date in Africa, but see great promise for success in the future. They call for more adaptive management in which activities are monitored, evaluated, and reformulated in an interactive fashion.

NO: Roderick P. Neumann, associate professor and director of graduate studies in the department of international relations at Florida International University, argues that protected area buffer zone programs have not lived up to their initial intent of greater participation and benefit sharing. Rather, these programs duplicate more coercive forms of conservation practice associated with parks and facilitate the expansion of state authority into remote rural areas.

A number of national parks were established in African countries during the colonial era. While these parks ostensibly were established for the preservation of natural resources, they also served to sequester resources for the European population. In the postcolonial era, national park systems have persisted and have been expanded in many instances, particularly in East and Southern Africa where relatively larger numbers of charismatic megafauna still reside. African park systems have been bolstered by a global environmental movement as well as a burgeoning ecotourism industry. In countries such as Kenya, Tanzania, Zimbabwe, Botswana, and South Africa, Western tourists flock to see the "big five," a term used to refer to the biggest, rarest, or most cherished animals traditionally sought after by trophy hunters (elephant, lion, rhinoceros, leopard, and African or Cape buffalo). Nature tourism has become big business. In Kenya, for example, it is the leading source of foreign exchange. Here, Richard Leakey, the former head of the Kenyan Wildlife Service and famous archeologist, had established a shoot-to-kill policy to combat against suspected poachers found in national parks.

The poaching problem is symptomatic of a much deeper set of social issues (numbering at least three) surrounding parks and protected areas in Africa. First, local people often were evicted without compensation from areas where national parks were established. This led to feelings of resentment and compromised livelihoods in many instances; i.e., local people did not have the same resource base to rely on in their new location. Second, feelings of resentment and the inability of many national governments to effectively patrol park borders has led local people to encroach on parks in search of sustenance. Some local people may view parks as open-access resources, i.e., resources with no particular owner (as opposed to private property (belonging to an individual) or common property (controlled by a group)). In the absence of a legitimate controlling force or owner (government may be viewed as an illegitimate force), open access resources tend to be overexploited as everyone tries to maximize their personal gain with little to no regard for the overall ecological health of the resource. Finally, big game animals rarely respect park boundaries and may wander onto the lands of communities abutting national parks. This is problematic because large animals may pose safety risks and destroy field crops. Elephants in particular are known for their ability to inflict a substantial amount of crop damage.

In lieu of the aforementioned problems, a number of conservation programs have been initiated that take into consideration the needs of local people. Part of the incentive for these programs is a genuine concern about the welfare of local people, but there is also recognition that many conservation initiatives, including parks, are doomed to failure unless they enlist the support of local people. A key way of securing such support has been to share ecotourism revenues with local people in exchange for their participation in protecting wildlife resources. Such programs typically work with the communities neighboring national parks and may even involve the establishment of buffer zones (i.e., areas surrounding national parks where the activities of local people are restricted).

In the following selections, William D. Newmark and John L. Hough assert that they see great promise in integrated conservation and development programs in Africa. In contrast, Roderick P. Neumann states that these programs duplicate more forceful forms of conservation practice associated with parks and make possible the increase of state authority in remote rural areas.

William D. Newmark
and John L. Hough

 **YES**

Conserving Wildlife in Africa: Integrated Conservation and Development Projects and Beyond

Conservationists in Africa are struggling to develop new approaches to protect the continent's spectacular natural heritage. The challenge is to design strategies that not only will ensure the long-term viability of species and ecosystems but also will be politically and economically acceptable to local communities and governments. One approach that has gained considerable attention in recent years is the integrated conservation and development project (ICDP), which attempts to link the conservation of biological diversity within a protected area to social and economic development outside that protected area. In ICDPs, incentives are typically provided to local communities in the form of shared decision-making authority, employment, revenue sharing, limited harvesting of plant and animal species, or provision of community facilities, such as dispensaries, schools, bore holes, roads, and woodlots, in exchange for the community's support for conservation.

The ICDP approach to conservation in Africa began in earnest in the 1980s and 1990s, although efforts to link wildlife conservation with local development go back to the 1950s in a few protected areas in Africa, such as Ngorongoro Conservation Area in Tanzania. Currently, much of the funding by major bilateral and multilateral donors to protected areas in Africa is in the form of ICDPs. A recent review (Alpert 1996) suggests that there have been more than 50 such projects in 20 countries.

Given the popularity of ICDPs, it is discouraging that so many reviews (Kiss 1990, Hannah 1992, Wells et al. 1992, Kremen et al. 1994, Western et al. 1994, Barrett and Arcese 1995, Gibson and Marks 1995, Oates 1995, Alpert 1996) indicate that most ICDPs have had only limited success in achieving both conservation and development objectives. Thus, a lively and important debate about the appropriateness of the ICDP model is under way in the conservation and development community (Kramer et al. 1997). Recent critiques of ICDPs in Africa (Kiss 1990, Hannah 1992, Stocking and Perkin 1992, Wells et al. 1992, Kremen et al. 1994, Western et al. 1994, Barrett and Arcese 1995, Gibson and Marks 1995, Oates 1995, Alpert 1996, Hofer et al. 1996) highlight many of the problems associated with these projects. Based on our own field observations in more than 15 African countries and the critiques of other workers, as well as a review of many project proposals, reports, and evaluations, we discuss these problems. In addition, we argue that the lack of success of many ICDPs is attributable in part to a series of erroneous assumptions made frequently by many designers of ICDPs. Finally, we suggest that ICDPs need to be viewed as just one of a variety of tools available to conservationists and development workers, and that both alternatives to ICDPs and tools and techniques that complement ICDPs need to be actively explored.

Rationale for the ICDP Approach

The ICDP approach to conservation in Africa has gained popularity for several reasons. One reason is the recognition that wildlife populations have declined dramatically throughout Africa over the last 30 years, primarily because of habitat loss. Surveys suggest that over 65% of the original wildlife habitat in Africa has been lost (Kiss 1990) as a result of agricultural expansion, deforestation, and overgrazing, which have been fueled by rapid human population growth and poverty. Given the underlying determinants of habitat loss, it has been argued that conservation activities in the field must be intimately linked with development (IUCN 1980).

A second reason for the popularity of ICDPs relates to the challenges of conserving biological diversity within existing protected areas. Throughout Africa, protected areas are becoming increasingly ecologically isolated as a result of agricultural development, deforestation, human settlement, and the active elimination of wildlife on adjacent lands. This phenomenon, in combination with the small size of most protected areas, indicates that in the absence of intensive management, most protected areas in Africa will not be large enough to conserve many species, as illustrated by recent patterns of extinction of large mammals in Tanzanian parks (Newmark 1996) as well as large carnivores in southern and East African protected areas (Woodroofe and Ginsberg 1998). Additionally, rural poverty and external markets will continue to encourage both subsistence and commercial poaching of many species within protected areas. Analysis in Zambia suggests that it costs $200 per km^2 per year to effectively control commercial poaching of species such as elephant and rhinoceros in protected areas (Leader-Williams and Albon 1988). Unfortunately, few, if any, African countries have such financial resources, and central governments are unlikely to allocate significantly more funds for wildlife management in the future, given the many other competing demands for governmental resources. Recognition of these problems has led many workers to argue that the only way to enlarge and link existing protected areas (Newmark 1985, 1996) and control commercial poaching (Owen-Smith 1993) is to develop cooperative relationships with adjacent communities.

A third reason for the popularity of ICDPs is that such programs are perceived as an effective mechanism for addressing problems of social injustice. Protected areas have adversely affected many indigenous people in Africa. For example, all of the large savanna parks of East Africa have been established on former Masai rangelands (Århen 1985, Parkipuny and Berger 1993). Many donors view ICDPs as a means to develop supportive relationships with the communities that must bear much of the social costs of protected areas.

Finally, ICDPs are attractive because of the recognition that past methods of management have been ineffective in curbing poaching and have frequently created confrontational relationships with local communities. The former "fences and fines" approach to conservation is viewed as anachronistic and counterproductive, and many conservationists view the ICDP approach as a valid alternative.

Critiques of ICDPs in Africa

A number of assessments of the effectiveness of ICDPs in Africa have been conducted. Two things are striking about these reviews: the consensus among workers that nearly all ICDPs have either not achieved their objectives or that progress has been modest, at best, and the multiple explanations given for the limited success of ICDPs. These explanations fall into three broad categories: assessment problems, internal constraints, and external forces.

Assessment problems Project evaluators have identified two important constraints that have hindered the objective assessment and demonstration of success of many ICDPs. One is that many projects were at an early stage of implementation when they were assessed. The early evaluations (Kiss 1990, Hannah 1992, Wells et al. 1992) of ICDPs in Africa concluded that success was limited in meeting both conservation and development objectives, but also that most of these projects had not been under way long enough to be fairly evaluated. Reviewers noted that the normal 3–5 year project cycle may be inappropriate for ICDPs, as it was found to be during the 1970s for rural development projects, which required considerably longer project cycles to achieve project objectives. Given that a number of ICDPs in Africa have now been in operation for more than a decade, this issue should be less of a constraint; however, there is as yet little substantive evidence of improvement in success.

A second constraint on assessment is the absence of ecological monitoring. Kremen et al. (1994) examined 36 projects worldwide, 23 of them from Africa, and found that over half of the projects had no ecological monitoring and only two contained a comprehensive ecological monitoring component. The lack of ecological monitoring in most projects has prevented a rigorous evaluation of the impacts of development activities, particularly resource exploitation, on biological diversity. The lack of ecological monitoring has also meant that feedback useful for guiding the future course of project activities is frequently absent (Kremen et al. 1994). Wells et al. (1992) noted that few of the 18 ICDPs they studied in Africa, Asia, and Latin America were able to demonstrate—largely because of the absence of ecological monitoring— that the development activities occurring outside of the protected areas enhanced the conservation of biological diversity within the protected areas.

Internal constraints Project evaluations have also identified four internal constraints common to many ICDPs. First, public goods may not alter the behavior of individuals, as Gibson and Marks (1995) have suggested; they maintain that many ICDPs in Africa will fail in their goal of conservation because the incentives presented to communities are public goods and are insufficient to alter individual behavior. Furthermore, these incentives may have differential effects on different groups within the communities (Noss 1997). Gibson and Marks (1995) also argue that the economic incentives that many ICDPs offer are often ineffective because project designers frequently overlook the social importance of many activities, such as hunting. Metcalfe (1994) also highlights the difficulty of distributing public benefits to individuals as one of the key challenges facing the Communal Areas Management Programme for Indigenous Resources (CAMPFIRE) in Zimbabwe.

A second internal constraint is that the organizational structure of many ICDPs often mimics earlier ineffective colonial structures. Gibson and Marks (1995) suggest that many local people remain disenfranchised from most ICDPs in Africa because the ultimate authority for wildlife continues to reside with the state. They maintain that although a number of ICDPs have devolved authority over wildlife to local communities, that authority is limited and local communities should have greater control over the use of wildlife. Most wildlife departments accept the rhetoric of such a change in approach, but they can find it difficult to effect that change because doing so demands new sets of skills, a shift from competitive to collaborative relationships with other agencies and institutions, and changes in the internal institutional culture (Hough 1994a). These difficulties have been problematic for ICDPs in Madagascar; government and donor efforts to overcome them have resulted in a number of changes in institutional mandates and structure (Hough 1994a, McCoy and Razafindrainibe 1997).

A third internal constraint is that the offtake associated with many harvesting schemes may be unsustainable over the long term. Barrett and Arcese (1995) and Hofer et al. (1996), for example, have argued that the large mammal harvesting schemes associated with many ICDPs in savanna ecosystems in Africa may be unsustainable because wildlife populations in these ecosystems are inherently variable. They suggest that because managers are frequently under considerable political pressure to maintain a constant flow of benefits (in this case, meat, skins, or revenues) to local communities, they may find it extremely difficult to reduce the offtake when wildlife populations are declining. They also suggest that if wildlife managers do reduce offtake, the project could lose community support. Less work has been done on the sustainability of plant and animal harvesting in nonsavanna biomes in Africa, but some research on woodlands in southern Africa (Shackleton 1993) and forests in East and West Africa (Fa et al. 1995, FitzGibbon et al. 1995, Slade et al. 1998, Wilkie et al. 1998) indicates that the current offtake for many species in those areas is likewise unsustainable.

A fourth internal constraint is that development activities frequently conflict with conservation objectives. In many projects, such conflicts are a result of the inability of managers to effectively control resource exploitation by communities or individuals (Stocking and Perkin 1992), the nonsustainable use of resources, or the ecologically disruptive nature of the development activities. For example, one ICDP in Tanzania placed fish ponds in an important wetland habitat in the East Usambara Mountains. These ponds, although effective in providing additional protein to villagers, severely disrupted scarce riparian habitat (William D. Newmark, personal observation).

External forces   Finally, project evaluations have identified three external forces that adversely affect many ICDPs in Africa. First, sources of potential revenues for communities are usually unreliable and insufficient. Because exchange rate fluctuations and political turmoil often make tourist revenues unreliable, basing cash inducements to communities on tourism is unwise (Barrett and Arcese 1995). The dramatic decline in tourism in recent years in Uganda, Kenya, Comoro Islands, and Zimbabwe highlights the high vulnerability of this industry to political unrest and economic downturns. Additionally, as Barrett and Arcese (1995) noted, there are few protected areas in Africa where the revenues from gate receipts exceed the cost of management; thus, it is unlikely that many communities will ultimately benefit from such revenue-sharing practices. Furthermore, as Norton-Griffiths and Southey (1995) have pointed out, if opportunity costs are taken into account, protected areas and their buffer zones may impose economic penalties on their surrounding communities that far outweigh any potential financial advantages from revenue-sharing arrangements.

Second, external market forces are increasingly manipulating resource use patterns in Africa. The urbanization that is taking place in Africa has created a growing demand in many cities and towns for resources such as meat, timber, and firewood (Barrett and Arcese 1995). These urban markets will produce increasingly strong market incentives to exploit rural natural resources, which could circumvent or undermine ICDP activities. For example, regional urban market forces have encouraged the commercial poaching of large mammals in and around Serengeti National Park for meat (Hofer et al. 1996): Between 1970 and 1992, the population of Cape buffalo in Serengeti National Park declined between 50% and 90% over portions of their range (Campbell and Borner 1995, Hofer et al. 1996). Similarly, Hannah et al. (1998) found that distant market forces have had significant negative impacts on the success of ICDPs in Madagascar.

Third, ICDP development activities may induce migration into the project area (Wells et al. 1992, Barrett and Arcese 1995, Noss 1997). Evidence for such in-migration comes from other rural development projects in Africa. For example, a United Nations–supported irrigation project that was initiated in the early 1980s near Lake Manyara in Tanzania was largely responsible for the 40% growth in population in the area between 1978 and 1988 (Yanda and Mohamed 1990).

Why ICDPs' Success Has Been Limited

There are, in our opinion, several overarching factors responsible for the limited success of ICDPs in Africa. These include erroneous assumptions, unintended social relationships, and inadequate knowledge about the project environment.

Erroneous assumptions   That local communities are hostile to protected areas, that raising living standards will inevitably result in conservation, and that buffer zones are panaceas have proved to be erroneous assumptions that are detrimental to the success of ICDPs. Because protected areas in Africa have historically excluded local people and have a colonial legacy (Anderson and Grove 1987, Neumann 1998), it is generally assumed that these areas are surrounded by hostile communities and enjoy little, if any, support among local people (Lusigi 1981, Wells 1996). The attitudinal research that has been conducted in Africa indicates that this assumption is overly simplistic.

Surveys in South Africa (Infield 1988), Rwanda (Harcourt et al. 1986), Tanzania (Newmark and Leonard 1991, Newmark et al. 1993), and Nigeria (Ite 1996) have found that an overwhelming majority of people living adjacent to protected areas in these countries agreed on the need for the protected area or were opposed to abolishing the parks or making them available for agriculture. On the other hand, surveys showed that most people living adjacent to protected areas in South Africa (Infield 1988), Botswana (Parry and Campbell 1992), and Tanzania (Newmark et al. 1993) held negative or neutral attitudes toward managers of protected areas. Furthermore, surveys in South Africa, Botswana, and Tanzania found that local people's support or opposition to protected areas, managers of protected areas, and wildlife is based on utilitarian values (Infield 1988, Mordi 1991, Parry and Campbell 1992, Newmark et al. 1993). In these countries, local people expressed support for protected areas because national parks and related reserves protect important watersheds, generate foreign exchange, or maintain critical hydrological functions. Similarly, local people expressed support for wildlife primarily because wildlife is viewed as a source of food. However, those who held negative or neutral attitudes toward managers of protected areas did so because they felt that managers provided few services or benefits for their communities.

Thus, the documented instances of the unpopularity of ICDPs with local people (e.g., the Cross River National Park project in Nigeria; Ite 1996) and the overall lack of success of many ICDPs do not result from local people's opposition to conservation or protected areas per se. Rather, they are a result, in part, of the inherent limited capacity of ICDPs and—in the eyes of many local people—managers of protected areas to provide sufficient tangible incentives to alter the attitudes and behavior of local people toward the ICDPs (see, e.g., Ferraro and Kramer 1997, McCoy and Razafindrainibe 1997).

A second erroneous assumption of the ICDP model is that improving the living standards of people living adjacent to protected areas will necessarily enhance conservation within the protected area (Wells et al. 1992, Wells 1996). Studies of conservation attitudes of people in South Africa (Infield 1988) and Tanzania (Newmark and Leonard 1991, Newmark et al. 1993) have found a positive correlation between affluence and conservation attitudes, but it is unlikely that an improvement in the living standards of communities near protected areas will inevitably lead to enhanced long-term viability of many species within the protected areas. For example, although providing employment to local people in Zambia improved living standards and reduced hunting pressures on species in protected areas (Lewis et al. 1990), such correlations do not always hold. Ferraro and Kramer (1997) found that the hiring of poachers at Ranomafana National Park in Madagascar actually increased levels of poaching because these new employees used their earnings to hire more people to expand their poaching operations. It is also unclear whether species in protected areas that are threatened indirectly by habitat loss outside of these reserves, perhaps by agricultural intensification, would be helped by an improvement in the living standards of local communities. Thus, encouraging landscape-wide compatible land use adjacent to protected areas may be more important for conserving species in protected areas than simply stimulating local economic development.

A third erroneous assumption is that buffer zones are panaceas. These management zones are promoted frequently in many ICDPs as peripheral areas where living conditions of local communities are to be enhanced through selective resource use and where habitat degradation will be reduced through habitat restoration. However, it is unclear how those goals are to be achieved: None of the ICDPS that promote the use of buffer zones have explained how an already overexploited area can be used to increase productivity and provide additional habitat for wildlife (Little 1994).

Unintended social relationships   Aside from the problems caused by problematic assumptions underlying the ICDP approach are those that stem from ICDPs' creation of unintended social relationships with local communities. In the effort to win the support of local communities for conservation, ICDPs frequently share park revenues, provide employment, or permit access to plant and animal resources. However, most provide only nominal opportunities for community-wide participation and often fail to link development benefits directly to community conservation obligations. The result is that many ICDPs may unintentionally promote dependency rather than reciprocity and have often treated local communities as recipients of aid rather than partners in development.

Inadequate knowledge about the project environment   Finally,   in   our opinion, many ICDPs have had limited success because the social and ecological environment surrounding the project is often poorly understood and dynamic. This inadequate understanding of the project environment has contributed greatly to the difficulty in transferring seemingly successful components of ICDPs from one region to another. In most ICDPs, scientific input is normally limited to a "rapid" preproject ecological and social appraisal of the project area. However, these appraisals, by their very nature, have a limited capacity to capture the complex ecological and social (Gezon 1997) relationships that surround most projects. Moreover, they provide a tenuous baseline for subsequent project monitoring, assessment, and adaptation.

ICDP designers are often reluctant to incorporate a significant research component into these projects. Part of this reticence stems from the crisis nature of most conservation initiatives: Research is often viewed as a hindrance to action and an expensive luxury. Yet incorporating a significant research component into ICDPs is essential if the ecological and social dynamics encompassing each project are to be accurately defined and if conservation and development are to be truly integrated.

Lessons Learned

Several lessons can be drawn from our own and others' observations. One is that multiple ecological, social, political, economic, and institutional problems confront ICDPs. Not only are ICDPs themselves complex, but so is the environment in which they operate. However, ICDPs seem to rarely build in mechanisms for analyzing and adapting to these changes. Furthermore, project designers and scientists' understanding of the mechanisms governing this environment is generally inadequate. For example, little is known about the long-term primary and secondary impacts of resource harvesting on the structure and function of most tropical ecological communities. Similarly, many social scientists counsel that it is unwise to devolve total authority to local communities (West and Brechin 1991), but little is known about how much authority over the use of natural resources should be transferred to local communities or how to ensure that project benefits are equitably distributed and not captured by local elites (Lutz and Caldecott 1996). A second lesson, related to the first one, is that more thorough, and ongoing, ecological and social assessment and analysis is required, both during the design phase of ICDPs and during their implementation.

A third lesson is that project planners need to examine in more detail the effects of external factors such as markets, land tenure, and population growth on proposed project activities. ICDPs may need to include project components or explicit linkages to other initiatives, which address external constraints well beyond the limited geographic focus of the ICDP. For example, efforts to control commercial meat poaching in protected areas may require not only upgraded law enforcement within protected areas and improved grazing management in the buffer zones but also favorable pricing and marketing systems for domestic livestock in distant urban areas.

A fourth lesson is that although linking conservation with development may be desirable, the simultaneous achievement of these two objectives may be impossible because of inherent contradictions. In these cases, success may be enhanced by addressing each of these objectives separately but in parallel, tightly linked interventions, rather than within the same project. Decoupling these two objectives does not negate the importance of development to conservation and conservation to development; rather, it implies that protected-area organizations, which have been responsible for implementing most ICDP rural development activities so far, should delegate these activities to organizations with the appropriate mandate, expertise, and experience. The implications are that protected-area institutions should serve more as facilitators than as implementers of rural development activities, although they must work closely with local communities to attract assistance that addresses the needs of local communities without adversely affecting the protected areas. Some protected-area institutions, such as the Kenya Wildlife Service and Tanzania's Division of Wildlife, appear to have already adopted this approach for revenue-sharing schemes between protected areas and local communities, but it needs to be extended to cover the full range of development activities. Another implication of decoupling conservation and development objectives is that an ongoing mechanism is needed within ICDPs for negotiating the compromises and seeking out the win–win solutions that meet both conservation and development needs.

Future Direction?

Several immediate challenges need to be addressed in designing future conservation initiatives in Africa. One is the need to develop mechanisms for ensuring that ICDPs respond to the real complexity of their ecological and social environments and that they effectively monitor, analyze, and adapt to this environment as it changes.

A second challenge is the need to assess, implement, and evaluate alternative and complementary approaches to ICDPs that address the external forces affecting ICDPs through actions such as economic and land-tenure policy reform, landscape-wide conservation planning, conflict resolution, community-based natural resources management, and enhanced management capacity of protected-area institutions. Although project experience with and evaluation of these approaches is insufficient for a rigorous assessment of their overall effectiveness in comparison to (or as complements of) ICDPs, some preliminary observations can be considered now.

- **Economic and land tenure policy reform.** Such reforms can greatly assist in reducing external environmental pressures on protected areas, particularly external market forces and in-migration. For example, the international ban on ivory trading has significantly reduced elephant poaching throughout Africa.
- **Landscape-wide conservation planning.** Given that most protected areas in Africa are small and that many are becoming ecologically isolated, it is important that land-use activities that are compatible with wildlife conservation be encouraged on a landscape-wide scale adjacent to protected areas, and activities that are incompatible must be actively discouraged. It is particularly important that land use be controlled within wildlife corridors linking existing protected areas as well as within wildlife dispersal zones. In most savanna ecosystems in Africa, pastoralism is considerably more compatible with wildlife conservation than agriculture; thus, efforts should be made to maintain existing pastoral systems adjacent to protected areas. Similarly, for use adjacent to protected areas in tropical forest ecosystems, native hardwood plantations and multilayer perennial agroforestry are better choices than agricultural monocultures and pastoralism (Thiollay 1995, Perfecto et al. 1996, Greenberg et al. 1997).
- **Conflict resolution.** Promoting dialogue between managers of protected areas and local communities, involving affected stakeholders in protected-area project planning and implementation, identifying areas of common interest between protected areas

and local communities, and including community representatives on advisory management boards for protected areas can greatly assist in reducing conflicts between parks and local people (Hough 1988, Lewis 1996). Such programs are attractive not only because they are relatively easy to implement but also because they are fairly inexpensive. Recent conflict resolution initiatives in areas adjacent to the Bwindi Impenetrable and Mgahinga Gorilla National Parks in Uganda indicate that such activities can greatly reduce tensions between local communities and park authorities (Wild and Mutebi 1996).

- **Community-Based Natural Resources Management (CBNRM).** Considerable success in generating compatible land-use regimes around protected areas has been claimed in Zambia, Zimbabwe, and Namibia through the use of CBNRM approaches, the most notable of which is the CAMPFIRE program (Murphree 1993, Metcalfe 1994). CBNRM differs from the normal ICDP approach in that, instead of offering development services in exchange for conservation, it devolves management responsibility for natural resources—wildlife—to local communities. Its success depends on communities seeing more value in managing their wildlife on a long-term sustainable basis than in pursuing short-term exploitation or alternative land uses. Yet a number of scientists associated with these projects believe that local communities will eventually be forced to forsake wildlife conservation for more intensive agriculture development because of demographic and social pressures (Hackel 1999). Therefore, complete devolution of authority to local communities may be unwise (West and Brechin 1991).

- **Enhancing the management capacity of protected-area institutions.** The capacity of most African protected-area institutions to address complex interactions between protected areas and local communities is limited (Hough 1994a, 1994b). The development of scholarships, courses, exchange programs, training manuals, and technical assistance that focus on ecological and social monitoring, conflict resolution, park planning, and modern law enforcement techniques would greatly enhance the capacity of protected-area institutions to address many of the protected-area–local community conflicts.

Although ICDPs in Africa have had only limited success, we feel that a refined ICDP approach may be appropriate in some circumstances, especially when protected areas and local communities are highly codependent; that is, when local communities control the habitat abutting protected areas—habitat that is vital to the long-term viability of protected-area species and ecological processes—and protected areas control resources used historically by local communities, the use of which could be managed to be both sustainable and ecologically nondisruptive. An argument for an ICDP is compelling in this case because, unlike most of the alternative approaches discussed above, an ICDP can simultaneously address issues of conservation and development on the ground.

However, the ICDP approach needs to be both refined and enhanced. Improvements to the ICDP model include increasing flexibility and enhancing the use of adaptive management, which is a process by which management activities in a complex biophysical and social environment are monitored, evaluated, and reformulated in an iterative fashion so as to evaluate alternative hypotheses, accumulate knowledge about the system, and reassess long-term objectives (Holling 1978, Walters 1986). Central to this approach is the formulation of well-articulated objectives and the rigorous testing of management activities, which typically entails incorporating adequate samples, replicates, and controls. Additional refinements of the ICDP model should include the incorporation of a comprehensive ecological and social monitoring component; a more rigorous assessment of resource-harvesting schemes; more use of ecological and social research as a basis for identifying and addressing the ecological, social, and economic links that affect ICDPs; and the recognition that protected-area institutions need to act as facilitators of development assistance.

Obviously, effective conservation of wildlife in Africa and elsewhere will depend on the willingness and capacity of both national institutions and donors to embrace a broad package of interventions. These interventions might well be applied in conjunction with improved ICDPs on a landscape-wide scale.

NO ↩

Roderick P. Neumann

Primitive Ideas: Protected Area Buffer Zones and the Politics of Land in Africa

Introduction

The objective of this article is to critically evaluate the conceptualization and implementation of participatory, integrated conservation and development programmes in Africa. The focus of the paper is directed specifically at the interventions of international NGOs [nongovernmental organizations] into rural land use and access in communities bordering protected areas. These interventions are planned and implemented by conservation organizations such as the World Conservation Union (IUCN) and the World Wide Fund for Nature (WWF), headquartered in Europe and North America and operating on a global scale. The conservation programmes of these organizations are in turn increasingly funded by bi-lateral and multi-lateral donors like the World Bank, the European Community, and various national agencies from the First World. The geographic extent of protected areas alone would make an examination of international interventions crucial: nine African countries, including Namibia, Tanzania, the Central African Republic and Botswana, have 9 per cent or more of their land under strict protection in national parks and game reserves. Tanzania's total of nearly 130,000 km^2 exceeds the combined territories of Holland, Slovakia and Switzerland.

It is not merely the size of the land area under question, however, that makes an analysis of conservation interventions important. Efforts by conservation NGOs to include the lands surrounding protected areas as buffer zones under the jurisdiction of the state have major implications for the politics of land. In the cases of the international conservation interventions under examination, land politics can be viewed as operating at two geographical scales. The first is global: it raises questions about the relations of power between rural communities in Africa and international conservation NGOs, and about how power relations between local communities and the state are affected by global environmental agendas. In their conceptualization, global conservation strategies tend to gloss over the magnitude of political changes involved and invest international conservation groups and allied states with increased authority to monitor and investigate rural communities. Recent studies indicate that pro-

From Roderick P. Neumann, "Primitive Ideas: Protected Area Buffer Zones and the Politics of Land in Africa," *Development and Change*, vol. 28, no. 3 (July 1997). Copyright © 1997 by The Institute of Social Studies. Notes and references omitted.

grammes attempting to integrate conservation with development serve to extend state power into remote and formerly neglected rural areas. The second scale at which land politics are affected is at the intra-community level. Many of the programmes and projects under review here emphasize land registration and tenure reform in general as key to stimulating the adoption of more resource-conserving land use in buffer zones. Research indicates that land conflict in rural Africa has often been heightened by land tenure reform and registration efforts. Conservation interventions will therefore undoubtedly engage with and influence ongoing negotiations and struggles over land ownership and access within communities. . . .

The 'New' Approach to Conservation in Africa

Calls to include 'local participation' and 'community development' as part of a comprehensive strategy for biodiversity protection in Africa are now ubiquitous, with organizations ranging from the World Bank to grassroots human rights activists offering endorsements. In outlining its lending policies, the World Bank emphasized that it would seek to integrate 'forest conservation projects with . . . macroeconomic goals' and involve 'local people in forestry and conservation management'. Writing for the World Conservation Union (IUCN), Oldfield asserted that 'new ideas are needed' in biodiversity conservation because '[l]ocal people all too often see parks as government-imposed restrictions on their traditional rights'. In short, the redistribution of the material benefits of conservation and the resolution of conflicts between conservationists and local communities are central elements in a purported 'new approach' to conservation in Africa.

The revamped conservation philosophy in Africa is manifested in the proliferation of integrated conservation-development projects (ICDPs). ICDPs take various forms, but all embody the idea that conservation and development are mutually interdependent and must be linked in conservation planning. An important rationalization for these initiatives is that 'conservation policies will work only if local communities receive sufficient benefits to change their behavior from taking wildlife to conserving it'. In other words, 'the basic notion of an exchange of access for material consideration is central to ICDPs'. 'Benefits' to local communities include those directly related to wildlife management (wages, income, meat), social services and infrastructure (clinics, schools, roads), and political empowerment through institutional development and legal strengthening of local land tenure. Additionally, ICDPs are often linked with cultural survival efforts and thus seek to incorporate indigenous knowledge and practices in conservation management. Indigenous peoples, so the argument goes, have been living sustainably in relatively undisturbed habitats for generations and can thus be active participants in implementing conservation policy.

The main features of ICDPs are embodied in protected area buffer zones, a particular land use designation that is gaining increasing currency within conservation circles in Africa. Government and non-government conservation officials support buffer zones as an ideal means to promote environmental protection while simultaneously improving socio-economic conditions on reserve boundaries.

Buffer zones are now included in virtually all protected area plans and are viewed, along with other participatory ICDPs, as the key strategy for the future of biodiversity maintenance in Africa. The buffer zone idea is most directly traceable to UNESCO's 'Man and the Biosphere Programme' (MAB) biosphere reserve model, first proposed in 1968. There are now numerous published definitions for buffer zones. Generally they are lands adjacent to parks and reserves where human activities are restricted to those which will maintain the ecological security of the protected area while providing benefits to local communities. Though ecological and biological concerns have typically driven conservationists' designs for buffer zones and related strategies, they are increasingly presented as a means to strengthen local land and resource claims. The buffer zone idea originally entailed the legal demarcation of boundaries which would separate land uses in transitional stages, though sometimes authors use the term less discriminatingly.

Much of the writing on buffer zones has been light on analysis and evaluation, tending to be more 'philosophical and prescriptive'. At the foundation of this 'philosophy' is the notion that conservation will not succeed unless local communities participate in management of and receive material benefits from protected areas. Participation in buffer zones can best be accomplished by first securing local people's rights to land and resources. Writing in a World Bank Technical Paper, Cleaver argues that a 'key to success in better forest management [in Africa] will be local people's participation . . . This is best done through their ownership of land and of resources on the land . . . '. An additional rationale for supporting tenure reform as part of conservation planning is 'that private investment in environmental protection increases with security of tenure'. Thus, many new conservation proposals seek to integrate land surveying, titling, and registration efforts to improve land tenure security for buffer zone residents.

The issue of local land tenure in buffer zones is also seen to converge with cultural survival/indigenous rights efforts among conservationists and development experts. Writing for the IUCN, Oldfield suggests that where 'tribal and indigenous peoples' have customary land and resource rights, 'buffer zones should be established by vesting title to the lands with the local communities at the level of either the village or ethnic group'. Similarly, Cleaver recommends that '[w]here traditional authority still exists, group land titles or secure long-term user rights should be provided'. Rather than individual titling, most proposals suggest group titling to communities, so that '[l]and within the community can continue to be allocated according to customary practice'. In general, the policy rhetoric of institutions and organizations such as the IUCN and the World Bank presents indigenous land rights as complementing the goals of ICDPs.

A Kinder, Gentler Conservation?

Despite the sympathetic treatment of local land rights and emphasis on benefit sharing by buffer zone proponents, land alienations and local impoverishment seemingly continue apace. Many of the projects sound alarmingly similar to the fortress-style approach to protected areas which they supposedly replace. There are more reports of forced relocations, curtailment of resource access, abuses of power by conservation authorities, and increased government surveillance, than of successful integrations of local people into conservation management. Rather than representing a new approach, many buffer zone projects and other ICDPs more closely resemble colonial conservation practices in their socio-economic and political consequences. In actuality, many buffer zones constitute a geographical *expansion* of state authority beyond the boundaries of protected areas and into rural communities. Given the already substantial proportion of land placed in protected areas across Africa, the potential for spatially extending the reach of the state is tremendous. A few examples will illustrate.

In Madagascar, proposals to integrate conservation with rural development in buffer zones in fact involve new forms of state intervention and restrictions on land use. The Madagascar Environmental Action Plan, developed with the assistance of the World Bank, aims: 'to help farmers to sedentarize and to incite them to invest in the medium term in soil conservation, agroforestry and reforestation . . . To discourage shifting cultivation and other forms of deforestation, via integrated development in the zones surrounding protected areas'. The rationale of the Bank and the Madagascar government is virtually identical to ill-fated colonial efforts across Africa to convert shifting cultivators into 'progressive farmers'. Paradoxically, current conservation advocates, like their colonial predecessors, conceive of *tavy* (the local term for shifting cultivation in Madagascar) not as 'indigenous knowledge' in practice, but as a 'long-lived habit' which must be eliminated. Increased monitoring of land use activities by the state is required to implement conservation agendas in buffer zones. In the country's Mananara Biosphere project, the state has substantially increased the number of forest guards, engaged the support of local police, and placed forestry extension agents with surveillance duties in buffer zone communities. In general, Madagascar's present conservation policies 'stress the need to remove villagers from within protected areas [and] to create larger buffer zones'. At Montagne d'Ambre National Park, the government has recently added a buffer zone which has expanded the park authority's control over village lands and resources. In effect, park management has been 'encroaching upon local forest and land resources'.

In Tanzania, too, several buffer zone projects have been proposed or implemented with similar ramifications for local land and resource control. For instance, a buffer zone project is underway at the Selous Game Reserve, already the largest protected area on the continent at 50,000 km2. In the 1980s, the Selous Conservation Programme was implemented under the aegis of the German organization Deutsche Gesellschaft Für Technische Zusammenarbeit (GTZ) in an attempt to address some of the conflicts between reserve authorities and local communities. A 1988 study produced for GTZ recommended that a buffer zone be established along the perimeter of the game reserve. The authors of the study recommended that within the buffer zone, '[t]he Game Authorities should have the final say. It should not be considered as part of village land'. The government subsequently established a buffer zone encompassing 3630 km^2 of adjacent forest, grazing pasture, and settlement under the jurisdiction of the reserve authorities. Similarly, a proposed buffer zone at Lake Manyara National Park, Tanzania, would be managed by park authorities who would oversee land use. In this case, restrictions on adjacent land uses are seen as essential '[t]o minimize conflicts across boundaries between the Park and adjacent villages'. As a final example, the Serengeti Regional Conservation strategy, on the boundaries of Serengeti National Park, was launched in 1985. The strategy includes three types of buffer zones including 'mandatory' buffer zones. In these areas, the ultimate resolution for land use conflicts is 'the removal of land uses that are incompatible with conservation'.

A final case comes from Cameroon. Korup National Park and its 'support zone' encompass 4500 km2 of tropical rainforest in southwest Cameroon. The implementation of the Korup project, though formulated as a participatory ICDP, has meant an increase in the policing capacity of the state. Consequently, the buffer zone now has a much higher concentration of law enforcement officials than any other nearby government lands. Once again, when compliance with conservation objectives is not forthcoming, eviction and relocation are the ultimate solution. As Colchester points out, 'the same laws that made resettlement from [Korup National Park] necessary would also apply in the buffer zones to which the populations were relocated, making their presence there equally illegal'.

The above cases serve to reveal the relations of power between First World conservationists and rural African communities which are embodied within the new approach to conservation. As long as a 'tradition' of living 'in harmony with nature' is maintained in a manner suitable to buffer zone planners, local communities may remain on the land. However, it is the prerogative of First World conservationists (backed up by the power of the state) to determine whether land uses are compatible with their interests or suitable for the purposes of the buffer zones. A recent IUCN publication uses an example from Nigeria to describe how this works in practice. 'The SZDP [Support Zone Development Programme] and the Park Management Service will thus work closely together to monitor village behaviour, and to administer appropriate "rewards" and "punishments".' . . . In essence, these buffer zone management guidelines call for the geographical expansion of park authority to monitor and regulate the daily lives of local community members and to force compliance through systems of rewards and punishments.

In sum, though the documents of international conservation NGOs present ICDPs and buffer zones as participatory and locally empowering, the power to propose, design, and enforce buffer zones lies far distant from rural African communities. The concept of participation is severely limited and frequently based on an assumption that local indigenous communities live in harmony with their environment. In many proposals which suggest a place for people in buffer zones, the image of the Other as closer to nature is central. This image is best exemplified in an IUCN publication:

> Traditional lifestyles of indigenous people have often evolved in harmony with the local environmental conditions . . . Retaining the traditional lifestyles of indigenous people in buffer zones, where this is possible and

appropriate, will encourage the long-term conservation of tropical forest protected areas. Protecting the rights of local communities ensures that they remain as guardians of the land and prevents the incursion of immigrants with less understanding of the local environment.

'They' belong in buffer zones because they have co-evolved with the environment and will serve as protectors against the incursions of 'outsiders' who have lost that harmonious relationship with nature. Indigenous peoples thus bear a tremendous burden—to demonstrate to outsiders (i.e. Western conservationists) a conservative, even curative, relationship with nature while risking the loss of their land rights should they fail. As Stearman observes, there is a growing danger that indigenous peoples 'must demonstrate their stewardship qualities in order to "qualify" for land entitlements from their respective governments'. Their lifestyles must allow them to do what immigrants and, significantly, Westerners, cannot—produce and reproduce in an ecologically benign way. Conservationists' ideas for indigenous participation in buffer zones are structured by a long history of western notions of the non-western 'primitive'. . . .

Conclusion

. . . First, we need to recognize that past and present conservation policies are complicit in creating the climate of land tenure insecurity within which many rural African communities operate. The establishment of virtually every national park in sub-Saharan Africa required either the outright removal of rural communities or, at the very least, the curtailment of access to lands and resources. As a result buffer zones extend the authority of the park to monitor and restrict land and resource uses of populations already displaced by protected areas. Policies need to be reconceptualized as mechanisms for power-sharing between local communities and state and international institutions rather than as opportunities for extending state control. Research needs to be directed toward identifying and developing institutional mechanisms for controlling access and use of lands and resources that are seen as legitimate by affected communities and that have a detectable effect on conservation goals.

Second, research and policy needs to be directed toward identifying the lines of fracture in rural communities and how segments of the community are differentially and even adversely affected by conservation proposals. Specifically, we need to recognize that local communities are not homogeneous entities whose members share a common set of interests regarding land and resource rights and that conservation interventions, almost by definition, will produce winners and losers in struggles over access. Local politics in rural Africa often revolve around the competing land claims of men versus women or the poor versus more well-to-do peasants, within villages or even within households. Most importantly, we need to problematize the notion of traditional or customary land tenure as the product of years of intra-community struggle over rights, not a set of ancient laws frozen in time.

Finally, we need to understand how the development interventions in buffer zones relate to conservation. Many of the projects reviewed are designed not to improve livelihoods, but merely to defuse local opposition. This is a very short-sighted and short-lived 'solution' and simply 'buys' the support of (some segments of) local communities rather than integrating conservation with development. Whether the 'benefits' from conservation are reaching the people most directly involved in activities which threaten protected areas or, if they are, whether they have any marked effect on their land and resource decisions remains an open question. Research focused on the politics of land is needed to demonstrate the link between conservation and the improvement of local livelihoods. Moving in these directions will, I believe, lead us closer to a truly 'new approach' to biodiversity conservation.

POSTSCRIPT

Are Integrated Conservation and Development Programs a Solution to Conflicts Between Parks and Local People?

This debate tugs at a couple of deeper philosophical issues, including the chasm between social and physical sciences in thinking about biodiversity protection and the ongoing debate within the environmental community regarding preservationist versus conservationist approaches.

While it may be an obvious point, the natural sciences have tended to prioritize wildlife in their design and evaluation of conservation programs, whereas the social sciences generally have emphasized the welfare of people. While some advocates of the sustainable development paradigm argue that their approach integrates the two concerns (development leading to better conservation, and sustainable use of resources leading to enhanced development), the reality is that sustainable development is conceptualized in very dissimilar ways by different constituencies, e.g., economists versus deep ecologists. Some African intellectuals complain that environmental concerns have been used to unfairly constrain their development prospects, a problem sometimes referred to as "green imperialism." In his 1997 article (January/February issue) in *The Ecologist*, entitled "The Authoritarian Biologist and the Arrogance of Anti-Humanism: Wildlife Conservation in the Third World," Bamchandra Guha, an Indian scholar, asserts that biologists have been overly influential in environmental policy making. According to Guha, "Biologists have a direct interest in species other than humans. . . . This interest in other species, however, sometimes blinds them to the legitimate interest of the less fortunate members of their own." In contrast, many environmentalists complain that the World Bank, for example, supports a view of sustainable development that is overly anthropocentric.

Within the environmental community itself, there is an ongoing debate about the effectiveness of preservationist versus conservationist approaches to biodiversity protection. Preservation calls for the total nonuse, or nonconsumptive use, of natural resources, an approach typically associated with parks. Conservation allows for the use of natural resources to meet human needs within certain biological limits. This debate is directly relevant to discussions in Africa regarding protected areas. Some countries, such as Kenya, have opted for a more park-based approach, whereas others, such as Namibia, rely on more of an integrated conservation and development model. The preservation-conservation debate has also influenced views toward trade in ivory. Until recently, there was a total ban on ivory trade under the Convention on International Trade in Endangered Species (CITES). Kenya, with a declining elephant population, argued that this was necessary to eliminate elephant poaching and the associated illegal trade in ivory. It was further suggested that limited legal trade in ivory would be unenforceable. In contrast, countries like Zimbabwe, Botswana, and South Africa, with stable or growing elephant populations, argued that the sanctioned culling of elephants would help fund conservation efforts and maintain elephant populations at sustainable levels. Against the wishes of many environmental organizations, CITES allowed for the limited sale of legal ivory beginning in the late 1990s.

ISSUE 12

Is Sub-Saharan Africa Experiencing a Deforestation Crisis?

YES: Kevin M. Cleaver and Götz A. Schreiber, from *Reversing the Spiral: The Population, Agriculture, and Environment Nexus in Sub-Saharan Africa* (The World Bank, 1994)

NO: Thomas J. Bassett and Koli Bi Zuéli, from "Environmental Discourses and the Ivorian Savanna," *Annals of the Association of American Geographers* (March 2000)

ISSUE SUMMARY

YES: World Bank economists Kevin M. Cleaver and Götz A. Schreiber argue that Africa is engaged in a downward spiral of population growth, poor agricultural performance, and environmental degradation.

NO: Academic geographers Thomas J. Bassett and Koli Bi Zuéli counter that it is dominant perceptions of environmental change, rather than concrete evidence, that lie behind the widely held belief that Africa is engaged in an "environmental crisis of staggering proportions."

It has long been assumed that Africa is experiencing high levels of deforestation and that drastic measures must be undertaken to curb this disturbing trend. While this characterization still pervades much of the literature on environmental change in Africa, this view has been challenged in recent years by a series of books and articles questioning the degree and nature of deforestation in Africa.

One may gain perspective on debates concerning the nature and extent of environmental degradation in Africa by considering a number of broader, theoretical viewpoints. Contemporary scholars who believe that population growth is the main cause of environmental degradation in Africa are often described as neo-Malthusians. The neo-Malthusian label stems from the work of the original Malthusian, Thomas Malthus, and his 1798 treatise entitled *Essay on the Principle of Population*, as well as the subsequent and related work of neo-Malthusians such as Paul Ehrlich and his book entitled *The Population*

Bomb (Simon and Schuster, 1968). Malthus suggested that human population will tend to expand until it has outstripped the capacity of the land to support it. Neo-Malthusians have updated this idea by accounting for improvements in agricultural productivity and family planning technologies, while still maintaining that high rates of population growth lie behind most forms of environmental degradation. During the colonial era in Africa, many European administrators, foresters, and academics adopted Malthusian-leaning viewpoints, portraying Africa as a scene of environmental destruction driven by excessive population expansion and poor management practices. Since independence, the neo-Malthusian perspective has tended to flourish following natural disasters (such as the Sahelian droughts of 1968–1972 and 1984–1985) and during periods of heightened international attention to environmental issues (such as that surrounding the 1992 United Nations Conference on Environment and Development in Rio de Janeiro).

There have been a number of scholarly traditions countering the neo-Malthusian perspective. In Africa, cultural ecologists (an interdisciplinary field examining human-environment interactions in developing-country settings) have conducted field studies demonstrating that many traditional natural resource management practices are ecologically sound. Another closely related line of scholarship was developed in the wake of the pioneering work of Ester Boserup, who, in her 1965 book, *The Conditions of Agricultural Growth* (G. Allen and Unwin), argues that population increase leads to sustainable increases in agricultural production via a process of intensification over the medium to long term. In Africa, scholars such as Michael Mortimore have documented agricultural intensification in northern Nigeria and the highlands of East Africa.

More recently, scholars working in the tradition of political ecology have focused on the effect of broad-scale political and economic processes on local-level ecological dynamics (both real and perceived). Political ecologists have often drawn on Marxist-inspired discourse theory to highlight the role of political and economic power, rather than "neutral" empirical observation, in shaping our understanding and diagnosis of environmental problems.

In this issue, Kevin M. Cleaver and Götz A. Schreiber present deforestation as a major problem in sub-Saharan Africa and in West Africa in particular. While acknowledging that data on forest resources and rates of extraction are imperfect, the authors argue that this information is reliable enough to describe the scale and trend of the problem. Cleaver and Schreiber suggest that the causes of deforestation include a number of activities driven by population growth and international demand, especially forest conversion to farmland, road construction in environmentally fragile areas, timber extraction, and commercial fuelwood harvesting.

Thomas J. Bassett and Koli Bi Zuéli contend that there is only shaky evidence to support the perception of Africa as physically disintegrating due to the destructive practices of its inhabitants. They are particularly critical of National Environmental Action Plans (NEAPs) that the World Bank has sponsored in a number of African countries. NEAPs that misdiagnose the nature and causes of environmental change may, in fact, lead to policy prescriptions that acerbate, rather than assuage, real environmental problems.

Kevin M. Cleaver
and Götz A. Schreiber

 **YES**

Reversing the Spiral: The Population, Agriculture, and Environment Nexus in Sub-Saharan Africa

Introduction

Over the past thirty years, most of Sub-Saharan Africa (SSA) has experienced very rapid population growth, sluggish agricultural growth, and severe environmental degradation. Increasing concern over these vexing problems and the apparent failure of past efforts to reverse these trends led the authors to take a fresh look at the available research findings and operational experience. The objective was not to compile and address all of the agricultural, environmental, and demographic issues facing Africa or simply to juxtapose these three sets of problems. It was to gain a better understanding of the underlying causes and to test the hypothesis that these three phenomena are interlinked in a strongly synergistic and mutually reinforcing manner.

The need to survive—individually and as a species—affects human fertility decisions. It also determines people's interactions with their environment, because they derive their livelihood and ensure their survival from the natural resources available and accessible to them. Rural livelihood systems in SSA are essentially agricultural, and agriculture is the main link between people and their environment. Through agricultural activities people seek to husband the available soil, water, and biological resources so as to "harvest" a livelihood for themselves. Such harvesting should be limited to the yield sustainable from the available stock of resources in perpetuity so as to ensure human survival over successive generations. Improvements in technology can increase the sustainable yields or reduce the resource stock required. Population growth should thus be matched or surpassed by productivity increases so as to safeguard the dynamic equilibrium between the stock of resources and the human population depending on it for survival. Over the past thirty years, this has not been the case in most of Sub-Saharan Africa.

This study's findings confirm the hypothesis of strong synergies and causality chains linking rapid population growth, degradation of the environmental resource base, and poor agricultural production performance. Traditional African crop and livestock production methods, traditional methods of obtaining woodfuels and building materials, traditional land tenure systems and land use arrangements, and traditional gender roles in rural production and household maintenance systems were well suited to survival needs on a fragile environmental resource endowment when population densities were low and populations growing slowly. But the persistence of these traditional arrangements and practices, under severe stress from rapid population growth in the past thirty to forty years, is causing severe degradation of natural resources which, in turn, contributes further to agricultural stagnation.

Rapid population growth is the principal factor that has triggered and continues to stimulate the downward spiral in environmental resource degradation, contributing to agricultural stagnation and, in turn, impeding the onset of the demographic transition. The traditional land use, agricultural production, wood harvesting, and gender-specific labor allocation practices have not evolved and adapted rapidly enough on most of the continent to the dramatically intensifying pressure of more people on finite stocks of natural resources.

Many other factors also have a detrimental impact on agriculture and the environment. These include civil wars, poor rural infrastructure, lack of private investment in agricultural marketing and processing, and ineffective agricultural support services. Inappropriate price, exchange rate, and fiscal policies pursued by many governments have reduced the profitability and increased the risk of market-oriented agriculture, prevented significant gains in agricultural productivity, and contributed to the persistence of rural poverty.

A necessary condition for overcoming the problems of agricultural stagnation and environmental degradation will be, therefore, appropriate policy improvements along the lines suggested in the 1989 World Bank report on Sub-Saharan Africa's longer-term development prospects (World Bank 1989d). These policy changes will be instrumental in making intensive and market-oriented agriculture profitable—thus facilitating the economic growth in rural areas necessary to create an economic surplus usable for environmental resource conservation and to provide the economic basis for the demographic transition to lower population fertility rates. That this can occur has been demonstrated in a few places in Africa that pursued good economic and agricultural policy, invested in agriculture and natural resource conservation, and provided complementary supporting services to the rural population. This study provides evidence for both the causes of the problem and its solution.

The Three Basic Concerns

Population Growth
Sub-Saharan Africa lags behind other regions in its demographic transition. The total fertility rate (TFR)—the total number of children the average woman has in a lifetime—for SSA as a whole has remained at about 6.5 for the past twenty-five years, while it has declined to about 4 in all developing countries taken together. As life expectancy in Sub-Saharan Africa has risen from an

average of forty-three years in 1965 to fifty-one years at present, population growth has accelerated from an average of 2.7 percent per annum for 1965–1980 to about 3.0 percent per year at present. Recent surveys appear to signal, however, that several countries—notably, Botswana, Kenya, and Zimbabwe—are at a critical demographic turning point. This study discusses the factors that have contributed to the beginning of the demographic transition in these countries.

Agricultural Performance

Agricultural production in Sub-Saharan Africa increased at about 2.0 percent per annum between 1965 and 1980 and at about 1.8 percent annually during the 1980s. Average per capita food production has declined in many countries, per capita calorie consumption has stagnated at very low levels, and roughly 100 million people in Sub-Saharan Africa are food insecure. Food imports increased by about 185 percent between 1974 and 1990, food aid by 295 percent. But the food gap (requirements minus production)—filled by food imports, or by many people going with less than what they need—has been widening. The average African consumes only about 87 percent of the calories needed for a healthy and productive life. But as with population growth, a few African countries are doing much better, with agricultural growth rates in the 3.0 to 4.5 percent per annum range in recent years (Nigeria, Botswana, Kenya, Tanzania, Burkina Faso, and Benin). The policies of these countries help show the way forward.

Environmental Degradation

Sub-Saharan Africa's forest cover, estimated at 679 million ha in 1980, has been diminishing at a rate of about 2.9 million ha per annum, and the rate of deforestation has been increasing. As much as half of SSA's farmland is affected by soil degradation and erosion, and up to 80 percent of its pasture and range areas show signs of degradation. Degraded soils lose their fertility and water absorption and retention capacity, with adverse effects on vegetative growth. Deforestation has significant negative effects on local and regional rainfall and hydrological systems. The widespread destruction of vegetative cover has been a major factor in prolonging the period of below long-term average rainfall in the Sahel in the 1970s and 1980s. It also is a major cause of the rapid increase in the accumulation of carbon dioxide (CO_2) and nitrous oxide (N_2O), two greenhouse gases, in the atmosphere. Massive biomass burning in Sub-Saharan Africa (savanna burning and slash-and-burn farming) contributes vast quantities of CO_2 and other trace gases to the global atmosphere. Acid deposition is higher in the Congo Basin and in Côte d'Ivoire than in the Amazon or in the eastern United States and is largely caused by direct emissions from biomass burning and by subsequent photochemical reactions in the resulting smoke and gas plumes. Tropical forests are considerably more sensitive than temperate forests to foliar damage from acid rain. Soil fertility is reduced through progressive acidification. Acid deposition also poses a serious risk to amphibians and insects that have aquatic life cycle stages; the risk extends further to plants that depend on such insects for pollination.

Unlike the situation of population growth and agriculture, there are few environmental success stories in Africa, although there remain large parts of Central Africa that are little touched. In looking closely, however, places can be found, such as Machakos District in Kenya, where environmental improvements have occurred along with rapidly expanding population. Good agricultural and economic policy, and investment in social services and infrastructure, are found to be the critical ingredients to such success (English and others 1993; Tiffen and others 1994). These positive experiences form the empirical basis for an action program to overcome the downward spiral elsewhere. . . .

Agricultural Stagnation and Environmental Degradation

The Deteriorating Natural Resource Base and Ecological Environment

Much of Sub-Saharan Africa's natural resource base and ecological environment is deteriorating. If present trends continue, this deterioration will accelerate. The most pressing problem is the high rate of loss of vegetative cover—mainly the result of deforestation and the conversion of savanna to cropland—which in turn leads to loss of soil fertility and soil erosion. Global and regional climatic changes and deviations from longer-term average conditions are also causal factors—but human impact on the environment in Sub-Saharan Africa may itself be an important element contributing to these climatic changes.

Deforestation

In much of Sub-Saharan Africa, deforestation is a major problem—with significant local, national, and global consequences. Forests provide a multitude of products and serve many functions, including essential environmental ones. With deforestation, these are lost. Forests and woodlands are cleared for farming and logged for fuelwood, logs, and pulp wood. Data on forest resources and rates of extraction and clearing are imperfect, as are data on most of Africa's environmental resources, but information is continually improving and reliable enough to suggest the scale of the problem. In 1980, there were about 646 million hectares of forests and woodlands in Sub-Saharan Africa. A 1980 FAO/UNEP [Food and Agriculture Organization/United Nations Environment Programme] study estimated that 3.7 million hectares of tropical Africa's forests and open woodlands were being cleared each year by farmers and loggers (Lanly 1982). More recent estimates suggest that close to 2.9 million hectares were lost each year during the 1980s, mainly through conversion to farm land, but the rate of deforestation may be accelerating as the aggregate area still under forests continues to shrink. Reforestation during the 1980s amounted to 133,000 hectares per year, only about 5 percent of the area lost each year to deforestation.

Aggregate data obviously obscure important differences among regions and countries. Deforestation has been particularly rapid in West Africa, with East Africa and southern Africa also suffering substantial losses in forest cover. Large tracts of tropical forest still remain, especially in Zaire, Gabon, Congo, the Central African Republic, and Cameroon. It would take many years for Central Africa's forests to be completely destroyed, but the process has started. In most of East Africa and southern Africa, as well as in the West African coastal countries, the process is far advanced. . . .

Managing the Natural Resource Base

Forests

About 30 percent of Sub-Saharan Africa's land area is classified as forests or woodlands. But only about 28 percent of this area is closed forest—compared with about two-thirds in Latin America and in Asia. About 34 percent is shrubland and 38 percent is savanna woodland; both are multiple-use resource systems, utilized for meeting local requirements for fuelwood and other tree and forest products as well as for farming and forage.

. . . The most important causes of deforestation are conversion to farmland, infrastructure development in environmentally delicate areas, timber extraction, and commercial fuelwood harvesting. Growing and migrating human populations as well as international demand for tropical timber drive these processes. Timber exports from Sub-Saharan Africa amount to about US$700 million per year at present. Cropland is expanding at a rate of 1 million ha annually—to a large extent at the expense of forest areas and woodlands. A number of agricultural development projects supported by external aid donors, including the World Bank, have facilitated the conversion of forest and rangelands into cropland.

The most important areas for action to stop the degradation of Sub-Saharan Africa's forest resources lie outside the immediate purview of forestry sector policy. They are: (a) reducing population growth, and (b) intensifying agricultural production at a rate which exceeds population growth, in order to encourage sedentary agriculture and livestock raising and to discourage further invasion of the remaining forests. Rapidly growing numbers of people, barely surviving in land-extensive agricultural systems, have no option than to continue to invade and destroy forests. This points again to the complex mutual dependency of agricultural and nonagricultural activities.

For the forests that remain, improved management for multiple uses will be vital. These uses range from the provision of critical environmental services to the supply of timber and nontimber products, and from tourism and recreational uses to mineral extraction. It is unrealistic to expect that all forests can be conserved in their present state. For almost all of Africa's forests the issue is not whether to use them or not to use them—but how to use them. If people (and governments) feel that there is little benefit from forests, they will continue to be mined for urgently needed export revenue or converted into agricultural land.

To address these problems effectively, there is no alternative to planning, orchestrated by governments. This can be done within Tropical Forestry Actions Plans (TFAPs), National Environmental Action Plans (NEAPs), or simply forestry master plans. Each will involve some form of land use and natural resource planning. Land use plans for forest areas should identify conservation areas, parks, areas designated for sustainable logging, mining areas, farming and grazing areas, and areas designated for infrastructure development. . . .

National Environmental Action Plans

The development of national environmental resource management strategies must be a national affair. The main instrument for this process is the National Environmental Action Plan (NEAP). NEAPs are currently being prepared or implemented with World Bank support by most African countries. They should contain strategies for addressing all of the issues of the nexus. The NEAP concept is multisectoral in approach, and oriented to bottom-up participatory planning and implementation. It provides a framework for integrating environmental concerns with social and economic planning within a country. The objective is to identify priority areas and actions, develop institutional awareness and processes, and mobilize popular participation through an intensive consultation process with NGOs and community representatives. Donor collaboration can also be effectively mobilized in this manner.

A successful national approach to environmental concerns involves several important steps:

- Establishing policies and legislation for resource conservation and environmental protection that are integrated into the macroeconomic framework and, if possible, assessing the costs of. degradation. These were, for example, estimated to be between 5 and 15 percent of GNP [gross national product] in Madagascar and more than 5 percent of GDP [gross domestic product] in Ghana.
- Setting up the institutional framework, usually involving a ministerial or higher-level environmental policy body, developing mechanisms for coordination between agencies, building concern in these agencies, balancing private and public sector concerns, decentralizing environmental management, and assuring continuous contact with local people. The preparation of regional land use plans could be an important component. The basic framework needed to guide the implementation of land tenure reform, forest policy reform, and other elements discussed above can also be included in NEAPs.
- Strengthening national capacity to carry out environmental assessments and establishing environmental information systems. This can be done to some extent by restructuring existing data and making them available to users. Pilot demand-driven information systems should also be initiated to strengthen national capacity to monitor and manage environmental resources. Local and regional research capacity will be crucial to the development of plant varieties and technologies which are truly adapted to local conditions.
- Developing human resources through formal and on-the-job training; introducing environmental concerns into educational curricula and agricultural extension messages; and increasing public awareness through media coverage, general awareness campaigns, and extension services.

- Establishing Geographical Information Systems (GISs) that incorporate adequate environmental information. Lack of operationally meaningful and reliable environmental data is a major problem. It tends to result in misconceptions about natural resource problems and the consequent risk that policy measures will be misdirected. Urgent needs include assessments of forest cover, soil erosion and soil capability, desertification risks, and the distribution of human and livestock populations. This is clearly an area in which donors can provide support and expertise and governments need to act. It is important to develop national capacity to gather and analyze information in-country: properly designed and operated Geographical Information Systems can be extremely helpful in this regard. GISs make use of aerial photography, remote sensing, and actual ground inspections and data collection. GISs will be particularly useful not only to monitor the progress of natural resource degradation and destruction, but—more importantly—to assess land capability for various uses and, thus, to provide the basis for sound land use planning.

NEAPs are intended to be evolutionary—developing policies through field experience as well as national-level analysis. They should lead to the empowerment of the nongovernmental sector, not just by providing funds for small-scale community activities through national environmental funds, but also by drawing large numbers of village and district representatives into consultative forums. A nongovernmental advisory body was part of the institutional arrangements set up, for example, under the Lesotho NEAP.

Considerable external support has been provided for the NEAP process, from bilateral and multilateral agencies and NGOs [nongovernmental organizations] (such as the World Wildlife Fund, the World Resources Institute, and the International Institute for Environment and Development). External expertise is made available to the countries undertaking NEAP preparation, and aid agency policies are coordinated in the process, with the NEAP forming the basis for coordination. Where NEAPs have led to the preparation of national environmental investment plans (as in Madagascar and Mauritius), donors have substantially oversubscribed the programs. A National Environmental Action Plan can therefore become the major preparatory instrument for addressing the issues discussed [here].

Thomas J. Bassett
and Koli Bi Zuéli

Environmental Discourses
and the Ivorian Savanna

The image of an entire continent physically disintegrating due to the destructive land-use practices of its inhabitants conveys the magnitude of Africa's environmental problems—at least in the eyes of the World Bank. Yet there remains considerable uncertainty about the very processes generating this assumed degradation of the environment. As the Bank notes for Côte d'Ivoire. . . , "little data exist to confirm this fact." This is also the case for other parts of Africa (Watts 1987; Stocking 1987, 1996). Despite a lack of reliable evidence, the World Bank considers environmental degradation to be so widespread, that "the business" of environmental planning and regulation is now seen as a global affair, and one that falls within its own purview (Falloux and Talbot 1993: xiii–xiv). Indeed, since the late 1980s, the Bank has required low-income countries that receive International Development Association (IDA) funding to draw up national environmental-action plans (NEAPs).

As demonstrated in World Bank policy papers and country reports, the link between environmental planning and development assistance is articulated within the discourse of sustainable development (Williams 1995). The fuzzy green notion of sustainable development is readily adopted by the Bank because of its compatibility with its basic "technocratic, managerial, capitalistic, and modernist ideology" (Adams 1995: 93). Under the banner of sustainable development, the Bank now promotes a "win-win" strategy of combining economic growth with environmental conservation (World Bank 1992: 2–3; Biot et al. 1995). Never considering that its past policies and interventions are in any way implicated in the so-called environmental crisis, the Bank presents itself as an impartial observer and promoter of good stewardship. It is currently assisting dozens of African governments to develop NEAPs which, in assembly-line fashion, are being produced according to a blueprint (Greve et al. 1995). NEAPS are heralded as modern vehicles that will lead its member countries down the road to rational and orderly sustainable development.

In this [selection], we examine the contents of the NEAP for Côte d'Ivoire with special attention given to how environmental problems are constructed for the northern savanna region. Our objectives are [two]fold. The first is to highlight the problem of data gaps in the environmental-planning

From Thomas J. Bassett and Koli Bi Zuéli, "Environmental Discourses and the Ivorian Savanna," *Annals of the Association of American Geographers*, vol. 90, no. 1 (March 2000). Copyright © 2000 by The Association of American Geographers. Notes and references omitted.

and sustainable-development discourses. Determining if an environmental problem exists would appear to be a critical first step in the planning process. Yet what is striking about the NEAP process is how quickly environmental problems are identified and prioritized on the basis of so little data. We confront this data problem by contrasting the image of a highly degraded savanna environment found in Côte d'Ivoire NEAP reports with the actual landscape as experienced by farmers and herders and confirmed by our analysis of aerial photographs and land-cover changes.

Our second objective is to address some of the policy implications related to the disjuncture between local and regional patterns of environmental change and national and global environmental discourses. One result of this disjointed scale problem is that the actual dynamics of environmental change are being overlooked. We consider, in turn, the ecological and human consequences of ignoring ongoing biophysical changes while planners are busy addressing imaginary environmental problems. . . .

Research Area and Methods

. . . We have collected information on land-cover and land-use patterns using a variety of field research and analytical techniques. Survey-research methods were used to administer a questionnaire on environmental perceptions to a sample of 38 Senufo and Jula households in Katiali and to 42 Senufo households in the Tagbanga region. Group interviews were also held with Fulbe pastoralists in the Katiali area. To assess whether local perceptions of environmental change were congruent with scientific findings, we reviewed the specialist literature on human-induced modifications of savanna vegetation. We then examined aerial photographs located in Côte d'Ivoire and France for different time periods to compare land use/cover patterns for the two research sites. Geographic information systems (GIS) techniques were utilized to quantify land-cover trends. To gain a clearer understanding of vegetation change dynamics on the ground, we inventoried species along 50-m transects and in 10 3 10-meter plots following the contact-point method adapted from Daget and Poissonnet (1971) by César and Zoumana (1995). Finally, we collected environmental policy and planning documents and interviewed individuals involved in the NEAP process in government ministries and at the World Bank's regional headquarters in Abidjan. . . .

Discourses on Environmental Change

Before examining the contents of the Ivorian NEAP, it is useful to provide some information on its origins.

The NEAP Process

According to the World Bank, the NEAP process involves four stages: the identification of environmental problems and their underlying causes; setting priorities; establishing goals and objectives; and proposing new policies, institutional and legal reforms, and priority actions. The Bank considers this process to be straightforward. "It is relatively easy to identify problems and formulate appropriate responses to them" (Greve et al. 1995: 8–16). The more difficult phase, it argues, centers around the implementation of reforms and other policy actions.

The elaboration of a National Environmental Action Plan for Côte d'Ivoire began on the eve of the U.N.-sponsored conference on the environment and development held in Rio de Janeiro, June 3–4, 1992. The Ministry of the Environment and Tourism organized a national conference (May 19–21, 1992) during which a rationale for a NEAP was presented. The World Bank worked closely with and helped to train the staff members who organized this meeting and who subsequently carried out the first "civilian phase" in the preparation of the NEAP (World Bank 1994: 4). This stage involved holding regional meetings at which local civic and political leaders, government officials, and selected farmers and herders were invited to present their views on regional environmental issues. This form of "participatory planning" did not involve consultations with ordinary men and women living in rural areas about what they considered to be the most important environmental issues. At the Korhogo regional meeting, a small number of peasants were invited to participate in a setting that was dominated by civil servants representing the agricultural services, planning, and rural development. If "participation" means "the ability of people to share, influence, or control design, decision-making, and authority in development projects and programs which affect their lives and resources" (Peters 1996: 22), then this so-called civilian phase of the Ivorian NEAP process involved very limited participation. As the Korhogo region NEAP report reveals (see below), the voices that were heard and the stories that were ultimately accepted suggests that "participatory" planning in the NEAP process is more rhetoric than reality.

A second national conference took place on November 28–30, 1994, where the NEAP coordinating committee presented its *White Paper on the Environment* that summarized the results of these regional meetings (RCI 1994a). This document became the basis of the Côte d'Ivoire National Environmental Action Plan [NEAP-CI] whose appearance in June 1995 capped the second phase of the NEAP process. At the same meeting, the World Bank presented its own report on Ivorian environmental problems and policy recommendations, *Côte d'Ivoire: Towards Sustainable Development*, which it later revised and distributed in December 1994 (World Bank 1994). A comparison of the outlines and content of the two reports suggests that both the Bank and NEAP coordinating committee worked closely together. The Ivorian government approved the NEAP in 1996, thus bringing the formal planning phases to completion. The execution of the plan, however, quickly ran aground when the Ministry of Housing and the Environment established its own environmental agency to coordinate environmental projects estimated to cost $112 million. Aid donors, led by the World Bank, were critical of the structure of the agency, especially the lack of inter-Ministry coordination and the exclusion of NGOs [Nongovernmental Organizations] from its operations. They also expressed serious concerns about the competence of the individuals appointed by the Minister to head the agency (World Bank 1998). The NEAP proposed the establishment of a National Environmental Agency that would be placed under the control of a Management Council, comprising twelve representatives from government and the private sector, including a representative of Ivorian NGOs. The NEAP process also envisioned the creation of regional commissions and departmental committees in which different social groups would participate in various environmental planning activities. In contrast to this partially decentralized planning apparatus, the Minister of the Environment "viewed environmental planning as a *business* and could only see millions of dollars falling from the sky," according to a well-placed member of the World Bank (World Bank 1998).

Discourse 1: The NEAP Report

What image of environmental change in the savanna emerged from this NEAP process? The most detailed picture is contained in the report summarizing the findings of the northern regional meeting held in Korhogo and published in March 1994. The Korhogo report presents a grim scene of environmental degradation in which peasants and pastoralists are blamed for the deforestation of wooded savannas. According to the report's authors, "vegetative cover is declining due to the practice of shifting cultivation, bush fires, and the anarchic exploitation of forests and overgrazing" (RCI 1994b: 14). This change in plant cover is specifically characterized by "a replacement of the tree savanna by the grass savanna." The report goes on to paint a portentous picture of this process:

> More generally, the progressive widening towards the south of (grassy) plant formations has climatic repercussions (temperature, rainfall. . .) which in turn affects vegetation cycles. To compensate for the corresponding lowering of productivity, the one recourse has been to use chemical fertilizers which engenders certain problems such as soil acidification, and the contamination of surface and subsurface waters (RCI 1994b: 14).

This image of a southerly advancing boundary of a vegetation type associated with more arid climates is similar to the "marching desert" view found in the desertification literature. That is, in the absence of field studies, it is assumed that the forms of environmental transformation purportedly taking place in the Sahel are also occurring in humid savannas. Bush fires and indigenous land-rights systems are signaled out as major forces in this assumed environmental devastation:

> We are increasingly witnessing a decline in vegetation cover, essentially due to bush fires used in an intensive and excessive manner leading to the disappearance of certain varieties . . . these assaults on the environment are essentially linked to the abuses of customary rights, the exaggerated interpretation of the declarations of [the former] President Félix Houphouet-Boigny such as *"Land belongs to the person who improves it"* and *"that which has been planted by the hand of man must not be destroyed, no matter where;"* and especially the absence of a rural land code (RCI 1994b: 12).

According to this analysis, and that of the World Bank (Cleaver and Schreiber 1994: 8–10), "traditional" land-rights systems are inadequate for the task of modern environmental planning. They may have worked in the past, but contemporary land conflicts and insecurity have prevented farmers from investing in land improvements that might increase agricultural output and conservation practices. The assumption is that only when customary rights give way to modern (i.e., freehold) tenure systems will the incentive to conserve natural resources exist. Indeed, the transformation of land-holding systems to freehold arrangements is considered in the Ivorian NEAP to be an important step towards addressing all sorts of environmental problems. [T]his modernization model of tenure change, environmental conservation, and agricultural growth, which informs the Ivorian NEAP and which is at the heart of World Bank rural-development policies in Africa. The model points to the extent to which environmental crises are integral to neoliberal development discourses. These policies only have meaning with reference to agricultural stagnation and/or environmental decline. The desertification narrative serves such a need. This is not to suggest that environmental degradation is not occurring in sub-Saharan Africa. There is ample evidence of it (Batterbury and Bebbington 1998), whether it be soil erosion on the Borana plateau of southern Ethiopia (Coppock 1993), soil-fertility decline in southwestern Burkina Faso (Gray 1997), or rangeland degradation in southern Botswana (Abel and Blaikie 1989). Yet all of these examples are situated in local-level dynamics of resource access, control, and management. They emphasize, as do the case studies of environmental conservation in the Kano Close-Settled Zone of northern Nigeria (Mortimore 1998) and in Machakos District, Kenya (Tiffen et al. 1994), the importance of approaching natural resource management at multiple and nested scales (both biophysical and social). In the policy arena, these examples point to the need to provide "locationally and culturally appropriate technical and economic options" to different groups of land users and the necessity of moving away from "regulation and intrusive administration" (Mortimore 1998: 190–93). In contrast, blueprint development and cookie-cutter planning models like NEAP tend to be highly regulatory and intrusive. The case of Côte d'Ivoire's NEAP is indicative.

With reference to preserving the country's biodiversity, the Ivorian NEAP makes a number of forestry policy recommendations. These include outlawing logging (*l'exploitation forestière*) above the eighth parallel, intensifying village tree planting, controlling bush fires, and creating a Forestry Police to enforce these new regulations (RCI 1996). The first recommendation is strikingly reminiscent of E. P. Stebbing's shelterbelt scheme, proposed more than sixty years ago (Stebbing 1935). The link between bush fires and desertification is commonly made in Côte d'Ivoire newspapers. An editorial in the ruling party's newspaper warned that dry-season bush fires "each year contribute to the desert's advance in our country" (Gooré Bi 1999). A National Committee for Forest Protection and Bush Fire Control was organized in 1996 to raise public awareness about the assumed social and environmental costs of bush fires. The committee organizes a national awareness day each year in which statements are made linking bush fires with desertification. A national arbor day is also held each year, during which public officials and billboards urge citizens to plant trees to stop the purportedly advancing desert.

The image of an increasingly degraded wooded savanna giving way to a grass savanna and, ultimately, desert-like conditions not only persists in the minds of environmental planners, journalists, and public officials but is also firmly implanted in the perception of Ivorian environmental nongovernmental organizations (ENGOs). For example, Côte d'Ivoire's leading ENGO, the Green Cross of Côte d'Ivoire, devoted a special issue of its monthly information magazine to bush fires and forests. In his editorial, Green Cross President Gomé Gnohité Hilaire emphasized the importance of educating the citizens of Côte d'Ivoire about the urgency of protecting the nation's remaining forests. He exclaimed that the paucity of funds going to environmental education was having disastrous consequences:

> We have forgotten that raising awareness, that environmental education, is a daily and unending task. We have continued more than ever to utilize the forest as the green gold of our development without concerning ourselves with the consequences. Our forest ecosystem has continued to degrade, forests are savannized. The savannas are desertified (Gomé Gnohité 1998:).

How accurate is this image of environmental change in the northern savanna of Côte d'Ivoire found in national environmental planning documents and in the pages of NGO publications? Has the expansion of livestock raising and the area under cultivation led to an increase in grass savannas and a decline in tree cover? Is fire the great destructive force that environmental planners and NGOs believe it to be? . . .

The Lessons of the Katiali and Tagbanga Case Studies

A major finding of this comparative research on land-cover changes in the Katiali and Tagbanga areas is that, contrary to received wisdom, the savanna has become more wooded over the past thirty years. This finding runs counter to the dominant narrative, which assumes that the savanna has become less wooded and increasingly dominated by grass savannas. It also extends, both geographically and analytically, the findings of Fairhead and Leach on the expansion of wooded landscapes in the forest-savanna transition zone of Guinée (Fairhead and Leach 1996) to the sudanian savanna.

A second finding points to the diversity of savanna vegetation communities in the Korhogo region. The similarities and differences in the transformation of the Tagbanga and Katiali savanna areas underscore the importance of temporal and spatial variations in environmental change. This finding conforms to the scientific literature on savanna ecology that points to a wide range of plant communities, which are commonly distributed in mosaic form across the landscape. The most important factors influencing the nature and direction of vegetation change are farming systems, grazing pressure, population density, and changing fire regimes. These factors, which are themselves linked to changing political and economic processes extending beyond the region (e.g., cotton-development policies, immigration of Fulbe herders, or farmer-herder conflicts), interact with a host of biophysical factors such as soil type, slope, and rainfall to create temporally and locationally specific outcomes.

A third finding of this research is its relevance to environmental planning. Despite its problematic scientific status, the desertification narrative currently guides environmental policy. For example, NEAP-CI recommendations to combat the assumed reduction in tree cover include the regulation of bush fires through a range of increasingly coercive measures, restrictions on wood cutting, and the promotion of village-level tree planting (RCI 1994a). In light of the findings of this case study, such policy recommendations can be seen as misconceived and a waste of limited resources. The disjuncture between national and global environmental discourses and actual vegetation-change patterns is alarming. Our findings show that although desertification is not taking place, heavy grazing and early fires have significantly reduced the quality of the savanna for livestock raising. Tree and shrub invasion and a highly degraded herbaceous layer were evident in both the Katiali and Tagbanga study areas. Since livestock development is a priority of the Ministry of Agriculture, one would think that rangeland rehabilitation would be a centerpiece of the Côte d'Ivoire NEAP. Not surprisingly, it is nowhere to be found in NEAP documents which are more concerned with reforestation than range condition. While environmental analysts and planners are occupied with an imaginary environmental problem, tree and bush encroachment continues unabated. This disjointed scale problem also produces its contradictions. For example, the Ivorian NEAP's recommended regulation, permitting only *early*-dry-season fires, would result in further bush invasion. To improve range conditions, degraded areas will have to be protected from grazing for at least two or three years, and woody growth must be controlled by extremely hot (i.e., *late*) bush fires (César 1994).

Conclusion

Given the extraordinary amount of environmental planning currently underway in Africa and its far-reaching implications on land use, access and management, one obvious conclusion of this study is that further research on environmental-change dynamics is of utmost importance. Indeed, the World Bank places the identification of environmental problems and their underlying causes as the first step in the NEAP process. Yet, from all indications, the Bank does not consider this to be a particularly challenging phase. Despite the glaring gaps in our knowledge, the Bank believes that most environmental issues are easy to identify and can be classified along a simple color scheme. A conclusion of this [selection] is that identifying environmental problems and their causes is one of the most difficult and time-consuming stages in environmental planning and policy making.

One of the challenges in confronting the environmental-data problem is that so little data exist with any meaningful time depth. Even where data like aerial photographs do exist, their relatively small scale rarely permits one to make little more than very general statements. This situation demands that multiple approaches be pursued to determine the spatial and temporal dynamics of environmental change that are not apparent in aerial photos. In this study, we have combined household-survey research focused on farming systems and environmental perceptions with aerial-photo interpretation and vegetation transects to identify the general trends in vegetation change. This multiscale, multimethod approach yielded different results from the so-called "participatory approach" followed in the NEAP process, in which the opinions of selected individuals from different social strata were solicited in public meetings. Not surprisingly, peasants and herders were reticent in such fora.

A third point centers on competing discourses on environmental change. In contrasting the environmental narratives expressed in World Bank and NEAP documents with those of rural land users, it would be misleading to suggest that a homogeneous view prevails on either side. For example, peasant farmers downplayed their own role in transforming savanna vegetation through their agricultural activities by pointing their finger at Fulbe herders as the primary agents of environmental change. This tendency to "blame" the Fulbe must be contextualized in the often bitter conflicts that exist between farmers and herders in northern Côte d'Ivoire. Similarly, the tendency of the Fulbe to deny their use of fire as a range management tool and to "blame" farmers and hunters for bush fires must be seen in light of these land-use conflicts.

Fourth, it is also clear that the environmental-crisis lexicon is wide spread. Despite the disparate goals of the World Bank, the Ministry of the Environment, and environmental nongovernmental organizations, they share an environmental-crisis imaginary that gives meaning and an immediacy to their missions. The visual imagery of an expanding desert is a powerful framing device that demands equally dramatic solutions, such as the establishment of green belts along the eighth parallel and imprisonment as punishment for lighting bush fires.

Finally, there are striking historical parallels between colonial-era writings on land degradation and control and contemporary environmental planning. Both blame farmers and herders for recklessly destroying the land and altering local climates, programmatic statements abound while good data are hard to come by, and proposed conservation measures invariably involve increased state intervention in the countryside with an emphasis on transforming land-rights systems, specifically the exclusion of local people from protected areas. These recurring themes, principal players, and silences regarding the goals and resource management strategies of farmers and herders suggest that we are operating within a regional discursive formation. What is different between the 1930s and the 1990s is the number of contestants involved in environmental management. In addition to the state, there are NGOs and development-aid organizations seeking to establish their authority and legitimacy as environmental advocates and stewards. The desertification narrative persists in part because it serves to mobilize support for these groups' varied agendas. This [selection] has privileged the voices and experiences of farmers and herders whose understanding of environmental change is more nuanced and sophisticated than the dominant narrative. From all indications, this local understanding of the nature and direction of environmental change is not reflected in the Côte d'Ivoire National Environmental Action Plan. As in the past and despite the rhetoric of decentralization and participatory planning (Little 1994; Ribot 1999; Schroeder 1999), this case study shows that the perceptions of ordinary men and women are marginalized in contemporary environmental planning in sub-Saharan Africa.

POSTSCRIPT

Is Sub-Saharan Africa Experiencing a Deforestation Crisis?

It is important to note that while Bassett and Zuéli question the accuracy of perceptions of deforestation in northern Côte d'Ivoire, they acknowledge that grassland degradation is occurring. The distinction they make between deforestation and degradation is critical because it is often assumed that deforestation equates with degradation, and that afforestation is a positive environmental trend. In the Ivorian savanna, the increase in woody species may actually be undermining the health of grasslands. As Bassett and Zuéli suggest, misperceived forest cover trends in the Ivorian savanna may, ironically, lead to policy prescriptions that exacerbate grassland degradation.

Another significant issue to keep in mind when evaluating these two selections is the question of scale. Cleaver and Schreiber are discussing deforestation at the scale of the African continent, whereas Bassett and Zuéli are examining vegetation trends at the scale of the savanna ecosystem in northern Ivory Coast. Is it possible that deforestation is occurring at the broad, continental scale while quite different, and even contrary, trends are operating in specific bioregions and localities? As Bassett and Zuéli suggest, it is critical not to assume that macro-scale trends are always reflected at the local level.

The findings of Bassett and Zuéli are not inconsistent with others who have come out in recent years with books and articles reassessing landscape change in Africa. Examples of these works include those by James Fairhead and Melissa Leach, *Misreading the African Landscape* (Cambridge University Press, 1996); Michael Mortimore, *Roots in the African Dust* (Cambridge University Press, 1998); and Jeremy Swift, "Desertification: Narratives, Winners and Losers," in Melissa Leach and Robin Mearns, eds., *The Lie of the Land: Challenging Received Wisdom on the African Environment* (Oxford & Heinemann, 1996). Newer work on African savannas suggests that, in addition to misrepresented biomass trends, the character of these ecosystems has been misunderstood. For example, a volume edited by Roy H. Behnke, Ian Scoones, and Carol Kervan, entitled *Range Ecology at Disequilibrium: New Models of Natural Variability and Pastoral Adaptation in African Savannas* (Westview Press, 1993), argues that African savannas may actually be more resilient than originally perceived. The book further asserts that transhuman pastoral livelihoods, rather than European modes of livestock rearing, are better suited to handle the inherent variability of African savannas.

Despite emerging new evidence to the contrary, Cleaver and Schreiber are in the majority when they sound the alarm about deforestation in Africa. Environmental organizations and the World Bank have been the most outspoken about their deforestation concerns. Examples of recent books and articles expressing apprehension about deforestation trends in Africa include Uma Lele et al., *The World Bank Forest Strategy: Striking the Right Balance* (World Bank, 2000); K. Boahene, "The Challenge of Deforestation in Tropical Africa" (1998); Claude R. Heimo et al., *Strategy for the Forest Sector in Sub-Saharan Africa* (World Bank, 1994); and Alan Durning, *Saving the Forest: What Will It Take* (Worldwatch Institute, 1993).

Wherever the truth may lie, the contrasting perspectives presented in this set of selections suggest that it is important not to make assumptions about forest cover change in Africa. Among other issues, students may more thoughtfully read assessments of environmental change in Africa by paying attention to the scale of analysis and suppositions regarding appearance of degradation on the landscape.

On the Internet . . .

Ethnologue Country Index: Languages of Africa

The Ethnologue Country Index: Languages of Africa is a comprehensive source on the languages of Africa, including linguistic heritage and geographical distribution of the listed languages.

`http://www.ethnologue.com/country_index.asp?place=Africa`

Minnesota State University's E-Museum, African Cultures Section

This site offers useful background information on over 60 ethnic groups in Africa. It includes information on each group's geographic location, language, history, religion, and typical livelihood strategies.

`http://www.mnsu.edu/emuseum/cultural/oldworld/africa.html`

Population Council: Africa

The Population Council's Africa page explains population and family planning issues, reproductive health, HIV/AIDS, and other issues by country and for the African continent as a whole.

`http://www.popcouncil.org/africa/index.html`

Washington Post: AIDS in Africa

The Washington Post has an ongoing "Special Report" on the HIV/AIDS issue that contains news on the HIV/AIDS epidemic from African countries, debate and information on U.S. actions to fight the epidemic, and world HIV/AIDS information.

`http://www.washingtonpost.com/wp-dyn/world/issues/aidsin-africa/index.html`

World Health Organization

The World Health Organization offers information on diseases and epidemiological facts for African countries (as well as other areas of the world).

`http://www.who.int/en/`

The University of Pennsylvania's African Studies Center, Women's Issues

The women's issues page of this Web site offers links to several other reputable sites dealing with women and gender.

`http://www.africa.upenn.edu/About_African/ww_wmen.html`

PART 4

Social Issues

*P*erhaps more than any other set of contested African issues, those pertaining to the social sphere tend to provoke deep-seated emotional responses. This is also an area where differences in perspective between Africanists and non-Africanists tend to be more apparent. Such a degree of contestation is not surprising as these are, after all, deeply personal and culturally specific issues dealing with sexuality, gender roles, intra-household dynamics, customs, and language. Despite the highly private nature of some of the topics, this is also a realm that has come under incredible public scrutiny given concern about the global AIDS pandemic and the increasingly global nature of the human rights and feminist movements.

- Should Female Genital Cutting Be Accepted as a Cultural Practice?

- Are Women in a Position to Challenge Male Power Structures in Africa?

- Should International Drug Companies Provide HIV/AIDS Drugs to Africa Free of Charge?

- Is Sexual Promiscuity a Major Reason for the HIV/AIDS Epidemic in Africa?

ISSUE 13

Should Female Genital Cutting Be Accepted as a Cultural Practice?

YES: Fuambai Ahmadu, from "Rites and Wrongs: Excision and Power among Kono Women of Sierra Leone," in B. Shell-Duncan and Y. Hernlund, eds., *Female 'Circumcision' Africa: Culture, Controversy, and Change* (Lynne Reiner, 2001)

NO: Liz Creel et al., from "Abandoning Female Genital Cutting: Prevalence, Attitudes, and Efforts to End the Practice," A Report of the Population Reference Bureau (August 2001)

ISSUE SUMMARY

YES: Fuambai Ahmadu, an anthropologist at the London School of Economics, finds it increasingly challenging to reconcile her own experiences with female initiation and circumcision and prevailing (largely negative) global discourses on these practices. Her main concern with most studies on female initiation is the insistence that the practice is necessarily harmful or that there is an urgent need to stop female genital mutilation in communities where it is done. She suggest that "the aversion of some writers to the practice of female circumcision has more to do with deeply imbedded western cultural assumptions regarding women's bodies and their sexuality than with disputable health effects of genital operations on African women."

NO: Liz Creel, senior policy analyst at the Population Reference Bureau, and her colleagues argue that female genital cutting (FGC), while it must be dealt with in a culturally sensitive manner, is a practice that is detrimental to the health of girls and women, as well as a violation of human rights in most instances. Creel et al. recommend that African governments pass anti-FGC laws, and that programs be expanded to educate communities about FGC and human rights.

When examining the issue of female genital cutting in Africa (also known as female circumcision, female genital mutilation, or female genital alteration), it is difficult for many Westerners not to have an emotional reaction. In order to carefully evaluate the topic, the reader should try to keep as open a mind as possible.

This issue tugs at a deeper debate between those who believe there are certain universal rights and wrongs, and that female genital cutting is just wrong, irrespective of the cultural context, and cultural pluralists who believe we need to evaluate a practice within its own cultural context. Advocates of the universality of certain norms often depict female genital cutting as a violation of basic human rights. They may further disparage defenders of female genital cutting as cultural relativists. Cultural relativism is often cast as problematic because it may be used as an excuse to say that anything goes. For example, some individuals have and continue to argue that slavery is appropriate in some cultural contexts.

Others would argue that, despite one's personal objections to the practice, that female genital cutting must be viewed within the context of cultural pluralism. Cultural pluralists assert that there are separate and valid cultural and moral systems that may involve social mores that are not easily reconcilable with one another. In contrast to cultural relativists, however, cultural pluralists would argue that everything does not go, and that there are certain universal norms (e.g., murder is wrong). The challenge for cultural pluralists is to determine if a practice violates a universal norm when it is viewed in its proper cultural context (rather than in the cultural context of another). The result of this deep philosophical divide is that we often see Western feminists pitted against multiculturalists (two groups that frequently function as intellectual allies in the North American context) over this controversial African issue.

In this issue, Fuambai Ahmadu, an anthropologist at the London School of Economics, reflects on her own position as a Western trained academic, as a member of an ethnic group that practices female initiation and as someone who underwent the procedure herself. She is troubled by the ethnocentric insistence of outsiders that the practice is necessarily harmful or that there is an urgent need to stop female genital cutting in communities where it is done. Research and personal experience lead her to conclude that the positive aspects of initiation outweigh the negative ones. She argues that "initiation was the 'acting out' and celebration of women's preeminent roles in history and society." She believes the practice should not be banned, but medicalized. Liz Creel et al. argue that female genital cutting (FGC), while it must dealt with in a culturally sensitive manner, is a practice that is detrimental to the health of girls and women, as well as a violation of human rights in most instances. They recommend that African governments pass anti-FGC laws and that programs be expanded to educate communities about FGC and human rights. They also believe that the use of medical professionals to perform the procedure should be discouraged.

Fuambai Ahmadu  **YES**

Rites and Wrongs: Excision and Power among Kono Women of Sierra Leone

The issue of female initiation and circumcision is of significant intellectual and personal interest to me. Like previous anthropologists, I am fascinated by social, ideological and religious/symbolic dimensions of these rituals, particularly from indigenous perspectives. I also share with feminist scholars and activists campaigning against the practice a concern for womens physical, psychological and sexual well-being, as well as with the implications of these traditional rituals for womens status and power in society. Coming from an ethnic group in which female (and male) initiation and circumcision are institutionalized and a central feature of culture and society and having myself undergone this traditional process of becoming a "woman," I find it increasingly challenging to reconcile my own experiences with prevailing global discourses on female circumcision.

Most studies on FGC [female genital cutting] in Africa have been conducted by "outsiders" or individuals who are not from the societies they analyze and who have no personal experience of any form of the operation. The limited number of African women who have written about FGC either come from ethnic groups where female genital operations are not practiced (i.e. Thiam, Dorkenoo, Koso-Thomas) or have never undergone the procedures themselves (Toubia, El-Nadeer). There is an unfortunate and perturbing silence among African women intellectuals who have experienced initiation and circumcision. This reticence however is understandable given the venomous tone of the "debate" and unswerving demand that a definitive stance be taken—evidently, if one is educated—*against* the practice. However, "insider" voices from initiated/circumcised African women scholars can go a long way in providing fresh approaches to our understanding of these practices and their continued significance to the bulk of African women.

This essay is an attempt at reconciling "insider" representations with "outsider" perspectives. I seek to contextualize my own experience within the broader framework of initiation in Sierra Leones Kono society and then contrast dominant Kono paradigms with conflicting international debates which focus on female circumcision as a peculiar manifestation of womens global subordination.

My main quarrel with most studies on female initiation and the significance of genital cutting relates to the continued insistence that the latter is necessarily "harmful" or that "there is an urgent need to stop female genital mutilation in communities where it is done." . . . Both of these assertions are based on the alleged physical, psychological and sexual effects of female genital cutting. I offer, however, that the aversion of some writers to the practice of female circumcision has more to do with deeply imbedded western cultural assumptions regarding womens bodies and their sexuality than with disputable health effects of genital operations on African women. For example, one universalized assumption is that human bodies are "complete" and that sex is "given" at birth. A second assumption is that the clitoris represents an integral aspect of femininity and has a central erotic function in women's sexuality. And, finally, through theoretical extension, patriarchy is assumed to be the culprit—that is, women are seen as blindly and wholeheartedly accepting "mutilation" because they are victims of male political, economic and social domination. According to this line of analysis, excision is necessary to patriarchy because of its presumed negative impact on womens sexuality. Removal of the clitoris is alleged to make women sexually passive, thus enabling them to remain chaste prior to marriage and faithful to their husbands in polygynous households. This supposedly ensures a husband sole sexual access to a woman as well as certainty of his paternity over any children she produces. As victims, then, women actively engage in "dangerous" practices such as "female genital mutilation" to increase their marriageability . . . , which would ultimately enable them to fulfill their honored, if socially inferior, destiny of motherhood.

When attempting to reconcile Kono practice with dominant anti-"FGM" discourses, a number of problems arise, starting with the alleged physical harm resulting from the practice. Part of the problem . . . is the unjustified conflation of varied practices of female genital cutting and the resulting over-emphasis on infibulation, a rare practice which is associated with a specific region and interpretation of Muslim *purdah* ideology. Kono women practice *excision*, removal of the clitoris and labia minorae. . . . The purported long-term physical side-effects of this procedure may have been exaggerated. It can be argued, as well, that although there are short-term risks, these can be virtually eliminated through improved medical technology. . . .

Furthermore, among the Kono there is no cultural obsession with feminine chastity, virginity nor with womens sexual fidelity, perhaps because the role of the biological father is considered marginal and peripheral to the central "matricentric unit." Finally, Kono culture promulgates a dual-sex ideology, which is manifested in political and social organization, sexual division of labor and, notably, the presence of powerful female and male secret societies. The existence and power of *Bundu*, the womens secret sodality, suggest positive links between excision, womens religious ideology, their power in domestic relations, and their high profile in the "public" arena.

The Kono example makes evident underlying biases of such culturally loaded notions as the "natural" vagina or "natural female body." The word "natural" is uncritically tossed around in the Female Genital Mutilation (FGM) literature to describe an uncircumcised woman when actually it needs definition and clarification. Kono concepts of "nature" and "culture" differ significantly from western assumptions and it is these local understandings which compel female (and male) genital cutting. In essence, what this paper amounts to is a critique of a profound tendency in western writing on female circumcision in Africa to deliver male-centered explanations and assumptions. Scholars must be wary of imposing western religious, philosophical and intellectual assumptions which tend to place enormous emphasis on masculinity and its symbols in the creation of culture itself. In traditional African societies, as is the case with the Kono, womb symbolism and imagery of feminine reproductive contributions form the basis of meanings of the universe, of human bodies, of society and its institutions—social organization, the economy, and even political organization can be viewed as extensions of the "matricentric core" or base of society. Female excision, I propose, is a negation of the masculine in feminine creative potential, and in the remainder of this essay I will show how the Kono case study demonstrates this hypothesis.

This paper is a culmination of several years of informal inquiry as well as formal research into the meaning of female circumcision and initiation, particularly among my parental ethnic group, the Kono, in northeastern Sierra Leone. This study constitutes an analysis of five stages: (1) my subjective experience of initiation in December/January 1991-92 which lasted just over month; (2) indigenous interpretations from other participants, mainly ritual leaders and their assistants, recorded at the time; (3) later academic study, when I returned to Kono for an additional 2 months in December 1994 and December 1996; (4) a total of nine months conducting formal and informal interviews among Kono immigrants in and around the Washington, D.C. area; and finally, (5) approximately three months spent between January and July of 1998 traveling back and forth between Conakry and Freetown talking to Kono refugees and women activists, mainly about their more immediate survival concerns but also about circumcision, initiation, and the future of womens secret societies. These discussions included informal interviews, as well as formal semi-structured interviews with three ritual officials: two traditional circumcisers, or *Soko* priestesses, and one *digba*, or ranking assistant to the *Soko*.

The cumulative data is drawn from interviews with a broad range of Kono men and women: young, old, university educated professionals in Freetown and in the U.S., as well as illiterate villagers and traditional rulers in Kono. If I have sacrificed quantification, it has been for the benefit of collecting detailed qualitative data which would enable my search for meaning and significance, both of which I felt could be best obtained through carefully selected, knowledgeable informants. What this study attempts to explain are the views, beliefs, and rationales of *supporters* of initiation and circumcision. The extent to which these attitudes reflect those of all or the majority of Kono women is left open for future research. . . .

The "Debate": Physical, Sexual and Psychological Effects

Anthropologists have not been the only ones interested in initiation and female genital cutting. In the last decade or so many others—feminists, politicians, international aid organizations, international medical community etc. within Africa and without—have produced a plethora of literature and convened conferences and the like on the subject of the effects of various forms of genital cutting on womens bodies, their sexuality and psychological well-being. My intention in this section is to interrogate some of the major assumptions in prevailing international discourses on female circumcision in light of my own experiences and the data collected from other Kono women, primarily but not limited to immigrants residing in the U.S.

First, as regards the health implications of excision, several short and long-term risks have been associated with the practice. . . . I have personally interviewed several male and female Sierra Leonean gynecologists who profess that although they regard excision as "medically unnecessary" the practice does not pose any significant adverse long-term effects to women and that, moreover, traditional circumcisers are on the whole "very well trained" and are "experts" at what they do. None had personally treated women with long-term problems related to excision but all stated that they had come across "reports" of horror cases.

Each of the doctors I have spoken to, irrespective of their position on the legitimacy of the practice, agree that short-term risks can be significantly reduced if not altogether eliminated through the use of antiseptic instruments, anesthetics to reduce pain, and skilled traditional officials. Also, it must be noted that most Kono women I have spoken to maintain that excision has existed in their society for hundreds of years and the practice has not adversely affected their fertility nor has it been giving their womenfolk the types of gynecological or obstetrical problems which have been over the past decade become associated with the operation. Thus, if some medical practitioners are saying that safe excisions are possible under the right conditions and if many Kono women do not attribute gynecological/obstetrical problems to their operations and choose to continue to uphold their tradition, a genuine case for limited medicalization can be made on this basis. . . . Such steps may reduce the immediate risks of the operation for young girls, until such a time that women are collectively convinced to give up the practice.

Second, my research and my experience contradict received knowledge regarding the supposed negative impact of removing the clitoris on womens sexuality. Much of this taken for granted information comes perhaps from popular misconceptions about the biological significance of the clitoris as the source of female orgasms. It is probable that such myths evolved as a result of the heightened focus on female clitoris during the 1960s sexual revolution and subsequent discourses regarding womens sexual autonomy. The clitoris has come to be seen in western societies as not only the paramount organ responsible for womens sexual pleasure but it has also been elevated as *the* symbol of womens sexual independence—the latter suited womens objectives in asserting their sexual agency and rejecting previous constraining notions of their roles as wives and mothers.

However, the presumptions which inform Kono womens values regarding female sexuality, as in other aspects of socio-cultural life, emphasize sexual interdependence and complimentarity, principles which are profoundly heterosexual. Western womens notions of the importance of the clitoris to female sexual autonomy can be contrasted with *Bundu* officials stress on vaginal stimulation which implies male penetration, and this glaringly suggests heterosexual intercourse which, because the latter leads to reproduction, is considered the socially ideal form of sexual relations. My informants consider vaginal orgasm as independent of the clitoris but still fundamental to a womans sexuality. Perhaps because women believe that the "internal" vagina is the appropriate locus of womens sexual pleasure, they profess that the clitoris is redundant and leads to excessive "sexiness." Also, as the clitoris is associated with androgyny and "nature," its presence signifies lack of self-control or self-discipline which are attributes of "culture." *Bundu* officials insist that the clitoris is "no good" and that it leads to uncontrolled masturbation in girls and sexual insatiability in adult women. It is believed to be a purely superfluous erotic organ, unlike a "proper" adult penis, its sex-corollary, which at least has reproductive functions. It is thus understandable, even if one does not agree, how some Kono women can claim that while excision curbs a womans desire for sex, the operation itself does not reduce her enjoyment of sexual pleasure.

. . . There can be no way to "objectively" test the evidence regarding the impact of excision on womens sexuality as the latter is subjective and individually variable. Notwithstanding, an interesting finding in the Hite report is that the external clitoris constitutes a small fraction of total nerve endings which account for sensations for the entire appendage. . . . This suggests that excision leaves uncut most of the nerve endings which are beneath the vaginal surface. Thus, paradoxically, even according to "objective" biological science, it is possible for a womans sensitivity to remain for the most part undiminished after excision. This would probably explain how it is that many women who had sexual experiences *prior* to excision, the author included, perceive either no difference or increased sexual satisfaction following their operation. In any case, most contemporary, urban educated as well as rural Kono women are just as interested in their sexuality as are their counterparts in western countries, and they do not perceive of excision as inhibiting them in any way. Also it is worth noting, especially since it is usually omitted, that significant numbers of western women, despite having their clitorises intact, experience their own difficulties in achieving any kind of orgasm, clitoral or vaginal.

Finally, as regards to the psychological well-being of young girls and women who have undergone initiation and excision, more research is needed before any credible generalizations can be made. A small but growing number of African female activists against various forms of circumcision have detailed the pain and trauma they underwent and the lasting impact such negative experiences have had on their lives and thus, they campaign against what they rightfully believe to be an affront to their human rights and womanhood. I have spoken to a few young Kono women who are adamantly opposed to initiation because of their experiences of pain, abuse and mal-treatment by female elders in the "bush." However, the bulk of women I have interviewed fervently support the practice and my ground observations confirm that not only do most girls continue to look forward to their initiation but, further, they demonstrate their on-going support for the practice by actively participating in later ceremonies involving younger female friends and relations.

Conclusion

The question is often put to me: "How can a Western-bred and educated African woman *support* a practice which degrades women and deprives them of their humanity?" Notwithstanding the ethnocentrism in this remark, and the fact that I prefer to consider myself "neutral" in terms of the continuation of the practice, I am aware of many educated, professional circumcised African women gracefully negotiating their way through culturally distinct settings. There are those, the author included, who refuse to privilege one presumably objective, scientific model of personhood over supposedly "misguided" local interpretations but, rather, seek to juggle "modern" and "traditional" identities according to appropriate cultural context. Educated circumcised African women, like most people of multicultural heritage, maneuver multiple identities depending on the specific circumstances in which they find themselves. Personally, I do not see any conflict or contradiction in being educated and being circumcised, as the contexts which require each of these cultural idio-syncracies are separate and distinct.

For me, the negative aspect of excision was that it was a physically excruciating experience, for which, given my relatively cushioned Western upbringing, I was neither emotionally nor psychologically prepared. This is in contrast to most of the prepubescent Kono girls with whom I was "joined." As with the young Mandinka girls in the Gambia among whom I am currently conducting fieldwork, they "took" excision "bonically" (Krio term used to describe sheer human strength, strength of the flesh) and in a few hours were up, laughing and playing. After one or two days, they were jumping up and down dancing the "bird dance" to the rhythm of makeshift drums in preparation for their big "coming out" dance. To impose on my research what was my own experience of "pain" would be a gross distortion of the experiences of most of the other novices and thus, a certain disservice to anthropological knowledge in general.

The positive aspects have been much more profound. Initiation was the "acting out" and celebration of womens preeminent roles in history and society. Although I could not at the time put together all the pieces, I felt I was participating in a fear-inspiring world, controlled and dominated by women, which nonetheless fascinated me because I was becoming a part of it. In the years since, I have managed to make sense of much of the ritual symbolism and acting-out, enough to understand that women claim sole credit for everything from procreation to the creation of culture, society and its institutions, and, most important, they maintain a "myth of male dominance" so that their fundamental prerogatives are not threatened by increasing masculinization of religion, culture and society in Africa.

One such prerogative is the virtual deification of mothers among the Kono (and most African societies for that matter). This is not only symbolically important for women, but it gives them "real" power in inter- and intra-domestic lineage and immediate family relations, by virtue of the moral privilege women have over sons and daughters. I agree with Diops assertion that the greatest abomination of any African, male or female, high or low, is the curse of his or her mother. This could also explain the findings of Skramstad and Hernlund indicating that Gambian Mandinka women continue "circumcision" first and foremost out of respect for their mothers and grandmothers. Even for the few Kono women who have second thoughts about "joining" their own daughters, the idea of eradication never comes up. It is not so much that an unexcised woman is unfathomable to them, but the public defiance and condemnation that abolition campaigns require would constitute a most unfathomable "insult" against their mothers and grandmothers.

Another feature of excision is the way in which the scar itself symbolizes womens sameness or common female identity. In effect, the operation rite is what defines and, thus, essentializes womanhood. Unlike in Western society, there is no confusion or fruitless intellectualizing about the definition of "woman." Among the Kono, a woman is a woman by virtue of the fact that she has been initiated and nothing else. But initiation also creates a hierarchical ordering of women in society. At the apex is, of course, the *Soko*, the mother of the community, then an individuals mother, after which is her mother-in-law, and then all other older women in the community. A womans equals are her age-mates, those with whom she was initiated and/or those falling within the same age group. Thus, sameness is not always tantamount to equality, and neither does it imply strict conformity to dominant values of womanhood, such as motherhood. For example, my grandmother often nags me about not yet having children and about the importance of motherhood to a woman but, for her, as for the entire community, it was my initiation which "made" me into a "woman". This is perhaps how it is possible for some circumcised African women to be educated, westernized and yet not view the practice as an affront to their womanhood. In short, initiation/excision has the positive value of creating sameness among all women and maintaining equality within age-groups as well as a general hierarchy of female authority in society.

Other advantages of initiation include beliefs about womens esoteric knowledge and their monopoly over powerful "medicines." Although excision cannot be said to be a marker of ethnicity today (most ethnic groups in Sierra Leone practice excision), what does distinguish Kono *Bundu* from those of other groups are the "medicines" which are used. According to a high-ranking *Bundu* official, even more important than excision itself is women's "medicine" which is used in ritual. The more powerful a sodality's "medicine" is reputed to be, the more feared, and thus, influential are the women leaders of such a group. Kono women often assert the power of their own "medicine" and claim that this is how they dominate their men and "keep them home." Also, it is believed that the medicine which is used for the novices during initiation will protect them against all sorts of witchcraft and other malevolent supernatural practices which may be aimed at them throughout their lives.

Finally, and more subjective, is my shared view of the aesthetics of excision and (male) circumcision. I propose that the basis of Kono appreciation of male/female genital modifications is the latters compatibility and harmony with basic principles of complimentarity and interdependence. These ideals underpin cosmological beliefs regarding sex and gender difference and are manifested in the dual-sex organization of culture and society. As long as there are deeply implanted mental associations of the clitoris with masculinity, then the former will continue to be regarded as dirty, abnormal, unclean, and harmful by a culture which sees "male" and "female" as fundamentally separate and distinct moral categories.

To Cut or Not to Cut?: The Future of Excision

While location and identity may establish who is an "outsider" as opposed to an "insider" with respect to studies on FGC, these factors do not automatically determine the position of any writer regarding abolition. For example, not a few anthropologists—who are by discipline western scholars and often by nationality "outsiders"—have been bitterly criticized for their attempts to represent the cultural viewpoints and values of their informants. Conversely, indigenous African female activists or "insiders," fighting against "FGM" often promulgate the same messages contained in global discourses that link the practice to women's social, sexual and psychological oppression. What is certain is that the future of FGC will depend on the extent to which "insiders" themselves are convinced of purported negative effects of the practice.

The medical evidence as well as the speculations regarding adverse effects on womens sexuality do not tally with the experiences of most Kono women. It is the immediate physical pain and risk of infection which concern most mothers and both of these hazards can be reduced, if not eliminated, through medicalization, education and general modernization of the operation. A compelling point has been made, however, that all the eradication mechanisms, such as policies of international organizations and local NGOs devoted to change peoples attitudes and behaviors, have already been set in place and that most likely there can be no going back. . . . But the virtually universal resistance to change after several decades of international and internationally sponsored local campaigning, conferencing and legislating suggests that what is seriously needed is a re-thinking of previous eradication strategies and a deeper appreciation of the historical and cultural relevance of this ancient practice and its symbolically dynamic and fluid links to womens changing sources and notions of power.

In my opinion, if eradication has become an irreversible "international" political compulsion, then the ideal of "ritual without cutting" . . . seems to be a reasonable middle-ground. The ritual without cutting model positively values many cultural aspects and beliefs underlying female genital operations and initiation while attempting to eliminate the actual physical cutting. Perhaps what *is* needed to replace the physical act of cutting is an equally dynamic symbolic performance which will retain the same fluidity in associated meanings, that is eschewal of masculinity, womanhood, fertility, equality, hierarchy, motherhood, and sexual restraint. However, for rural Kono women in particular, the "cutting" and "medicine" are all-important. Also, as I discussed earlier, "ritual without cutting" can be very dangerous when taken out of context such as in the recruitment and "training" of child rebels in Kono.

I continue to support, however, the goal of medicalizing and modernizing initiation and "circumcision"—not necessarily in a full sense of institutionalizing female circumcision or transferring the practice from the "bush" to hospitals, as in male circumcisions today, because this would reduce the power and authority of female ritual leaders and female elders—but rather by making available basic, modern hygienic equipment and medications to traditional officials to use during rituals. I support change which will promote safe, sanitary environments, so that initiates are given adequate, modern medical assistance to reduce pain and risks of infection. The position that this only legitimizes the practice is dangerously arrogant: the practice is already seen as legitimate by its proponents, who have themselves undergone excision, and denying them the benefits of medicalization only continues to endanger the health and lives of innocent young girls. Modernization should also include impartial, neutral education within primary and secondary schools. Such education should entail both positive historical and cultural significance of initiation/circumcision as well as possible negative health effects. Emphasis should be on preparing young girls to make informed choices about their futures and the futures of their own girl-children.

What direction individual women take should be left to them and their immediate family members. Just as much as die-hard "traditionalists" must relinquish their insistence that uncircumcised women are not socially and culturally "women" who therefore must be denied legal rights and dignity within society, hard-line efforts by abolitionists to coerce women against the practice and stigmatize those who uphold their ancestral traditions as "illiterate," backward, and against "womens rights" and "progress" are unacceptable. It is the bulk of circumcised African women who are unfortunately caught between a rock and a hard place, as the adage goes: Either break traditional customary laws and face the consequences of "not belonging," or ignore increasing efforts to ban the practice and face possible legal penalties instigated by eradicators at the national and international level. Today, it seems that the pressure on circumcised African women, educated or not, is to choose between these two extremist positions—to be either "anti-culture" or "anti-progress."

Change may indeed be occurring gradually, but I do not believe this is necessarily a direct result of "anti-FGM" campaigning. In my grandmothers days, excision was a universal *rite-de-passage*. For my educated, Christian mother who has spent over thirty years in the United States, initiating her daughters was a matter of judgment, an expedient choice to enable us to easily navigate between worlds. My generation is faced with a dramatically different and greater complexity of issues and other priorities (i.e. the complete destruction of Kono through civil war) and, as a result, initiation and excision can hardly be said to be the most pressing preoccupation of young, contemporary Kono women. In the event that I ever have a daughter I would like her to be well-informed about the socio-cultural and historical significance of the operation as well as its purported medical risks so that she can make up her own mind, like I had the opportunity to do. Mbiti has noted regarding female initiation and circumcision in Africa: "If they are to die out, they will die a long and painful death." However, through more culturally sensitive and appropriate "education" as well as limited medicalization strategies, the "death" of female circumcision could be more gradual, more natural, and a lot less painful for millions of future African women and girls. . . .

Abandoning Female Genital Cutting: Prevalence, Attitudes, and Efforts to End the Practice

Introduction

More than 130 million girls and women worldwide have undergone female genital cutting [FGC]—also known as female circumcision and female genital mutilation—and nearly 2 million more girls are at risk each year. The practice often serves as a rite of passage to womanhood or defines a girl or woman within the social norms of her ethnic group or tribe. The tradition may have originated 2,000 years ago in southern Egypt or northern Sudan, but in many parts of West Africa, the practice began in the 19th or 20th century. No definitive evidence exists to document exactly when or why FGC began. FGC is an ancient practice but has also been recently adopted, for example, among adolescents in Chad.

FGC is generally performed on girls between ages 4 and 12, although it is practiced in some cultures as early as a few days after birth or as late as just prior to marriage, during pregnancy, or after the first birth. Girls may be circumcised alone or with a group of peers from their community or village. Typically, traditional elders (male barbers and female circumcisers) carry out the procedure, sometimes for pay. In some cases, it is not remuneration but the prestige and power of the position that compels practitioners to continue. The practitioner may or may not have health training, use anesthesia, or sterilize the circumcision instruments. Instruments used for the procedure include razor blades, glass, kitchen knives, sharp rocks, scissors, and scalpels. A discouraging trend is the use of medical professionals (physicians, nurses, and midwives) in some countries (e.g., Egypt, Kenya, Mali, and Sudan) to perform the procedure due to growing recognition of the health risks associated with FGC and heightened concern regarding the possible role of FGC in HIV transmission. WHO [World Health Organization] has strongly advised that FGC, in any of its forms, should not be practiced by any health professional in any setting—including hospitals and other health centers.

FGC has health risks, most notably for women who have undergone more extreme forms of the procedure (see Box 1). Immediate potential side effects include severe pain, hemorrhage, injury to the adjacent tissue and organs, shock, infection, urinary retention and tetanus—some of these side effects can lead to death. Long-term effects may include cysts and abscesses, urinary incontinence, psychological and sexual problems, and difficulty with childbirth. Obstructed labor may occur if a woman has been infibulated. This involves cutting off the external genitalia and sewing together the two sides of the vulva, leaving a small hole for urination and menstruation. If the woman's genitalia is not cut open (defibulated) during delivery, labor may be obstructed and cause life-threatening complications for both the mother and the child, including perineal lacerations, bleeding and infection, possible brain damage to infants, and fistula formation.

TYPES OF FEMALE GENITAL CUTTING

Female genital cutting (FGC) refers to a variety of operations involving partial or total removal of female external genitalia. The female external genital organ consists of the vulva, which is comprised of the labia majora, labia minora, and the clitoris covered by its hood in front of the urinary and vaginal openings. In 1995, the World Health Organization classified FGC operations into four broad categories described below:

Type 1 or **Clitoridectomy:** Excision (removal) of the clitoral hood with or without removal of the clitoris.

Type 2 or **Excision:** Removal of the clitoris together with part or all of the labia minora.

Type 3 or **Infibulation:** Removal of part or all of the external genitalia (clitoris, labia minora, and labia majora) and stitching and/or narrowing of the vaginal opening, leaving a small hole for urine and menstrual flow.

Type 4 or **Unclassified:** All other operations on the female genitalia including

- pricking, piercing, stretching, or incising of the clitoris and/or labia;
- cauterization by burning the clitoris and surrounding tissues;
- incisions to the vaginal wall; scraping or cutting of the vagina and surrounding tissues; and introduction of corrosive substances or herbs into the vagina.

Note:
1. World Health Organization, *Female Genital Mutilation: Report of a Technical Working Group* (Geneva: WHO, 1996): 9.

All of these possible side effects may damage a girl's lifetime health, although the type and severity of consequences depend on the type of procedure performed (see Box 1). Infibulation or Type 3 is the most invasive and damaging type of FGC. Operations research studies conducted in Burkina Faso and Mali have shown that women who were infibulated were nearly two and a half times more likely to have a gynecological complication than those with a Type 2 or Type 1 cut. Risks during childbirth also increased according to the severity of the procedure. For instance, in Burkina Faso, women with Types 2 or 3 cutting had a higher likelihood of experiencing hemorrhaging or perineal tearing during delivery.

While it is difficult to determine both the number of women who have undergone FGC and how many have undergone each type of circumcision, WHO has estimated that clitoridectomy, which accounts for up to 80 percent of all cases, is the most common procedure. Fifteen percent of all circumcised women have been infibulated—the most severe form of circumcision.

FGC is practiced in at least 28 countries in sub-Saharan and north-eastern Africa but not in southern Africa or in the Arabic-speaking nations of North Africa, with the exception of Egypt. It is practiced at all educational levels and in all social classes and occurs among many religious groups (Muslims, Christians, animists, and one Jewish sect), although no religion mandates it. For countries presented here with DHS [Demographic and Health Surveys] data, prevalence varies from 18 percent in Tanzania to nearly 90 percent or more in Egypt, Eritrea, Mali, and Sudan. According to WHO estimates, 18 African countries have prevalence rates of 50 percent or more. Through migration, the practice has also spread to Europe, North and South America, Australia, and New Zealand. Although doctors, colonial administrators, and social scientists have documented the adverse effects of FGC for many years, governments and funding donors have become increasingly interested in the practice because of the public health and human rights implications.

Global efforts to end FGC have used legislation to provide legitimacy for project activities, to protect women, and to discourage circumcisers and families who fear prosecution. In the 1960s, WHO was the first United Nations (UN) specialized agency to take a position against female genital cutting. It began efforts to promote the abandonment of harmful traditional practices like FGC in the 1970s, focusing largely on gathering information about FGC's epidemiology and health consequences and speaking out about FGC at international, regional, and national levels. In 1982, WHO issued a formal statement to the UN Commission on Human Rights and recommended several actions:

- Governments should adopt clear national policies to end FGC, and educate and inform the public about its harmful aspects.
- Anti-FGC programs must consider the practice's association with difficult social and economic conditions and respond to women's needs and problems.
- Women's organizations at the local level should be encouraged to take action.

In 1988, WHO began to integrate FGC into the development context of primary health care. Over the intervening years, WHO shifted its position on FGC from addressing the practice only in terms of health to acknowledging it as both a health and human rights issue. In the 1990s, FGC gained recognition as a health and human rights issue among African governments, the international community, women's organizations, and professional associations. The 1993 Vienna Human Rights Convention, the 1994 International Conference on Population and Development, and the 1995 Fourth World Conference on Women called for an end to the practice. When performed on girls and nonconsenting women, FGC violates a number of recognized human rights protected in international conventions and conferences, such as the Convention on Children's Rights, the Convention on the Elimination of All Forms of Discrimination against Women, and recommendations of the Committee on the Elimination of Discrimination against Women (CEDAW). These conventions explicitly recognize harmful traditional practices such as FGC as violations of human rights, including the right to nondiscrimination, the right to life and physical integrity, the right to health, and the right of the child to special protections.

Respect for international human rights law does not require that every culture use an identical approach to abandoning FGC. One Muslim scholar suggested that respecting different cultures means accepting "the right of all people to choose among alternatives equally respectful of human rights," and that human rights must include life, liberty, and dignity for every person or group of people.

In Africa, 10 countries–Burkina Faso, the Central African Republic (CAR), Côte d'Ivoire, Djibouti, Ghana, Guinea, Niger, Senegal, Tanzania, and Togo—have enacted laws that criminalize the practice of FGC. The penalties range from a minimum of six months to a maximum of life in prison. In Nigeria, three of 36 states (as of 2000) had also enacted legislation regarding FGC. In Burkina Faso, Ghana, and Senegal, these laws are enforced and circumcisers are imprisoned. In these countries, various groups educate the public about the law, use a variety of strategies (e.g., public service announcements and watchdog committees) to denounce FGC, and stop circumcisers by going to the police. Several countries also impose fines. In Egypt, the Ministry of Health issued a decree declaring FGC unlawful and punishable under the Penal Code. There have been several prosecutions under this law, which include jail time and fines. In addition, seven more developed countries that receive immigrants from countries where FGC is practiced—Australia, Canada, New Zealand, Norway, Sweden, the United Kingdom, and the United States— have passed laws outlawing the practice. Enforcement of these laws, however, is extremely uneven. France, on the other hand, consistently enforces general penal code provisions against providers of FGC but has not adopted specific legislation regarding FGC.

Why is FGC Performed?

The traditions surrounding FGC vary from one society to another. In some communities, FGC is a rite of passage to womanhood and is performed at puberty or at the time of marriage. In other communities, it may be performed on girls at a younger age for other reasons such as a celebration of womanhood, preservation of custom or tradition, or as a symbol of ethnic identity. The ritual cutting is often an integral part of ceremonies, which may occur over several weeks, in which girls are feted and showered with presents and their families are honored. It is described as a joyous time with many visitors, feasting, dancing, good food, and an atmosphere of freedom for the girls. The ritual serves as an act of socialization into cultural values and an important connection to family, community, and earlier generations. The ceremonies often involve three interrelated aspects:

- **Educational**   A girl learns her place in society and her role as woman, wife, and mother.
- **Physical** A girl must undergo physical pain to prove she is capable of assuming her new role courageously without showing suffering or pain; the pain is experienced both through the actual cutting and through punishment received by girls in complete submission throughout weeks of initiation.
- **Vow of silence**   Each girl must make a solemn pledge not to speak about her experience during the ceremony.

The reasons for performing FGC differ, but many practicing communities believe that it preserves the girl's virginity and protects marital fidelity because it diminishes her sexual desire. Practicing communities cite reasons such as giving pleasure to the husband, religious mandate, cleanliness, identity, maintaining good health, and achieving good social standing. At the heart of all this is rendering a woman marriageable, which is important in societies where women get their support from male family members, especially husbands. A circumcised woman will also attract a favorable bride price, thus benefiting her family. The practice is perceived as an act of love for daughters. Parents want to provide a stable life for their daughters and ensure their full participation in the community. Many girls and women receive little formal education and are valued primarily for their role as sources of labor and future producers of children. For many girls and women, being uncircumcised means that they have no access to status or a voice in their community. Because of strong adherence to these traditions, many women who say they disapprove of FGC still submit themselves and their daughters to the practice.

Understanding Why the Practice Continues

FGC is a cultural practice. Efforts to end it require understanding and changing the beliefs and perceptions that have sustained the practice over the centuries. Irrespective of how, where, and when the practice began, those who practice it share similar beliefs—a "mental map"—that present compelling reasons why the clitoris and other external genitalia should be removed. The details of these mental maps vary across countries, and there are distinctive features to each culture that providers, community workers, and others involved with anti-FGC campaigns need to take into consideration.

Figure 1 provides a conceptual framework for understanding the role of FGC in society. This mental map shows the psychological and social reasons, and the religious, societal, and personal (hygienic and aesthetic) beliefs that contribute to the practice. These beliefs involve continuing long-standing custom and tradition; maintaining cleanliness, chastity, and virginity; upholding family honor (and sometimes perceived religious dictates); and controlling women's sexuality in order to protect the entire community. In the countries surveyed by Demographic and Health Surveys, good custom/tradition is the most frequently cited reason for approving of FGC. Bad custom/tradition is also mentioned as one of the primary reasons for discontinuing the practice.

To encourage abandonment of FGC, health care providers, community workers, and others involved with anti-FGC programming need to understand the mental map in the communities where they are working. Communities have a range of enforcement mechanisms to ensure that the majority of women comply with FGC. These include fear of punishment from God, men's unwillingness to marry uncircumcised women, insistence that women from other tribes get circumcised when they marry into the group, as well as local poems and songs that reinforce the importance of the ritual. In some

Figure 1

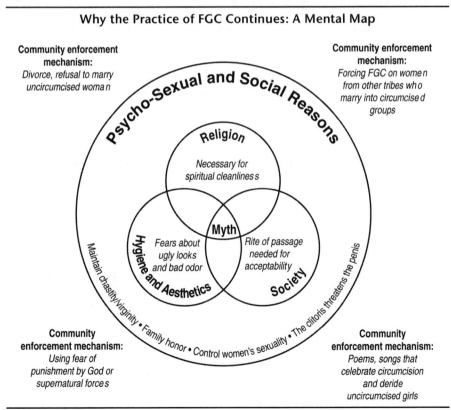

Why the Practice of FGC Continues: A Mental Map

Source: Asha Mohamud, Nancy Ali, Nancy Yinger, World Health Organization and Program for Appropriate Technology in Health (WHO/PATH), *FGM Programs to Date: What Works and What Doesn't* (Geneva: WHO, 1999):7.

cases, women who are not circumcised may face immediate divorce or forced excision. Girls who do undergo FGC sometime receive rewards, including public recognition and celebrations, gifts, potential for marriage, respect and the opportunity to engage in adult social functions. In other instances, girls and women are cut without an accompanying ceremony; thus, importance is attached to being circumcised rather than to having gone through a ritual.

The desire to conform to peer norms leads many girls to undergo circumcision voluntarily, yet frequently girls (and sometimes infants) have no choice in whether they are circumcised. A girl's family—typically her mother, father, or elder female relatives—often decides whether she will undergo FGC. Due to the influence of tradition, many girls accept, and even perpetuate, the practice. In Eritrea, men are more likely than women to favor ending the practice.

FGC could continue indefinitely unless effective interventions convince millions of men and women to abandon the practice. Many African activists, development and health workers, and people following traditional ways of life recognize the need for change but have not yet achieved such an extensive social transformation. . . .

Recommended Actions to End FGC

Data on attitudes, practices, and prevalence can provide important background information on opportunities for intervention. In addition, lessons from program experiences provide an important context for formulating abandonment campaigns. PATH [Program for Appropriate Technology in Health] and WHO developed the following recommendations for policymakers and program managers.

Recommendations for Policymakers

Policymakers are those who are in a position to influence policies and provide funding related to FGC.

> 1. *Governments and donors need to support the groundswell of agencies involved in FGC abandonment with financial and technical assistance.*

An increasing number of agencies, especially NGOs [nongovernmental organizations], are involved in efforts to end FGC. However, programs tend to be small, rely heavily on volunteers and funds from foreign donors, and reach a small proportion of the people in need. Additional support is needed to make the growing network of agencies more effective and expand their reach.

In Egypt, 15 NGOs, including the Egyptian Fertility Care Society, the Task Force Against FGM, the Cairo Institute for Human Rights Studies, and CEOSS [Coptic Evangelical Organization for Social Services] have been instrumental in advocating the abandonment of FGC. In order to become more effective, these groups need to collaborate with one another, enhance training in advocacy and communications skill building, and evaluate the impact of their programs.

2. Governments must enact and use anti-FGC laws to protect girls and educate communities about FGC and human rights.

Passing anti-FGC legislation is one of the most controversial aspects of the FGC abandonment movement. It is extremely difficult to enforce anti-FGC laws. There is fear that heavy-handed enforcement may drive the practice underground. In fact, this has occurred in some countries. Still, most program planners and activists agree that anti-FGC legislation can demarcate right from wrong, provide official legal support for project activities, offer legal protection for women, and ultimately, discourage circumcisers and families for fear of prosecution. The key is to use the law in a positive fashion—as a vehicle for public education about and community action against FGC.

3. National governments need to be active both in setting policy and in expanding existing programs.

A key role for governments is to "scale up" successful community-based FGC abandonment activities. To date, most governments have provided support in the form of in-kind contributions to NGOs working in the communities. The excellent program models that NGOs have carried out on a pilot basis need to be expanded, either by direct government interventions or by increased support for the NGO networks.

4. To sustain programs, governments need to institutionalize FGC abandonment efforts in all relevant ministries.

Currently, none of the anti-FGC efforts underway are sustainable over the long run, in part because they have failed to change the social norms underlying FGC. The integration of FGC issues into government programs, however, has met with some success. In Burkina Faso, the National Committee to Fight Against the Practice of FGC has effectively promoted FGC abandonment through participation in national events such as the international day of population, by integrating FGC abandonment into all of the relevant ministries, and through training and awareness raising activities.

Efforts in other countries, such as Mali, have encountered more difficulties. While various ministries have expressed their support for anti-FGC activities, they have not been integrated into the relevant ministries, particularly in programs carried out by Mali's Ministry of Health. The primary nursing and medical schools in Mali do not include FGC as an adverse health practice in their curricula. Presently, PRIME II, a partnership of U.S.-based organizations, is working with the Ministry of Health to develop a national curriculum integrating FGC.

Governments have a responsibility to make political decisions and place FGC abandonment in the mainstream of reproductive health and development programs. Limited success has been achieved through increased fundraising, greater integration of anti-FGC activities into government and civil society programs, and through solicitation of community support.

5. *Health providers at all levels need to receive training and financial sup-*
port to treat FGC complications and to prevent FGC.

A key foundation for FGC abandonment is to make health providers aware of the extent and severity of FGC-related complications and to give them the skills and resources to treat these problems. Health providers often encounter women and girls suffering from FGC-related complications, yet they are often not prepared to treat and counsel women, or to prevent recurrence of the circumcision practice. Because there is limited training on clinical treatments for circumcised women or counseling women suffering from psychological or sexual problems, women lack access to high quality, relevant services in most countries.

A 1998 operations research study in Mali sought to assess the use of health personnel to address FGC. The study, which was conducted by an NGO, Association de Soutien au Developpement des Activités de Population (ASDAPO), and the Ministry of Health, evaluated the effectiveness of a three-day training course on identifying and treating medical complications related to FGC and counseling patients about the problem. The study focused on 14 urban and rural health centers in Bamako and the Ségou region and included 107 health providers from experimental and control sites. Results indicated that the course was highly effective in changing provider attitudes toward FGC. After receiving training, three in four trained providers knew at least three immediate and long-term complications of FGC. The study also indicated that providers felt they had limited competence in caring for FGC complications (even after receiving training) and needed further training in how to discuss FGC with their clients.

6. *Governments, donors, and NGOs working on FGC abandonment should*
continue to coordinate their efforts.

Findings from field assessments reveal an impressive array of cooperative efforts and exchanges of information and resources among NGOs, government institutions, and donors. Agencies typically invite each other to meetings and training activities and coordinate at program sites to avoid duplication of efforts. Although occasional conflicts arise over funding and strategies, they should not discourage agencies from continuing to coordinate and build on each other's strengths.

7. *International agencies should assist staff of NGOs and government to*
develop their advocacy skills.

Advocacy is essential to ensuring that FGC abandonment programs are established and maintained until the practice of FGC ceases. Agencies involved in abandonment efforts increasingly use advocacy for public education and to influence legislation, but they need to improve their skills.

POSTSCRIPT

Should Female Genital Cutting Be Accepted as a Cultural Practice?

After reading the different arguments in this issue, there are at least five different points that one may want to ponder before taking an informed stance on topic. First, female genital cutting covers a very broad range of practices in the African context. In some instances, apparently contradictory statements from either author may have as much to do with the specific practices they have in mind as with the fact that they have differing views on the general topic.

Second, the whole notion of choice, the prospect of giving girls and women the option of undergoing or not undergoing the procedure, implies that they are aware that there is a choice. Many girls and women may just assume that this is what is done, or what is normal.

Third, if a girl or young women opts not to undergo female genital cutting, there could be serious social consequences in some settings. Within the context of the educational programs advocated by Creel et al., is there an obligation to make sure individuals are made aware of the medical dangers of the procedure as well as the social consequences of not being initiated?

Fourth, some African countries (e.g., Kenya) have a mix of ethnic groups that may or may not practice female genital cutting. In other nations, such as Mali or Eritrea, the vast majority ethnic groups, and the population in general, practice female genital cutting. This level of homogeneity or heterogeneity could have implications for people's exposure to different practices (particularly in urban areas where ethnic groups tend to mix) as well as the chances of success or failure of education programs in this domain.

Finally, the different authors have very different views on medicalizing FGC in Africa. Ahmadu contends that this will minimize health problems whereas Creel et al. fear that this may help perpetuate the practice. How likely is making the procedure safer going to contribute to its spread?

For more information on this debate, see Richard Scweder's article "What about 'Female Genital Mutilation'?" and "Why Understanding Culture Matters in the First Place" in *Daedalus* (Fall 2000) or Monica Antonazzo's paper "Problems with Criminalizing Female Genital Cutting" in *Peace Review* (2003). For a publication questioning the medical evidence against female genital surgeries, see an article by Carla M. Obermeyer in *Medical Anthropology Quarterly* (no. 13, 1999) with the title "Female Genital Surgeries: The Known, The Unknown, and the Unknowable." Finally, for more of an anti-FGM perspective, see *Eradicating Female Genital Mutilation: Lessons for Donors* (by Susan Rich and Stephanie Joyce, Wallace Global Fund for a Sustainable Future, 1990).

ISSUE 14

Are Women in a Position to Challenge Male Power Structures in Africa?

YES: Richard A. Schroeder, from *Shady Practices: Agroforestry and Gender Politics in The Gambia* (University of California Press, 1999)

NO: Human Rights Watch, from "Double Standards: Women's Property Rights Violations in Kenya," A Report of Human Rights Watch (March 2003)

ISSUE SUMMARY

YES: Richard A. Schroeder, an associate professor of geography at Rutgers University, presents a case study of a group of female gardeners in The Gambia who, because of their growing economic clout, began to challenge male power structures. Women, who were the traditional gardeners in the community studied, came to have greater income-earning capacity than men as the urban market for garden produce grew. Furthermore, women could meet their needs and wants without recourse to their husbands because of this newly found economic power.

NO: Human Rights Watch, a nonprofit organization, describes how women in Kenya have property rights unequal to those of men, and how even these limited rights are frequently violated. It is further explained how women have little awareness of their rights, that those "who try to fight back are often beaten, raped, or ostracized," and how the Kenyan government has done little to address the situation.

As is the case in other parts of the world, African women suffer from discrimination and inequality. According to the World Bank, the female adult illiteracy rate in Africa in 2001 was 46 percent as compared to 38 percent for the general population. Girls also continue to attend primary school in lower numbers than boys in many African countries (although this ranges from near equality in nations such as South Africa, Zimbabwe, and Namibia to great disparities in countries like Benin, Chad, and Guinea). Despite these disadvantages, women are the backbone of the rural economy in many African settings where it is estimated that they produce, on average, 70 percent of the food supply.

The inequities faced by many women in the African context led to the rise of the women in development (WID) movement in aid circles in the late 1970s and 1980s. These WID programs were also instigated because of a general recognition that many aid programs had not addressed the needs of women or had excluded them entirely. Many agricultural development programs catered almost exclusively to men. In many instances, such programs exacerbated economic disparities between men and women. WID programs were specifically designed to counteract these problems, including a number of initiatives related to gardening, income generation, health care, and education.

In promoting these initiatives, development agencies occasionally exploited the image of African women as a downtrodden class of people who undertake a disproportionate share of the work, yet are severely disadvantaged in terms of access to education, health care, land, and legal protection. While there may be some truth to this generalization, it is problematic because it denies African women "agency." In other words, it could negate or understate the ability of African women to change their situation. This is not to say that African women should not form alliances with outside groups to work for transformation, but those peddling the assistance need to be careful that they are not trafficking images and stereotypes that may be disempowering.

In this issue, Richard A. Schroeder presents a case study of a group of female gardeners in The Gambia. These women, who were the traditional gardeners in the community, benefited from outside funding for fencing and wells during the heyday of WID programming in the 1980s. They eventually came to have greater income-earning capacity than men as the urban market for garden produce grew, and they adeptly intensified production. As a result, men were often forced to turn to their wives for loans. This allowed women to "purchase" freedom of movement and social interaction. Furthermore, women with growing economic clout could challenge male power structures because they were capable of meeting their needs and wants without recourse to their husbands. They also were less susceptible to the threat of divorce (which historically implied the nearly impossible obligation of repaying one's bride-price) because women were now capable of repaying their bride-price with their gardening income.

In contrast, the selection from Human Rights Watch contains the assertion that in Kenya "discriminatory property laws and practices impoverish women and their dependents, put their lives at risk by increasing their vulnerability to HIV/AIDS and other diseases, drive them into abhorrent living conditions, subject them to violence, and relegate them to dependence on men and social inequality." The Kenyan government is castigated for having done little to address this situation.

Richard A. Schroeder   **YES**

Shady Practices: Agroforestry and Gender Politics in The Gambia

Introduction

Some sixty kilometers upriver along the North Bank of The River Gambia lies the Mandinka-speaking community of Kerewan (ke´-re-wan). The dusty headquarters of The Gambia's North Bank Division is located on a low rise overlooking rice and mangrove swamps and a ferry transport depot that facilitates motor vehicle transport across Jowara Creek (Jowara Bolong), one of The River Gambia's principal tributaries. Since the Kerewan area was dominated by opposition political parties throughout the nearly thirty-year reign of The Gambia's first president, Al-Haji Sir Dawda Jawara (1965–1994), it became something of a developmental backwater. Before 1990, Kerewan town had no electricity or running water beyond a few public standpipes. For a community of 2,500 residents, there were no restaurants and only a poorly stocked market that lacked fresh meat. Indeed, from the standpoint of the civil servants assigned to the North Bank Division, Kerewan was considered a hardship post. Mandinka speakers sarcastically referred to the divisional seat as "Kaira-wan," a place where "peace" (Mandinka: *kaira*) reigned to the point of overbearing stagnation. Neighboring Wolof speakers, meanwhile, disparaged the community by dubbing it "Kerr Waaru"—"the place of frustration."

Kerewan's reputation was only partially deserved, however, for the community was actually the center of a great deal of productive economic activity. Over two decades beginning in the mid-1970s, the town's women transformed the surrounding lowlands into one of the key sites of a lucrative, female-controlled, cash-crop market garden sector. A visitor to Kerewan as recently as 1980, when I made my first trip to The Gambia, would have found that vegetable production on the swamp fringes ringing Kerewan on three sides was decidedly small-scale. Most gardeners, virtually all of whom were women, worked single plots that were individually fenced with local thorn bushes or woven mats. Outside assistance in obtaining tools, fences, and wells was minimal. Seed suppliers were not yet operating on a significant scale, and petty commodity production was largely confined to tomatoes, chili peppers, and onions. The market season, accordingly, stretched only a few weeks, and sales outlets were all but nonexistent. Most Kerewan produce was sold directly to end users in the nearby Jokadu District by women who transported their fresh vegetables by horse or donkey cart and then toted them door to door on their heads (a marketing strategy known as *kankulaaroo*).

By 1991, when I completed the principal phase of research for [my] book, large gardens on the outskirts of Kerewan had come to dominate the landscape. Each morning and evening during the October–June dry season, caravans of women plied the footpaths connecting a dozen different fenced perimeters to the village proper. Over the course of nearly twenty years, the number of women engaged in commercial production rose precipitously from the 30 selected to take part in a pilot onion project in the early 1970s to over 400 registered during an expansion project in 1984, and some 540 recorded in my own 1991 census. The arrival of the first consignments of tools and construction materials donated by developers for fencing and wells in 1978 initiated an expansion period which saw the area under cultivation more than triple in size, growing from 5.0 ha to 16.2 ha in ten years. Between 1987 and 1995, a second wave of enclosures nearly doubled that area again. At least a dozen separate projects were funded by international NGOs, voluntary agencies, and private donors. These donations were used toward the construction of thousands of meters of fence line and roughly twenty concrete-lined irrigation wells. In addition, there were some 1,370 hand-dug wells and nearly 4,000 fruit trees incorporated within Kerewan's garden perimeters. Growers purchased seed, fertilizer, and other inputs directly from an FAO [Food and Agriculture Organization]-sponsored dealership in the community and sent truckloads of fresh produce to market outlets located up and down the Gambia-Senegal border, which thrived on the vegetable trade. In sum, the Kerewan area developed over two decades into one of the most intensive vegetable-producing enclaves in the country. . . .

Theories Connecting Gender, Development, and the Environment

The image most widely used to capture the "plight" of Third World women is that of an African peasant woman toting an improbably large and unwieldy bundle of firewood on her head. She may or may not have a young child tied to her back, but the image is always meant to convey that she has traveled a great distance to gather her load. As a metaphor, this feminine icon suggests the incredible burdens women shoulder, and the great lengths they go to, to satisfy the multiple and competing demands society and their families place on them. The implication is that women suffer these conditions universally, as a class, and that pure, selfless motives drive them to undertake routinely dull, repetitive, and ultimately thankless tasks. At the same time, the graphic portrayal of firewood collectors is meant to underscore the idea that close connections exist between women and the natural environment. It suggests that women forced to gather wood from the countryside lead a hand-to-mouth existence, where knowledge of the landscape is bred of necessity and deep personal experience, and where the vagaries of climate and ecology have profound and immediate implications for human well-being. Thus, by virtue of their collective lot in a singular division of labor, women mediate the relationship between nature and society, and they feel the brunt of natural forces as a consequence.

Such images convey a stark reality: life for peasant women is often filled with considerable toil and drudgery. Yet if these women suffer a common plight, it resides not in any particular niche in some all-encompassing division of labor but in the countless ways the range and variety of their lived experiences are distorted in the words and images conveyed by outsiders. The wood-gathering icon represents Third World women as Africans, African women as peasants, and peasant women as a single type. There is no geographical detail at either localized or macropolitical scales that might serve as an explanation for the plight thus portrayed. Moreover, to render such women as beasts of burden, dumb, stolid, unwavering in their support of their families, unstinting in their service of same, is to acquiesce in the notion that they are perpetual victims, steeped in need, and incapable or disinclined to contest their lot creatively.

This tension between images of women as victims and women as autonomous actors traces back to the earliest efforts of developers to promote Women in Development (WID) programs in the Third World. The United Nations–sponsored convocation in Mexico City in 1975 proclaimed an International Decade for Women and initiated efforts within the major development agencies to address a broad agenda of issues deemed especially pertinent to Third World women. . . .

Gone to Their Second Husbands: Domestic Politics and the Garden Boom

One of the offshoots of the surge in female incomes and the intense demands on female labor produced by the garden boom was an escalation of gender politics centered on the reworking of what [Anne] Whitehead once called the "conjugal contract." In Kerewan, the political engagement between gardeners and their husbands can be divided into two phases. The first phase, comprising the early years of the garden boom, was characterized by a sometimes bitter war of words. In the context of these discursive politics, men whose wives seemed preoccupied with gardening claimed that gardens dominated women's lives to such a degree that the plots themselves had become the women's "second husbands." Returning the charge, their wives replied, in effect, that they may as well be married to their gardens: the financial crisis of the early 1980s had so undermined male cash-crop production and, by extension, husbands' contributions to household finances, that gardens were often women's only means of financial support during this period.

As the boom intensified, so, too, did intra-household politics. The focus of conflict in the second phase—which extended into the mid-1990s—was the role of garden income in meeting household budgetary obligations. Several studies have examined "non-pooling" households in Africa, that is, households in which men and women tend to engage in distinctly different economic activities and control their own incomes from these enterprises. The garden boom offers a case study in which women, by virtue of their new incomes, entered into intra-household negotiations over labor allocation and income disposition with certain economic advantages. The upshot of these negotiations was not, however, quite so simple. In terms of budgetary obligations, women in the garden districts assumed a broad range of new responsibilities from their husbands. Moreover, they frequently gave their husbands part of their earnings in the form of cash gifts. This outcome appears in some respects as a capitulation on the part of gardeners. I argue, . . . however, that it can also be read as symbolic deference designed to purchase the freedom of movement and social interaction that garden production and marketing entailed. In effect, gardeners used the strategic deployment of garden incomes to win for themselves significant autonomy and new measures of power and prestige, albeit not always at a price of their own choosing.

. . . Before the garden boom, men in Mandinka society had powerful economic levers at their disposal which they could, and did, use to "discipline" their wives. They controlled what little cash flowed through the rural economy due to their dominant position in groundnut production and were able to fulfill or deny a range of their wives' expressed needs at will. These included such basic requirements as clothing, ceremonial expenses (naming ceremonies, circumcisions, and marriages for each individual woman's children), housing amenities, and furnishings. The power vested in control over cash income was only enhanced by polygamous marital practices and the opportunities they afforded to play wives off against one another. A second advantage was derived from the husband's rights in divorce proceedings. In the event of a divorce, Mandinka customary law requires that the bride's family refund bridewealth payments. Consequently, when marital relations reach an impasse, divorce is not automatic; the financial arrangement between the two families must first be undone. Typically, the woman flees or is sent back to her family so that they can ascertain to their own satisfaction whether she has made a good faith effort to make her marriage work. The onus is on the woman to prove her case, however, and she is not infrequently admonished by her own family to improve her behavior before being returned to her husband.

The advent of a female cash-crop system reduced the significance of both these sources of leverage, not least because women's incomes had outstripped their husbands' in many cases. A rough comparison of the garden incomes of women in Kerewan and Niumi Lameng and the earnings their husbands reported from groundnut sales showed that 81 percent and 47 percent of women in the Niumi Lameng and Kerewan samples, respectively, earned more cash than their husbands from sales of these crops. This reversal of fortunes changed fundamentally the way male residents of the garden districts dealt with their wives:

> *Before gardening started here, if you saw that your wife had ten dalasis you would ask her where she got it. At that time, there was no other source of income for women except their husbands. . . . But nowadays a woman can save more than two thousand dalasis while the husband does not even have ten dalasis to his name. So now men cannot ask their wives where they get their money, because of their garden produce.*

Gardener's husband

Indeed, the garden boom reduced male authority ("If she realizes she is getting more money than her husband, she may not respect him"), and the extent of gardeners' economic influence expanded proportionately. The simple fact that women could largely provide for themselves ("If we join [our husbands] at home and forget [our gardens in] the bush, we would all suffer. . . . Even if he doesn't give you [what you want], as long as you are doing your garden work, you can survive") constituted a serious challenge to the material and symbolic bases of male power. In the first phase of conflict brought on by the boom, men openly expressed their resentment in pointed references to female shirking and selfishness. Their feelings were also made plain in actions taken by a small minority who forbade their wives to garden, or agitated at the village level to have gardening banned altogether. In the second phase, men dropped their oppositional rhetoric, became more generally cooperative, and began exploring ways to benefit personally from the garden boom. Sensing the shift in tenor of conjugal relations, women, accordingly, began a prolonged attempt to secure the goodwill necessary to sustain production on a more secure basis.

     . . . Survey data show that both senior members of garden work units and women working on their own took on many economic responsibilities that were traditionally ascribed to men. Fifty-six percent of the women in the Kerewan sample, for example, claimed to have purchased at least one bag of rice in 1991 for their families. The great majority bought all of their own (95%), and their children's (84%), clothing and most of the furnishings for their own houses. Large numbers took over responsibility for ceremonial costs from their husbands, such as the purchase of feast day clothing (80%), or the provision of animals for religious sacrifice. Many paid their children's school expenses. In a handful of cases, gardeners undertook major or unusual expenditures such as roofing their family's living quarters, providing loans to their husbands for purchasing draught animals and farming equipment, or paying the house tax to government officials. There are, once again, unfortunately no baseline data that could be used to gain historical perspective on this information. Nonetheless, several male informants stated unequivocally that, were it not for garden incomes, many of the marriages in the village would simply fail on the grounds of "non-support." . . .

Gone to Their Second Husbands

It is fair to say that domestic budgetary battles did not originate with the garden boom in Mandinka society; nor are they wholly unique to either The Gambia or Africa. Nonetheless, the Gambian garden boom clearly produced dramatic changes in the normative expectations and practices of marital partners in the country's garden districts. . . .

     The price of autonomy notwithstanding, women in The Gambia's garden districts succeeded in producing a striking new social landscape—by embracing the challenges of the garden boom, they placed themselves in a position to carefully extricate themselves from some of the more onerous demands of marital obligations. Indeed, in a very real sense, they won for themselves "second husbands" by rewriting the rules governing the conjugal contract. Thus the product of lengthy intra-household negotiations brought on by the garden boom was not the simple reproduction of patriarchal privilege and prestige; it was instead a new, carefully crafted autonomy that carried with it obligations and considerable social freedoms.

Double Standards: Women's Property Rights Violations in Kenya

Summary

Shortly after Emily Owino's husband died, her in-laws took all her possessions—including farm equipment, livestock, household goods, and clothing. The in-laws insisted that she be "cleansed" by having sex with a social outcast, a custom in her region, as a condition of staying in her home. They paid a herdsman to have sex with Owino, against her will and without a condom. They later took over her farmland. She sought help from the local elder and chief, who did nothing. Her in-laws forced her out of her home, and she and her children were homeless until someone offered her a small, leaky shack. No longer able to afford school fees, her children dropped out of school.

—Interview with Emily Owino, Siaya, November 2, 2002

When Susan Wagitangu's parents died, her brothers inherited the family land. "My sister and I didn't inherit," said Wagitangu, a fifty-three-year-old Kikuyu woman. "Traditionally, in my culture, once a woman gets married, she does not inherit from her father. The assumption is that once a woman gets married she will be given land where she got married." This was not the case for Wagitangu: when her husband died, her brothers-in-law forced her off that homestead and took her cows. Wagitangu now lives in a Nairobi slum. "Nairobi has advantages," she said. "If I don't have food, I can scavenge in the garbage dump."

—Interview with Susan Wagitangu, Nairobi, October 29, 2002

Women's rights to property are unequal to those of men in Kenya. Their rights to own, inherit, manage, and dispose of property are under constant attack from customs, laws, and individuals—including government officials—who believe that women cannot be trusted with or do not deserve property. The devastating effects of property rights violations—including poverty, disease, violence, and homelessness—harm women, their children, and Kenya's overall development. For decades, the government has ignored this problem. Kenya's new government, which took office in January 2003, must immediately act to eliminate this insidious form of discrimination, or it will see its fight against HIV/AIDS (human immuno-deficiency virus/ acquired immune deficiency syndrome), its economic and social reforms, and its development agenda stagger and fail.

This report recounts the experiences of women from various regions, ethnic groups, religions, and social classes in Kenya who have one thing in common: because they are women, their property rights have been trampled. Many women are excluded from inheriting, evicted from their lands and homes by in-laws, stripped of their possessions, and forced to engage in risky sexual practices in order to keep their property. When they divorce or separate from their husbands, they are often expelled from their homes with only their clothing. Married women can seldom stop their husbands from selling family property. A woman's access to property usually hinges on her relationship to a man. When the relationship ends, the woman stands a good chance of losing her home, land, livestock, household goods, money, vehicles, and other property. These violations have the intent and effect of perpetuating women's dependence on men and undercutting their social and economic status.

Women's property rights violations are not only discriminatory, they may prove fatal. The deadly HIV/AIDS epidemic magnifies the devastation of women's property violations in Kenya, where approximately 15 percent of the population between the ages of fifteen and forty-nine is infected with HIV. Widows who are coerced into the customary practices of "wife inheritance" or ritual "cleansing" (which usually involve unprotected sex) run a clear risk of contracting and spreading HIV. The region where these practices are most common has Kenya's highest AIDS prevalence; the HIV infection rate in girls and young women there is six times higher than that of their male counterparts. AIDS deaths expected in the coming years will result in millions more women becoming widows at younger ages than would otherwise be the case. These women and their children (who may end up AIDS orphans) are likely to face not only social stigma against people affected by HIV/AIDS but also deprivations caused by property rights violations.

A complex mix of cultural, legal, and social factors underlies women's property rights violations. Kenya's customary laws—largely unwritten but influential local norms that coexist with formal laws—are based on patriarchal traditions in which men inherited and largely controlled land and other property, and women were "protected" but had lesser property rights. Past practices permeate contemporary customs that deprive women of property rights and silence them when those rights are infringed. Kenya's constitution prohibits discrimination on the basis of sex, but undermines this protection by condoning discrimination under personal and customary laws. The few statutes that could advance women's property rights defer to religious and customary property laws that privilege men over women. Sexist attitudes are infused in Kenyan society: men that Human Rights Watch interviewed said that women are untrustworthy, incapable of handling property, and in need of male protection. The guise of male "protection" does not obscure the fact that stripping women of their property is a way of asserting control over women's autonomy, bodies, and labor—and enriches their "protectors."

Currently, women find it almost hopeless to pursue remedies for property rights violations. Traditional leaders and governmental authorities often ignore women's property claims and sometimes make the problems worse. Courts overlook and misinterpret family property and succession laws. Women often have little awareness of their rights and seldom have means to enforce them. Women who try to fight back are often beaten, raped, or ostracized. In response to all of this, the Kenyan government has done almost nothing: bills that could improve women's property rights have languished in parliament and government ministries have no programs to promote equal property rights. At every level, government officials shrug off this injustice, saying they do not want to interfere with culture.

As important as cultural diversity and respecting customs may be, if customs are a source of discrimination against women, they—like any other norm—must evolve. This is crucial not only for the sake of women's equality, but because there are real social consequences to depriving half the population of their property rights. International organizations have identified women's insecure property rights as contributing to low agricultural production, food shortages, underemployment, and rural poverty. In Kenya, more than half of the population lives in poverty, the economy is a disaster, and HIV/AIDS rates are high. The agricultural sector, which contributes a quarter of Kenya's gross domestic product and depends on women's labor, is stagnant. If Kenya is to meet its development aims, it must address the property inequalities that hold women back.

Unequal property rights and harmful customary practices violate international law. Kenya has ratified international treaties requiring it to eliminate all forms of discrimination against women (including discrimination in marriage and family relations), guarantee equality before the law and the equal protection of the law, and ensure that women have effective remedies if their rights are violated. International law also obliges states to modify discriminatory social and cultural patterns of conduct. Kenya is violating those obligations.

With a new government in office and a new draft constitution containing provisions that would enhance women's property rights set for debate, this is a pivotal time for Kenya to confront the deep property inequalities in its society. It must develop a program of legal and institutional reforms and educational outreach initiatives that systematically eliminates obstacles to the fulfillment of women's property rights.

Conclusion

Women's property issues touch deeply the ways people live, think, and organize their social and economic lives. It's not just a matter of getting a few women in parliament. People feel threatened.

—Professor Yash Pal Ghai, chairman, Constitution of Kenya Review
Commission, Nairobi, October 23, 2002

Property rights abuses inflicted on women in Kenya should be recognized for what they are: gross violations of women's human rights. Discriminatory property laws and practices impoverish women and their dependents, put their lives at risk by increasing their vulnerability to HIV/AIDS and other diseases, drive them into abhorrent living conditions, subject them to violence, and relegate them to dependence on men and social inequality.

Despite the slow recognition that property rights violations harm not just women and their dependents but Kenya's development as a whole, little has been done to prevent and redress these violations. Averting these abuses in a country where dispossessing women is considered normal will be difficult. A concerted effort is needed not just to improve legal protections, but to modify customary laws and practices and ultimately to change people's minds. With extreme poverty, a moribund economy, rampant violence, and catastrophic HIV/AIDS rates, Kenya can no longer afford to ignore women's property rights violations. Eliminating discrimination against women with respect to property rights is not only a human rights obligation; for many women, it is a matter of life and death.

POSTSCRIPT

Are Women in a Position to Challenge Male Power Structures in Africa?

In many ways, the viewpoints presented in this issue get at a deeper debate about social change and the best way to improve the situation of women in Africa. The selection by Human Rights Watch presents the local situation for women in Kenya as deplorable and intractable, suggesting that a top-down, legislative solution is the best course of action. Critics of this approach might argue that, while this is all well and good, it is largely ineffectual as the reach of government is fairly limited in many African contexts. The case study presented by Schroeder about women in The Gambia provides ammunition for those who suggest that a bottom-up approach that is focused on economic empowerment is the best avenue to greater gender equality in Africa. Imagine, for example, what type of social change might occur in the United States if women earned more on average than men (the situation in Kerawan). This can be compared with U.S. Bureau of Labor Statistics survey results showing that American women earned 77 percent of their male counterparts' salaries in 1999. However, it should be noted that a reading of Schroeder's entire volume (of which a small portion was excerpted for this issue) reveals that the situation was later constrained because women's access to land for gardening was somewhat tenuous. Many men who had temporarily loaned land to women for gardening began reasserting their rights to these plots in the 1990s. As such, it may be that both top-down (i.e., legislative) and bottom-up approaches are needed in order to improve the situation of women in Africa.

The case presented by Schroeder is not an isolated incident of economically empowered women in Africa. Another classic example concerns the "Nanas-Benz" of Togo who are wealthy cloth merchants. They are emblematic of how successful women can be in the West African marketplace. *Nanas* means "established woman" or "woman of means." Benz refers to the type of auto preferred by these market women. The most successful of these merchants can turn over about $600,000 in cloth per month. They act as agents between importers and wide-ranging clientele in West Africa. Successful Nanas-Benz make sure that their children attend university. The girls study economics, management and administration while the boys become architects, teachers, and bankers. The business is often passed down to a woman's female children.

While WID programs still exist today, there has been an effort to move beyond stand-alone programs focused on women to attention and awareness of the situation and needs of women in all types of programs and policy initiatives. This broader approach is often simply referred to as "gender" or "gender and development." For examples of the WID and gender approaches, see relevant sections of the Web sites of the United States Agency for International Development `http://www.usaid.gov/wid/links.htm` and the World Bank `http:// www.worldbank.org/gender/`.

ISSUE 15

Should International Drug Companies Provide HIV/AIDS Drugs to Africa Free of Charge?

YES: Akin Jimoh, from "'Raise the Alarm Loudly': Africa Confronts the AIDS Pandemic," *Dollars and Sense* (May/June 2001)

NO: Siddhartha Mukherjee, from "Take Your Medicine," *The New Republic* (July 24, 2000)

ISSUE SUMMARY

YES: Akin Jimoh, program director of Development Communications, a non-governmental organization (NGO) based in Lagos, Nigeria, argues that the AIDS epidemic in Africa is linked to a number of factors, including the high cost of drugs. He describes how some of the big drug companies, in the face of international protests, begrudgingly agreed to lower the price of anti-HIV medications in Africa. "The companies, however, remain steadfast about keeping their patent rights, which would leave ultimate control over prices and availability in their hands."

NO: Siddhartha Mukherjee, a resident in internal medicine at Massachusetts General Hospital and a clinical fellow in medicine at Harvard Medical School, asserts that the availability of cheap anti-HIV drugs in Africa, without adequate health care networks to monitor their distribution and use, is dangerous. If such medications are not taken consistently and over the prescribed length of time, new strains of HIV are likely to develop more quickly that are resistant to these drugs. He states that investment in health care infrastructure must accompany any distribution of cheap anti-HIV medications.

Patents provide the inventor of a new product with exclusive rights to its sale for a specified time period before competitors may produce the same product under a generic label. Patents are seen as a critical element of the free market system in the United States as they provide an incentive to invent new products. As patent protection is not equally viewed across the globe, the

United States has consistently sought to expand and enforce its view of this concept through international trade agreements, most notably via the World Trade Organization (WTO). The Agreement on Trade-Related Aspects of Intellectual Property (TRIPS), ratified in 1995, required countries to implement strict U.S.-style patent rules within a five to ten year period for a variety of products, including pharmaceuticals.

An important provision in this agreement was an exception for countries in a state of national emergency to be able to resort to compulsory licensing and parallel imports. In the case of pharmaceuticals, compulsory licensing allows a country to require a patent holder to grant authority to another company to produce the drug in exchange for a reasonable royalty. Parallel importation involves importing a product from another country, without permission of the original seller, for resale in another. This practice is officially forbidden under normal conditions because drug companies charge different prices (depending on market conditions) for the same product in different countries.

South Africa angered the United States in 1997 when it adopted a Medicines Act that allowed for both compulsory licensing and parallel importing (although the government's initial intent was to allow parallel importing only). Fearing that similar legislation might be passed in other countries, the Pharmaceutical Researchers and Manufacturers Association, a U.S. trade association, filed suit in South African courts against certain provisions of the legislation. In the face of considerable pressure from the pharmaceutical industry as well as the U.S. government, the South Africans were unyielding, insisting that their citizens should not have to pay more for anti-HIV drugs than, for example, Australians. A series of well-publicized protests from 1999 to 2001 in South Africa, and by AIDS activists in the United States, actually led the pharmaceutical industry and the U.S. government to back down.

In the following selections, Akin Jimoh contends that the AIDS epidemic in Africa can be linked to the high costs of drugs. Big drug companies agreed to lower the price of anti-HIV medications in Africa, however, they have kept their patent rights. Therefore, availability and pricing are still under the control of the drug companies. Siddhartha Mukherjee states that adequate health care networks are needed to monitor the distribution and use of anti-HIV drugs in Africa. Such medications must be taken consistently and over the prescribed length of time so that new strains of HIV will not develop that are resistant to these drugs. The health care infrastructure must be invested in rather than simply providing free anti-HIV medications.

Akin Jimoh

➡ **YES**

"Raise the Alarm Loudly": Africa Confronts the AIDS Pandemic

We were both standing on the sidewalk, watching the convoy of return-ing soldiers on their way to the military hospital in Victoria Island, Lagos, Nigeria. Amid the noise from the heavy-duty military vehicles and downtown traffic, my companion, Mohammed Farouk Auwalu, a former soldier in the Nigerian army, shook his head and muttered, "Many of them will most likely die soon or be out of the army like me with little or nothing to show for it. A lot of people don't know that many have died, others are dying, and many are walking in the shadow of death."

The convoy was returning from one of Nigeria's many peacekeeping missions elsewhere on the continent, but African wars were far from Auwalu's mind. He was talking about the specter of AIDS. In his mid thirties and married, Auwalu is now retired, not because he cannot perform his assigned duties, but because he is living with HIV. He currently heads the Nigeria AIDS Alliance, an awareness group formed by people living with HIV/AIDS.

The Pandemic

So far, AIDS has killed 17 million Africans. It has orphaned about 12 mil-lion children. And about 25.3 million Africans (about 9% of the conti-nent's total population) now live, like Auwalu, with HIV. According to the World Bank, the HIV infection rate in pregnant women in Blantyre, Malawi, increased from less than 5% in 1985 to over 30% in 1997. In Francistown, Botswana, the rate climbed from less than 10% in 1991 to 43% in 1997. New figures from the United Nations Joint AIDS Program (UNAIDS) show that 3.8 million people in sub-Saharan Africa became infected with HIV during 2000. Meanwhile, 2.4 million Africans died of AIDS that year.

From the Horn of Africa to the Cape of Good Hope, HIV/AIDS is crip-pling national economies. Many African countries now face the enormous costs of fighting the epidemic and caring for the millions orphaned by AIDS, even as the most productive generation is decimated by the disease. A study published in the *South African Journal of Economics* in July 2000 concluded that, as a result of HIV/AIDS, South Africa's national income would be 17% lower in 2010 than it would have been otherwise. Overall, the World Bank estimates that HIV/AIDS has cut economic growth in Africa by about two thirds.

"The AIDS situation in Africa is catastrophic and sub-Saharan Africa continues to head the list as the world's most affected region," says Dr. Peter Piot, executive director of UNAIDS. "One of the greatest causes for concern is that over the next few years, the epidemic is bound to get worse before it gets better." AIDS has struck virtually all sectors of society. Families have been devastated; husbands, wives, brothers, and sisters are dead or dying. Women, young people, and children are among the hardest hit.

How did it get this bad?

- *Migrant labor.* The prevalence of migrant labor in Southern Africa has greatly contributed to the high infection rates in Botswana, South Africa, Malawi, Namibia, Zambia, and Zimbabwe. As migrant laborers move from one work site to another, leaving their families behind, many engage in multiple sexual relationships.
- *Low social status of women.* Women account for half of Africa's HIV-positive population, according to the UN, and the infection rate for women is on the rise. Data from several African countries show infection rates for teenage girls five to six times the rates for teenage boys. Poverty forces many girls and women to trade their bodies for money. Meanwhile, the low social and economic status of women, argues UN Secretary General Kofi Annan, results in a "weaker ability to negotiate safe sex."
- *Lack of open discussion.* Cultural and religious inhibitions on the discussion of sex-related issues hindered AIDS prevention at an early stage. Repression against the media also inhibited the flow of information. At an HIV/AIDS meeting in Mexico in 1988, U.S. journalist and science writer Laurie Garrett saluted by name a Kenyan journalist who had broadcast AIDS information over an independent radio station. He was arrested within hours. The Zimbabwean and South African governments have also routinely targeted journalists disseminating information about AIDS.
- *Lack of quick government action.* Olikoye Ransome-Kuti, a pediatrician and former health minister of Nigeria, says that, even in the mid 1990s, the Nigerian military regime allocated a mere $3,000 annually to AIDS control programs. Now, 5.4% of Nigerians between the ages of 15 and 49—about 2.6 million people—live with HIV/AIDS. In many African countries, political turmoil and war contributed to a delayed government response.
- *Weak health-care systems.* In the mid 1980s, most African countries achieved child-immunization rates, to take just one indicator of basic public-health provision, of over 80%. In the following decade, rates fell below 20% in many African countries. Lack of access to basic health services has increased the rate of non-sexual (mother-to-child) HIV transmission.

- *Economic austerity programs.* The AIDS epidemic began its full onslaught in the mid-to-late 1980s, when the International Monetary Fund imposed structural adjustment programs (SAPs) on many African countries. Under the SAPs, national currencies were devalued and subsidies to critical sectors of the economy discontinued. With minimal funds available to governments, social infrastructure and services, including health services, suffered. Keith Hansen, deputy head of the World Bank's AIDS Campaign Team for Africa, admitted that SAPs had weakened African economies. Austerity has deprived African countries of the means to fight the epidemic.
- *The high cost of drugs.* Pharmaceutical companies like Bristol-Myers Squibb of the United States, Glaxo-SmithKline of Great Britain, and Boerhinger Ingelheim GMBH of Germany sell their patented AIDS drugs for $10,000-15,000 per patient per year, three to five times the per capita income of South Africa (the highest in Africa).

Uganda, the place where AIDS first struck in Africa, now offers a model for combating the epidemic. The Ugandan government has helped bring about a mini-sexual revolution. In the mid 1980s, it began prevention campaigns on HIV/AIDS and other sexually transmitted diseases, and started promoting sex education generally. President Yoweri Museveni personally championed the AIDS-control program. Meanwhile, some debt relief and the creation of an anti-poverty program has resulted in a revival of the health system.

"When a lion comes to your village you must raise the alarm loudly," Museveni says. "This is what we did in Uganda; we took it seriously and achieved good results. AIDS . . . is not like small pox or Ebola. AIDS can be prevented as it is transmitted through a few known ways. If we raise awareness sufficiently, it will stop." Between 1997 and 2000, while the HIV infection rate climbed from about 13% to nearly 20% in South Africa and from about 25% to over 35% in Botswana, it has actually decreased in Uganda, from 9.5% to 8.3%. Since there is no cure for AIDS, lower infection rates reflect the deaths of some people who already had AIDS—but also a lower rate of new HIV infections.

The Patents War

In Pretoria, South Africa, this past March [2001], thousands of AIDS activists and HIV-positive youths descended on the country's High Court and the U.S. Embassy. Wearing "HIV-positive" T-shirts and baseball caps, hands locked together in solidarity, they marched in angry protest against the high cost of AIDS drugs. Their placards expressed their rage: "Lives Before Profits" and "AIDS Profiteer Deadlier Than The Virus." The battle over AIDS-drug patents had begun.

A new cocktail of generic AIDS drugs developed by the Indian drug company CIPLA threatens the big drug companies' lucrative monopolies. CIPLA has offered the drug at a cost of $350 per year per patient to the humanitarian organization Doctors Without Borders, and $600 per year per patient to African governments. In March, thirty-nine of the big pharmaceutical companies went to court to challenge the South African government's go-ahead on the sale of generic AIDS drugs, provoking the March protests.

A few weeks after the court battle began, Doctors Without Borders approached Yale University to convince it to release its patent on the AIDS drug dT4. Two Yale professors had developed dT4, which the University then licensed to Bristol-Myers Squibb. Professor William Prusoff, one of the developers, wrote during the height of the controversy that the drug should be either free or very inexpensive in sub-Saharan Africa, and expressed disappointment that it was not reaching the millions of people who desperately needed it. Not long after, Bristol-Myers announced that it would reduce the cost of d4T by 15% in the United States and 85% in the rest of the world, and that it would offer the drug for 15 cents per daily dose in the most afflicted areas of Africa. The other two pharmaceutical giants, GlaxoSmithKline and Boerhinger Ingelheim GMBH, are also expected to cut their AIDS-drug prices. The companies, however, remain steadfast about keeping their patent rights, which would leave ultimate control over prices and availability in their hands.

In response, the AIDS-devastated countries of Africa may resort to "compulsory licensing," ignoring the patents and proceeding with generic drugs. International convention recognizes the right of countries in states of national emergency to obtain or manufacture generic drugs, even in breach of drug-company patents. So far, President Thabo Mbeki of South Africa has resisted an official declaration of national emergency, though he promises to go forward with generic drugs. The U.S. government, under both former President Bill Clinton and current President George W. Bush, has promised not to challenge laws passed by African countries to improve access to AIDS drugs, even if U.S. patent laws are broken. It has not, however, pressed U.S. pharmaceutical firms to renounce their patent rights—which is why protestors targeted the U.S. embassy.

The battle is far from over. Even at 15 cents per day, or about $55 per year, AIDS drugs will remain beyond the means of most Africans. At the 8th Conference on Retroviruses and Opportunistic Infections in February 2001, doctors, scientists, and policymakers proposed that rich nations pay for drugs and other means to combat AIDS in Africa, with the United States paying $3 billion. Harvard economist Jeffrey Sachs explained that $3 billion would only cost the United States about $10 per person, the cost of a movie ticket and a bag of popcorn. Dr. Peter Piot of UNAIDS believes that this additional $3 billion would go a long way towards coping with the epidemic in sub-Saharan Africa—with half going to basic care for those already infected, the other half to prevention efforts.

Donors cannot, however, dictate how the battle against AIDS will be fought. A recent report issued by the Africa-America Institute, which champions a greater U.S. commitment to the fight against AIDS in Africa, concludes that donors need to support national priorities set by Africans themselves. Local circumstances vary greatly from country to country, the AAI argues, so international donors need to learn more about Africa and adapt their programs to the needs of each country. "If the U.S. and other donors want to make a difference in the fight against HIV/AIDS in Africa," AAI President Mora McLean says, "they need to listen to Africans and involve them as full partners in the global battle against the epidemic."

NO ◄

Siddhartha Mukherjee

Take Your Medicine

Last week's [July 2000] International AIDS Conference in Durban, South Africa, was a spectacularly glum affair. While angry protesters outside the conference railed against greedy pharmaceutical companies, delegates inside recited dismal statistics about the plague, each more alarming than the last. In South Africa, approximately one in ten adults is HIV-positive; in Africa as a whole, AIDS now takes three times as many lives as the next most common cause of death. Of all the depressing numbers, there was only one that health officials felt confident about changing any time soon: the $15,000 it currently costs to treat just one person with anti-HIV drugs for a year.

The reason is something called "tiered pricing" or "equity pricing," a concept that UNAIDS, the United Nations agency dealing with AIDS, began promoting recently and that elicited considerable excitement in Durban, even winning the endorsement of Bill Gates. Under the scheme, Western pharmaceutical companies, like Merck and Glaxo Wellcome, would set different prices for drugs in rich and poor countries. The same pill—say, AZT—could be sold for $4 in New York but only 40 cents in Johannesburg. With tiered pricing, Africans could finally afford the anti-HIV medicines they desperately need, and drug companies could still turn a reasonable profit.

A great idea? Actually, no—at least not by itself. What the enthusiasts seem not to realize is that without adequate health care networks to monitor their distribution, potent new medicines are worse than useless; they're dangerous. Consider Russia's recent experience with anti-tuberculosis drugs. In the 1990s, physicians in the former Soviet Union unleashed a torrent of anti-tuberculosis drugs on the population. The drugs were great, but the patients taking them weren't adequately supervised; in many hospitals, as many as 50 percent of patients strayed from the prescribed regimen. Soon, upwards of five percent of patients in some Russian clinics began to exhibit a strain of tuberculosis completely resistant to all drugs. Subsequently, millions of dollars had to be spent to contain the deadly strain. As Dr. C. Robert Horsburgh, a public health expert from Boston University, recently warned in the *Journal of American Medicine*, "The genie of multi-drug-resistant TB [was] irreversibly out of the bottle."

The HIV genie is even more ominous. HIV's secret—one reason the wispy virus is now a continent-hopping Goliath—is that it mutates rapidly, quickly becoming resistant to drugs. If anti-HIV drugs are not taken properly—a missed capsule here, a forgotten pill there—a low level of viral reproduction continues within the body. And the viruses brewed while the antiviral medicines are still present in a patient's system can be especially lethal, as they are selected to carry mutations that render them resistant to the original drug. Even in the United States, where an excellent health care network monitors most drug regimens, about ten percent of patients already harbor HIV strains resistant to AZT, the most common anti-HIV drug. And if such potent drugs are dumped unsupervised on Africa—where health care networks cannot afford to be as vigilant—then a virulent, drug-resistant strain of HIV may emerge very quickly and could even boomerang back to the West.

⋯◉⋯

Fortunately, there is an alternative to the solution hyped . . . in Durban. Since the safety of anti-HIV drugs depends on a country's health care infrastructure, pharmaceutical companies could pay to develop in Africa some of the infrastructure necessary to make sure their anti-HIV drugs are taken properly.

Why would drug companies do something so altruistic? Because it's not altruistic at all. After all, drug companies can only squeeze profits out of Africa by selling Africans their anti-HIV drugs over a long period of time. Right now, with about 22 million Africans infected with HIV, the demand for anti-viral drugs seems inexhaustible. But, if a viral strain immune to a company's drug emerged, the drugmakers would no longer have medicine Africans wanted to buy. Even worse, the resistant virus might spread into more profitable Western markets. Only by making an investment in health care infrastructure—and thus preventing drug-resistant strains of HIV from coming to life—can a pharmaceutical company ensure that its cash-cow drug isn't rapidly made worthless by new mutations.

Glaxo Wellcome, at least, seems to understand this. In May, the company announced it would enter an unusual collaboration with UNAIDS to make sure its discounted anti-HIV drugs would be sold only in selected areas—places that "address[ed] the health care infrastructure and drug distribution aspects" and where there was "access to safe and effective ongoing treatment" for HIV. Glaxo also agreed to foot some of the bill for building these infrastructures through direct training and technical support of AIDS advocacy groups.

No one can be sure the Glaxo-UNAIDS scheme will work, because nothing like it has ever really been tried. There isn't much precedent for such public and private collaborations actually creating safe environments for selling discounted drugs. But, then again, there isn't much precedent for a recalcitrant virus infecting whole swaths of an entire continent. HIV is so deadly because it is enormously resourceful, crafty, and even creative. To defeat it, we will have to be, as well.

POSTSCRIPT

Should International Drug Companies Provide HIV/AIDS Drugs to Africa Free of Charge?

Mukherjee brings up the issue that the health care systems in most African countries are incapable of effectively monitoring the wide-scale use of anti-HIV drugs. While Mukherjee suggests that drug companies have a self-interested stake in supporting these systems, many others have decried the role of structural adjustment programs and debt in facilitating funding cuts to these systems. Structural adjustment programs, largely implemented by the World Bank and the International Monetary Fund, call for the balancing of government budgets through, among other things, reductions in social service spending and contractions in the civil service. Debt (with African countries accounting for 34 of the 41 most indebted countries in the world) also reduces current spending on social services, as a growing proportion of state revenues must be spent on debt service. For more on this topic see Laura Dely, "Aiding and Abetting an Epidemic," in *Sojourners* (November 1999).

Much of the HIV/AIDS work in Africa has been focused on prevention as opposed to treatment. As Mukherjee describes, Uganda is an excellent example of a country that has aggressively pursued prevention strategies and has consequently seen an amazing reduction in the prevalency rate of AIDS. As a result of the exorbitant cost of anti-HIV drugs (even with the price concessions of pharmaceutical companies), some may conclude that investing in drugs that merely prolong the lives of infected individuals is less of a priority than prevention efforts. This position may be tempered by a knowledge of Africa's already large and growing problem of AIDS orphans, that is, children for whom both parents have died from AIDS, as well as the issue of mother-to-child transmission of HIV during birth or through breastfeeding. In the case of the former, drugs that prolong the life of a parent also enhance the life of a child. In the case of the latter, drugs taken shortly before the birth of a child by an HIV-infected mother greatly reduce the chances of transmission. For more on the issue of mother-to-child transmission, see a 2001 World Health Organization technical consultation entitled "New Data on the Prevention of Mother-to-Child Transmission of HIV and Their Policy Implications." A good book on the AIDS orphan problem in Uganda, Zambia, and South Africa is Emma Guest's *Children of AIDS: Africa's Orphan Crisis* (Pluto Press, 2001).

One cannot conclude a discussion of this issue without mentioning George Bush's announcement in his 2003 State of the Union Address that the United States would be committing $15 billion over the next five years to combat AIDS in Africa. Of this money, roughly half will be spent on AIDS drugs with the hope of offering antiretroviral drugs to two million people. This is the largest commitment to fighting AIDS in Africa that we have seen to date. No mention, however, was made concerning the role (if any) of drug companies in this initiative.

ISSUE 16

Is Sexual Promiscuity a Major Reason for the HIV/AIDS Epidemic in Africa?

YES: William A. Rushing, from *The AIDS Epidemic: Social Dimensions of an Infectious Disease* (Westview Press, 1995)

NO: Joseph R. Oppong and Ezekiel Kalipeni, from "A Cross-Cultural Perspective on AIDS in Africa: A Response to Rushing," *African Rural and Urban Studies* (1996)

ISSUE SUMMARY

YES: William A. Rushing, late professor of sociology at Vanderbilt University, explains the high prevalence of HIV/AIDS in Africa in terms of how Africans express and give social meaning to sex. He argues that the confluence of a set of sex-related behavioral patterns and gender stratification explains the HIV/AIDS infection rate. According to Rushing, these behavioral patterns include polygamous marriage practices, weak conjugal bonds, the transactional nature of sexual relations, the centrality of sexual conquest to male identity, and sex-positive cultures.

NO: Joseph R. Oppong, associate professor of geography at the University of North Texas, and Ezekiel Kalipeni, associate professor of geography at the University of Illinois at Urbana-Champaign, take issue with Rushing's conclusions. They contend that his analysis is Americentric, suffers from overgeneralizations, and problematically depicts Africans as sex-positive (and by implication, promiscuous and immoral). They assert that Rushing's cultural stereotypes are far too general to provide any meaningful insight into the AIDS crisis in Africa. An understanding of historical and contemporary migration patterns, as well as associated phenomena, better explain the spread of the virus.

Halting the spread of HIV/AIDS is one of the greatest challenges facing contemporary Africa. Unlike some other diseases, AIDS is particularly problematic because it strikes the working-age population and thus has serious economic and social consequences. In 1999 AIDS became the leading cause of death in Africa, overtaking malaria. As of 2002 the United Nations AIDS program (UNAIDS) reported that 29.4 million adults were infected with the HIV virus in sub-Saharan Africa, which accounts for about 70 percent of the infected population worldwide. Through 2001 approximately 21.5 million Africans had lost their lives to AIDS. The overall infection rate among adults in sub-Saharan Africa is estimated at 8.8 percent (compared with 1.2 percent worldwide), although this rate varies considerably throughout the region. Twelve countries, mostly in eastern and southern Africa, have infection rates above 10 percent. Botswana leads the continent with an infection rate of 38.8 percent, while Zimbabwe, Swaziland, and Lesotho also have infection rates above 30 percent. South Africa, Zambia, and Namibia have rates between 20 and 25 percent. West Africa has been hit less hard by the disease. Notable exceptions are Ivory Coast with an infection rate of 9.7 percent and Nigeria with a rate of 5.8 percent. The case of Nigeria is particularly worrisome because it is the most populous country in Africa.

The spatial pattern of the disease has changed over time. Initially, it was distributed along major highways and in the urban centers of eastern and central Africa. More recently, the epicenter of the virus has moved to southern Africa. In Africa, the disease is largely transmitted through unprotected heterosexual sex and unsafe medical practices. Truck drivers, prostitutes, and military personnel all have above-average infection rates and are believed to play a significant role in the spread of the virus. Women comprise 58 percent of those infected in Africa.

In the following selections, William A. Rushing argues that it is the confluence of a set of sex-related behavioral patterns and gender stratification that explains the HIV/AIDS infection rate in Africa. Joseph R. Oppong and Ezekiel Kalipeni maintain that historical and contemporary migration patterns, as well as associated phenomena, are a major reason for the HIV/AIDS epidemic in Africa.

A nice aspect of the readings selected for this issue is that Oppong and Kalipeni wrote their selection directly in response to the chapter in Rushing's book dealing with Africa. An additional benefit is that the writings capture the two main lines of argumentation used to interpret the spread of HIV/AIDS in Africa, that is, those based on cultural factors and those based on political/economic factors.

William A. Rushing  **YES**

The AIDS Epidemic: Social Dimensions of an Infectious Disease

The Cross-Cultural Perspective

AIDS in Africa

Statistics show that since 1985, AIDS has been increasing faster in Africa than in any other region of the world (Mann et al., 1992:893–901). Surveys indicate that as many as 5 percent of the populations of Uganda, Rwanda, and Ivory Coast are infected. More than 20 percent of pregnant women in some urban areas are infected (Mann et al., 1992:41–47, 65), and extrapolation to the general population in one city (Kigali) gives an estimated *annual incidence* of 3–5 percent (Bucyendore et al., 1993). The International AIDS Center of the Harvard School of Public Health estimated that in 1992 more than 8 million Africans were infected, which would be about 65 percent of all cases worldwide (Mann et al., 1992:89–90). HIV-AIDS is about evenly distributed between males and females (Mann et al., 1992:76).

Several factors account for the pattern of high rates and balanced sex distribution. Poor nutrition and many infectious diseases compromise immune systems and possibly make people susceptible to HIV. Medical technology to screen donor blood for HIV and disposable hypodermics are quite limited. HIV-contaminated needles may be reused without being properly sterilized (Mann et al., 1992:433–434; Root-Bernstein, 1993:301–309).

In addition, STDs [sexually transmitted diseases] are exceedingly prevalent in Africa. For example, in a review of STDs in developing countries, Robert Brunham and Alan Ronald (1991:61) concluded that in some African countries STDs are one of the top five diseases for persons seeking health services. STDs are especially high for persons (men and women) infected with HIV (Allen et al., 1991:1660; Plummer et al., 1991:236; Plourde et al., 1992:89–90; Dallabetta et al., 1993:40). An epidemic of STDs appeared in the years preceding the AIDS epidemic in Africa (Arya and Bennet, 1976; Osoba, 1981; Mann et al., 1992:167), just as it did among American gays. One study in the early 1980s revealed that as many as 20 percent of Zimbabwe's urban population had an STD (Ungar, 1989:331). Another study showed that 10 percent of Ugandans had gonococcal infections in 1981; in comparison, only 0.4 percent of American and Europeans had these infections, and differences of similar magnitude for syphilis and other STDs were reported (Root-Bernstein, 1993:165, 301–303). Given the presence of HIV, the high rate of STDs assures that HIV will be widely transmitted in heterosexual intercourse, which may account for 90 percent of HIV infections (Williams, 1992:46).

But high rates of STDs do not act alone. Polygamous behavior spreads STDs and hence HIV, whereas monogamous behavior limits the spread. Most experts agree that polygamous behavior is a major factor in African HIV-AIDS, and from a sociological point of view, it is the most relevant factor. It is also the focus of this [selection].

That STDs are so widespread is indirect evidence that polygamous behavior is also widespread. Ethnographic studies leave no doubt that having multiple sexual partners is a common cultural practice in many groups in Africa (Caldwell et al., 1989:205–216; see also Southall, 1961:52; Gregersen, 1983:190; Hrdy, 1987; Larson, 1989; Bledsoe, 1990). For this reason many Westerners claim Africans are "promiscuous." This view is ethnocentric. Sexual behavior varies widely across societies (Davenport, 1977; Gregersen, 1983; Becker, 1984), and there is simply no universal cultural standard against which sexual practice can be judged as promiscuous and excessive (or repressive); what is appropriate in one society may be deviant in others. Sociologically, if the customs of a particular society approve polygamous behavior, such behavior is normal and appropriate by the standards of that society. To call it promiscuous simply reflects the view of persons who belong to sex-negative societies in which monogamous relations are the normative ideal and having multiple partners is viewed as deviant and immoral. Such moralizing does nothing to enhance our understanding of the practice. Analysis based on the cross-cultural perspective does.

The Cross-Cultural Perspective and Sex

The central idea in the cross-cultural perspective is that behavior patterns that exist in one society but not in others or in varying degrees in different societies are the result of differences in the way societies structure and give meaning to behavior. This is true for sexual behavior no less than other types. Eroticism and, for heterosexual sex, reproduction are universal. But although the biological dynamics of sex are universal because the biology of sex does not vary with society, the social dynamics—how society structures the way sex is expressed and gives it social meaning—are not universal. Therefore, to understand why polygamous behavior is so common in Africa (and a major reason for the pattern of HIV-AIDS in Africa), we must understand why sexual expression is structured this way in African societies, or "tribes," and the social meaning sex has for members of most of these societies.

. . . Commonalities in the social dynamics of sex derive from (1) the traditional marriage institution and kinship ties, (2) cultural norms and beliefs about sexual expression (sexual culture), and (3) gender stratification. The descriptions that follow are for rural tribal societies, even though HIV is more serious in urban areas, because sexual practices in towns and cities are patterned on rural customs. In addition, the rates of HIV-AIDS in rural Africa are low only when compared to rates in urban Africa. In comparison to most places in the world, the prevalence of HIV-AIDS in many rural areas in Africa is very high.

Marriage and Kinship

Polygyny. Traditionally, in most African societies polygamy has been the preferred form of marriage. Polygyny is still widespread, though polyandry is (and traditionally has been) rare (Gregersen, 1983:190; see also Southall, 1961:52; Molnos, 1968:50–51; Caldwell et al., 1989:201; Bledsoe, 1990:117). In certain regions in Europe and Asia, polygamous (mostly polygynous) marriage is also normatively approved, but only about 3–4 percent of marriages are in this form, whereas according to the World Fertility Survey, up to 30–50 percent of all marriages in Africa are polygamous (Caldwell et al., 1989:201). Consequently, the proportion of all women involved in a polygynous marriage at some stage during their lives is very high. Since multiple wives increase the spread of STDs in a population, polygyny obviously contributes to the high HIV-AIDS rate as well as the balanced rate between males and females.

Patrilineage.   Typically, after marriage the couple lives embedded in a compound or adjacent huts usually belonging to the husband's extended family, subclan, or clan. This makes for cohesive kinship ties, which are valued more than marital ties. Children are usually descended patrilineally and belong to the husband's kinship unit. They are valued as economic assets (to perform field labor and take care of parents and other relatives in old age) (Molnos, 1968:50; Lamb, 1987:33–34; Ungar 1989:184). Children also increase the numerical strength of clan and tribe. And a man's personal status within the clan-tribe rises as his progeny increases; traditionally, "the key measure of a man's wealth [has been] the number of dependents in his household" (Henn, 1984:5). Patrilineage thus gives men strong social incentives to acquire many wives (Southall, 1961:52; Caldwell et al., 1989:202).

It also promotes polygamous behavior outside marriage. Wives are valued largely for their potential as "baby machines" (Lamb, 1987:39). The respect they receive in the clan-tribe depend on the number of children they bear. Children are social and economic assets to women no less than to men. Consequently, the physical and emotional aspects of sex in marriage are subordinate to childbearing (Molnos, 1968:58, 79). This makes for weak conjugal bonds (Caldwell et al., 1989:199–189, 200; see also Radcliffe-Brown, 1950:51–54; Larson, 1989:722; Bledsoe, 1990:117; O'Connor, 1991:51), so that extramarital sex is common, normal, and even expected, though more so for men than women (Caldwell et al., 1989:212). And the fact that children born from such unions belong to the husband and his kinship group is an incentive for men to engage in extramarital affairs. Thus, since patrilineage encourages men to acquire wives and to engage in polygamous nonmarital behavior, it is a major etiological factor in the African pattern of HIV-AIDS.

Sexual Culture

Sexual culture refers to the cultural beliefs, attitudes, and norms regarding sex. In contrast to Americans, who usually view sex morally and think that people who have multiple partners (even if unmarried) are immoral and unfaithful, most Africans do not judge sexual behavior in such terms at all. They experience little guilt about sex, and they enter into sex more casually and have more sexual partners than Westerners do. The cultural beliefs and norms that do bear most directly on sex are the transactional element in sexual relations, a masculine sexual ideology, and sex-positive beliefs.

The transactional element in sexual relations. In general, Africans view sex as an ordinary activity, much like work (Caldwell et al., 1989:194, 209, 218). Traditional sexual ethics are similar to those that regulate other services, namely, the ethic of exchange (Caldwell et al., 1989:203). Sexual relations are characterized by a "transactional element" (Caldwell et al., 1989:202–205), which is especially explicit in the traditional marriage.

Marriage is primarily an arrangement between kinship groups rather than individuals (Radcliffe-Brown, 1950:41–54; Little, 1971:17–20, 1974:4–8; La Fontaine, 1974:112). In return for loss of the daughter's labor as well as for her sexual favors and the children she will produce for the husband and his clan, the wife's family receives a bride-price (traditionally in the form of cattle). The transaction is negotiated by family elders who have little, if any, concern for the wishes and passion of the couple (Lamb, 1987:37). (Indeed, in some instances marriages are arranged early in the couple's life and sometimes before birth). This approach to marriage contributes to weak conjugal bonds, so that divorce, separation, and desertion are common (Caldwell et al., 1989:201; Larson, 1989:720); see also Pankhurst and Jacobs, 1988).

In extramarital and premarital affairs, men are expected to give women money and gifts as an expression of affection, respect, and gratitude (Larson, 1989:723; Caldwell, et al., 1989:203; see also Shoumatoff, 1988:155). And for women, such affairs are important sources of income. Extramarital sex is less common for women than premarital sex (Larson, 1989:721), though a wife sometimes has several lovers, serially or concurrently (Obbo, 1980:151). This (or the threat thereof) may give her leverage over the husband and thus access to his economic resources (Caldwell et al., 1989:204). (This tactic may well backfire, however, especially if the husband has several wives.)

In general, then, in most sexual relations—whether casual liaisons, premarital relations, extramarital affairs, or marriage—"there is an economic core," with women "exchanging sexual favours and often also reproductive potential for economic benefits" (Barnett and Blaikie, 199:77). This exchange is explicitly acknowledged and normatively accepted. In some groups mothers may actually encourage their daughters to trade sexual favors for money and gifts as a way to provide for themselves (Caldwell et al., 1989:203–204).

Although many Westerners have difficulty seeing how this arrangement differs from prostitution, Western anthropologists who study African societies disagree on how prostitution should even be defined in the African context (Molnos, 1968:79; Little, 1973:84; Caldwell et al., 1989:218–219; Dirasse,

1991:10). The usual definition of prostitution holds that a prostitute is a woman whose income is derived more or less exclusively from payment for brief impersonal encounters with all comers, most of whom are strangers, in which no services or activities beyond the sex act are involved. (Many Westerners use "prostitute" more loosely to refer to all women who use sex to elicit money and other material favors from men.) By this definition, prostitution in Africa appears to have been most limited; in fact, prior to colonization in most groups prostitutes as a category of women were not even recognized (Gregersen, 1983:15; Hrdy, 1987:1112; Caldwell et al., 1989:220–221). Even so, the transactional element in sex increases the spread of HIV, as the following example reveals.

In a study of lakeside trading villages in the Rakai district of Uganda, Tony Barnett and Piers Blaikie (1992:78) observed that women commonly support themselves through commodity trading. However, they also "set up independent households," with "one or more regular lovers who help them financially." These woman are obviously involved in sexual transactions (financial help for sex) but they are not prostitutes. Although lovers may give them money, nonsexual activity is central to the relationship; sexual activity is simply integrated in a round of other activities that the partners share. In addition, such relationships are not the sole (or even primary) source of women's livelihood. And these relationships involve more than a single sexual encounter, the partners are not strangers, and a degree of affection may be assumed. Little (1973:81) observed the same pattern in African towns. Similar arrangements do exist in the West, or course, though they are less common and less open. More significantly, the arrangement in the West in almost always limited to one partner extending over a period of time. In contrast, in Africa "the rate of partner change can be assumed to be fairly rapid" (Barnett and Blaikie, 1992:78). Although many Americans would consider this immoral, even as prostitution, Africans do not; this arrangement is best viewed as part of the transactional cultural norm in sex rather than as either promiscuity or prostitution. The implications for the transmission of HIV are clear. Barnett and Blaikie (1992: 32, 69) reported that in the Rakai district, around 40 percent of men and women between twenty and thirty are seropositive for HIV.

Masculine sexual ideology and the status of men. In most African societies a plurality of sexual partners is a male right (Southall, 1961:52; Molnos, 1968:66; Caldwell et al., 1989:202; Larson, 1989:721; Barnett and Blaikie, 1992:77–78). This right is related to polygyny (if only as a rationalization for it) (Davenport, 1977:125). But it goes beyond polygyny since the right does not end with marriage. It is socially acceptable for a married man to have mistresses and "outside wives" (concubines) (Little, 1974b:17–18; Obbo, 1980:89; Larson, 1989:720). Men's extramarital relations are "taken for granted" and simply "expected of the normal man" (Caldwell et al., 1989:212). Indeed, sexual conquest and fatherhood are central to male identity, and children enhance a man's social status. This reinforces women's use of sex for material gain (Barnett and Blaikie, 1992:44, 77–78).

Masculine sexual ideology combines with the transactional element such that the more wealth a man has, the more sexual partners he can get. For example, a bride-price must be paid for a wife. Thus, traditionally "the key measure of a man's wealth [has been] the number of [wives and children] in his household" (Henn, 1984:5). Some chiefs are known to have hundreds of wives (Molnos, 1968:50). The association of number of female partners with male wealth suggests that HIV infection rates are higher among men with higher status than among men with lower status.

Sexual relations and a sex-positive culture. Most groups in Africa have sex-positive cultures. Sex is viewed as a part of courtship and a form of recreation, and relations between lovers are viewed as affairs between friends (Larson, 1989:723, 727). Despite the emphasis on sex for reproduction, New Yorker reporter Alex Shoumatoff (1988:154–155), who is married to a Rwandan, stated that most African societies "are unquestionably sex-positive." This is especially so for men, who tend to be "womanizers." Women "put up with it or participate in it depending on how much freedom they are allowed by their culture." (See also Barnett and Blaikie, 1992:77–78). And by all accounts, as the existence of the transactional element in sex would indicate, in many groups women are allowed considerable freedom indeed (Molnos, 1968:58). Premarital sex for females is accepted (Molnos, 1968:58–59; Caldwell et al., 1989:195, 197, 203–205; Larson, 1989:727), as is female adultery (Caldwell et al., 1989:197, 199, 212; Larson, 1989:723). According to Laketch Dirasse (1991:57), in at least one tribe (the Borana), men allow their wives "to have as many lovers as they want" (see also Bledsoe, 1990:123). Wife sharing is also reported for a number of societies, which permit or even require a wife to have sex with persons besides her husband, most frequently distant relatives of the husband's clan, sometimes as a form of hospitality to guests (Gregersen, 1983:190; Caldwell et al., 1989:213). In some groups a widow is inherited by one of her husband's brothers (levirate), and a woman may have sex with each brother to see which one would please her most in case her husband dies (Schuster, 1979:14).

In sum, for females as well as males, "fairly permissive . . . sexual attitudes are found generally across sub-Saharan Africa" (Caldwell et al., 1989:222). Many scholars of African society have observed that a "wide range of all types of unstable and occasional [sexual] unions" are widespread in Africa (Molnos, 1968:79). Beyond polygamous relations, sex is simply "regarded . . . positively [and as] normal and good for the health, and which, if not experienced, might well result in ill health" (Caldwell et al., 1989:209). In short, sex is viewed in sex-positive terms.

At the same time, sex is socially regulated. That the traditional African marriage is an economic arrangement between families limits the choices individuals have in mate selection. Family decisions are constrained by the custom of exogamy, and lovers usually must also be selected from outside the clan, subclan, or tribe (Davenport, 1977:125; Lamb, 1987:11). In other instances groups stipulate that the wife may have sex only with her husband's relatives or members of his age group (Gregersen, 1983:190; Caldwell et al., 1989:213). The nature of village life puts women under the surveillance of the husband's relatives and clan, and any deviation from the duties of wife and mother are apt to be quickly detected, as are deviations from restrictions on the tribal affiliation of sex partners. Even so, for most of Africa social norms permit and even encourage sex with multiple partners. Polygamous sexual relations are thus widespread for the married no less than the unmarried (Gregersen, 1983:186). This is the hallmark of a sex-positive culture. It also facilitates the spread of HIV.

NO ⬅ Joseph R. Oppong and
Ezekiel Kalipeni

A Cross-Cultural Perspective on AIDS in Africa: A Response to Rushing

Introduction

Data compiled by the World Health Organization and from various surveys seem to indicate that HIV/AIDS in Africa has reached epidemic proportions, particularly in the so-called AIDS epicenter in central African countries. It is usually noted that anywhere from 5 to 10 percent of the urban population may be infected. Rates of infection are assumed to be even higher for certain sectors of society such as commercial sex workers, pregnant women in urban areas, and truck drivers. The share of the disease between the sexes is equal and heterosexual contact is considered the main mode of transmission. Over the past decade research has shown that HIV/AIDS infections have increased at a faster rate in Africa than anywhere else. It is estimated that in excess of eight million Africans are believed to be infected with the deadly virus and more than 1.5 million have full-blown AIDS (Tastemain and Coles 1993). This is about 65 percent of all cases worldwide. Although Africa's share of HIV-infected persons is expected to decrease from the current two-thirds to one-half of the world's total by the year 2000, Good (1995) points out that this relative decrease cannot be celebrated, because the "long wave" character of the AIDS epidemic will continue to spiral out of control in many African countries. It is undeniable that the socioeconomic and demographic conse-quences of the epidemic are serious, since it strikes at the heart of the work force, mostly young men and women in their prime productive and repro-ductive years. Yet most Western approaches to the study of the factors that facilitate the transmission of the disease tend to be largely overgeneraliza-tions and too simplistic. Indeed, as [Angus] Nicoll and [Phyllida] Brown (1994) point out, the images of Africa conjured in Western minds, perpetu-ated by the biased media, have been those of an oversimplified exotic place variously depicted as a game park or an apocalyptic vision of famine and civil war. Recent ominous accounts by notable journalists such as [R. D.] Kaplan (1994) have tended to perpetuate such stereotypes.

In the medical and epidemiological arena, the different pattern of AIDS infection exhibited by African countries has resulted in the development of a

From Joseph R. Oppong and Ezekiel Kalipeni, "A Cross-Cultural Perspective on AIDS in Africa: A Response to Rushing," *African Rural and Urban Studies,* vol. 3, no. 2 (1996). Copyright © 1996 by The Michigan State University Press. Reprinted by permission. Notes and references omitted.

plethora of research on AIDS in Africa which, as [Randall M.] Packard and [Paul] Epstein (1991) note, resembles earlier narrow-minded colonial efforts to understand the epidemiological patterns of TB and syphilis. Indeed, current research on the AIDS epidemic in Africa has tended to focus on why Africa exhibits a different epidemiological pattern than that found in the West and elsewhere. Explanations of the different pattern invariably lay blame on the peculiarities of African customs, traditions, and behaviors that relate to issues of sexuality and reproduction at the expense of a range of other equally significant factors such as the colonial historical context, poverty, dependency, and underdevelopment (Packard and Epstein 1991).

In this [selection] we take issue with [William A.] Rushing's recent work titled "The Cross-Cultural Perspective of AIDS in Africa," which appears as chapter 3 in his book *The AIDS Epidemic: Social Dimensions of an Infectious Disease,* published in 1995 by Westview Press. The discussion contained in Rushing's paper follows the overgeneralization syndrome, as overly Americentric, and depicts Africans as being sex-positive and, by implication, promiscuous and immoral while Americans are sex-negative and morally upright and hence less akin to HIV infection. In our response to Rushing's stereotypical assertions, we argue that Rushing's cultural stereotypes are far too general to be of any meaningful use to the understanding of the AIDS epidemic in Africa, and that such careless propositions tend only to encourage a premature narrowing of research questions as happened during the colonial era in the cases of tuberculosis (TB) and syphilis (see for example, Fendell 1963; Packard 1987; Packard and Epstein 1991).

The Overgeneralization Syndrome

[Benjamin] Ofori-Amoah (1995) has correctly observed that overgeneralization frequently characterizes research on Africa. First, studies based on specificnational or people groups assume an African or sub-Saharan Africa title when it comes to publication of results. Thus, a study on AIDS in Uganda with a special focus on Rakai District or Buganda region is called *AIDS in Africa* (Barnett and Blaikie 1992). Second, despite the rich cultural mosaic and differences in geographical, economic, and historical experiences, Africa is portrayed as culturally homogenous. Rushing's (1995) work is replete with several excellent examples of overgeneralization as he portrays a sex-positive African culture, which sees sex as a recreation activity, and thus, "guides women into prostitution more easily than Western culture does" (73–74) as a major causal factor of AIDS in Africa. While generalizing results is a critical step for theory development in the search for universalism in social science (Nachimas and Nachimas 1981), loose generalizations can be inappropriate.

Rushing creates the impression that Africans are homogeneously promiscuous, that perhaps sexual promiscuity is the one attribute common to Africa's numerous cultures. Africa is discussed as though it were one country, not some 50 nations with hundreds of different ethnic groups, each with a complex set of traditions in as far as issues of sexuality, reproduction, and inheritance are concerned. No serious consideration is given to the many cultural influences

African peoples have been subjected to during the colonial era. His discussion ignores the reality that on top of the many traditions, one finds Western and in some cases Islamic cultural influences, all operating within the same locality, a fact which [Ali P.] Mazrui (1986) calls Africa's *triple heritage.* . . .

The Cross-Cultural Perspective

Rushing begins his paper by advancing four main factors that contribute to the proliferation of the AIDS epidemic in Africa. . . . The fourth factor, which Rushing considers to be the most important factor and hence the preoccupation of his paper, is the omnipresent polygamous behavior among all African societies. . . . Drawing upon outdated ethnographic studies such as those by [Alfred Reginald] Radcliffe-Brown (1950), [Aidan] Southall (1961), and a few recent ones by prominent Western Africanist scholars such as [John C.] Caldwell et al. (1989), and [Caroline] Bledsoe (1990), Rushing concludes that such studies leave no doubt that having multiple sexual partners is a universal cultural practice in many African societies and that such behavior is culturally determined and considered normal and appropriate by Africans, and hence the proliferation of HIV/AIDS. In so doing Rushing invokes the behavioral paradigm to account for the widespread nature of the HIV/AIDS epidemic in Africa. It is this kind of rush to find a cause, i.e., "the sexual life of the natives" and to prescribe an immediate solution, i.e., "modification of sexual behavior," that obscures the real risk factors, namely, the historical, social, political, and economic contexts within which such risk behaviors are played out.

Once the central factor in the proliferation of HIV/AIDS in Africa is identified as promiscuous behavior, Rushing tries to rationalize it through the cross-cultural framework. The central idea in this framework is that "behavior patterns that exist in one society but not in others or in varying degrees in different societies are the result of differences in the way societies structure and give meaning to behavior." In the context of African societies, exotic or almost primitive marriage, and sexual and kinship arrangements are highlighted as the culprits for the proliferation of AIDS in both rural and urban settings. . . .

Marriage and Kinship

. . . In terms of polygyny, it is noted that in most traditional societies the preferred form of marriage is polygamy whose prevalence is given as being 30 to 50 percent of all marriages, according to the World Fertility Surveys of the 1970s, compared to 3–5 percent elsewhere in the world. Based on this fact it is concluded that since multiple wives increase the spread of STDs [sexually transmitted diseases] in a population, polygyny contributes to the high HIV/AIDS rate as well as the balanced rate between males and females. If indeed polygamy was such a potent means of proliferation, then the Islamic societies of northern Africa should exhibit larger than usual HIV rates since polygamy is the normative form of marriage in these societies. Yet evidence suggests otherwise. In North Africa and the Middle East HIV is spreading, but more slowly than elsewhere in the world (Tastemain and Coles 1993). In short a culture can be polygamous, but that does not automatically result in the rapid transmission of sexually transmitted diseases; it all depends on marital norms. Furthermore, the 30–50 percent prevalence rate of polygamy is not broken down by age. Recent data from censuses and the Demographic and Health Surveys (DHS) of the mid-1980s and early 1990s indicate much lower rates of polygamous unions in most African countries. For example, in most southern and east African countries, marriage for women is universal but mostly monogamous. In Malawi census data show that only 20 percent of men over 40 years of age have more than one wife (World Bank 1992). In the DHS data only 9 percent of men reported having more than one wife and 20 percent of women reported being in polygamous unions (Malawi National Statistical Office 1994). In a number of African countries such as Ghana, Malawi, Zambia, Namibia and Botswana, the proportion of husbands in a polygamous union is around 10 to 15 percent among those less than age 30 and about 40 percent for those over age 50 (Ghana Statistical Service 1989; Malawi National Statistical Office 1994; Gaisie 1993; Lesetedi et al. 1989; Katjiuanjo et al. 1993). Younger men and women are more likely to be in monogamous unions than polygamous ones. Paradoxically, HIV/AIDS rates are much lower among the most polygamous age group, those over 50 years, in comparison to the less polygamous group, those below age 40.

In typical traditional society, women in polygamous unions were expected to be faithful to their husbands and so were husbands expected to be faithful to their wives, since not to do so would result in tragedy of one sort or another such as the husband or child dying. For example, among the Chewa found in central Malawi, Zambia, and parts of Mozambique, there is a disease called *Tsempho* which has been discussed at great length in ethnographic studies (Hodgson 1913, p. 129–31; Rangeley 1948, pp. 34–44; Williamson 1956; Marwick 1965, pp. 66–68). Tsempho is considered to be a particular kind of wasting disease which may have fatal consequences, and it is related to promiscuous sexual relationships, or to the indulging of sexual intercourse by spouses during prohibited periods. The disease affects both men and women, as well as young children, and is caused by another's social transgression. Thus wives and husbands were forewarned of the dangers of promiscuity. There are certain variations of the *tsempho* sexual taboo among other ethnic groups of central, southern and eastern Africa such as the Bemba, Luapula, Tonga, Ndembu, etc. (Richards 1956; Cunnison 1959; Colson 1958, 1960; Colson and Gluckman 1961; Maxwell 1983; Gibbs 1988; Ouma 1996). In other words, traditional societies were not predominantly promiscuous or sex-positive as Rushing and others would like us to believe.

Underlying polygamy and promiscuity, the patrilineal kinship system is blamed as one of the major etiological factors in the African pattern of HIV/AIDS. All of Africa is considered to be patrilineal in descent, and matrilineal societies are relegated to a tiny footnote as an insignificant group. It is argued that patriarchy gives men the incentive to acquire as many wives as possible because of the value placed in children as economic assets and, as such, promotes polygamous behavior outside of marriage. But when one reads ethnographic studies such as those relied upon by Rushing, it becomes clear that many groups in central Africa and parts of West Africa such as Ghana, practice the matrilineal system of descent. Often men have to move to the wife's village, sometimes in a subservient position. In these societies women have been known to rise to positions of power in society, and generally enjoy some autonomy in comparison to women in patrilineal societies (Chilivumbo 1975). In both patrilineal and matrilineal societies premarital sex is taken very seriously. Although rules of chastity differ radically, in patrilineal societies (such as the Tumbuka, Ngonde, Sukwa, and Ngoni of central Africa) stress is laid on a girl's chastity before marriage. In the orthodox form of chastity rules, the girl's virginity on the eve of a wedding determines the value of bridewealth (Southall 1961; Chilivumbo 1975). Among the Bemba and Chewa (matrilineal groups) girls go through an initiation ceremony called *Chisungu* or *Chinamwali*, a puberty rite that initiates girls through the symbols of life and death in order to give social form and meaning to their sexuality (Richards 1956; Yoshida 1993; Helitzer-Allen 1994; 1997). One of the worst things that could happen to a girl in Bemba traditional society was to bear a child before she had been initiated, a sign that premarital sex was not condoned. Such a child was considered a creature of ill-omen and both the father and mother could be banished.

In short, there are several social and religious sanctions on sexual behavior in both patrilineal and matrilineal societies. Sex is not merely a transactional process or an ordinary activity in which men are expected to give women money and gifts as an expression of affection, respect, and gratitude for sexual favors. Sex is never considered as a form of recreation as Rushing claims; it is much more than this, a sacred undertaking in most traditional societies. Premarital sex, pregnancy out of wedlock, homosexuality, and other forms of sexual deviance are considered to be abhorrent behaviors and are never encouraged. Thus to argue, as Rushing does, that Americans usually view sex morally and think that having multiple partners constitutes immorality and unfaithfulness, while most Africans do not judge sexual behavior in such terms and have a positive-sex culture, is indeed to go against reality. If anything, it could be argued that Americans are more sex-positive than Africans. In the United States and Europe, commercials on TV and billboards often utilize seminude if not completely nude models. In the United States and other Western nations, business in pornographic movies, sexually explicit TV programs, and pornographic magazines is lucrative and vigorous. If indeed most Americans were morally upright in matters of sex are concerned, such activities would have been banned long ago. The French scientist Luc Montagnier, who was the first to isolate HIV, supports the theory that a mycoplasma, a bacterium-like organism, is the trigger that turns a slow-growing population of AIDS viruses into killers. Montagnier believes that the explosion of *sexual activity* (our emphasis) in the United States during the 1970s fostered the spread of a hardy, drug resistant strain of the mycoplasma and that the AIDS epidemic began when the mycoplasma got together with HIV, which had been dormant in Africa (Ungeheuer 1993). . . .

Toward a Reformulation

. . . We suggest that more plausible explanations of the HIV/AIDS epidemic in Africa may be found in the migrant labor thesis (Hunt 1996; Bassett and Mhloyi 1991; Jochelson et al. 1991) which provides a social, historical, and economic context for urban sexuality and unsafe medical practices. The migrant labor thesis asserts that the establishment of wage labor on the continent, particularly in eastern, central and southern Africa, to support mining, agricultural plantations, and other economic activities of the colonialists, created a situation where migrant labor, mostly young men were contracted for long-term work (1 to 3 years). Because families were not encouraged to accompany the laborer, farming and traditional activities such as raising, feeding, and educating children became the responsibility of women (without husbands) in rural areas. The women's limited ability to increase productivity of the land led to declining fertility of the land and, ultimately, absolute shortage of food and malnutrition. When agricultural production becomes untenable as a means of survival, such women often migrate to the city where some engage in one of the very few options open to them—prostitution—"an activity that with a morbid irony serves as their only lifeline to economic survival in the short term at the same time that it poses an enormous risk of curtailing their survival in the long term" (Craddock 1996).

Male migrant workers, away from their families for long periods of time, use alcoholism and frequent visits to prostitutes to deal with their loneliness and boredom. For men and women in eastern, central, and southern Africa, these long separations lead to breakdown in the stability of the family, divorce, and a definitive increase in the numbers of sexual partners for both men and women. Thus, the relatively high number of sexual partners is not the result of a long-standing cultural attribute of Africans, or an innate craving of Africans for more sex, or promiscuity, but is directly a consequence of the economic and labor markets. Definitely, women do not turn to prostitution because African culture "encourages prostitution more easily than Western culture does" as Rushing argues. As [Susan] Craddock (1996) shows, women living in households where there is chronic undernutrition, who are most nutritionally at risk, are the ones most likely to seek other options including prostitution, for survival. . . .

Conclusion

The issue is not that HIV does not spread through polypartner sexual activity, whether as polygamy or simply multiple-partner sexual activity within or outside a marriage relationship. Wherever polypartner sexual activity is practiced, whether in Africa, Australia, or the United States, participants are undisputedly at an increased risk of getting the HIV virus. What is at stake is whether Africans are polysexual by nature, and whether African culture (if we can think about one homogenous African culture) promotes and rewards polysexual behavior. Is being promiscuous and polysexual an African culture trait or is polypartner sexual activity a survival response dictated and enhanced by a vicious political economic system? Our approach to solving the problem hinges critically on our answer to this question. Rushing's work incorrectly assumes and attempts to prove the former is true.

We have argued that this view is erroneous, based on ethnocentrism and overgeneralization. It fails to explain the geographical variations in the incidence of HIV/AIDS across the continent. The simplistic solutions that result from such explanations that advise on behavior modification and condom distribution that may provide little help to rural women, who out of necessity are unable to turn away paying customers who refuse to use condoms. They do not reach rural residents who get HIV while getting injections from an IDV or bush doctor, the only source of health care, to cure malaria. They do not protect the many people privileged to receive services in urban health facilities who face unsterile procedures including injections, blood tests, and transfusions daily. Moreover, this approach fails to stop the spread of HIV.

Why do such ridiculous explanations as Rushing's persist? Obviously, there is an urgent need to find quick answers that can be easily translated into programs. After all, it is a lot easier to distribute condoms in urban Africa than to change the sociopolitical and economic contexts that condition the spread of HIV. Nevertheless, any interventions that fail to address the broader issues of African social and economic life, not merely the sexual promiscuity of Africans, are bound to fail.

POSTSCRIPT

Is Sexual Promiscuity a Major Reason for the HIV/AIDS Epidemic in Africa?

The two sides presented in this issue clearly have little to agree on. However, it is interesting to note that while Oppong and Kalipeni attack Rushing's cultural characterizations as overly generalized and ethnocentric, they do not raise issue with his concern that gender stratification (namely limited empowerment of women in many instances) may be contributing to the problem. Furthermore, they do not categorically dismiss cultural factors as unimportant in the spread of the disease (they just disagree with Rushing's analysis and characterization of these factors). The reality is that a thorough understanding of the spread of HIV/AIDS in Africa probably should include an analysis of cultural and political/economic factors. An interesting point, however, and one brought up by Oppong and Kalipeni at the end of their selection, is that much of the analysis and associated HIV/AIDS prevention programming has focused on cultural and behavioral issues as opposed to political/economic issues. This may be because donors believe that there is a better chance of changing behavioral patterns than political/economic conditions. It might also be related to the ideological orientation of donors that causes them to focus on one set of factors over another.

There are other factors contributing to the spread of HIV/AIDS in Africa that neither of the selections spend much time focusing on. For example, part of the reason that HIV/AIDS may be spreading less rapidly in some West African countries (e.g., Senegal and Guinea-Bissau) is that a different strain of the virus predominates there (HIV-2), as opposed to HIV-1, which is the major strain in other parts of Africa. Unlike HIV-1, HIV-2 does not appear to be spread as easily, is less likely to convert to full-blown AIDS, and tends to attack an older segment of the population. Also frequently mentioned as contributing to the AIDS problem in Africa are high levels of poverty, food insecurity, and armed conflict in some areas. In 2000 South African President Thabo Mbeki drew a firestorm of criticism when he appointed a committee of scientists to re-examine the AIDS epidemic in Africa. Included on the committee were several dissident specialists who argued that HIV is not the cause of AIDS, but factors such as malnutrition and poor hygiene are. It is the former assertion (that HIV does not cause AIDS) that was roundly condemned by the scientific community. For more on this issue, see several articles in the *New York Times*, including Rachel Swarns, "South Africa in a Furor Over Advice About AIDS" (March 19, 2000) and "In Debate on AIDS, South Africa's Leaders Defend Mavericks" (April 21, 2000).

It may be easy for the student to become depressed or overwhelmed when studying the AIDS crisis in Africa. As such, it is worth pointing out that there have been successful attempts at combating the disease in Africa, most notably in Uganda. While many African leaders were denying that HIV/AIDS was a problem in the 1980s and 1990s, President Yoweri Museveni (in power since 1986) jumped on this issue early. He constantly spoke about the issue in public addresses, putting considerable stress on prevention and health education. The result is that Uganda's infection rate dropped from around 30 percent to 6 percent. This decline, however, is not only related to a decreasing rate of new infections. There is also a decrease in the death of those who had the disease. Furthermore, it should be noted that Uganda has also experienced an economic recovery during this period, suggesting that improving political/economic conditions may also have contributed to the improved situation.

For more general information on the AIDS situation, see "AIDS Epidemic Update," *UNAIDS/WHO* (December 2002), which has a significant number of pages devoted to Africa.

AllAfrica Global Media

AllAfrica Global Media is the largest provider of African news online with offices in Johannesburg, Dakar, Abuja, and Washington, D.C. Over seven hundred stories are posted daily in French and English, in addition to multimedia content.

http://allafrica.com

African Governments on the WWW

African Governments on the WWW catalogues Internet links to many government organizations in Africa.

http://www.gksoft.com/govt/en/africa.html

Africa Action

Africa Action provides information on political movements related to a wide variety of African issues. It hosts its own information and contains links to other Internet sites.

http://www.africaaction.org/index.php

Centre for Democracy and Development

The Centre for Democracy and Development is a U.K.-based non-governmental organization (NGO) promoting democracy, peace, and human rights in Africa.

http://www.cdd.org.uk/

African Union

The Web site of Africa's premier pan-African organization, the African Union (formerly the Organization of African States)

http://www.africa-union.org

PART 5

Politics, Governance, and Conflict Resolution

*T*he terrain of politics, governance, and conflict resolution is simultaneously one of the most hopeful and distressing realms in contemporary African studies. While more contested elections have been held in the last 10 years than at any other time in the post-colonial period, the African continent also suffers from more instances of civil strife than other world regions. Scholars and commentators intensely debate the connections between contemporary political developments, historical patterns of governance, global geopolitics and local traditions of decision making, public discourse, and conflict resolution.

- Is Multi-Party Democracy Taking Hold in Africa?
- Is Foreign Assistance Useful for Fostering Democracy in Africa?
- Is Corruption the Result of Poor African Leadership?
- Are International Peacekeeping Missions Critical to Resolving Ethnic Conflicts in African Countries?

ISSUE 17

Is Multi-Party Democracy Taking Hold in Africa?

YES: Michael Bratton and Robert Mattes, from "Support for Democracy in Africa: Intrinsic or Instrumental?" *British Journal of Political Science* (July 2001)

NO: Joel D. Barkan, from "The Many Faces of Africa: Democracy Across a Varied Continent," *Harvard International Review* (Summer 2002)

ISSUE SUMMARY

YES: Michael Bratton, professor of political science at Michigan State University, and Robert Mattes, associate professor of political studies and director of the Democracy in Africa Research Unit at the University of Cape Town, find as much popular support for democracy in Zambia, South Africa, and Ghana as in other regions of the developing world, despite the fact that the citizens of these countries tend to be less satisfied with the economic performance of their elected governments.

NO: Joel D. Barkan, professor of political science at the University of Iowa and senior consultant on governance at the World Bank, takes a less sanguine view of the situation in Africa. He suggests that one can be cautiously optimistic about the situation in roughly one-third of the states on the African continent, nations he classifies as consolidated democracies and as aspiring democracies. He asserts that one must be realistic about the possibilities for the remainder of African nations, countries he classifies into three groups: stalled democracies, those that are not free, and those that are mired in civil war.

There was a great deal of enthusiasm among Africanists in the early 1960s when more than 40 African nations gained independence and formed popularly elected governments. This enthusiasm was tempered when a large proportion of these countries succumbed to one-party rule or military regimes by the end of the decade. The 1970s and 1980s were largely characterized by the persistence of undemocratic forms of governance. Lacking popular support, undemocratic regimes and guerilla movements often sought Soviet or American patronage within the context of the cold war. The United States, in the name of anti-communism, financially and militarily backed a number of unsavory political leaders and guerilla insurgents during this period. These ranged from Mabuto Sese Seko in former Zaire to UNITA rebels in Angola. Seko, perhaps one of the most corrupt of African dictators, plundered his country for over 20 years during the cold war with the full support of the United States. In Angola, the U.S. and then-white-ruled South Africa sustained a bloody civil war by supporting UNITA rebels in the late 1980s.

The end of the cold war largely led to the end of perverse outside intervention in African affairs. Combined with this change in the external environment was a groundswell of internal support for political reform, which some commentators attribute to the democratic changes occurring in Eastern Europe in the late 1980s that many Africans observed through the international media. The result has often been referred to as Africa's "second wave" of democratization in which, between 1991 and 2000, multiparty elections were held in all but 5 of Africa's 47 states.

In this issue, Michael Bratton and Robert Mattes find as much popular support for democracy in Zambia, South Africa, and Ghana as in other regions of the developing world. However, citizens of these countries tend to be less satisfied with the performance of their elected governments than those in comparable non-African nations. The authors interpret these results to mean that support for democracy in Africa is more intrinsic (an end in itself) than instrumental (a means to an end—such as improving material standards of living). This finding highlights the importance that Africans attach to the basic political rights afforded by democracy. It also contradicts other research indicating that governments in new democracies mainly legitimate themselves through economic performance.

In contrast, Joel D. Barkan takes a more sober view of the situation in Africa. He states that those assessing the political situation in Africa roughly break down into two camps, the optimists and the realists. These two groups tend to draw very different conclusions because they focus their attention on different countries in Africa. Barkan contends that one can be cautiously optimistic about the situation in roughly one-third of the states on the African continent, nations he classifies as consolidated democracies (Botswana, Mauritius, and South Africa) and as aspiring democracies (15 countries). The prospects for the remainder of African nations are much more uncertain. Barkan classifies these states into three groups, the stalled democracies (13 countries), those that are not free (10 countries), and those that are mired in civil war (roughly 6 countries). As a realist, he believes that there is a tendency to over celebrate progress in the first two groups and to retreat from the challenges in the third, fourth, and fifth groups.

Michael Bratton
and Robert Mattes

➡ **YES**

Support for Democracy in Africa: Intrinsic or Instrumental?

Popular support for a political regime is the essence of its consolidation. By voluntarily endorsing the rules that govern them, citizens endow a regime with an elusive but indispensable quality: political legitimacy. The most widely accepted definition of the consolidation of democracy equates it squarely with legitimation. In a memorable turn of phrase, Linz and Stepan speak of democratic consolidation as a process by which all political actors come to regard democracy as 'the only game in town'. In other words, democracy is consolidated when citizens and leaders alike conclude that no alternative form of regime has any greater subjective validity or stronger objective claim to their allegiance.

This article explores how the general public in new multiparty political regimes in sub-Saharan Africa is oriented towards democracy. What, if anything, do Africans understand by the concept? Do they resemble citizens in new democracies elsewhere in the world in their willingness to support a regime based on human rights, competing parties and open elections? And beyond democracy as a model set of rights and institutions, are citizens in Africa satisfied with the way that elected regimes operate in practice? All of these questions are coloured by the fact that many of Africa's democratic experiments are taking place in countries with agrarian economies, low per capita incomes and minuscule middle classes. Under such unpropitious conditions, observers have every reason to wonder whether elected governments have the capacity to meet citizen expectations and, if they cannot, whether citizens may therefore quickly lose faith in democracy.

We assume that citizens will extend tentative support to neo-democracies, if only because they promise change from failed authoritarian formulae of the past. But what is the nature of any such support? Is it *intrinsic*, based on an appreciation of the political freedoms and equal rights that democracy embodies when valued as an end in itself? Or does support reflect a more *instrumental* calculation in which regime change is a means to other ends, most commonly the alleviation of poverty and the improvement of living standards?

The resolution of this issue has direct implications for regime consolidation. Intrinsic support is a commitment to democracy 'for better or worse'; as such, it has the potential to sustain a fragile political regime even in the face of economic downturn or social upheaval. By contrast, instrumental support is conditional. It is granted, and may be easily withdrawn, according to the temper of the times. If citizens evaluate regimes mainly in terms of their capacity to deliver consumable benefits or to rectify material inequalities, then they may also succumb to the siren song of populist leaders who argue that economic development requires the sacrifice of political liberties.

Let us be clear. We do not dispute that evaluations of democracy in new multiparty regimes are likely to be based in good part on the performance of the government of the day. After all, it is very unlikely that citizens in neo-democracies would possess a reservoir of favourable affective dispositions arising from a lifetime of exposure to democratic norms. If democracy is a novel experience, how could such socialization have taken place? Instead of bestowing 'diffuse support', citizens fall back on performance-based judgements of what democracy actually does for them.

We wish to divide regime performance, however, into distinct baskets of goods: an *economic* basket (that includes economic assets, jobs and an array of basic social services) and a *political* basket (that contains peace, civil liberties, political rights, human dignity and equality before the law). The African cases provide a critical test of the importance of political goods to evaluations of democracy. If the denizens of the world's poorest continent make 'separate and correct' distinctions between 'a basket of economic goods (which may be deteriorating) and a basket of political goods (which may be improving)', then citizens everywhere are likely to do so. And if political goods seem to matter more than economic goods in judging democracy, then we can cast light on the 'intrinsic v. instrumental' debate. If democracy is valued by citizens as an end in itself in Africa, then this generalization probably holds good universally.

In this study we find that citizen orientations to democracy in Africa are most fully explained with reference to both baskets of goods. With one interesting country exception, satisfaction with democracy (the way elected governments actually work) is driven just as much by guarantees of political rights as by the quest for material benefit. Support for democracy (as a preferred form of government) is rooted even more deeply in an appreciation of new-found political freedoms, a finding that runs counter to the conventional view that the continent's deep economic crisis precludes regime consolidation. At least so far, new democratic regimes in Africa have been able to legitimate themselves by delivering political goods.

Scope of the Study

Our substantive focus is intentionally restricted—to attitudes to democracy, among masses rather than elites—because our geographical coverage is broader than most studies in Africa. This article uses standard survey items to compare political attitudes in Ghana, Zambia and South Africa, thus bridging the major regions of the sub-Saharan sub-continent and situating public opinion in Africa in relation to other new democracies in the world.

All three countries underwent an electoral transition to multi-party democracy during the last decade but their political trajectories have since diverged. Both of South Africa's competitive polls (in April 1994 and June 1999) were ruled substantially free and fair by independent observers. By contrast, Zambia's founding elections of October 1991 were far more credible than its dubious second contest of November 1996. For its part, Ghana experienced improved electoral quality, with flawed elections in November 1992 being followed by a December 1996 poll that drew almost universal praise. Thus, with reference to the institution of elections alone, South Africa's democracy has stabilized, Ghana's is gradually consolidating, and Zambia's is slowly dying.

In reality, democracy is a fragile species throughout Africa. It is far from clear that a pervasive political culture exists to promote and defend open elections, let alone any other democratic institution. Regime transitions in Africa commonly resulted from intense struggles between incumbent and opposition elites, whose interest in self-enrichment was sometimes more palpable than their commitment to democracy. Even elected leaders have tampered with constitutional rules in order to prolong a term of office or to sideline rivals. And the armed forces continue to lurk threateningly in the wings: about half a dozen of Africa's new democracies succumbed to military intervention within five years of transition. Only in places like South Africa in 1994 (and possibly Nigeria in 1999), where transitions were lubricated by pacts among powerful insiders, are there signs that a culture of compromise and accommodation has penetrated the ranks of the political elite.

The extent to which a commitment to democracy has radiated through the populace is also open to question. After all, regime transitions in Africa were sparked by popular protests that were rooted in economic and political grievances. While the protesters had clear ideas about what they were *against* (the repressions and predations of big-man rule) they did not articulate an elaborate or coherent vision of what they were *for*. Judging by the issues raised in the streets, people seemed to want accountability of leaders and to eliminate the inequities arising from official corruption. To be sure, these preferences loosely embodied core democratic principles. And multiparty elections quickly became a useful rallying cry for would-be political leaders. But, during the tumult of transition, relatively little attention was paid to the institutional design of the polity. Emerging from life under military and one-party rule, citizens could hardly be expected to have in mind a full set of democratic rules or to evince a deep attachment to them.

This article takes stock of what has been learned from the first generation of research on political attitudes in new African democracies in the 1990s. . . .

The Meaning of Democracy in Africa

In considering the meaning of 'democracy' in Africa, the first possibility is that the term has not entered popular discourse, especially where indigenous languages contain no direct semantic equivalent. Some cultural interpretations emphasize that the word changes its meaning in translation, sometimes even signifying consensual constructs like community or unity. Or, because African languages borrow new terminology from others, a phonetic adaptation from a European language (like 'demokrasi') may have become common currency.

In one form or another, democracy seems to have entered the vocabulary of most African citizens. When the 1997 Ghanaian survey asked respondents 'What is the first thing that comes to mind . . . when you think of living in a democracy?', 61.5 per cent were able to provide a meaningful response, rising to 75 per cent in 1999. Interestingly, even more respondents felt that Ghana was a democracy in 1997, implying that some people who could not specify a meaning for democracy could nevertheless recognize one if they saw one. In both countries, the salience of the concept was a function of education, with democracy having meaning in direct proportion to a respondent's years of schooling.

Contrary to cultural interpretations, we contend that standard liberal ideas of civil and political rights lie at the core of African understandings of democracy. In Zambia in 1993 and 1994, participants in two rounds of focus groups were asked 'What does democracy mean to you?' In the ensuing discussions, democracy was most commonly decoded in terms of the political procedure of competitive elections in which 'people are free to vote if they want to' and 'have a right to choose their own leaders'. Informants described how they resented having been forced to vote for the former ruling United National Independence Party (UNIP) and decried the political intimidation exerted by the party's youth wing. They favourably compared a choice of candidates under a multi-party regime with the system of 'appointed representatives' under a one-party state.

An open-ended question in the 1999 survey in Ghana about 'the first thing that comes to your mind . . . when you hear the word "democracy"' elicited the following responses, in frequency order: civil liberties and personal freedoms (28 per cent of all respondents), 'government by the people' (22 per cent), and voting rights (9.2 per cent). The only other major response was 'Don't know' (24.8 per cent) and very few respondents offered a materialistic interpretation (2.5 per cent). These findings seem to suggest that Ghanaians view democracy almost exclusively in political terms, with an emphasis on selected civil liberties (especially free speech), collective decision-making and political representation.

Survey findings point to a much more materialistic world view in South Africa. In 1995, South Africans were asked to choose from a list of diverse meanings (both political and economic) that are sometimes attached to democracy. At the top of the popular rankings, 91.3 per cent of respondents equated democracy with 'equal access to houses, jobs and a decent income' (with 48.3 per cent seeing these goods as 'essential' to democracy). This earthy image of democracy far outstripped all other representations: for example, regular elections (67.7 per cent), at least two strong parties (59.4 per cent), and minority rights (54.5 per cent). To be sure, a majority of South Africans did associate democracy with procedures to guarantee political competition and political participation, but their endorsement of these political goods was far less ringing than the almost unanimous association of democracy with improved material welfare. Tellingly, only small minorities found it 'essential' to democracy to hold regular elections (26.5 per cent) or guarantee minority rights (20.6 per cent).

Because South Africa is a deeply divided society with mutually reinforcing fault lines of race and class, one would expect that various social groups would hold disparate views of democracy. We have noted elsewhere 'massive racial differences in agreement with regime norms'. Whites are much more likely than blacks to agree that regular elections, free speech, party competition and minority rights are essential to democracy. This procedural interpretation of democracy most likely reflects their own minority status and their reliance for protection on constitutional and legal rules. South African blacks, for their part, attach just as much or more importance to narrowing the gap between rich and poor. And while many South Africans of all races say they accept the necessity of redistributing jobs, houses and incomes, blacks seem to focus more on 'equality of results' while whites stress 'equality of opportunity'.

We reach four working conclusions based on recent research on citizen conceptions of democracy in three African countries. First, Africans here are more likely to associate democracy with individual liberties than with communal solidarity, especially if they live in urban areas. Secondly, popular conceptions of democracy have *both* procedural *and* substantive dimensions, though the former conception is more common than the latter. Thirdly, citizens rank procedural and substantive attributes in different order across countries. Zambians place political rules at the top of the list of democratic attributes, whereas South Africans relegate such guarantees behind improvements in material living standards. Finally, rankings differ even within the category of political goods: whereas Zambians (and to a lesser extent South Africans) grant primacy to elections, Ghanaians elevate freedom of speech to the top of their own bill of democratic rights.

These cross-national differences can be interpreted in terms of the life experiences of citizens under each country's old regime. Zambians may regard democracy mainly in terms of competitive multi-party elections because of their disappointing experiences with the ritual of 'elections without choice' under Kenneth Kaunda's one-party state. Ghanaians, for their part, emphasize freedom of speech as a reaction against the tight controls over communication imposed by the previous military regime, whose populist ideology was the only approved form of political discourse. Finally, South Africans place socio-economic considerations at the heart of their notion of democracy because of the integrated structure of oppression experienced under apartheid. Impoverished under the old regime, they see the attainment of political freedom as only the first step in rectifying manifold inequalities in society. In this conception, democracy has an inclusive meaning; it is as much a means to social transformation as a politically desirable end in itself.

Support for Democracy in Africa

The best way to ask questions about popular support for democracy is in concrete terms and in the form of comparisons with plausible alternatives. Since democracy has motley meanings, it is not useful to ask whether people support it in the abstract. It is far better to elicit opinions about a real regime with distinctive institutional attributes, such as a 'system of governing with free elections and many parties'. And if citizens support democracy as the 'least worst' system (the so-called 'Churchill hypothesis'), it is worth testing their levels of commitment against other regime forms that they have recently experienced or could conceive of encountering in the future.

Table 1 reports results of survey questions of this sort from various world regions, with sub-Saharan Africa represented by Ghana, Zambia and South Africa. In so far as these countries are representative of the region, Table 1 shows that the level of public commitment to democracy is much the same in Africa as in other regions of the world that have recently undergone regime change. Excluding Southern Europe, almost two out of three citizens in new democracies extend legitimacy to elected government as their preferred political regime: the relevant mean figures are 65 per cent for East and Central Europe, 63 per cent for South America, and 64 per cent for the three countries of sub-Saharan Africa. Indeed, the average level of support in Africa (64.3 per cent) is virtually identical to the combined mean for Latin America and post-Communist Europe (64.2 per cent).

Moreover, deviation in support for democracy around the regional mean is lower for the three African countries than for other parts of the world. The countries with the lowest and highest levels of support for democracy are separated by just 18 percentage points in the African cases, but by 27 points for Eastern Europe and 39 points in South America. We interpret this to mean

Table 1

Public Attitudes to Democracy: Preliminary Cross-National Comparisons

	Support democracy	Satisfied with democracy	Supportive and satisfied	Supportive but not satisfied
European Union	78	53	–	–
Southern Europe	84	57	79	11
Greece	90	52	84	11
Portugal	83	60	77	9
Spain	78	60	75	12
East and Central Europe	65	60	72	6
Czech	77	56	70	8
Poland	76	61	70	4
Romania	61	77	68	4
Bulgaria	66	61	75	2
Slovakia	61	49	62	14
Hungary	50	53	79	4
South America	63	50	45	22
Uruguay	80	54	57	29
Argentina	77	53	55	28
Chile	53	48	38	17
Brazil	41	46	32	16
Sub-Saharan Africa	64	48	41	18
Ghana (1997)	74	53	46	13
Zambia (1996)	63	53	49	14
South Africa (1997)	56	38	29	13
South Africa (blacks)	61	45	35	11
South Africa (whites)	39	7	5	18

Note: Regional means are raw estimates, uncorrected for proportional population size of countries. Further fnn. to Table 1 can be found in the electronic version of the journal available at www.cup.cam.ac.uk

that authoritarian regimes have been widely discredited across the continent. Although the citizens of Ghana and Zambia may not have committed themselves to democracy as firmly as the citizens in Uruguay and the Czech Republic, they evince less nostalgia for hardline rule than citizens in Hungary and Brazil. Once again, though, South Africa is an exception. And we would need many more confirming cases before we could be sure that legitimating sentiments are evenly spread across all African countries.

Indeed, variations are evident within Africa in the extent to which citizens support new regimes. Of the three cases under review, Ghana displays the highest levels of citizen commitment to democracy. In 1997, fully 73.5 per cent of citizens thought it somewhat or very important for Ghana to 'have at least two political parties competing in an election'. The intensity of this support appears to be strong, as reflected by the 55.9 per cent of respondents who thought these institutions 'very important'. And the quality and depth of this support is underlined by the even higher proportions who granted importance to the right of citizens to form parties representing diverse viewpoints (82.5 per cent), to the openness of the mass media to political debate (89.3 per cent), and to the regular conduct of honest elections (92.7 per cent). While there is some possibility that respondents are acquiescing here to non-controversial 'motherhood' questions, Ghanaians nonetheless appear to consistently favour a full basket of liberal political rights.

Among the countries considered, legitimation of the new regime was lowest in South Africa, where citizens do not yet feel a widespread attitudinal commitment to democracy. A 1997 survey asked respondents to choose between the following statements: '[When] democracy does not work . . . some say you need a strong leader who does not have to worry with elections. Others say democracy is always best'. Since only a bare majority chose the democratic option (56.3 per cent, up from 47 per cent in 1995, but dropping back again below 50 per cent in 1998), support for democracy appeared to be weaker there than in the other African countries. Other responses underscore the shallowness of democratic legitimacy and the appeal of authoritarian alternatives in South Africa. In 1997, about one-third of the population thought that, under democracy, 'the economic system runs badly' (29 per cent), order is poorly maintained (30.2 per cent), and leaders are 'indecisive and have too much squabbling' (35.1 per cent). And more than half of all South Africans (53.8 per cent) stated that they would be 'willing to give up regular elections if a non-elected government or leader could impose law and order and deliver jobs and houses'.

Thus, the potential constituency for forceful rule appears to be larger in South Africa than in South America, where an average of just 15 per cent of citizens considers that 'in some circumstances an authoritarian government can be preferable to a democratic [one]'. Sentiments for a strong man were higher in South Africa (30.8 per cent) than in Chile (19 per cent) and Brazil (21 per cent), where authoritarian nostalgia is usually considered to be high. Question wording may have had a significant effect, with the cue of higher material living standards ('jobs and houses') inducing even some of democracy's supporters to abandon it. But, at minimum, this finding draws attention to the role of instrumental calculations in the assessments of democracy by many South African citizens.

South Africa's deviance is explicable again, however, in terms of its cultural diversity. White South Africans were much less likely to judge that 'democracy is always best' (39 per cent) than the country's African citizens (61 per cent). And, while 'coloureds' situated themselves between blacks and whites when granting such support to democracy (53 per cent), Asian South Africans were the least supportive of all (27 per cent). Thus the cautious, even retrogressive, attitudes of ethnic minorities tended to depress overall levels of commitment to democracy in South Africa. Examined alone, African citizens can be seen to support this form of regime at the highest level of any ethnic group in South Africa (61 per cent), a level not too different from citizens in Zambia (63 per cent) and the sub-Sahara region as a whole (64 per cent).

In Zambia, the question on support for democracy differed slightly, while still focusing on a political system featuring elections and posing a comparison with a realistic alternative regime. Respondents were asked to choose: Is 'the best form of government . . . a government elected by its people' or 'a government that gets things done'? On the assumption that support erodes as regimes mature, especially if citizens' expectations are not fully realized, we thought that support for 'elected government' would decline over time. To date this has not happened in Zambia. Public support for democracy held steady, at 63.4 per cent in 1993 and 62.9 per cent 1996. As in Ghana, other related items bespoke an electorate with a relatively firm syndrome of democratic commitments. In 1996, 73 per cent preferred 'a choice of political parties and candidates' to 'a return to a system of single-party rule'.

Satisfaction With Democracy in Africa

Democracy looks better in theory than in practice. In elected regimes worldwide, more citizens support democracy as their preferred form of government than express satisfaction with the way that it actually works. This generalization holds true not only for Third Wave neo-democracies but, even more so, for the established regimes of Western Europe. . . .

Unlike support for democracy, satisfaction with democracy is not as widespread in the three African countries as it is in South America and Eastern Europe. Satisfaction lags support by a wider margin in the sub-Saharan region (16 per centage points) than in the other two world regions (13 and 5 per centage points respectively). Substantively, fewer than half (48 per cent) of the citizens in these new African democracies report satisfaction with key aspects of the performance of elected regimes. Once more, the African average is pulled down by South Africa, with Ghana and Zambia displaying popular approval of regime performance at levels similar to consolidating democracies like Uruguay and Argentina. Although different racial groups in South Africa again evince distinct levels of satisfaction (45 per cent for blacks versus just 7 per cent for whites), black South Africans in this instance trail their fellow citizens elsewhere on the continent in their contentment with democracy in practice (39 per cent). Instead, they tend to more closely resemble the citizens of Brazil (41 per cent), more of whom are unhappy with democracy than are satisfied with it. . . .

Explaining Satisfaction With Democracy

. . . Satisfaction with democracy among African citizens appears to depend upon their assessment of the performance of government, particularly its performance at delivering *both* economic *and* political goods. Taken together, these factors explain between a quarter and two-fifths of the variance in expressed satisfaction in three African countries. Apart from social background, no set of factors–whether general performance, economic goods or political goods—can be discarded without a significant loss of explanatory power. Any ecumenical explanation of satisfaction with democracy in Africa must make reference to government performance in *both* its political *and* economic dimensions.

But what about the relative weight of economic and political explanations? We note that the delivery of economic goods sometimes has large independent effects on satisfaction with democracy in individual countries. Cross-nationally, however, such effects are rather inconsistent. We therefore conclude that economic effects are subject to the exigencies of time and place, such as gradual economic recovery in Ghana and persistent economic crisis in Zambia. We therefore doubt that a general explanation of satisfaction with democracy can be constructed from economic data alone. At the same time, we note that the effects of political factors, while occasionally weaker than those of economic factors, prevail more consistently across countries. This observation suggests that the delivery of political goods is a more reliable general predictor of satisfaction with democracy and a more promising foundation on which to construct a theory of democratic consolidation. This line of argument is explored further in the next section.

Explaining Support for Democracy

We turn, finally, to explain support for democracy as a preferred regime type. As Table 2 shows, our analysis accounts for 12 to 17 per cent of the variance in popular support (see adjusted R^2 statistics). Our explanation was less complete in this case perhaps because of the impalpability of the issue at hand: citizens may find it more difficult to assess the qualities of abstract constitutional rules than the concrete performance of actual governments. In any event, public opinion in Africa seems to be less fully formed, and more contradictory, when it comes to support for democracy.

Nevertheless, Table 2 does reveal interesting findings. First, it reconfirms that attitudes to democracy cannot be inferred from standard social background characteristics. Again, gender and age were irrelevant to the legitimation of democracy in all countries studied and education had a positive impact only in Zambia. These findings are consistent with the observations

Table 2

Multiple Regression Estimates of Support for Democracy

	S. Africa			Ghana			Zambia		
	B	(s.e.)	Beta	B	(s.e.)	Beta	B	(s.e.)	Beta
Social background factors									
Gender			0.028			-0.014			0.048
Age			-0.019			0.000			0.042
Education			-0.009			0.001	0.064	(0.010)	0.200***
General performance factors									
Approval of government performance	0.084	(0.014)	0.145***	0.368	(0.064)	0.169***	0.122	(0.030)	0.128***
Satisfaction with democracy	0.082	(0.011)	0.196***	0.393	(0.052)	0.195***			-0.010
Economic factors									
Assessment of current economic conditions			-0.013			0.038			0.001
Assessment of current personal QOL			-0.017			0.023			-0.021
Assessment of future personal QOL	0.035	(0.011)	0.077***			-0.023			0.067
Support for market reforms			0.038			-0.006			0.017
Delivery of economic goods			-0.002	0.066	(0.031)	0.062***			0.059
Political factors									
Interest in politics	0.054	(0.015)	0.077***			0.015	0.115	(0.025)	0.144***
Trust in government institutions			0.032			-0.003			0.018
Perception of government responsiveness			0.031			-0.008			0.012
Perception of official corruption			-0.003	-0.140	(0.072)	-0.045*			-0.020
Delivery of political goods			0.028	0.158	(0.025)	0.153***	0.461	(0.080)	0.181***
N		3,500			2,005			1,182	
R		0.349			0.417			0.382	
R^2		0.122			0.174			0.146	
Adjusted R^2		0.120			0.171			0.142	

(*)Significant at 0.05
(**)Significant at 0.01
(***)Significant at 0.001

that 'the more education a person has, the more likely he or she is to reject undemocratic alternatives' but that, overall, 'social structure [has] little influence . . . on attitudes towards the new regime'. If African societies do not contain entrenched pockets of generational or gender-based resistance to democratization, then the prospects for the consolidation of democratic regimes would seem to be slightly brighter than is sometimes thought.

Secondly, regime legitimacy in Africa depends upon popular appraisals of government performance. Consistently, in all three countries, support for democracy was strongest among citizens who felt that elected governments were generally doing a good job. But approval of government performance was closely connected to party identification, with supporters of the ruling party in each country being much more approving. Thus we must investigate further whether citizens are accrediting government performance—and thereby supporting democracy—out of 'knee-jerk' loyalty to a ruling party rather than a rational calculation that democratic governments deserve legitimation because they are more effective.

In Ghana and South Africa, support for democracy also was accompanied by expressions of satisfaction with democracy. We take this as further evidence that regime legitimation in Africa rests squarely upon performance considerations. On the up-side, popular demand for government performance increases the likelihood that citizens will make use of the rules of democratic governance to hold their leaders accountable. On the down-side, it also raises the possibility that citizens may conflate the performance of governments (that is, the achievements of incumbent groups of elected officials) with the performance of regimes (that is, the rules by which governments are constituted). The risk thus arises that, faced with continued mismanagement by ineffective governments, Africans may throw the baby out with the bath-water. By punishing government under-performance, they may inadvertently dismiss democracy.

Thirdly, and notwithstanding what has just been said about performance, we find little systematic evidence from Africa that citizens predicate support for democracy on the delivery of economic goods. Generally speaking, the legitimation of democratic regimes does not depend on citizen assessments of personal or national economic conditions, either now or for the future. Only in South Africa are assessments of future personal conditions linked positively to support for democracy. Strikingly too, when other relevant factors are controlled for, citizen perceptions of economic delivery have no discernible effects on the endorsement of democracy in either Zambia or South Africa. The delivery of economic goods only seems to matter in Ghana, though the influence of this instrumental consideration is far from the strongest in the Ghana model.

Instead, we are led back again to the impact of political factors. For the first time, we find that citizen interest in politics had a positive effect on attitudes to democracy in two out of the three countries (Zambia and South Africa). It stands to reason that democracy will not consolidate where citizens remain disinterested in, and detached from, the political process; before people can actively become democracy's champions, they must orient themselves towards involvement in political life. One wonders why Ghanaians, who display the highest levels of interest in politics among the Africans surveyed, do not automatically support democracy. The answer appears to lie, at least in part, in the popular perception of rampant official corruption in that country. Many persons who are predisposed by their interest in politics to become active citizens are 'turned off' from democracy by what they see as the illicit machinations of civilian politicians. As one would expect, perceptions of official corruption are negatively associated with support for democracy in all three African countries; only in Ghana, however, is this relationship statistically significant.

Finally, and most importantly, the delivery of political goods bears a strong and significant relationship to the popular legitimation of democracy. In judging democracy, the Africans that we surveyed think of government performance first and foremost in political terms. Unlike the delivery of economic goods, a factor that is relevant in only one country, this relationship holds in at least two country cases. . . .

Conclusion

In this [selection,] we have established that levels of popular support for democracy are roughly similar in three neo-democracies of sub-Saharan Africa as in other Third Wave countries. Almost two-thirds of eligible voters in these African countries say that they feel some measure of attachment to democratic rules and values. Under these circumstances, the popular consolidation of democracy in at least some African countries does not seem an entirely far-fetched prospect.

Yet the African cases stand apart from other new democracies in terms of lower levels of mass satisfaction with actual regime performance. The fact that African survey respondents support democracy while being far from content with its concrete achievements suggests a measure of intrinsic support for the democratic regime form that supersedes instrumental considerations. But, although support for democracy may be quite broad, we cannot confirm that it is deep. We do not yet know if citizens will vigorously defend the political regime if economic conditions take a decisive turn for the worse or if rulers begin to backtrack on hard-won freedoms.

NO ⤶

Joel D. Barkan

The Many Faces of Africa: Democracy Across a Varied Continent

A decade ago, seasoned observers of African politics including Larry Diamond and Richard Joseph argued that the continent was on the cusp of its "second liberation." Rising popular demand for political reform across Africa, multiparty elections, transitions of power in several countries, and negotiations toward a new political framework in South Africa led these experts to conclude that the prospects for democratization were good. Today, these same observers are not so sure. They describe Africa's current experience with democratization in terms of "electoral democracy," "virtual democracy," or "illiberal democracy," and are far more cautious about predicting what is to come. What is the true state of African democracy? And what is its future?

Governance Before the 1990s

Africa's first liberation was precipitated by the transition from colonial to independent rule that swept much of the continent, except the south, between 1957 and 1964. The West hoped that the transition would be to democratic rule, and more than 40 new states with democratic constitutions emerged following multiparty elections that brought new African-led governments to power. The regimes established by this process, however, soon collapsed or reverted to authoritarian rule—what Samuel Huntington has termed a "reverse wave" of democratization. By the mid-1960s, roughly half of all African countries had seen their elected governments toppled by military coups.

In the other half, elected regimes degenerated into one-party rule. In what was to become a familiar scenario, nationalist political parties formed the first governments. The leaders of these parties then destroyed or marginalized the opposition through a combination of carrot-and-stick policies. The result was a series of clientelist regimes that served as instruments for neopatrimonial or personal rule by the likes of Mobutu Sese Seko in Zaire or Daniel Arap Moi in Kenya—regimes built around a political boss, rather than founded in a strong party apparatus and the realization of a coherent program or ideology.

This pattern, and its military variant (as with Sani Abacha in Nigeria), became the modal type of African governance from the mid-1960s until the early 1990s. These regimes depended on a continuous and increasing flow of patronage and slush money for survival; there was little else binding them together. Inflationary patronage led to unprecedented levels of corruption, unsustainable macroeconomic policies that caused persistent budget and current account deficits, and state decay, including the decline of the civil service. Most African governments still struggle with this structural and normative legacy, which has obstructed the process of building democracy.

Decade of Democratization?

Africa's second liberation began with the historic 1991 multiparty election in Benin that resulted in the defeat of the incumbent president, an outcome that was replicated in Malawi and Zambia in the same year. The results of these elections raised expectations and created hopes for the restoration of democracy and improved governance across the continent. By the end of 2000, multiparty elections had been held in all but five of Africa's 47 states— Comoros, the Democratic Republic of Congo, Equatorial Guinea, Rwanda, and Somalia.

Along with the new states of the former Soviet Union, Africa was the last region to be swept by the so-called "third wave" of democratization, and as with many of the successor states of the former Soviet Union, the record since has been mixed. In stark contrast to the democratic transitions that occurred in the 1970s and 1980s in Southern and Eastern Europe and Latin America (excluding Mexico), most African transitions have not been marked by a breakthrough election that definitively ended an authoritarian regime by bringing a group of political reformers to power. While this type of transition has occurred in a small number of states, most notably Benin and South Africa, the more typical pattern has been a process of protracted transition: a mix of electoral democracy and political liberalization combined with elements of authoritarian rule and, more fundamentally, the perpetuation of clientelist rule. In this context, politics is a three-cornered struggle between authoritarians, patronage-seekers, and reformers. Authoritarians attempt to retain power by permitting greater liberalization and elections while selectively allocating patronage to those who remain loyal. Meanwhile, patronage-seekers attempt to obtain the spoils of office via electoral means, as reformers pursue the establishment of democratic rule. The boundaries between the first and second of these groups, and sometimes between the second and third, can be blurred because political alignments are very fluid. Liberal democracy is unlikely to be consolidated until reformers ascend to power.

The result is what Thomas Carothers has termed a "gray zone" of polities, describing countries where continued progress toward democracy beyond elections is limited and where the consolidation of democracy, if it does occur, will unfold over a long period, perhaps decades. This characterization does not necessarily mean that the third wave of democratization is over in Africa. Rather, we should expect Africa's democratic transitions to be similar to those of India or Mexico. In the former, the party that led the country to independence did not lose an election for three decades, and periodic alternation of power between parties did not occur until after 40 years. In the latter, the end of one-party rule and its replacement by an opposition committed to democratic principles played out over five elections spanning 13 years rather than a single founding election. Such appears to be the pattern in Africa, where two-thirds of founding and second elections have returned incumbent authoritarians to power, but where each iteration of the electoral process has usually resulted in a significant incremental advance in the development of civil society, electoral fairness, and the overall political process.

That many African polities fall into the gray zone is confirmed by the most recent annual *Freedom in the World* survey conducted by Freedom House. Of the 47 states that comprise sub-Saharan Africa, 23 were classified by the survey as "partly free" based on the extent of their political freedoms and civil liberties. Only eight (Benin, Botswana, Cape Verde, Ghana, Mali, Mauritius, Namibia, and South Africa) were classified as "free" while 16, including eight war-torn societies (Angola, Burundi, the Democratic Republic of Congo, Ethiopia, Eritrea, Liberia, Rwanda, and Sudan) were deemed "not free."

The overall picture revealed by these numbers is sobering. Less than one-fifth of all African countries were classified as free, and of these, only two or three (Botswana, Mauritius, and perhaps South Africa) can be termed consolidated democracies. On the other hand, if one excludes states in the midst of civil war, one-fifth of Africa's countries are free, one-fifth not free, and three-fifths fall in-between. That is to say, four-fifths of those not enmeshed in civil war are partly free or free, a significant advance over the continent's condition a decade ago. Only a handful are consolidated democracies, but few are harsh dictatorships of the type that dominated Africa from the mid-1960s to the beginning of the 1990s. As noted by Ghana's E. Gyimah-Boadi, "Illiberalism has persisted, but is not on the rise. Authoritarianism is alive in Africa today, but is not well."

Optimists and Realists

The current status of democracy in Africa varies greatly from one country to the next, and one should resist generalizations that apply to all 47 of the continent's states; one size does not fit all. Notwithstanding this reality, those who track events in Africa have divided themselves into two distinct camps: optimists and realists. Those in the United States who take an optimistic view—mainly government officials involved in efforts to promote democratization abroad, former members of President Bill Clinton's administration responsible for Africa, members of the Congressional Black Caucus, and the staff of some Africa-oriented nongovernmental organizations—trumpet the fact that multiparty elections have been held in nearly 90 percent of all African states. They note that most African countries have now held competitive elections twice and that some, including Benin, Ghana, and Senegal, have held genuine elections three times, at least one of which has resulted in a change of government. The optimists further note that the quality of these elections has improved in some countries, both in terms of efficiency and of fairness. Electoral commissions seem to have been more independent, even-handed, and professional in recent elections than in the early 1990s. Opposition candidates and parties have greater freedom to campaign and have faced less harassment from incumbent governments. The presence of election observers, both foreign and domestic, is now widely accepted as part of the process. Perhaps most significant, citizen participation in elections has been fairly high, averaging just under two-thirds of all registered voters.

Recognizing that elections are a necessary but insufficient condition for the consolidation of democracy, the optimists also point to advances in several areas, listed below in their approximate order of accomplishment. First, there has been a re-emergence and proliferation of civil society organizations after their systematic suppression during the era of single-party and military rule. Second, an independent and free press has also re-emerged, spurred on by the privatization of broadcast media in several countries. Third, members of the legislature have increasingly asserted themselves in policymaking and overseeing the executive branch. Fourth, the judiciary and the rule of law have been strengthened in countries such as Tanzania, and human rights abuses have also declined. Fifth, there have been new experiments with federalism—the delegation or devolution of authority from the central government to local authorities—to enhance governmental accountability to the public and defuse the potential for ethnic conflict, most notably in Nigeria but also in Ethiopia, Ghana, Tanzania, Uganda, and South Africa. One or more of these trends, especially the first two and perhaps the third, can be found in most African countries that are not trapped in civil war.

Optimists also point to less exclusive membership in the governing elite, which has expanded into the upper-middle sector of society far more than during the era of authoritarian rule. In country after country, repeated multi-party elections have resulted in significant turnover in the national legislatures and local government bodies, sometimes as high as 40 percent per cycle. While the quality of elected officials at the local level remains poor, members of national legislatures are younger, better educated, and more independent in their political approach than the older generation they have displaced. Although further research is needed to confirm any major change in the composition of these bodies, new politicians and legislators also appear more likely than their predecessors to be democrats and to focus on issues of public policy and less likely to be patronage seekers.

Finally, public opinion across Africa appears to prefer democracy over any authoritarian alternatives. Surveys undertaken for the Afrobarometer project in 12 African countries between 1999 and 2001 found that a mean of 69 percent of all respondents regarded democracy as "preferable to any other kind of government," while only 12 percent agreed with the proposition that "in certain situations, a non-democratic government can be preferable." Moreover, 58 percent of all respondents stated that they were satisfied" or "very satisfied" with the "way democracy works" in their country.

Realists—who criticize what they contend was a moralistic approach to US foreign policy by the Clinton administration and disparage the use of democratization as a foreign policy goal—take a far more cautious view of what is occurring on the continent. Considering the same six developments that optimists cite as examples of democratic advances, realists note that all six are present in fewer than six countries. They also see much less progress than the optimists when nations are considered one by one. First, regular multi-party elections across the continent have resulted in an alternation of government in only one-third of the countries that have held votes. Moreover, only about one-half of these elections have been regarded as free and fair, with results accepted by those who have lost. It is also debatable in most of these countries whether recent elections have been of higher quality than those held in the early 1990s.

Second, although the re-emergence of civil society and the free press is a significant advance from the era of authoritarian rule when both were barely tolerated or systematically suppressed, civil society remains very weak in Africa compared to other regions and is concentrated in urban areas. Political parties are especially weak and rarely differentiate themselves from one another on the basis of policy. Apart from the church, farmers' organizations, or community self-help groups in a smattering of countries (such as Kenya, Côte d'Ivoire, and Nigeria), civil society barely exists in rural areas where most of the population resides. The press, especially the print media, is similarly concentrated in urban areas and thus reaches a relatively small proportion of the entire population. Only the broadcast media penetrates the countryside, but it is largely state-owned. Although private broadcasting has grown in recent years, especially in television and FM radio, stations cater almost exclusively to urban audiences. With a few exceptions, AM and short- and medium-wave radio—the chief sources of information for the rural population—remain state monopolies.

Third, while the legislature holds out the promise of becoming an institution of countervailing power in some countries, it remains weak and has rarely managed to effectively check executive power. Fourth, the judicial system in most countries is ineffectual, either because its members are corrupt or because it has too few magistrates and too poor an infrastructure to keep pace with the number of cases. Human rights abuses also continue, though less frequently and with less intensity than a decade ago. Fifth, Africa's experiments with federalism, though apparently successful, are confined to six states. Finally, the extent to which Africans have internalized democratic values is hard to judge. Although the Afrobarometer surveys indicate broad support for democracy, the results also suggest that such support is "a mile wide and an inch deep." An average of only 23 percent of respondents in each country described their country as "completely democratic."

Both optimists and realists are correct in their assessments of what is occurring in Africa. But how can both views be valid? The answer is that each presents only one side of the story. On a continent where the record of democratization is one of partial advance in over one-half of the cases, those assessing progress toward democratization, or lack of it, tend to dwell either on what has been accomplished or on what has yet to be achieved. These divergent assessments are proverbial examples of those who view the glass as either half-full or half-empty. Optimists and realists also draw their conclusions from slightly different samples. Whereas optimists focus mainly on states that are partly free or free, realists concentrate on states that are partly free or not free.

Optimists and realists are also both right because there are several Africas rather than one. In fact, at least five Africas cut across the three broad categories of the Freedom House survey. First are the consolidated and semi-consolidated democracies—a much smaller group of countries than those classified as free. This category presently consists of only two or three cases, such as Botswana, Mauritius, and perhaps South Africa. The second group consists of approximately 15 aspiring democracies, including the remaining five classified by Freedom House as free but not yet consolidated democracies plus roughly 10 classified as partly free where the transition to democracy has not stalled. All these states have exhibited slow but continuous progress toward a more liberal and institutionalized form of democratic politics. In this group are Benin, Ghana, Madagascar, Mali, Senegal, and possibly Kenya, Malawi, Tanzania, and Zambia. Third are semi-authoritarian states, countries classified as partly free where the transition to democracy has stalled. This category consists of approximately 13 countries including Uganda, the Central African Republic, and possibly Zimbabwe. Fourth are countries that are not free, with little or no prospect for a democratic transition in the near future. About 10 countries make up this group, including Cameroon, Chad, Eritrea, Ethiopia, Rwanda, and Togo. Finally, there are the states mired in civil war, such as Angola, Congo, Liberia, and Sudan. Each of these five Africas presents a different context for the pursuit of democracy.

Inhibiting Democracy

Several conditions peculiar to the continent make Africa a difficult place to sustain democratic practice. They explain why Africa lags behind other regions in its extent of democratic advance, why political party organizations are weak, and why the ties between leaders and followers are usually based on clientelist relationships. These conditions in turn create pressures for more and more patronage, a situation that undermines electoral accountability and leads to corruption.

Africa is the poorest of the world's principal regions: per capita income averages US$490 per year. This condition does not affect the emergence of democracy but does impact its sustainability. On average, democracies with per capita incomes of less than US$1,000 last 8.5 years while those with per capita incomes of over US$6,000 endure for 99. The reasons for this are straightforward. Relatively wealthy countries are better able to allocate their resources to most or all groups making claims on the state, while poor countries are not. The result is that politics in a poor country is likely to be a zero-sum game, a reality that does not foster bargaining and compromise between competing interests or a willingness to play by democratic rules.

Almost all African countries remain agrarian societies. With few exceptions like South Africa, Gabon, and Nigeria, 65 percent to 90 percent of the national populations reside in rural areas where most people are peasant farmers. Consequently, most Africans maintain strong attachments to their places of residence and to fellow citizens within their communities. Norms of reciprocity also shape social relations to a much greater degree than in urban industrial societies. In this context, Africans usually define their political interests—that is to say, their interests as citizens vis-à-vis the state—in terms of where they live and their affective ties to neighbors, rather than on the basis of occupation or socio-economic class.

With the exceptions of Botswana and Somalia, all African countries are multi-ethnic societies where each group inhabits a distinct territorial homeland. Africans' tendency to define their political interests in terms of where they live is thus accentuated by the fact that residents of different areas are often members of different ethnic groups or sub-groups.

Finally, African states provide much larger proportions of wage employment, particularly middle-class employment, than states in other regions do. African states have also historically been large mobilizers of capital, though to a lesser extent recently. Few countries have given rise to a middle class that does not depend on the state for its own employment and reproduction. In this context, people seek political office for the resources it confers, for their clients' benefit, and for the chance to enhance their own status. In the words of a well known Nigerian party slogan, "I chop, you chop," literally, "I eat, you eat."

POSTSCRIPT

Is Multi-Party Democracy Taking Hold in Africa?

In addition to the factors raised by Barkan as inhibiting democracy in Africa, which some would dispute, there are other conditions frequently evoked to foreground a discussion of multiparty democracy in Africa. First, prior to independence, most African nations had little to no experience with democracy (as it is conceived in the West) at the national scale. If anything, the colonial period served to reinforce undemocratic tendencies, as the main purpose of unelected colonial administrations was to extract resources. Second, most African nations inherited national borders from the colonial era that cut across ethnic boundaries. The "unnaturalness" of these boundaries has made African states more difficult to govern. Third, and a point alluded to in the introduction to this issue, external powers have meddled in African affairs, often to the detriment of more representative government. The French, in particular, have intervened on a number of occasions in their former colonies when the leadership was not supportive of French interests. Finally, the role of the military is very poorly defined in many African contexts. In the absence of strong civilian rule, there is a tendency for this institution to assert control when there are economic or political problems. Here again, the way in which the military was used in the colonial era probably has contributed to this ill-defined role. While some scholars are highly cognizant of the aforementioned factors when assessing political change in Africa, others assert that attempts to put the "blame" for Africa's nontransition to democracy on outsiders or former colonial powers is simply a convenient excuse for the corruption and mismanagement of African leaders.

For those interested in further reading, Claude Ake offers a different perspective on African democracy than Bratton and Mattes, arguing that "the democracy movement in Africa will emphasize concrete economic and social rights rather than abstract political rights." See *Democracy and Development in Africa* (The Brookings Institution, 1997). A good example of a more thoroughly pessimistic view (or realistic depending on your perspective) of the prospects for democracy in Africa is George Ayittey's *Africa in Chaos* (St. Martin's Press, 1998).

ISSUE 18

Is Foreign Assistance Useful for Fostering Democracy in Africa?

YES: Arthur A. Goldsmith, from "Donors, Dictators, and Democrats in Africa," *The Journal of Modern African Studies* (2001)

NO: Julie Hearn, from "Aiding Democracy? Donors and Civil Society in South Africa," *Third World Quarterly* (2000)

ISSUE SUMMARY

YES: Arthur A. Goldsmith, professor of management at the University of Massachusetts in Boston, examines the relationship between the amount of development assistance given to sub-Saharan African countries in the 1990s and the evolution of their political systems. He suggests that there is a positive, but small, correlation between donor assistance and democratization during this period. He views aid as insurance to prevent countries from sliding back into one-party or military rule.

NO: Julie Hearn, with the department of politics and international relations at Lancaster University, investigates democracy assistance in South Africa. She critically examines the role assigned to civil society by donors, questioning the "emancipatory potential" of the kind of democracy being promoted.

$\mathbf{S}$tarting in the early 1990s the international aid community began to more explicitly link donor assistance to democratic reform in Africa. This was in part due to a realization that, in the quest for constancy in strategically important African nations, the United States and other donor nations had often perpetuated the existence of corrupt and antidemocratic regimes that ultimately were unstable. Furthermore, the end of the cold war and the disintegration of the Soviet Union meant that the competing one-party, socialist ideology had lost most of its steam. Finally, there was a growing conceptual assertion that good governance was essential for economic growth and enhanced international trade. The way in which donors openly began to work to shape political structures in Africa was unprecedented. While covert attempts to influence the internal politics of African nations had always existed, it was once considered an infringement of national sovereignty for one nation to work actively and openly at shaping the political discourse in another.

The link between foreign assistance and democratic reform has taken two major forms to date. The first is "political conditionality," which links general foreign assistance (for all types of programs) to governance and democracy criteria. In other words, a country must meet certain standards of democracy as a condition for receiving any type of assistance. So, for example, the World Bank now requires its loan applicants to meet certain governance and economic criteria before it will release funds. The second type of assistance is designed specifically to promote the development and strengthening of democratic institutions and practices (often through technical assistance programs). For example, the United States Agency of International Development (USAID) works to advance democracy in Africa by funding programs that facilitate: 1)free and fair elections, 2) the rule of law, 3) a greater advocacy role for civil society, and 4) transparent, accountable, and participatory governance.

Proponents of this approach argue that it is better to rely on governance criteria than geopolitical considerations when dispensing aid. Critics suggest that the former is just a thinly veiled rationale for the latter, which will always dictate who receives foreign assistance and how much. Furthermore, they assert that democratic and economic conditionalities are now tightly woven into one package promoting a global neoliberal agenda that favors the interests of the wealthy nations over those of the poor.

In this issue, Arthur A. Goldsmith examines the relationship between the amount of development assistance given to sub-Saharan African countries in the 1990s and their levels of democratic reform. His assessment of such reform is based on a number of measures, including the staging of elections, electoral challenges to incumbent leaders, voter participation, the number of coup d'etats, and political indices (Freedom House index of political freedom and a democracy index). He states that there is a positive, but small, correlation between donor assistance and democratization during this period. Goldsmith views aid as analogous to "'maintenance therapy'—the long-term use of foreign assistance to forestall or postpone re-emergent authoritarian rule."

In contrast, Julie Hearn examines democracy assistance in South Africa and suggests that Western donors are largely concerned with establishing forms of governance that help maintain the international system. She asserts that U.S. assistance effectively has changed the debate on democracy in South Africa among civil society organizations, encouraging a focus on procedural democracy, and minimizing discourse related to economic justice. She is critical of this type of assistance because it has led to the maintenance of an "intensely exploitative economic system" in South Africa.

Arthur A. Goldsmith  **YES**

Donors, Dictators, and Democrats in Africa

Introduction

Sub-Saharan Africa (henceforth simply Africa) is marked by weak, often dictatorial states. They are also disproportionately among the states that receive the most aid per capita in the world. Is there a connection? A growing opinion assumes that there must be. It is probably no surprise when Doug Bandow (1997) of the libertarian Cato Institute asserts that fifty years experience proves that aid usually hurts political reform. More surprising, perhaps, is a study sponsored by the Swedish Foreign Ministry that documents how large amounts of aid delivered over long periods may reduce accountability and democratic decision-making among recipient states (Bräutigam 2000). Even the World Bank (1998: 84–8) raises questions about aid's impact on governments, concluding that the Bank has often given too much money to ineffective regimes and in the process has sometimes undermined their administrative capacity.

A common theme in these criticisms is that aid is like a narcotic, fostering addictive behaviour among states that receive it. States are thought to exhibit the symptoms of dependence—a short-run benefit from aid, but increasing need for external support that does lasting damage to the country (Azam et al. 1999). By feeding this 'addiction', the aid donors have supposedly weakened the resolve of African states to act on behalf of their citizens. Development assistance, in other words, has had the perverse and unintended political effect of reinforcing despotic rule in the region. The implication is that countries need to 'kick the habit' of aid before they can turn to the task of building authentic democratic institutions.

This article takes a sceptical look at these convictions, asking whether it is true that heavy reliance on aid has blocked democratic development in Africa. It focuses on the period after 1990, when many donors started making democratisation an explicit object of policy. Dissenting from the prevailing critique of aid, it finds that aid dependency has not systematically set back Africa's political evolution. The evidence suggests, to the contrary, that aid may have had a small favourable effect over the past decade, encouraging more responsible self-government in

From Arthur A. Goldsmith, "Donors, Dictators, and Democrats in Africa," *The Journal of Modern African Studies*, vol. 39, no. 3 (2001). Copyright © 2001 by Cambridge University Press. Reprinted by permission. Notes and references omitted.

some countries. . . . Getting Africa off the donor assistance 'drug' is a commendable goal, but it does not appear to be a prerequisite for democratisation in the region, as some people assume is true. Weaning countries abruptly from external financing and technical assistance might well have the opposite effect.

Foreign aid is an international transfer of resources that would not have taken place as the result of market forces. It includes grants and loans made at subsidised interest rates, provided by governments or by international financial institutions. It also includes technical assistance and debt relief. One goal of these transfers has been to encourage democracy, or pluralistic national political systems where people are reasonably free to express their political demands and to hold rulers to account. Democracy in this sense is not identical with competitive elections, held at regular intervals. The two do overlap, however, and elections are often the best tangible evidence of the extent to which a democratic system is in place. Accordingly, the discussion will concentrate on election procedures and outcomes.

The article starts by documenting the ways in which international donors have attempted to boost democracy in the region. Donors' forays into government reform have been criticised as inconsequential or counterproductive. However, analysis of the data suggests a clear, though small, correlation between the amount of aid received by a country in the 1990s, and the extent to which its political system opened up to greater accountability and competition. The issue for many African countries is how to consolidate and extend these moderate reforms on their own, with less external support.

Foreign Aid for Democracy

Africa has been using large amounts of foreign aid for years. Depending on the definition of aid, the average African country took between $600 and $1,500 (in 1995 prices) in aid per capita between the mid-1970s and mid-1990s. Starting about 1990, international donors began to link these resources expressly to democratic reform. Representative government had disappeared in most African countries following independence. Too often, African governments ignored or repressed their people. They failed to supply critical public goods—or if they did, they redirected them to the regime's narrow base of supporters. During the Cold War, the rich democracies were reluctant to say or do much about these governmental problems for fear of driving African countries into the socialist camp. The changed geopolitical scene in the late 1980s altered those calculations and freed public lenders to use their clout to extract domestic political concessions in Africa (Olson 1998).

The new official consensus on democratisation was clearly reflected in the Development Assistance Committee (DAC) policy statement in 1993. For the first time, the DAC specifically advocated that developing countries lay down procedures whereby ordinary people can help shape the policies that affect their lives. Communities and private organisations must be empowered so they can check the risk of arbitrary government, according to the DAC. Thus, client states should be encouraged to build institutions that assure the consent of the governed—and that allow the governed to withhold their consent so that their political leaders can be peacefully replaced (OECD 1993: 9–12).

To take at face value any official developed country policy statement about the importance of democratic government in a developing country would be naive. Since 1975, an amendment to the Foreign Assistance Act has made US aid conditional on respect for human rights and civil liberties. Yet, *realpolitik* often meant that human rights violations were overlooked, while national security issues dominated who got aid (Hook 1998). An oft-cited example was Zaire's Mobutu Sese Sekou, whose corrupt but reliably anti-communist regime for decades received American backing. With the 'Evil Empire' defeated, however, US foreign assistance policy turned more seriously to human rights as a basis for determining how to allocate resources (Meernik et al. 1998; Apodaca & Stohl 1999; Blanton 2000). The United States suspended aid to Mobutu in 1992.

There was economic logic behind making legislative and administrative reforms a centre of attention in development assistance. Greater participation and more debate in public life, the donors argued, would provide a sounder institutional grounding for economic advancement. Not only did democracy offer a better way to aggregate and employ local knowledge, the climate of open discussion would help move resources to their most productive uses. Democracy's built-in checks and balances can lead to greater public accountability, responsiveness and transparency—which can enhance the business and investment climate, and perhaps eventually make foreign assistance less important. Empirical evidence also exists that democracy helps less-developed countries make better use of the aid that they do get (Svensson 1995).

This is not the classic political defence of civil liberties and free and fair elections. The usual instrumental arguments for democratic procedures are that they give voice to majority demands and that they are a peaceful means for recruiting new leadership talent. The economic argument put forth by international financial institutions and bilateral aid agencies in the 1990s is different. Without denying the political advantages of pluralistic competition, the donors' economic argument concentrates on improving the environment for private investment and innovation.

How Aid Affects Recipient Country Politics

Foreign aid can help shape African domestic politics in four ways. The first way happens by accident. Some of the pressure for government reforms in Africa is a by-product of donor-inspired economic austerity schemes, also known as structural adjustment. Imposed with increasingly frequency since the 1980s, these market-based reforms aim to shake up moribund African economies. Yet, they also encourage political shake-ups by curbing the power of the state to pay off its partners and confidants in the private sector. Africa's hitherto 'silent majority' has been energised to begin exercising its voice—though ironically, it is sometimes to speak against the hardship associated with structural adjustment. Democratic political reforms may thus inadvertently undermine pro-market economic policies, and contradict the donors' economic aims for their African clients (Baylies 1995). Still, the political effect often is for greater mass participation in public life, especially among urban groups who have tended to see themselves as net losers under structural adjustment.

The second mode of donor political influence is through direct aid for political reform. A recent example is Chad, which held a constitutional referendum and a presidential contest in 1996. France provided the logistical support that allowed co-ordination of voting nation-wide. France also underwrote the cost of Chad's elections (May & Massey 2000: 122). The amounts the donors give directly for governance and civil service reform are limited—only 4.4 per cent of all bilateral official development assistance (ODA) commitments made world-wide in 1998 (DAC 1999, Table 19). The World Bank (1999, Appendix 12) reports that its cumulative spending for public sector management in Africa amounted to just 3.8 per cent of lending to the region as of 1999.

However, these figures grossly understate the degree of external support for political reform. They do not include additional resources that go to support non-government organisations (NGOs). NGOs are a third avenue for aid's influence on democratisation. Official donors are taking steps to strengthen these voluntary and community groups in Africa (Robinson 1995). About half the World Bank's development projects have some involvement of local and international NGOs, for example. Many bilateral donors make even greater use of NGOs. Worldwide, about $9 billion in official aid is funnelled annually through these groups, or 15 per cent of all aid, not including the private funds that NGOs raise and spend on charitable activities (Gibbs et al. 1999). These groups often advocate on behalf of underrepresented groups in society, which may lead to demands for changes in political institutions and procedures.

Modifying the political system is not usually the donors' immediate objective when they enter partnerships with NGOs. Sometimes the aid may have the opposite effect of politically neutralising the recipient groups by making them look like foreign agents (Robinson 1993). Critics charge that too many domestic democracy movements in Africa rely on external support for resources and validation (Ihonvbere 1996). Yet, over time, such groups may add to the domestic organisational endowment and social capital that are important foundations for democratic government. Case studies in Ghana, Uganda and South Africa find that aid-supported groups can become key players in setting the course of national political reform (Hearne 1999).

The fourth, and perhaps most important, way in which aid can affect a recipient country's politics is through specific political conditionalities. Donors put political strings on loans for seemingly unrelated projects and programmes, using the financial resources as a reward and punishment to induce political reform. Often working in collaboration, donors make plain to the client state that it must shape up politically or lose access to credit. Such pressure is common. After Niger's President Ibrahim Maïnassara was killed in a coup in April 1999, for example, France immediately cut off development assistance, pending a return to civilian rule. France, which is Niger's largest international patron, restored its support seven months later, after successful completion of the presidential election. When a recent study looked at World Bank and International Monetary Fund (IMF) programmes in Africa from 1997 to 1999, it found that nearly three fourths of the loan conditions (or about 80 per country) pertained to governance (Kapur & Webb 2000).

Direct political aid, NGO support, and political conditionalities are often used in concert to try to bring about a favourable result, as illustrated by Zimbabwe. The IMF and the World Bank suspended aid to Zimbabwe in 1998. There were several reasons, the most serious being the sending of troops to the Democratic Republic of Congo (DRC), which compromised efforts to control Zimbabwe's budget deficit. The IMF and World Bank offered to restore the money only if Zimbabwe showed a serious effort to curb its military and to undertake other administrative and political reforms.

President Robert Mugabe's subsequent land policies hardened the donors' position. In an effort to buttress political support in the run-up to legislative elections in 2000, Mugabe openly sanctioned illegal seizures of commercial farms. His government also drew up a list of properties to be taken officially without compensation. Opposition groups charged that these farms were earmarked for government cronies instead of people who really needed land. Britain signalled its willingness to release funds for land reforms and to organise a conference to solicit support from other Western countries to redistribute farms to the truly landless. However, first all unauthorised land invasions had to stop and legal procedures be restored.

The US Agency for International Development (AID) forged links in Zimbabwe with private groups on grounds that government institutions were too politicised to be effective. For the 2000 national elections, the US government funded the training of 10,000 domestic election monitors and helped the semi-independent Electoral Supervisory Commission to cope with the administrative demands of election logistics. In Washington, the United States Congress considered the Zimbabwe Democracy Bill. It would impose an embargo on the country pending a certified return to the rule of law, respect for ownership of property, and freedom of speech and association.

Doubts and Controversies

How effective have such activities been? Official statements usually reflect self-assurance. In recent testimony before Congress, for example, AID's assistant administrator for Africa, Vivian Lowery Derryck (1999) expressed the following position:

> As a whole, Africa has made major progress towards expanding and consolidating democracy during the past ten years. The widespread increases in freedom of speech and the media, freedom of assembly and association, competitive national and local elections, and the growth of civil society have given more Africans greater freedom and stability in their lives than at any time in the recent past . . . USAID has been involved in many of these transitions, and we are proud of the achievements of these new democracies.

When policymakers speak for themselves, however, they typically sound less confident about the political outcome of their work. Former chief economist at the World Bank, Joseph Stiglitz (1999) has said that policy conditionalities actually tend to undermine participatory processes in developing countries, which should be building their own capacity to make democratic decisions. Ex-deputy administrator for AID Carol Lancaster (1999: 66) goes farther, suggesting that foreign aid in Africa has encouraged poor governance, by giving dishonest and incompetent regimes a sense of security.

It is not hard to find anecdotal evidence to support scepticism about foreign aid's beneficial political impact. Consider the Zimbabwe case, just cited. Despite the pressure, President Mugabe remained defiant. He charged that the opposition Movement for Democratic Change was the surrogate of the British and American governments. Foreign observers were turned away from the 2000 elections. Challenger candidates and their supporters were intimidated. Zimbabwe defaulted on its foreign debt that year. The government refused to obey court rulings against the land seizures, and it kept its troops engaged in the DRC. World Bank and IMF credits remained on hold. Political conditionalities appear to work best when they are in response to a specific event or tip the balance towards domestic opposition groups (Crawford 1997)—neither of which were evidently the case in Zimbabwe.

Nor have donors been completely consistent about whom they help. They have pushed harder for civil rights with some clients than others. In June 1990, French President François Mitterrand warned African heads of state that French aid would henceforth be conditional on progress in the direction of democracy. France pointedly did not intervene to protect the dictator Hissène Habré of Chad in a coup six months later, despite having troops in his country. Yet France ignored human rights abuses by Habré's successor, Idriss Déby.

The problem with negative anecdotes like these is that one can find others that cast foreign pressure and support for democratisation in a more positive light. Though it never received much direct financial assistance, South Africa is perhaps the best example of how the international community has helped give birth to a liberal constitution and multiparty political system in Africa. To assess aid's political impact systematically, we cannot rely just on stories from selected countries; we need to look specifically for two things: (a) comprehensive indications of the degree of democratisation across Africa; and (b), if democratisation can be substantiated, for signs that aid contributed to it. . . .

Evidence of Democratisation

Political scientists who specialise on Africa tend to question the authenticity and depth of democracy in the region. The social context of electoral rules obviously differs from what is found in Europe or North America, and superficially similar institutions and procedures may hold very different meanings south of the Sahara. With most African political reforms so new, no one can make confident predictions about where they are heading. Nonetheless, three types of evidence can be cited in support of a bona fide democratic tendency.

One indication is that across the sub-continent more liberal rules of political engagement are being adopted. Second, is the growing number and competitiveness of elections in recent years. Third, are overall indexes of political freedom, which, because they capture the previous two types of evidence, have been on the rise in Africa. . . .

This article has looked into the relationship between foreign aid and steps towards democracy in African countries over the past decade and earlier. Among specialists in international relations, it is often considered axiomatic that aid has an addictive effect on government that subtly reinforces repression in countries with single party rule, even if the opposite result is intended. Many area experts also doubt the ability and good will of outsiders to sponsor human rights and authentic multiparty competition in Africa. The result is seen as 'donor democracy' without significant domestic bloodlines. Civil society critics of the international economic regime, such as the Fifty Years is Enough Coalition or the Jubilee 2000 movement, are apt to agree that aid (at least in its current forms) is anti-democratic in character. Even the donors sometimes concede the point that their efforts in Africa have been politically counterproductive.

This article's analysis suggests a somewhat more favourable outlook. First, the data indicates that democratisation is more than a false front put up for donors. In some countries, at least, meaningful though tenuous changes in governing style and substance look as if they are taking place. Second, while we must be cautious about attributing causation, foreign assistance appears to have a positive association with these welcome political trends. This conclusion is supported by statistical analysis of quantitative data. Donors, it seems, can work with some client states or with civil society groups to obtain somewhat greater democratisation in Africa. There is no evidence here for the prevalent view that the 'compulsive use' of aid has net perverse political effect, or that 'going cold turkey' with less aid would speed the pace of democratic reform. Rather than the metaphor of addiction, a closer analogy may be 'maintenance therapy'—the long-term use of foreign assistance to forestall or postpone re-emergent authoritarian rule.

The difficulty for development policymakers is that aid's political benefit appears to be quite small and perhaps transient. Local opposition to arbitrary leadership and public corruption seems far more important. With many other factors pulling against democratic reform, any gains won with the help of development funds can easily be undone. At issue for many African countries is whether they can find the means to use official assistance to greater political effect, consolidating and extending the modest progress made since 1990. Given pressure from the developed world to break the cycle of aid dependence in Africa, these societies probably will soon have far less external help for their efforts to head for more responsive and open systems of government.

NO ↩

Julie Hearn

Aiding Democracy? Donors and Civil Society in South Africa

Democracy Assistance: Promoting Stability

During the 1980s a new branch of the aid industry was born, democracy assistance. Although 'democracy' often entered the foreign-policy-making vocabulary of the North in the postwar period, it was not the dominant form in which the North related to the South. The principal form was the development of strategic alliances with authoritarian regimes. The new industry arose out of a major reconsideration of Western foreign policy towards the South, particularly within the USA. With the US defeat in Vietnam, the Nicaraguan revolution and other nationalist victories in the South, US foreign policy towards the Third World had reached crisis-point by the late 1970s. It had failed to stop popular anti-US regimes taking power in South East Asia, Central America and Southern Africa and its capacity to shape events abroad appeared severely curtailed. By the early 1980s, a new consensus began to emerge among policy-makers around the strategy of 'democracy promotion'. This involved two key elements.

First was the recognition that coercive political arrangements had failed to deal with the social movements that had challenged authoritarian rule and that formal liberal democracies were better able to absorb social dissent and conflict. It is important to understand that the rationale for turning to liberal democracy was that it was perceived to be a better guarantor of stability. The goal remained the same: social stability, it was simply that the means to achieve the end had changed. This becomes clear when we examine the kind of democracy being promoted in the Third World. It is about creating political structures that most effectively maintain the international system. It has no more to do with radical change than its predecessor, authoritarianism does. As Samuel Huntington, one of the most influential proponents of formal democracy, clearly states: 'The maintenance of democratic politics and the reconstruction of the social order are fundamentally incompatible.' At its core, the contemporary political and industry is about effective system maintenance.

From Julie Hearn, "Aiding Democracy? Donors and Civil Society in South Africa," *Third World Quarterly*, vol. 21, no. 5 (2000). Copyright © 2000 by *Third World Quarterly*. Reprinted by permission of Taylor & Francis, Ltd. http://www.tandf.co.uk/journals.

The second point is that, where earlier foreign policy had focused almost exclusively on the strength of the client state and its governmental apparatus, the new democracy strategy began to recognise the important role of civil society. It was from within civil society that opposition to authoritarian rule had emerged and therefore it was imperative 'to penetrate civil society and *from therein* assure control over popular mobilization' (emphasis in original). [William I.] Robinson continues:

> The composition and balance of power in civil society in a given Third World country is now just as important to US and transnational interests as who controls the governments of those countries. This is a shift from social control 'from above' to social control 'from below . . .'

This is an important part of democracy assistance. Aid is targeted at a country's most influential, modern, advocacy-orientated civil society organs which include: women's organisations, human rights groups, national or sectoral NGO [nongovernmental organization] for business associations, private policy institutes, youth and student organisations, and professional media associations. As commentators, including those who direct the new political aid, have pointed out, this is not very different from what the CIA used to do, particularly within the context of counter-insurgency and 'low-intensity conflict'. However, former CIA director William Colby makes a key point: 'Many of the programs which . . . were conducted as covert operations [can now be] conducted quite openly, and consequently, without controversy'.

As Robinson points out: 'Transferring political intervention from the covert to the overt realm does not change its character, but it does make it easier for policymakers to build domestic and international support for this intervention.' This is the trump-card of democracy promotion, it diffuses opposition to Northern intervention. Advisor to the State Department and academic, [Howard] Wiarda, clearly sums up:

> A US stance in favor of democracy helps get the Congress, the bureaucracy, the media, the public, and elite opinion to back US policy. It helps ameliorate the domestic debate, disarms critics (who could be against democracy?) . . . The democracy agenda enables us, additionally, to merge and fudge over some issues that would otherwise be troublesome. It helps bridge the gap between our fundamental geopolitical and strategic interests . . . and our need to clothe those security concerns in moralistic language . . . The democracy agenda, in short, is a kind of legitimacy cover for our more basic strategic objectives.

Since its inception in the early 1980s, democracy assistance has continued its take-off. In the 1990s this was fuelled by three important developments: the academic and donor preoccupation with 'governance' as the root of underdevelopment, the practice of political conditionality, that is, making aid conditional on political reforms, and the changing balance of power in North–South relations. During the 1980s an orthodoxy developed that Africa's development crisis was precipitated by a failure of the state and that 'governance' had to be reconstructed, from the bottom up. Shaping civil society became the road to reforming the state. Making aid dependent on such changes has been the site of sharp confrontations between the governments of many sub-Saharan African countries and donors. In South Africa, no such crude coercion was needed. As international opponents of apartheid, including Western states, united with domestic combatants, a broad consensus was forged over the form that a new liberal democracy would take. With the demise of nationalist and socialist ideologies, such foreign, overtly political, interference was no longer viewed with the same levels of distrust. The latter has allowed the North to intervene in the (civil) societies of the South with an unprecedented degree of perceived legitimacy.

South Africa has had a long history of Western support to civil society. The highly conflictual politics of apartheid, particularly of the late 1970s and 1980s, generated a 'vast array of more or less popular, more or less institutionalised organisations and initiatives in broad opposition to the apartheid state'. These included trade unions, community organisations, sectorally mobilised movements of youth, students and women, as well as business, lawyers and religious associations. It is these kinds of civil society organisations (CSOs) (although they were hardly ever referred to as such) that donors funded. This support began with Denmark in the mid-1960s and was followed by Norway and Sweden in the 1970s. It culminated in the mid-1980s with the imposition of sanctions by Western governments and the international isolation of the apartheid regime. The Nordic countries were joined at this time by the European Union and the USA, who each provided an unprecedented $340 million over a nine year period to CSOs, before the end of apartheid and the 1994 elections. Despite such a significant involvement, a comprehensive account of foreign assistance to civil society in this period is still to be written, not least because of the covert nature of that support. With the election of an internationally recognised government, foreign donors began to provide aid to the new South African state as well as continuing some funding to civil society, though on a smaller scale. Although this loss of finance has had a considerable impact, it has not been fully analysed and thus there is substantial dispute as to how much funding was withdrawn and how significant this was.

This article examines foreign assistance to civil society in South Africa since 1994. The premise of this research is that political aid is 'political', that it is about consciously influencing the 'rules of the game'. . . .

The Importance of Democracy Assistance

Unlike in other African countries, democracy assistance forms a major part of foreign aid to South Africa. The principal objective of aid programmes to the country is to influence the political transition and to focus on democratic consolidation. This kind of aid is in stark contrast to other donor programmes on the continent, which primarily supplement the meagre national budget of African governments so that they can provide basic services in the areas of welfare, agriculture, energy and infrastructure. These are the predominant categories of aid in most African countries, where democracy assistance on average accounts for less than 5% of total aid. South Africa, with an average per capita GNP [gross national product] of about $3200, is categorised as an upper middle income country, along with Brazil and Chile. As such it would normally be disqualified as an aid recipient. Danish aid, for example, is restricted to countries with an average GNP per capita of less than $2000. Aid to the country is seen as a temporary measure, because, as USAID/South Africa points out: 'South Africa has substantial resources to address its problems over the long term.' Donor programmes are termed 'transitional', mirroring South Africa's own transition, and were to end soon after the 1999 elections, commonly perceived as the formal end-point of the passage from one political system to another. In South Africa, nation-wide poverty is not the motivating force behind donor activity. The whole thrust of aid involvement is about deepening the political changes that have taken place since 1994 and ensuring that, as far as possible, 'a point of irreversibility' is reached before the ending of external assistance. Foreign aid to South Africa is very much a case of democracy assistance, and if we wished to study contemporary foreign intervention in a country's democratisation process, South Africa could not be a better case study. . . .

Such a strong emphasis on political aid in South Africa is hardly surprising. Since the beginning of the century, South Africa has been important to the West, both politically and economically. It has been described as 'a reliable, if junior, member of the Northern club'. The West's relationship with Africa was largely predicated on a long-term strategic alliance with the apartheid regime in South Africa. This continued throughout the 1970s and into the 1980s. At the same time South African capital, some of which was in the same league as that of any Northern-based corporation, became thoroughly intermeshed with capital originating in Europe, the USA and Japan. As globalisation advanced, South Africa became a key outpost of international capital. However, with the political unrest that began with the 1976 Soweto uprising, capital outside South Africa began to push its South African counterparts to search for a political solution that would involve a transition from racial to non-racial capitalism. . . . [P]riority [was] given to democracy building in South Africa by the West after 1994. . . .

In the situation proffered by 1994, civil society was not a priority. There are a number of reasons for this. In other African countries, aid to civil society is about establishing something that is not there. It is about creating a modern, advocacy-orientated civil society. In South Africa this already exists. Using the lowest common denominator of pluralist theory, which says the more civil society groups, the better, South Africa scores highly. It has a dense, long-standing associational life. Second, this associational life is modern, a key characteristic of the donor model. Third, it is strongly advocacy-orientated and has proven its lobbying abilities on the world stage. Fourth, in South Africa, in 1994 at least, donors did not need to convince the new government that civil society had a legitimate role to play and that the government must give it the political space in which to operate. That was already what the government believed, since many new government officials came from the NGO sector, and as a result there were unusually close and sympathetic relationships between civil society and the government.

However, perhaps most importantly, many donors had established close links with civil society throughout the 1980s and early 1990s. For example, a large number supported the work of IDASA [Institute for a Democratic South Africa] in the late 1980s and early 1990s. IDASA is arguably one of the most professional, effective and high profile CSOs in South Africa today, and thoroughly steeped in democratic liberalism. A 1994 annual report states that the 'personal credibility with international donors' of cofounder, Boraine, 'was pivotal in securing a generous funding base for the organisation, allowing it to expand country-wide and make interventions with national impact'. After the 1994 elections, IDASA was renamed the Institute for Democracy in South Africa. It now runs some 12 national programmes and projects and has a staff of 140. This close association with donors continues today, possibly making it the most donor-associated democracy NGO in South Africa. We have indicated how the German foundations developed strategic relationships with sections of civil society, how the Nordic countries were stalwart supporters of an underground civil society, and the enormous resources that the USA spent on cultivating links with CSOs. Already from the mid-1980s the USA had grasped the pivotal role that civil society would play in shaping the new South Africa. Subsequently, it began to attempt to influence it, checking the growing radicalism among the black population by developing counterweight forces conducive to the establishment of a liberal order. This was achieved by supporting an emergent black middle class of professionals who could be incorporated into a post-apartheid order; developing a network of grassroots community leaders who could compete with more radical leadership; and cultivating a black business class that would have a stake in stable South African capitalism. From the standpoint of 1994, donors had already made an impact in civil society. The next section suggests one important role that donors are financing civil society to play in the new South Africa.

What Role for Civil Society?

A report on the democratic outlook for South Africa by an influential South African think-tank concludes that the chief threat to democratic consolidation is:

> the limited capacity of the state to govern—and, more particularly, to cement a 'social contract' with society in which government protects the rights of citizens who, in turn, meet their obligations to democratic government.

The US National Democratic Institute (NDI) describes the situation facing South Africa in the following terms: 'the twin challenges of rebuilding a new united South Africa while simultaneously developing the institutions that will conduct the daily business of government'. We have shown how foreign aid has prioritised the institutional development of government, thereby attempting to meet the need to build the capacity of the state to govern. However, as both analysts note, the other side of the equation is to link society with this new institutional framework, to cement the social contract and to build, in the words of the then Deputy President, Thabo Mbeki, 'a democratized political culture'. This is where the role of civil society is so important to the architects, both domestic and external, of the new South Africa. It is a particular kind of civil society that can help to legitimise the new state in the eyes of the South African citizenry and help to build a culture where citizens meet their obligations to liberal democratic government. First we show why this is needed in South Africa if liberal democracy is to succeed. Then we examine which civil society institutions are available to fulfil this function and how donor organisations are supporting this very role for civil society.

The same South African report writes about 'widespread citizen non-compliance—reflected in, among other indicators, crime and widespread non-payment for public services'. It continues: 'A variety of factors produce outcomes in which citizen dissatisfaction is expressed in withdrawal from the public arena and in attempts to evade the reach of government'. It concludes: 'This threatens democracy as much as overt resistance to democratic order . . . ' An annual review of political developments in South Africa in 1997, produced for the quarterly journal of the South African Coalition of NGOs and Interfund, a consortium of Northern NGOs, mainly Nordic, provides the following commentary:

> Whether currently higher or merely consistent with historical trends, crime rates in South Africa are unusually high . . . Public insecurity aside, the effect of crime is to reduce citizens' confidence in public institutions at a point when the success of the democratic transition requires enhanced trust and participation.

And a report written for the consortium of non-governmental donors, Interfund, writes:

> A key challenge for actors in civil society is to capture and steer rising (and probably inevitable) frustration into constructive, non-violent forms of conflict, namely political pressure channeled through social movements.

The purpose of the transition was to provide the political settlement that would allow the passage from racial to non-racial capitalism in South Africa. As we have noted, aid programmes have maintained this focus on political stability rather than on socioeconomic transformation, as a result of which South Africa continues to be a highly unequal society with areas of extreme deprivation. Indeed [Robert] Mattes and [Hermann] Thiel assert that the inequality is worsening. [Hein] Marais points out how the kind of instability facing South Africa, described by the above commentators, is 'symptomatic of the extreme inequalities that scar the society'. In a situation of such contradiction between economic inequality and political stability, political stability or 'democracy' will be simply about managing that tension. Civil society is the lynchpin in holding together that tension by fostering support among citizens for a government that maintains the inequality that undermines their lives. This, in effect, is recognised by the above report where it identifies the need for civil society to capture and steer the rising frustration. Obviously, social concessions will be made from time to time to maintain stability, but the primary function of political society, that is the state and civil society, will be to manage the tension between the economic and political spheres. Constituents of civil society must understand that this is their function in the political economy of South Africa in the eyes of those who wish to maintain capitalism, and ask themselves is this the role that they want to play?

Civil society plays this role in two ways. First it is the key mediator between the new state in South Africa and its citizens. From the following ratings we can see how urgently this is needed. . . . [A]pproval of the government's performance dropped between 1995 and 1997. The national government's aparting fell from 57% to 47%; parliament's went from 53% to 46%; and overall approval of all the provincial governments declined from 42% to 36%. In 1997 the approval rating for the new local governments introduced at the beginning of 1996 stood at a meagre 30%. No wonder then that the Konrad Adenauer foundation asserts that 'if democracy is to be understood and accepted by South Africans it must be seen to work well, particularly at the local level'. Second, the CPS [Centre for Policy Studies] report points out that democratic consolidation can only occur when there is widespread agreement among political elites and citizens on institutional rules. They cite political development theorists [Juan] Linz and [Alfred] Stepan who see democracy as consolidated when democratic rules become 'the only game in town'. Civil society has a key role to play in creating among the population an adherence to the values of liberal democracy and an acceptance of the rules of the game. Mattes and Thiel argue that, as well as structural features, an attitudinal commitment to democracy is essential. They write: 'The level of elite and citizen commitment to democratic processes is the single direct determinant of the probability of democratic endurance or consolidation.' In their analysis of public opinion polls taken on 'democracy' they comment: 'The results raise important questions about South Africans' understanding of democracy.' While only 27% rated as 'essential' such key procedural elements of democracy as regular elections, 48% said that equal access to houses, jobs and a decent income was 'essential' to democracy. They go on to explain why this might be so:

> While 'one man, one vote' was always the goal, the key liberation movements subscribed to and spread to their poverty-stricken followers an economic, as opposed to a procedural view of democracy.

This is disturbing to the authors and, of course, to those, within and outside the country, who wish to maintain the distinction between the political and economic sphere and maintain the tension between gross inequality and political stability. This is the wrong kind of democracy. The authors advise the following re-education:

> Thus one might urge South Africa's educational system, civil society, and political parties to shift their emphasis . . . to the . . . task of teaching people to value democratic institutions and processes more for their own sake than for what they may deliver in terms of immediate and tangible benefits.

What is interesting in South Africa, compared with other African countries, is the number and calibre of CSOs geared towards doing precisely that, encouraging a popular commitment to procedural democracy. What is more, these kinds of CSOs feature predominantly in donor political aid programmes. In our research we asked over a dozen different foreign donors what kind of civil society organisations they funded through their democracy assistance. There were five main categories: democracy organisations, concerned with the overall relationship between states and citizens; human rights and legal aid groups; conflict resolution agencies; organisations servicing or representing the nongovernmental sector; and think-tanks. Of these categories, democracy organisations were the largest. Not only were they the most numerous, but they also received the largest amounts of aid and were supported by the broadest cross-section of donors.

This is not to suggest that donor focus on the other categories, particularly in the human rights and legal aid field, is unimportant. For example, the National Institute for Public Interest Law & Research (NIPLAR), a consortium, received $3.25 million from USAID between 1996 and 1998 to create 18 human rights and democracy centres nation-wide. Along with the Legal Resource Centre (LRC) and the Black Sash Trust, NIPLAR receives donor funds to provide free legal advice. Between 1996 and 1999 USAID funded the Independent Mediation Service of South Africa (IMSSA) with $3 million as an umbrella grantee providing subgrants to conflict resolution NGOs working with local government. Another significant grant from the USA in 1997 went to the Free Market Foundation, a core partner of the German liberal Friedrich Naumann Foundation. This was to fund a programme promoting market-orientated economic policies in the South African parliament and administration. Many of these internationally funded projects form part of a broad liberal democratic discourse; however, it is crucial to investigate what the specific category of democracy organisations do in civil society.

The most prominent is IDASA. It is fully committed to procedural democracy, for example, the manager of the public opinion service at IDASA co-wrote the above article. As we mentioned, it is now an organisation with a staff of 140. It is probably also the most donor-funded CSO in South Africa. The other organisations are the Institute for Multiparty Democracy, whose name could not be more indicative of procedural democracy, and Khululekani Institute for Democracy, aimed at bringing parliament closer to the people. A fourth, the Electoral Institute of South Africa, deals with that key aspect of procedural democracy. A fifth, the Helen Suzman foundation, undertakes similar democracy surveys to those of IDASA, and has a map of Southern Africa on the back of its quarterly enblazoned with 'promoting liberal democracy'. A sixth, the South African Institute of Race Relations has a foreign donor-funded Free Society project which aims to monitor South Africa's democratic development and to promote the rule of law, ethics, justice, the concept of limited government and economic freedom. As a 1995 project description, written by one of its foreign funders, the US National Endowment for Democracy, explains: the programme will inform key government and non-government officials on activities that hinder the development of a free society. The project seeks to achieve these aims through three principal means: (1) publishing *'Frontiers of Freedom'*, a quarterly newsletter; (2) sponsoring specific research projects; and (3) hosting and attending special events, including briefings and lectures, frequently in conjunction with other non-profit institutions. It is interesting to note how some of the language has changed in the 1997 project description, which introduces the relatively new term 'civil society organisations', talks explicitly about researching 'public policy alternatives', and replaces the ideologically unambiguous 'limited government' with the much more ambiguous and widely accepted term, 'good governance'.

It is not altogether surprising to find out that these civil society organisations at the forefront of promoting procedural democracy are very much part of the South African liberal landscape. The South African Institute of Race Relations is one of the oldest liberal institutions in the country. The Helen Suzman foundation is named after arguably the most prominent South African liberal politician. IDASA was started in 1987 by van Zyl Slabbert, former leader of the opposition and Alex Boraine, former Progressive Federal Party MP. What these CSOs have done is to put procedural democracy high up on the agenda for civil society, and for the nation, and to establish the terms of the debate. This is not surprising given the resources allocated to them by the international donor community. IDASA has received grants not simply of tens of thousands of dollars, but of $1 million. In 1996 it received $1.165 million from the Ford Foundation. This is an exceptionally large grant by the Foundation's standards, which normally provides grants from $200 000 to $50 000 to CSOs in Africa, and is by far the largest grant to any grantee in South Africa. At the same time IDASA received a $1 million grant from USAID for a two-year period. The South African Institute of Race Relations and the Institute for Multi-Party Democracy received similar grants from USAID over the same period.

Conclusion

As we have seen, since 1994 South Africa has received an unprecedented amount of international political aid aimed at consolidating its liberal democracy. Even without the benefit of an in-depth, detailed study, one can safely conclude that there are few, if any, aspects of the new South African political system that have not been shaped by donor input. The external involvement in the construction of the new South African state raises important questions. What is the nature of the state of a middle income country that has been so extensively 'advised' by a myriad of international players? How do we understand such a state within existing theoretical frameworks? Does a state that is so permeable and malleable to external shapers exhibit the same autonomy as the states of advanced economies? Does it change the nature of the state? Is it a case of autonomy compromised? What impact does it have on the state's foreign policy and, perhaps even more pertinently, on its domestic policy?

And what of civil society? This article suggests that political aid to civil society has had two major consequences. First it has changed the debate on democracy. During the past five years, it is possible to see a process in which democracy has been redefined. Although half of South Africans still believe that access to housing, jobs and a decent income are essential components of a democratic society, this residual belief in social democracy is being eroded and replaced by the norms and practice of procedural democracy. It is our argument that the North has played its role in this process by funding the liberal proponents of procedural democracy in civil society, and that, subsequently, political aid has successfully 'influenced the rules of the game'. The second consequence is that this has facilitated a newly legitimatised South African state to preside over the same intensely exploitative economic system, but this time unchallenged. External and domestic support for procedural democracy has successfully removed all challenges to the system. It has ensured that democracy in the new South Africa is not about reconstructing the social order but about effective system maintenance.

POSTSCRIPT

Is Foreign Assistance Useful for Fostering Democracy in Africa?

One aspect to be aware of when interpreting these articles is that Goldsmith's research was funded by USAID, the foreign assistance arm of the U.S. government that funds a number of democracy programs in Africa. The reader should also note that some of the differences in assessment boil down to fundamentally different views on the way democracy should be conceptualized.

Many scholars are critical of the type of democracy and governance assistance being offered by USAID in Africa. A major concern is that the United States has one particular view of what democracy is and how it should function. Many believe that it is culturally presumptuous for Western nations and international financial institutions to seek the universal imposition of one type of political system.

In many African countries, district- and provincial-level officials are appointed by a central government. As such these are, relatively speaking, highly centralized political and administrative systems. While this level of centralization is not an uncommon situation in some European countries, e.g., France, this is different than the federal system in the United States where local and state officials are directly elected. This type of reform is being pushed by donors (mainly the U.S. and international financial institutions) in Africa because of a belief that decentralized government is more efficient and more responsive to the people. Critics of these policies argue that it is less about transferring power to the people than an opportunity for central government to shed its responsibilities.

For those interested in further reading, Mark Robinson has written a paper concerning donor assistance to civil society organizations entitled "Strengthening Civil Society in Africa: The Role of Foreign Political Aid," *IDS Bulletin* (no. 26, 1995). Kent Glenzer also has a very interesting book chapter, under the title "State, Donor NGO Configurations in Malian Development 1960–1999," in which he looks at the decentralization question in Mali. See B. I. Logan, ed., *Globalization, the Third World State, and Poverty-Alleviation in the Twenty-First Century* (Ashgate 2002). Finally, Kempe Hope examines a new African initiative, the New Partnership for African Development (NEPAD), designed to foster good governance and democracy in Africa in an article in *African Affairs* (2002) entitled "From Crisis to Renewal: Towards a Successful Implementation of the New Partnership for Africa's Development." Gorm Rye Olsen describes how the European Union has backed away from direct support for the promotion of democracy in Africa in a 2002 article in *International Politics* entitled "Promoting Democracy, Preventing Conflict: The European Union and Africa."

ISSUE 19

Is Corruption the Result
of Poor African Leadership?

YES: Robert I. Rotberg, from "The Roots of Africa's Leadership Deficit," *Compass* (2003)

NO: Arthur A. Goldsmith, from "Risk, Rule, and Reason: Leadership in Africa," *Public Administration and Development* (2001)

ISSUE SUMMARY

YES: Robert I. Rotberg, director of the Program on Intrastate Conflict and Conflict Resolution at Harvard University's John F. Kennedy School of Government, holds African leaders responsible for the plight of their continent. He laments the large number of corrupt African leaders, seeing South Africa's Mandela and Botswana's Khama as notable exceptions. According to Rotberg, the problem is that "African leaders and their followers largely believe that the people are there to serve their rulers, rather than the other way around."

NO: Arthur A. Goldsmith, professor of management at the University of Massachusetts—Boston, suggests that Africans leaders are not innately corrupt but are responding rationally to incentives created by their environment. He argues that high levels of risk encourage leaders to pursue short-term, economically destructive policies. In countries where leaders face less risk, there is less perceived political corruption.

Rightly or wrongly, corruption is perceived to be a major obstacle to development in Africa. Transparency International's annual corruptions perceptions index (a survey of surveys on this issue) ranked Chad, Nigeria, Equatorial Guinea, Ivory Coast, Angola, and the Democratic Republic of Congo among the top ten countries perceived to be the most corrupt in the world in 2005. Chad tied for first with Bangladesh as the worst in the world of the 159 countries surveyed. Among those countries perceived to be the least corrupt in Africa were Botswana, Tunisia, South Africa, and Namibia.

Arguments about the genesis of corruption in Africa typically break into those that emphasize internal factors and those that stress structural or political economic conditions (often termed externalist explanations). The first type of argument typically looks to aspects of African culture, society, and tradition to explain the presence and persistence of corruption. For example, regional ties, ethnic allegiances, obligations to the extended family, patron-client relationships, and (occasionally) moralistic explanations are used to elucidate why corruption takes place in Africa. In contrast, structural arguments begin with the premise that a proclivity for corruption is universal, but that history and macro-level political economic conditions have created or reinforced opportunities for corruption in Africa. Examples of such factors include a colonial experience that reinforced anti-democratic traditions, cash-strapped governments that cannot afford to pay civil servants a living wage, or predatory international corporations that seek to access markets and resources through bribery rather than normal government channels. The two points of view presented in this issue represent the two sides of this debate, yet they approach a middle ground of explanation that is slightly more nuanced than the typical arguments heard from either side.

In this issue, Robert I. Rotberg, director of the Program on Intrastate Conflict and Conflict Resolution at Harvard University's John F. Kennedy School of Government, holds Africa's kleptocratic, patrimonial leaders, like Robert Mugabe of Zimbabwe, responsible for giving Africa a bad name, creating poverty and despair, and inciting civil wars and ethnic conflict. He attributes this problem to several factors, including the tendency of the African electorate to "acquiesce for long periods to the autocratic actions of their leaders," the lack of a hegemonic bourgeoisie that is independent of government, a weak civil society, little expectation for political leaders to be fair, and presidents who believe they are the embodiment of the state. He praises the ethical leadership of Botswana's Khama, South Africa's Mandela, and Mauritius' Ramgoolam.

Arthur A. Goldsmith, professor of management at the University of Massachusetts—Boston, suggests that Africans leaders are not innately corrupt, but are responding rationally to incentives created by their environment. In finding that there is a correlation between political risk and corruption, and between low political risk and liberal economic reform, he argues that high levels of risk encourage leaders to pursue short-term, economically destructive policies. He suggests that the risks of governing may be reduced by the spread of multi-party democracy, a form of governance that will make transitions in power more orderly and reduce the chances of execution or imprisonment for leaders upon departure from office.

Robert I. Rotberg   ➡ **YES**

The Roots of Africa's Leadership Deficit

Leadership in Africa is typified more by disfiguring examples—the Idi Amins and Robert Mugabes—than by positive role models such as Nelson Mandela and Seretse Khama. Other clusters of developing nations, such as Southeast Asia or Latin America, exhibit wide variations in leadership quality, but none is so extreme in its range. During the past three decades roughly 90 percent of sub-Saharan Africa's leaders have behaved despotically, governed poorly, eliminated their people's human and civil rights, initiated or exacerbated existing civil conflicts, decelerated per capita economic growth, and proved corrupt.

Why should sub-Saharan Africa show such an extensive disparity between the many nation-states that have been and are poorly led and those few that consistently have been led well? Are the distinctions particularly African? Are they a product of colonial misrule? Do they reflect a common problem of transition from dependency to independence? Do they emanate from deep-rooted poverty and a lack of economic growth? Is sub-Saharan Africa's lamentable leadership record, in other words, attributable to exogenous variables beyond its control, or does Africa respond less favorably to a leadership challenge of the same order as every other region's?

The positive examples of African leadership stand out because of their clear-minded strength of character, their adherence to participatory democratic principles, and their rarity. In contrast, the negative examples include so many varieties—predatory kleptocrats; autocrats, whether democratically elected or militarily installed; simple-minded looters; economic illiterates; and puffed-up posturers—that caricaturing or merely dismissing them would mislead. These single-minded, often narcissistic leaders are many and share common characteristics: they are focused on power itself, not on the uses of power for good; they are indifferent to the well-being of their citizens but anxious to receive their adulation; they are frequently destructive to and within their own countries, home regions excepted; unreachable by reason, they are quick to exploit social or racial ideologies for political and personal purposes; and they are partial to scapegoating, blame-shifting, and hypocrisy.

Good leaders globally, not only in sub-Saharan Africa, guide governments of nation-states to perform effectively for their citizens. They deliver high security for the state and the person; a functioning rule of law; education; health; and a framework conducive to economic growth. They ensure effective arteries

From *Compass*, vol. 1, no. 1, 2003, pp. 28-32. Copyright © 2003 by Center for Public Leadership. Reprinted by permission.

of commerce and enshrine personal and human freedoms. They empower civil society and protect the environmental commons. Crucially, good leaders also provide their citizens with a sense of belonging to a national enterprise of which everyone can be proud. They knit rather than unravel their nations and seek to be remembered for how they have bettered the real lives of the ruled rather than the fortunes of the few.

Less benevolent, even malevolent, leaders deliver far less by way of performance. Under their stewardship, roads fall into disrepair, currencies depreciate and real prices inflate, health services weaken, life expectancies slump, people go hungry, schooling standards fall, civil society becomes more beleaguered, the quest for personal and national prosperity slows, crime rates accelerate, and overall security becomes more tenuous. Corruption grows. Funds flow out of the country into hidden bank accounts. Discrimination against minorities (and occasionally majorities) becomes prevalent. Civil wars begin.

It is easy in theory and in practice to distinguish among good, less-good, bad, and despicable leaders everywhere, especially in subSaharan Africa. Good leaders improve the lives of their followers and make those followers proud of being a part of a new Camelot. Good leaders produce results, whether in terms of enhanced standards of living, basic development indicators, abundant new sources of personal opportunity, enriched schooling, skilled medical care, freedom from crime, or strengthened infrastructures. Bad and despicable leaders tear down the social and economic fabric of the lands; they immiserate their increasingly downtrodden citizens. Despicable rulers, particularly, oppress their own fellow nationals, depriving them of liberty, prosperity, and happiness.

Poverty within the context of resource abundance, as in oil-rich Nigeria from 1975 to 1999, indicates inadequate leadership. Despicable leadership is exemplified by Mugabe's Zimbabwe, a rich country reduced to the edge of starvation, penury, and fear. Economic growth from a low base in the aftermath of civil war and in a context of human resource scarcity, as in contemporary Mozambique, signals effective leadership. The opening of a long-repressed society, with attention to education and a removal of barriers to economic entrepreneurship, as in post-dictatorship Kenya, is another sign of progressive leadership.

Botswana is the paragon of leadership excellence in Africa. Long before diamonds were discovered, the dirt-poor, long-neglected desert protectorate demonstrated an affinity for participation, integrity, tolerance of difference and dissent, entrepreneurial initiative, and the rule of law. The relative linguistic homogeneity of Botswana may have helped (but compare Somalia, where everyone speaks Somali, is Muslim, and there are clans but no separate ethnic groups). So would the tradition of chieftainship and the chiefly search for consensus after discussion among a *kgotla*, or assembly of elders. The century-old, deeply ingrained teachings of the congregational London Missionary Society mattered, too, and infected the country's dominant political culture. Botswana stands out in subSaharan Africa as the foremost country (along with Mauritius and South Africa) to have remained democratic in form and spirit continuously since its independence (in 1966). Throughout the intervening years it has conspicuously adhered strictly to the rule of law, punctiliously observed human rights and civil liberties, and vigorously attempted to enable its citizens to better their social and economic standings. A numerically small population (1.6 million) doubtless contributes to Botswana's relative success, and exploiting the world's richest gem diamond lodes—since 1975—has hardly made achieving strong results more difficult. But Angola, Gabon, and Nigeria all have abundant petroleum, without the same striking returns for their peoples.

Any examination of Botswana, especially before 1975, shows the value of well-intentioned, clear-eyed visionary leadership. Seretse Khama, heir to the paramount chieftaincy of the country's most important and largest ethnic polity, completed his bachelor's degree at Fort Hare College in South Africa in 1944, spent a year reading law at Balliol College, University of Oxford, and then studied for the bar at the Inner Temple in London. In 1948, he married Ruth Williams, a Briton, and returned home to take up his chieftainship. But the British colonial authorities prevented him from exercising the rights of paramountcy, and he and Ruth were exiled to Britain in 1951. Five years later, they were allowed to return, officially as commoners.

Khama came from a family of Bamangwato chiefs who were well regarded for their benevolence and integrity. His studies and his marriage may conceivably have reinforced those family traits. Being exiled might have embittered him, but Khama seems instead to have viewed exile as a mere bump along the road to leadership within the evolving context of Botswana's maturity from protectorate to nation. Whatever the combination of nature and nurture, when Khama (later Sir Seretse Khama) founded the Botswana Democratic Party (BDP) in 1961 and led his country to independence, he already held dear those values of deliberative democracy and market economic performance that proved a recipe for his young country's political, social, and economic success. Modest, without obvious narcissism, non-ostentatious as a chief and leader (unlike so many of his African contemporaries), and conscious of achieving a national, enduring legacy, Sir Seretse was able to forge a political culture for the emergent Botswana—a system of values governing the conduct of political affairs—that has endured during the peaceful and increasingly prosperous presidencies of Sir Ketumile Masire and Festus Mogae, his successors.

Sir Seretse had a largely implicit, understated, but nevertheless substantial program for his people and his country. He put that program into place gradually, never succumbing to external political whims (such as the affinity for Afro-socialism or crypto-Marxism that infected his peers elsewhere in Africa), instant panaceas (such as nationalizing his productive mineral industries in the disastrous manner of neighboring Zambia), or posturing ineffectively against the hideous crimes of apartheid in nearby South Africa. Indeed, Sir Seretse and Sir Ketumile were deft and decisive in their disapproving but non-antagonistic approach to South Africa. Sir Seretse engineered his control of Botswana's diamond resources without frightening off or limiting investment from South Africa. He trained his own Botswanan successors and empowered them, but gradually, and without overstretching indigenous human resource capacities. Sir Seretse took no short-cuts. He and his successors abided no abridgements of citizen rights.

Sir Seretse could have done otherwise. As a paramount chief beloved by his people and respected for his learning, he could have behaved as so many of his African peers behaved during the 1960s and 1970s. If he had arrogated more and more power to himself, "for the good of his people," there would have been few critics. The rest of Africa had largely followed President Kwame Nkrumah, Ghana's first president from 1957–1966, in renouncing colonial traditions of representative government and becoming autocrats. Even gentle Julius Nyerere of Tanzania and equally gentle, modest Kenneth Kaunda of Zambia by the 1970s were abandoning inherited democratic forms and substituting single-party, single-man rule in place of broad participation. They were depriving judiciaries of independence and legislatures of auton-omy. Objectors were jailed. Newspapers were banned or bought out. State radio broadcast only the words of the rulers.

Not Sir Seretse. He adhered to the nostrums that were no longer in cur-rent use in nearly all of Africa. For him, there was an ethic of performance and good governance to which he adhered. Sir Seretse was conscious every day that he could do better than the leaders of next-door South Africa, where whites oppressed the majority and deprived most inhabitants of their human rights and civil liberties. For whatever set of personal and pragmatic reasons, Sir Seretse epitomized world-class qualities of leadership.

In very different circumstances, Sir Seewoosagur Ramgoolam, the first leader of Mauritius (an offshore member of the African Union), operated under the same internalized leadership rules as Sir Seretse. Ramgoolam was more explicit in charting his vision, however—more in the manner of Lee Kuan Yew of Singapore. When Sir Seewoosagur took the Mauritian prime ministerial reins immediately after independence in 1968 (remaining prime minister until 1976), he understood that the island nation's mélange of colors and peoples—a plurality of Tamil-speaking Hindu Indians, Urdu-and Hindi-speaking Muslims from India and Pakistan, Chinese, and indigenous Creole-speaking Franco-Mauritians, most of whom were descended from slaves—could not long survive in peace if he or others were anything but transparently democratic. He stressed open politics, nurtured social capital, welcomed a free press, and strengthened the rule of law inherited from Britain, and earlier from France. Sir Seewoosagur also sensed that Mauritius' economy, hitherto based entirely on exporting raw sugar, would have to be diversified and grow. He attracted new investors from Asia. Soon Mauritius was a major world textile manufacturer; an island without sheep became a dominant supplier of wool garments.

Once again, leadership was central to Mauritius' post-independence transition from a potentially explosive racial hothouse and a primary pro-ducer subject to the fluctuations of world markets into a bustling, prosper-ous, politically hectic sustainable democracy. Sir Seewoosagur could have attempted to follow the other possible road to peace and growth on a crowded island of 1.2 million—strong, single-man rule of the Lee Kuan Yew variety. But the tactics that worked so well among overseas Chinese in Sin-gapore might have been incendiary in Mauritius's multiethnic mix.

Likewise, without Nelson Mandela's inclusive leadership, black-run South Africa after 1994 would have been much more fractured and less successful in governing its apartheid-damaged peoples. Mandela's vision insisted on full rights for the majority, but without too abrupt a removal of minority economic privileges. It strengthened the rule of law, greatly broadened the delivery of essential services, largely maintained existing pillars of the economy such as transportation and communications networks, and slowly shifted away from the dominant command economy toward one that was more market driven.

Mandela, Khama, and Ramgoolam all led their nations democratically when they could have aggregated personal power. Their leadership model might have been more Asian—top-down, less open, less constitutional, and less multi-ethnic and multi-tribal—and still benevolent and thus accomplished. Instead, they demonstrated what few of their fellow African leaders then or since have demonstrated: that Africans are perfectly capable of building nations, developing sustainable democratic political cultures, and modernizing and growing their economies effectively. Given these particular individuals' disparate human and ethnic origins, and given their respective nations' very diverse colonial legacies, it makes no sense to assert that African traditional culture somehow inhibits the exercise of democratic leadership.

There must be other reasons for leadership gone wrong in Africa, especially for those men who begin as promising democrats and then emerge a term or two later as corrupt autocrats. Take Bakili Muluzi, president of Malawi, for example. After the thirty-year dictatorship of Dr. Hastings K. Banda ended, Muluzi led the new United Democratic Front (UDF) against Banda and his associates, promising a return to full-fledged democracy. Overwhelmingly victorious, the UDP and Muluzi took power in 1994 and governed reasonably effectively during their first five-year term. Educational and health services were expanded, civil society and an open press were embraced, the judges were released from their fetters, and serious steps were taken to improve the very poor country's economic performance. Muluzi presided genially over this peaceful and welcomed transition from autocracy in his country of twelve million people.

Muluzi's second term, from 1999, began well enough, although the sticky stain of corruption soon began to spread through the upper echelons of government and around the state house. Economic growth stagnated, not least because of decisions not made by the president and the arrangement of special deals for presidential associates. In 2002, he decided that Malawi would be better off if he broke the constitutional provision against a third presidential term, beginning in 2004. (President Frederick Chiluba, in Zambia, another post-dictatorial reformer, tried the same argument to keep his presidency, but was rebuffed by Parliament and the citizenry. In Namibia, however, President Sam Nujoma successfully breached his country's constitution and now serves a third term.)

Malawi's Parliament denied Muluzi the needed constitutional amendments twice, and Muluzi reluctantly backed away from a third-term attempt in 2003. Instead, he bulldozed the ruling party's executive committee into letting him hand-pick a questionable successor (illegal by party rules), and then compelled a suddenly called meeting of the UDF to amend the party's by-laws to give him that authority, and also to make him permanent chair of the party, in control of its finances. Key cabinet ministers resigned, and Malawi's politics were soon thrown into turmoil—all local matters which concern us little here. The main question is what causes a democrat to turn autocratic? Is it simply that absolute power corrupts absolutely, as Lord Acton said long ago?

Mugabe is another of many African leaders who began by governing plausibly (in 1980, in Mugabe's case), only to turn venal later. Admittedly, within a few years of assuming power in Zimbabwe, he had used a special military brigade to kill 20,000 to 30,000 followers of a key opponent. But the first eighteen years of Mugabe's prime ministerial and presidential leadership (the title changed in 1987) also brought enlarged educational and medical opportunities, economic growth, relatively modest levels of official corruption, and comparatively calm relations between the tiny white commercial farming community and black Africans. Throughout the period, Mugabe astutely gained more and more personal power. He used official terror to remove challengers, and state-supplied patronage to keep senior supporters in line. From about 1991, his onetime key backers say, Mugabe began behaving with more and more omnipotence and arrogance. He was reelected frequently as president, and his largely obedient party dominated Parliament. Every now and again one or two outspoken dissidents were tolerated.

By 1998, Mugabe was seventy-four years old, married for the second time, and increasingly cranky that Mandela's release from prison and assumption of the South African presidency had dimmed Mugabe's own attempt to be a major player in all-African politics. His second wife was known, too, to be avaricious, and by 1998 corruption at the highest levels of Zimbabwe had grown in scale and audacity. Mugabe sought to salt away wealth for his extended family. He also gave license to the corrupt activities of others so that he could control them, in the manner of Mobutu Sese Seko of the Congo. Then, in 1998, Mugabe unilaterally decided to send 13,000 soldiers to the Congo, ostensibly to assist Laurent Kabila, the rebel successor to Mobutu, to defend against a Rwandan-organized invasion. Mugabe also wanted to grab the diamonds, cobalt, cadmium, and gold of the Congo for himself.

With Zimbabwean troops in the Congo until 2003, and corruptly acquired funds fleeing to safe havens offshore, Mugabe and his cronies bled Zimbabwe until, by 2000, the foreign exchange coffers were largely empty and food and fuel shortages began to recur regularly. By then he had also unleashed thugs against commercial farmers, using an old tactic to mobilize indigenous support. This time, however, it failed to do so, especially in the cities. Mugabe lost a critical constitutional referendum in early 2000. By midyear he had also come within a few seats of losing his party's parliamentary majority in a national election. The Movement for Democratic Change (MDC), led by Morgan Tsvangirai, had posed a formidable challenge and, indeed, claimed that Mugabe's party had falsified the votes in several key constituencies.

Mugabe lashed out furiously against the MDC, and attacked whites and blacks suspected of supporting the opposition. The country's once formidable rule of law became the law of the jungle, with Mugabe packing the Supreme Court and threatening High Court judges until they retired or resigned. Legions of hired thugs attacked white farmers and forcibly occupied the farms (despite High Court injunctions), thus depressing agricultural productivity. When Tsvangirai stood against Mugabe in the 2002 presidential election, he was defeated in a poll widely believed in Europe, the U.S., and among Zimbabweans to have been rigged. Even after such a disputed triumph, Mugabe persisted in victimizing MDC members and their presumed supporters. Having driven Zimbabwe to the brink of starvation in 2002 and 2003, he and his lackeys sought to deprive areas that had voted for the MDC of relief shipments of food.

By late-2003, Zimbabweans faced constant shortages of food and fuel. Unemployment had reached 80 percent and inflation 500 percent. The U.S. dollar, worth 38 Zimbabwean dollars in 2000, was being traded on the street for 5,000 local dollars. Hospitals operated without basic medicines. Schools were closed. President Bush and Secretary of State Colin Powell called for Mugabe's ouster, an unusual step, and so did Prime Minister Tony Blair. Zimbabwe's Council of Churches also railed at Mugabe, a Jesuit-trained Catholic. Tsvangirai, meanwhile, was indicted for treason and served some time in jail, as did many of his senior MDC colleagues. Mugabe, throughout, resisted entreaties to retire, as the once proud, wealthy country spiraled into decay.

These appalling details are less relevant, here, than seeking to explain why Mugabe and Muluzi, Chiluba and Nujoma, and also former President Daniel arap Moi of Kenya and many other African leaders perform adequately during their early elected terms and then, in their second terms or beyond, become despots. Is it the inevitability of Acton's aphorism, or some law of diminished accountability? Most African leaders, the Botswanan and South African presidents and the Mauritian prime ministers aside, travel in pompous motorcades, put their faces on the local currencies, and expect to see photographs of themselves in every shop and office. Almost invariably, the less legitimate the office and the less robust the country, the more ostentatious their displays and the more stilted their bearing and manner.

Is it the African reverence for "big men," a hangover from pre-colonial reverence for chieftainship, that turns democrats into despots and persuades obedient electorates to support the pretensions of their peers turned potentates? Would it help if the new nations of sub-Saharan Africa abandoned executive presidencies on the American model and reverted to pure parliamentary governing systems with ceremonial heads of state?

African leaders are driven by instincts no baser than those of their colleagues in Asia, Europe, or the U.S. But African electorates tend to acquiesce for long periods to the autocractic actions of their leaders. That acquiescence may stem from the sheer rawness of democracy in Africa, and from the absence of a long period of preparation for democracy, unlike in colonial India or the West Indies. The African press's lack of sophistication and independence is a contributing factor. Civil society is also weaker. Extensive public-sector patronage in most African countries also allows leaders to escape criticism until their leadership excesses are obvious.

Africa for the most part lacks a hegemonic bourgeoisie—a business class that is independent of government and capable of thriving without patronage and contracts; such independence lessens the zero-sum quality of a rule. In those few countries where there is that independence, as in South Africa but not yet Nigeria, a leader approaching the end of his term in office does not have to worry about taking the perquisites with him and looting the country before he and his colleagues go. In many other countries in Africa, especially the poorer ones, the incentives to grab it all are great.

Throughout most of Africa there is little expectation, thus far, that successors will be fair, that an incoming political movement will not necessarily victimize its predecessors, and that there is an acceptable role for former presidents and prime ministers—except, notably, in Mauritius and Botswana. In many places, too, there is as yet no sustainable democratic political culture. That is, whereas American and European politicians might want to behave as autocrats, they are restrained by the norms of their dominant political cultures and the likelihood of being found out. In Africa, shame is less apparent than a kind of entitlement. Once elected, or once chosen by a military junta to rule, the president confuses himself with the state—in some way thinking of himself as embodying and being the state. It is only the exceptional individuals like Khama or Mandela who can escape the deep psychological trap of constant sycophancy. Like Louis XIV, others come to accept their own importance as the suns around which their little countries revolve. Except in a few places like Botswana, where an early leader knew better and emulated President Washington's refusal to be royal, African leaders and their followers largely believe that the people are there to serve their rulers, rather than the other way around.

Fortunately, there are a handful of very new leaders in Africa who espouse an ethic of good governance. They are distinguished from their less democratic peers by a willingness to govern transparently, to consult with interest groups within their populations that are not their own, to create an atmosphere of tolerance and fairness in their official operations, and to strengthen the institutions of their societies. These promising new leaders include Presidents Abdoulaye Wade of Senegal, who had opposed previous methods of rule for decades and now rules consensually; Mwai Kibaki of Kenya, in opposition from 1992 to his election in late 2002; John Kuffour of Ghana, who has begun reducing the corrupt climate of his autocratic predecessor; and Prime Minister Pakalitha Mosisili of tiny Lesotho, who has modernized his country's methods of governance through a process of laborious national consultation.

Africa is not yet ready to parse distinctions between transactional and transformational leadership. It needs leaders in the first instance who serve whole nations, not just their tribes or ethnic groups or extended families. It needs leaders who embrace responsibility for the commonweal, and not for a group of associates who live off and puff up a country's all-commanding autocrat. It desperately needs new leaders who take Khama and Mandela as their models and embrace the Washingtonian-like restraints that they embodied. Once there are a cadre of leaders who espouse and embody in their actions the democratic values that emboldened Khama, Mandela, and Ramgoolam, and now drive their successors and men like Wade, Kibaki, Koffour, and Mosisili, Africa will begin to move from despotism and denials of human rights to the era of democratic leadership. Given the timbre of Africa's younger leaders, and the spread throughout Africa of global bourgeois democratic values, that era may soon be at hand.

NO ↵   Arthur A. Goldsmith

Risk, Rule, and Reason: Leadership in Africa

Introduction

Sub-Saharan Africa is poorly led. The region has far too many tyrants and 'tropical gangsters', far too few statesmen, let alone merely competent office-holders. Too often, these leaders reject sound policy advice and refuse to take a long and broad view of their job. They persecute suspected political rivals and bleed their economies for personal benefit. With a handful of exceptions, notably South Africa under Nobel laureate Nelson Mandela, countries in the sub-Saharan area are set back by a personalist, neopatrimonial style of national leadership (Aka, 1997).

Better leadership is not the cure-all for Africa's lack of development, but it would be an important step in the right direction. A few years back some observers saw hope in a new generation of supposedly benevolent dictators, such as Isaias Afwerki in Eritrea, Meles Zenawi in Ethiopia, or Yoweri Museveni in Uganda (Madavo and Sarbib, 1997; Connell and Smyth, 1998). Subsequent events (war between Eritrea and Ethiopia, invasion of the Congo Republic by Uganda) chilled the optimism (McPherson and Goldsmith, 1998; Barkan and Gordon, 1998; Ottaway, 1998). In most countries, it seems progressive leadership soon reverts to the more familiar form of autocratic one-man rule.

There is no shortage of macro-level explanations for this pattern. Authoritarian political traditions, lack of national identity, underdeveloped middle classes and widespread economic distress are among the sweeping, impersonal forces cited as factors that produce poor leader after poor leader. Foreign aid may have enabled some of these leaders to hang on longer than they would have otherwise, especially during the Cold War. This article instead takes a micro-level view of leadership. Without denying that macro-level social and economic factors bear on leaders' behaviour, I find it also useful to look at these people as individuals and to speculate about the incentives created by their environment.

In the tradition of political economy, we can begin with the assumption that African leaders are usually trying to do what they think is best for themselves. We can posit that they choose actions that appear to them to produce

From Arthur A. Goldsmith, "Risk, Rule, and Reason: Leadership in Africa," *Public Administration and Development,* vol. 21 (2001). Copyright © 2001 by John Wiley & Sons, Ltd. Reprinted by permission. Notes and references omitted.

the greatest benefit at least cost, after making allowances for the degree of risk involved. Such a leader also is capable of learning, and takes cues from what is happening to other leaders in neighbouring countries. He can improve his behaviour if he has to.

While no African leader fully exemplifies this rational actor model, all these individuals' behaviour can be illuminated by it. After all, even the best leaders have mixed, sometimes egoistic motives. To the extent that it represents reality, the rational actor model also may suggest how changing the political incentive system might induce African leaders to behave less autocratically.

I start this article by speculating about how these leaders might react to perceived levels of risk in their political environment. Next, I investigate the actual level of risk, guided by a new inventory that covers every major leadership transition in Africa since 1960. Then, I assess how risk appears to have distorted the way African leaders act in office. Finally, I consider the ways in which democratization may be changing political incentives for the better.

Leadership and Individual Motivation

Perhaps the most troubling thing about African leaders is their tendency to reject (or simply not follow through on) conventional economic advice (Scott, 1998). Africa is the graveyard of many well-intended reforms. The vacillating public attitude of Kenya's President Daniel Moi is emblematic. In March 1993, he rejected an International Monetary Fund (IMF) plan for being cruel and unrealistic. One month later, he reversed himself, and agreed to the plan. In June 1997, the IMF cut off lending to Kenya after Moi refused to take aggressive steps to combat corruption. Again, his initial reaction was defiance, swiftly followed by a more accommodating line.

Why are African leaders apt to resist advice to carry out market-friendly reforms that could boost national rates of economic growth? If one accepts the premise that, with sufficient time, open market policies will work in Africa, such a choice can look senseless. Certainly, no African leader would prefer to perpetuate mass poverty and economic stagnation in his country, which can only make governing more difficult. More to the point, perhaps, cooperating with the international financial institutions is the best way to assure continued diplomatic support and financial credit. Yet, many African leaders apparently see political rationality in choosing policies that are economically damaging or irrational. Miles Kahler (1990) refers to this as the 'orthodox paradox.'

Political economy offers a theory of micro-level behaviour that may explain the paradox. Mancur Olson (1993) argues that time is the key. According to this theory, the predicament facing any individual national leader is that the pay-offs to most economic reforms lie in the future, but he also has to hold on to power now. An insecure power base is likely to encourage either reckless gambling for immediate returns or highly cautious strategies to preserve political capital; it is unlikely to promote measured actions to obtain long-range returns. Whether a leader acts for the short or the long term, therefore, is influenced by his sense of the level of threat to his career.

A more technical way to understand a leader's intertemporal choices is to think of a 'political discount rate'. One of political economy's core ideas is that future events have a present value, which one can calculate by using a rate of discount. That rate of discount rises with risk and uncertainty. When an outcome is doubtful over time, it makes sense to mark down its present value. The more doubtful the outcome, the more valuable are alternative activities that yield immediate dividends, even if the expected return of those activities is low. Thus, under conditions of political uncertainty, the narrowly 'rational' leader will systematically forgo promising political 'investments'—ventures whose benefits he may not survive to reap. Whenever he is given a choice, according to this argument, such a leader will usually prefer current political 'consumption'. It follows that free-market reforms look like a poor bargain, requiring immediate political pain in exchange for distant (and therefore questionable) gain.

High political discount rates are also a possible explanation for the extensive and destructive political corruption seen in Africa. The Democratic Republic of Congo's Mobutu Sese Sekou is the archetype. The late dictator erased the line between public and private property, accumulating a vast personal fortune and bankrupting his country. His is an extreme case, yet every national leader has opportunities to profit individually from his office. According to the premises of political economy, it is the leader with the least certainty about his fate who has the strongest incentives to take his rewards now—and to take as much as possible. A more self-assured leader may calculate that it is safe to defer most personal financial gain until after he has left office. Some of the misuse of public office also may be due to the need to buy support from friends and extended family members. Olson (1993), for example, postulates that leaders with an insecure grip on power have an incentive to take steps to patronize favoured ethnic groups, often at the expense of national economic health. This sort of pork-barrelling is well known in Africa.

Political economy thus presents a cogent theory for why African rulers act they way they do. Short-term policy making and political corruption are 'rational' ways of trying to manage the risks associated with governing in an unsettled political system, as we typically find in Africa. According to this thesis, overly cautious or corrupt leaders may simply be attempting to maximize utility under conditions of personal and political uncertainty. Their assessment of risk is affected by their personal experiences and by their perceptions about larger trends in their country and region. Unfortunately for the social welfare, their effort to protect their individual interests has spillovers that hurt everyone else.

The issue for this article is whether the facts support this theory. First, is it true that African leaders face a high degree of risk? We can reasonably assume these people are tolerant of risk, or they would not have chosen political careers. Thus, we need to look for evidence of extraordinary occupational hazards for leaders. The second question is whether political risk in Africa is associated with 'bad' (anti-market) economic policy choices or with corruption. As we will see below, the answers to both questions seem to be affirmative: there is significant physical risk for leaders, and that risk correlates with anti-market policies and with corruption. Those two findings, in turn, suggest scope for enhancing the area's national leadership by reducing the risks of governing, a goal that may be abetted by democratization. . . .

Risk and Leaders' Behaviour

There is little doubt . . . that holding high office in Africa poses acute risks. To what extent do those risks affect leaders' behaviour, specifically their behaviour in the areas of economic reform and corruption? . . . That question is difficult to answer fully without detailed case studies of the individuals involved. In the absence of such information, however, we can look for approximate answers in national indicators of economic policy and corruption. To the extent we believe that country leaders control public policy or set the tone for public honesty, aggregate data may give us clues about how these leaders conduct themselves.

To represent a country's commitment to free market economics, I use the Heritage Foundation's Index of Economic Freedom (Johnson et al., 1999). The index is calculated by aggregating country scores on 10 policy indicators and measures of the business climate. Depending on their scores, countries are categorized as free (none in Africa), mostly free, mostly unfree, or repressed. While I do not see eye to eye with the Heritage Foundation on many subjects, I suspect that these categories offer a good approximation for how fully countries comply with IMF-style structural adjustment programs. My grouping of countries is based on the average economic freedom rating for 1995–1999.

I hypothesized earlier in this article that low-risk environments would tend to produce more reform-minded leaders, or at least leaders who would be more willing to go along with economic reform in exchange for financial credit. . . . [A] correlation exists between the hazards of leadership and the degree of 'economic freedom'. Leaders in the so-called mostly free countries were the least likely to be overthrown, killed, arrested or exiled. Leaders in the mostly unfree and repressed countries, by contrast, experienced a greater number of negative outcomes. Low political risk and liberal economic programmes seem to go together in Africa.

Correlation does not prove causation, especially in making inferences about micro-level behaviour based on macro-level data. We cannot say whether a safer political environment encourages leaders to opt for the market, or conversely, whether leaders who opt for the market make their political environment safer (though the latter possibility seems less likely, at least in the short run). In either case, however, the results are consistent with political economy theory.

What is the relationship between political risk and corruption? For a measure of the latter, I use Transparency International's Corruption Perception Index for 1999. Transparency International is a watchdog organization formed to help raise ethical standards of government around the world. It compiles an annual index that assesses the degree to which public officials and politicians are believed to accept bribes, take illicit payment in public procurement, embezzle public funds, and otherwise use public positions for private gains. The index is based on several international business surveys, using different sampling frames and varying methodologies (Transparency International, 1999). While Transparency International is careful to point out that the rankings only reflect perceptions about corruption, I find it reasonable to assume that they correspond roughly to reality.

I have conjectured that leaders in the riskier African countries would have the greatest propensity to use their public offices for personal ends. Once more, the data lend support to my hypothesis. . . . The pattern is striking. There has never been a successful coup in the less corrupt group of countries. None of their ex-leaders has been arrested or exiled, and only one was killed while in office (South Africa's Verwoerd). The more corrupt countries, by contrast, have many coups and many leaders who suffered personally upon losing power.

As with the economic freedom index, these correlations do not prove that a hazardous political environment encourages leaders to become corrupt. The opposite is also plausible: corrupt rulers seem likely to invite coups and to bring personal suffering on themselves. To the extent that risk and corruption are related, the relationship between the two probably is mutually reinforcing. The important point for this article is that the observed association of risk and corruption conforms to what you would expect, based on the assumption of 'rational' behaviour among national rulers. Without overstating the case, the correlation lends support to a political economy account of poor leadership in Africa.

Democratization and Improved Leadership

Political economy also suggests that one solution to poor leadership is to make the political environment less hazardous. A safer environment would reduce the incentives to engage in political misbehaviour and, in principle, encourage more responsible and forward-looking activity. In this context, Africa's recent moves toward more pluralistic national political systems, where people can express their political opinions and take part in public decisions, are reasons for hope. It is fashionable—and correct—to observe that democracy has shallow roots in most African countries (Joseph, 1997; van de Walle, 1999). Much of the impetus for reform comes from abroad, from the region's creditors. Yet, when we observe the patterns of leadership transitions, it is hard to deny that genuine changes are taking place.

No sitting African leader ever lost an election until 1982, when Sir Seewoosagur Ramgoolam of Mauritius was voted out. Since then, 12 more incumbents have been turned out of office by voters—accounting for about one-sixth of the leadership transitions in the 1990s. The threat of losing an election also may account for the increasing rate of leader retirements—nine in the 1990s versus only eight in the previous three decades.

Democratization appears to be altering the outcomes of the many coups that still occur. In the past, the new heads of military juntas often declared themselves permanent leaders (sometimes after doffing their uniforms and becoming 'civilians'). Now, it is becoming the norm for coup leaders quickly to organize internationally acceptable elections—and, more importantly, to honour the results afterwards (Anene, 1995). Recent examples include Niger and Guinea-Bissau. . . . The fact we see more transitions of this type in the 1990s is an indirect reflection of the region's growing democratization.

[There are] additional reasons to think that contemporary presidential elections are not simply façades in many countries. The entire sub-Saharan region had only 126 elections for top national office in the 30 years through 1989. Most of those were show elections, with an average winner's share of close to 90%. Conditions have changed significantly in the 1990s. There were 73 leadership elections during that decade, or more than half as many as in the three prior decades. All but five of sub-Saharan countries were involved. Equally important, the winner's share dropped to an average of about two-thirds of the votes cast. Such results would be considered landslide victories in the developed world. No president in the history of the United States has ever reached two-thirds of the popular vote. Still, in African terms, the tendency clearly is toward greater competitiveness at the ballot box.

The classic liberal defences of free and fair elections are that they give voice to majority demands and that they are a means for recruiting new leadership talent. Political economy and African experience suggest three additional benefits, all associated with reducing the hazards leaders face.

First, elections have the virtue of softening the penalties of losing political office. The defeated candidate in an election campaign, as opposed to the victim of a coup plot, is far less likely to be executed, jailed or exiled by his successor. By providing a low-risk avenue of exit, elections thus reduce the stakes in political competition. If the arguments in this article are correct, that would free African leaders to take a more purposeful, pragmatic view of their jobs.

A second benefit occurs if elections become institutionalized, and take place according to a schedule. Countries that hold regular elections reduce speculation about when (and how) the next political transition is likely. Again, the probable impact in Africa would be to change the political calculations made by the region's chief power holders, to allow them to worry less about how to hold onto power and to think more about the long term. Predictable political transitions might also reduce anxiety among private investors, and thus mitigate the harmful political business cycle that exists in some countries.

The third benefit stems from the more rapid turnover among national rulers that results when elections become a regular part of political experience. As leaders come to see their jobs less as an entitlement and more as a phase in their careers, that actually may liberate them to 'do the right thing', and not always feel forced to do what is politically expedient. Merilee Grindle and Francisco Thoumi (1993) have remarked on this phenomenon among lame-duck presidents in Latin America. Knowledge that their positions are transitory can, somewhat ironically, concentrate the incumbents' attention on how best to leave a lasting legacy. Similar results are possible in Africa.

Concluding Observations

Before multi-party competition and elections can have these positive effects on leaders, Africa's competitive political systems must become institutionalized. This has yet to happen in most countries, according to the results of Samuel Huntington's (1968) 'two-turnover test'. Huntington notes that institutionalized democracies prove themselves by repeatedly carrying out peaceful transfers of power through the ballot box. The first time an opposition leader replaces an incumbent power holder does not necessarily establish a tradition of peaceful political change. It is only after the new incumbent is defeated and leaves office that one can begin to be confident that constitutional procedures have taken root.

Second turnovers are almost unheard of in Africa. Botswana has not had one. The same party has ruled that country since independence. Mauritius has had two election-based leadership turnovers, but many observers question whether that island nation properly deserves classification in the region. Bénin is the only other African country where incumbent power holders have twice lost elections. The dictator Mathieu Kérékou fell to Nicéphore Soglo in 1991, but he regained the presidency by defeating Soglo in the election 5 years later. Kérékou's continued role raises some doubt whether Bénin's second transition indicates much other than the persistence of narrow, personalistic politics in that country.

Nonetheless, the last decade does offer hope that some African societies will be able to establish more orderly systems of political competition. That could change the incentives for African leaders, and encourage them to act more responsibly and even-handedly. As a means of redressing decades of oppression and economic stagnation, that cannot happen soon enough.

POSTSCRIPT

Is Corruption the Result of Poor African Leadership?

In this issue, Robert Rotberg attributed Africa's troubles to the fact that "African leaders and their followers largely believe that the people are there to serve their rulers, rather than the other way around." In contrast, Arthur Goldsmith viewed the mismanagement and corruption of African leaders as a structural problem in which individual leaders are responding to the incentive structures around them. These two interpretations of the situation appear to be quite different. Yet, while Rotberg eschewed the political economy or structural perspective, he concluded his argument by both calling for new leaders who will serve whole nations, *and* pointing out the conditions that allow the base instincts of many African leaders to prevail. In pointing to the adage that "absolute power corrupts absolutely," Rotberg evokes a universal rather than particularistic (i.e., conditions unique to Africa) explanation. Furthermore, by asserting that this tendency is unleashed by a weak civil society and the lack of democratic traditions, he acknowledges that the environment in which African leaders operate contributes to the problem. This is quite different than other internalist arguments that often seek to explain corruption in Africa in terms of cultural factors. These conditions are also considered at a scale that is consistent with the micro-level sphere that Goldsmith investigates. In sum, the differences between the two arguments may be more about style and emphasis than substance.

A less-discussed element of corruption is the extent to which international corporations may contribute to the problem in their dealings with African governments. In some instances, it is standard business practice for companies to provide financial incentives (or bribes) to government officials in order to win contracts, obtain permits, or gain certain rights. Interestingly, it is the government officials who are often accused of corruption, while little is heard of the companies' role in this process. An example of an exception to this involves a Canadian company that was convicted by the Lesotho high court for bribing a senior Lesotho government official in order to win contracts on that country's $8 billion Lesotho Highlands Water Project (a joint project of the governments of Lesotho and South Africa). Commenting on the case, a South African official said that it is often assumed that corruption is "a peculiarly African problem. This case shows that such a perception is wrong. It takes two to tango." ("Government Cracks Down on Western Corruption," *New African*, December 2002.)

For those interested in further reading on this topic, good examples of the structural perspective on corruption include an article by M.M. Munyae and M.M. Mulinge in a 1999 issue of the *Journal of Social Development in*

Africa entitled "The Centrality of a Historical Perspective to the Analysis of Modern Social Problems in Sub-Saharan Africa: A Tale from Two Case Studies," and an article by N.I. Nwosu in a 1997 issue of the *Scandinavian Journal of Development Alternatives* entitled "Multinational Corporations and the Economy of Third World States." There are roughly two types of particularlistic or internalist explanations regarding corruption in Africa—one is negative and the other is positive. The first, essentially negative perspective, views internal African characteristics as flaws that contribute to a universally accepted problem known as corruption. An example of this perspective is an article by M. Szeftel in a 2000 issue of the *Review of African Political Economy* entitled "Clientelism, Corruption and Catastrophe." The second, more positive or postmodern interpretation often views "corruption" as a relative concept that is culturally defined. In other words, what is viewed as corruption in one culture is not necessarily corruption in another. Examples of this perspective include a volume by Chabel and Daloz entitled *Africa Works: Disorder as Political Instrument* (Indiana University Press, 1999) and a 2001 article by Jeff Popke in the *African Geographical Review* under the title "The 'Politics of the Mirror': On Geography and Afro-Pessimism."

ISSUE 20

Are International Peacekeeping Missions Critical to Resolving Ethnic Conflicts in African Countries?

YES: Tim Docking, from *Peacekeeping in Africa* (United States Institute of Peace, 2001)

NO: William Reno, from "The Failure of Peacekeeping in Sierra Leone," *Current History* (May 2001)

ISSUE SUMMARY

YES: Tim Docking, African Affairs Specialist at the United States Institute of Peace, presents the reactions of policymakers and academics to a report on UN peace operations. The group argues that the lack of political will by Western powers is the key impediment to successful UN peacekeeping. Furthermore, given the situation in Africa, the group implores the United States to re-engage with the United Nations and African affairs.

NO: William Reno, associate professor of political science at Northwestern University, argues that no peacekeeping is better than bad peacekeeping. In his discussion of the failed Lomé Peace Accords, a settlement negotiated between warring parties in Sierra Leone, he notes that "[m]any Sierra Leoneans regarded positions taken by the UN and foreign diplomats who stressed reconciliation as offensive." According to Reno, Sierra Leonean consternation stemmed from the fact that just a year earlier, the U.S. and Europeans had backed the Sierra Leone government to fight rebel groups known for human rights abuses, and now they wanted to include these same individuals in a coalition government. He asserts that what was driving the peace process from the U.S. side was a desire to appear that they had addressed an African problem while avoiding a commitment of resources and soldiers. As opposed to the more bureaucratic peacekeeping approaches taken by the United States and the UN, he lauds the hands-on tactics of the British.

Two watershed events for American peacekeeping efforts in Africa have been the failed military intervention in Somalia in 1993 and the lack of intervention during the Rwandan genocide in 1994. In the twilight of the first Bush administration in 1992, the U.S. intervened militarily in Somalia to dispense food aid that was not being effectively distributed due to the presence of armed militias. The American force was then reduced under the new Clinton administration and made part of a UN operation that had as a mandate to protect the delivery of humanitarian assistance and disarm the warring factions. Following the deaths of 26 Pakistani soldiers, the United States sent in army rangers and delta force commandos to try to capture a particularly problematic warlord named Mohammed Aideed. Then in October 1993, 18 U.S. soldiers were killed and 50 wounded in a street war that also cost the U.S. military two Black Hawk helicopters. With the sight of a dead U.S. army ranger being dragged through the streets of Mogadishu on international television, President Bill Clinton ordered the withdrawl of all U.S. troops. This debacle is now commonly referred to as "crossing the Mogadishu line." It resulted in a new U.S. presidential directorate (#25) stating that the United States should not become involved in a war unless there was a clear national interest and the conflict could be won.

The events in Somalia had a chilling effect on U.S. interest in addressing the humanitarian crisis in Rwanda in 1994. Following the death of Rwandan President Juvenal Habyarimana in a mysterious plane crash in April 1994, the systematic elimination of Tutsis and moderate Hutus was begun by hard-line elements in the military and Habyarimana government. With most expatriates having left the country, and the meager UN force ordered to protect itself, it is estimated that over a million Tutsis and moderate Hutus were murdered while hundreds of thousands fled the country as refugees. Following these atrocities, the minority Tutsis amassed their forces and began a process of retribution. While the situation in Rwanda was eventually quelled, the inaction of the United States and other foreign powers has been roundly condemned. The specter of Somalia and Rwanda continue to haunt U.S. peacekeeping efforts in Africa today, with a fear of failure lingering from the first case, and the regret of inaction from the latter.

In this issue, Tim Docking, African Affairs Specialist at the United States Institute of Peace, presents the reactions of policymakers and academics to a report on UN peace operations. The group argues that the lack of political will by Western powers is the key impediment to successful UN peacekeeping. Furthermore, given the situation in Africa, the group implores the United States to re-engage with the United Nations and African affairs.

In contrast, William Reno, associate professor of political science at Northwestern University, argues that no peacekeeping is better than bad peacekeeping. In this article, he describes the conflict between the government of Sierra Leone and the rebel Revolutionary United Front (RUF), as well as the connections between the RUF and Liberian leader Charles Taylor. In his discussion of the failed Lomé Peace Accords, he condemns the UN and the United States for pushing for acceptance of rebel leaders with known human rights violations in the new government. He asserts that the United States wanted to appear to have addressed an African problem while avoiding a commitment of resources and soldiers. As opposed to the bureaucratic peacekeeping approaches taken by the United States and the UN, which tend to accredit armed groups that prey on society, he lauds the more hands-on tactics of the British.

➡ **YES**

Peacekeeping in Africa

The Brahimi Report

In March 2000, the secretary general of the United Nations convened a high-level panel to conduct a thorough review of United Nations peace and security activities. The 10-person panel was chaired by the former minister of foreign affairs of Algeria, Lakhdar Brahimi, and comprised of an international cast of experts in the fields of peacekeeping, peacebuilding, development, and humanitarian assistance: Brian Atwood, Colin Granderson, Ann Hercus, Richard Monk, Klaus Naumann, Hisako Shimura, Vladimir Shustov, Philip Sibanda, and Cornelio Sommaruga. The panel undertook three months of extensive research that involved fieldwork in Kosovo and drew upon more than 200 interviews, including discussions with every department within the United Nations. The panel was given a straightforward yet comprehensive mandate: to present a clear set of concrete and practical recommendations to assist the United Nations to improve future peacekeeping activities.

In August, the panel published its report, a critical assessment of UN peacekeeping operations. The Brahimi Report thus represents the first comprehensive attempt to assess the evolution and effectiveness of UN peacekeeping missions over the years and to specify important ways to improve the UN Department of Peacekeeping Operations (DPKO).

At the core of the report is a call for change. Indeed, the report can be seen as a damning critique of the UN's "repeated failure" in its military interventions over the past decade. At one point, the report states bluntly, "No amount of good intentions can substitute for the fundamental ability to project credible force." Following earlier stinging assessments of UN failures in Rwanda and Srebrenica, the Brahimi Report is the most recent attempt by the UN to shine the light of self-criticism on itself in search of objective and constructive analysis.

The report's call for change is thus supported by a detailed blueprint for the creation of an enhanced peacekeeping structure. In brief, the Brahimi Report examines every aspect of UN peacekeeping activities, from its current capacities to far-reaching recommendations for technical change within the 189-member General Assembly. At the start of the report the panel makes its conclusions clear: "The key conditions for the success of future complex operations are political support, rapid deployment with robust posture and a sound peacebuilding strategy" (p. 1). Every recommendation that follows is designed to ensure that these three conditions are met in the future. . . .

The Changing Nature of UN Peacekeeping Operations: The Rationale for Brahimi

An analysis of past UN peacekeeping missions reveals a sharp increase in both the complexity and frequency of missions since the end of the Cold War. Between 1948 and 1988 the United Nations undertook just 15 peace operations around the world. Of the 15, only three missions received mandates that transcended ceasefire verification and force separation. Between 1989 and 1999, the number of peacekeeping missions jumped to 31, of which 24 involved mandates exceeding ceasefire observation and often involved the much more complex and dangerous tasks of weapons control, refugee relief work, post-conflict reconstruction, election certification, and many more difficult policing and encampment/demobilization activities (for more information, see the tables at: www.stimson.org/unpk/panelreport/unpkstimsondiscussion.pdf, pp. 8–9, prepared by William J. Durch of the Henry L. Stimson Center, Washington, D.C.).

The explosion of demands for peacekeepers during the 1990s tested both the capabilities and resources of the United Nations throughout the decade. The unprecedented need for peacekeepers was complicated by the changing role they would play. More and more frequently peacekeeping forces were called upon to intervene in hostile (that is, non-consensual) and dangerous situations to protect besieged populations. Unfortunately, in many cases the organization failed to meet these daunting challenges and UN military failures seemed to become commonplace.

To its credit, the Brahimi Report underscores this fact and describes the United Nations' inability to bring more men, money, and thought to the mission of peacekeeping. The report thus reveals the extent to which today the UN Secretariat is under-staffed and under-funded. At the time the report was completed (July 2000) the DPKO had only 32 military officers to plan, recruit, equip, deploy, support, and direct some 27,000 soldiers that comprised the 15 missions underway. UN police forces faced a similar situation: a staff of only nine police officers working out of UN headquarters were called upon to support 8,000 UN police in the field. The report thus concluded that the DPKO administrative budget (which was equal to 1/50th of the field teams' budget) was utterly insufficient to support the teams in the field.

These numbers illustrate a central point of the report: that the United Nations currently lacks the resources to effectively fulfill its peacekeeping mission. This point also makes clear the UN's lack of independence and inability to assume a leadership role in international crisis situations. Indeed, conference participants pointed out that the United Nations is a body that is in constant search of material and financial support and coherent political backing from member states.

Another factor crucial to the success of UN missions is the ongoing political support of influential member states. While the Brahimi Report fails to address this final point, participants drove home the fundamental importance of gaining international support (especially from the United States) for UN missions. Participants illustrated the cross-cutting character of this issue: (1) "All the recommendations contained in Brahimi for improving UN peacekeeping activities depend on the will of the U.S. Congress to fund the program," (2) "There is a consistent undercurrent within the UN of dissatisfaction and disappointment with U.S. failure to support the institution," and (3) this dynamic is "eroding America's international standing."

In summary, the rationale behind the Brahimi Report is three-fold: (1) to underscore the growing need for peacekeepers around the world, (2) to bring to light the UN's failure to ramp up administrative and logistical support of peacekeepers in the field, and (3) to propose a series of changes to improve the effectiveness of the DPKO.

The Current State of Affairs in Sub-Saharan Africa

Nowhere was the scope and intensity of violence during the 1990s as great as in Africa. While the general trend of armed conflict in Europe, Asia, the Americas, and the Middle East fell during the 1989–99 period, the 1990s witnessed an increase in the number of conflicts on the African continent. During this period, 16 UN peacekeeping missions were sent to Africa. (Three countries—Somalia, Sierra Leone, and Angola—were visited by multiple missions during this time.) Furthermore, this period saw internal and interstate violence in a total of 30 sub-Saharan states.

In 1999 alone, the continent was plagued by 16 armed conflicts, seven of which were wars with more than 1,000 battle-related deaths (*Journal of Peace Research*, 37:5, 2000, p. 638). In 2000, the situation continued to deteriorate: renewed heavy fighting between Eritrea and Ethiopia claimed tens of thousands of lives in the lead-up to a June ceasefire and ultimately the signing of a peace accord in December; continued violence in the Democratic Republic of Congo (DRC), Sierra Leone, Burundi, Angola, Sudan, Uganda, and Nigeria as well as the outbreak of new violence between Guinea and Liberia, in Zimbabwe, and in the Ivory Coast have brought new hardship and bloodshed to the continent.

Indeed, there was a consensus among conference participants that the level of violence present in Africa today suggests that the continent has reached a nadir. Furthermore, the group agreed that the potential exists that more civil wars, like those that gripped Sierra Leone and Liberia during the '90s, will occur on the continent.

In addition to the massive human suffering caused by war in Africa, conference participants pointed out that the long-term effects these conflagrations will have on development are profound. Conflict has already compounded a host of health, environmental, and economic ills. A recent report, "AIDS Epidemic Update 2000" from the joint UN Program on HIV/AIDS (UNAIDS) and the World Health Organization (WHO), reported that 3.8 million people became infected with HIV in sub-Saharan Africa during the last year, bringing the total number of people living with HIV/AIDS in the region to 25.3 million or 8.8 percent of the adult population. This year alone the pandemic will claim the lives of two million Africans; one million more will die from malaria and tuberculosis.

Experts at the conference agreed that among the plethora of conflicts on the continent today, perhaps the worst and most intractable war is in the DRC. Since 1998 this conflict has involved the armed forces of nine different states and at least nine rebel groups (*SIPRI Yearbook 2000*). The complexity of this conflagration, along with the vast territory in play, was seen by the group as a key reason why not to get involved in the conflict. Indeed no one expressed enthusiasm or even suggested a strategy for political engagement in the Congo (although several participants wondered aloud, "Who will help pick up the pieces in the DRC or another Rwanda?"). Finally, it was agreed that the DRC conflict will most likely continue to limit the social, political, and economic development of central and southern Africa for years to come.

In reviewing past UN missions to the continent, the participants agreed that UN successes in Namibia, Mozambique, and South Africa during the 1990s probably did not receive due credit in the international community. Meanwhile, UN failures (especially in Somalia '93 and Rwanda '94) became infamous, and in the United States these calamities became emblematic of a "failed organization" and provided grist for UN bashers in Washington.

As the devastating confluence of economic, health, and political problems continue to submerge the continent in poverty and conflict, the international community will continue to be called upon to act in Africa. With conflicts still raging across the continent and the threat of new outbreaks of violence in places like Zimbabwe, Kenya, Nigeria, Guinea, and Ivory Coast, it is difficult to imagine the need for peacekeeping operations diminishing in the near future. The challenges for the United Nations and the West vis-á-vis Africa are therefore multifold

Current Peacekeeping Operations in Africa

Sierra Leone (UNAMSIL, 1999–present)

Since the beginning of conflict in 1991, Sierra Leone's population has suffered greatly at the hands of the marauding Revolutionary United Front (RUF). During nearly a decade of fighting, the RUF has systematically killed and maimed tens of thousands of Leoneans. At the start of the war, Sierra Leone's army, with support from the Economic Community of West African States (ECOWAS) and its military observer group, ECOMOG, tried to defend the government and beat back the rebels.

The following year the Sierra Leonean army toppled its own government and held power until February 1996 when it relinquished control to the newly elected president, Ahmed Tejan Kabbah. Yet the military spent little time in their barracks, staging another coup in May 1997, this time joined by the RUF.

Following extensive negotiations and numerous broken peace agreements, the UN Security Council imposed an oil and arms embargo on Sierra Leone on October 8, 1997 and authorized ECOWAS to ensure its implementation through ECOMOG troops. After the continued failure of negotiations and repeated attacks on ECOMOG forces by the RUF, ECOMOG launched a military offensive that led to the collapse of the junta and its expulsion from the captial, Freetown. On March 10, 1998, President Kabbah was reinstated as president.

In June 1998, the Security Council established a UN Observer Mission in Sierra Leone (UNOMSIL) that documented human rights violations and war atrocities. Yet fighting in Sierra Leone continued, and by January 1999 the RUF held control of much of the countryside and most of Freetown. UNOMSIL personnel were evacuated before ECOMOG forces again retook the capital. By May 1999, negotiations between the government and rebels were underway and on July 7, the controversial Lomé Accords were signed, creating a government of national unity in Sierra Leone.

On October 22, 1999, the Security Council authorized the termination of UNOMSIL and the creation of the UN Mission in Sierra Leone (UNAMSIL), a new and much larger mission with a maximum of 6,000 military personnel, to assist the government and the parties in carrying out the provisions of the Lomé peace agreement. This group has been steadily reinforced since its creation and now carries a Security Council mandate to increase its numbers to 20,500.

Nevertheless, the UN mission has been plagued by missteps and failure. During the spring and summer of 2000, several UN soldiers were killed and hundreds more were captured and held hostage by the RUF. Only through the dubious support of Liberian strongman Charles Taylor (and the dramatically more effective bilateral military intervention of British forces acting outside of UNAMSIL) was the humiliating episode brought to an end and the UN presence rescued.

In recent months, UNAMSIL has been hit with further bad news: India, source of the largest multinational contingent, announced the withdrawal of its 3,150 soldiers by February 2001 after several of its soldiers were killed and its commander, Major General Vijay K. Jetley, became involved in a dispute with the mission's Nigerian leaders. Shortly after this announcement the Jordanian contingent, citing the conspicuous absence of Western soldiers in the mission, also announced the departure of its 1,800 soldiers by the end of the year.

The impending departure of nearly half of the UN forces on the ground in Sierra Leone is a blow to UNAMSIL, and will leave Bangladesh as the sole non-African actors involved in the mission. While Bangladesh and Ghana have offered to replace the lost troops and maintain the current level of 12,500, it looks unlikely that the Security Council and the secretary general will be able to increase the number of forces to the 20,000 mark. And many Sierra Leoneans worry that the pull-out of the departing forces along with the start of the dry season—typically a time of intense fighting—will lead to more bloodshed. Together, these events cast further doubt on the future of this important peacekeeping mission.

Ethiopia-Eritrea (UNMEE, 2000–present)

In August, the UN Security Council adopted Kofi Annan's proposal to send a strong contingent of 4,200 Blue Helmets to oversee the implementation of the June 18 Algiers ceasefire agreement. This agreement between Ethiopia and Eritrea halted two years of intermittent war that killed tens of thousands. The treaty followed Ethiopia's ferocious May offensive that pushed deep into Eritrean territory and forced a million Eritreans to flee at a time when regional drought threatened thousands of lives.

The United Nations Mission in Ethiopia and Eritrea (UNMEE) was established to monitor the cessation of hostilities in this border dispute, and the redeployment of forces to respective sides of a demilitarized zone. The UN mission of 4,500 is currently deploying.

Building a durable peace in the Horn of Africa is yet to be accomplished, although the peace effort received good news in the fall when both sides signed a formal peace treaty on December 12 in Algiers.

Congo (MONUC, 1999–present)

The 1997 ouster of Zaire's long-time despot, Mobutu Sese Seko, brought Laurent Kabila and his Rwandan backers to power in the new Congo. But fighting once again erupted in August 1998 when rebels, backed by Rwanda and Uganda, accused President Kabila's government of harboring Hutu militia who had fled Rwanda after committing genocide in 1994.

On July 10, 1999, the DRC along with Angola, Namibia, Rwanda, Uganda, and Zimbabwe came together in Lusaka to sign a ceasefire agreement to end hostilities in the DRC. Conspicuous in their absence from the talks were several Congolese rebel groups. Nevertheless, the Security Council proceeded with the peace process and in August 1999, authorized the deployment of up to 90 UN military liaison personnel to the capitals of the signatory states and other strategic military locations.

Since then the mandate of MONUC has grown to a maximum deployment of 5,537 military personnel, including up to 500 military observers. Nevertheless, the UN Security Council and Secretariat have not proceeded with this second phase deployment due to the failure by Congo's government, rebels, and neighbors to implement their commitments under the Lusaka Agreement. The war in the DRC thus continues unabated.

Western Sahara (MINURSO, 1991–present)

The mission to Western Sahara is the UN's oldest on the continent. This protracted conflict between Morocco and the Frente Popular para la Liberación de Saguia el-Hamra y de Río de Oro (Polisario Front) over a stretch of land southwest of Morocco began after the withdrawal of Spain as colonial administrator in 1976. At that time, both Morocco and Mauritania affirmed their claim to the territory, a claim opposed by the Polisario Front.

The United Nations became involved with seeking a peaceful resolution of the conflict in the Western Sahara after fighting broke out between the Moroccan army and the Algerian-backed Polisario Front. By 1979, Mauritania had renounced its claims to the territory, leaving the two sides to battle for control. In cooperation with the Organization of African Unity (OAU), the UN secretary general initiated a mission of good offices that led to "settlement proposals" between the two sides that were accepted in August 1988.

By 1991, a tentative ceasefire was established and the UN Security Council decided to establish the UN Mission for the Referendum in Western Sahara (MINURSO). The settlement plan called for a referendum in which people of Western Sahara would choose between independence and integration with Morocco. At full strength the mission was to consist of approximately 1,700 military personnel and a security unit of 300 police officers.

According to the settlement plan, the referendum was to take place in January 1992, but it was never held. At issue still for the two parties is the composition of the electorate. The United Nations has tried to intercede and facilitate the process of voter identification, but the exercise has been fraught with problems. Kofi Annan's personal envoy to the Western Sahara, James A. Baker III, continues to seek a negotiated settlement between the independence-seeking Polisario Front and Morocco, and UN-mediated talks on the referendum continue.

U.S. Policy toward Africa

Cataloging contemporary conflict and tension in sub-Saharan Africa is a difficult task. The array of conflicts facing Africans today is long (the risk of increased conflict remains high in Algeria, Angola, Burundi, DRC, Guinea, Guinea-Bissau, Ivory Coast, Kenya, Liberia, Nigeria, Rwanda, Senegal, Sierra Leone, Somalia, Sudan, and Zimbabwe) and presents Western policymakers with a daunting task: how to design foreign policy toward a region with the breadth and depth of socio-economic trouble and political instability that is currently found in Africa?

Conference participants agreed that the "lack of political will" by Western powers is the major impediment hindering the deployment and success of UN peacekeeping missions in Africa. Yet as one conference participant said, "It is just not here in the United States where political leaders have to sell peacekeeping missions to their populations, it happens in all democracies." In short, few foreign leaders are willing to risk the loss of soldiers in poorly understood lands where there may be no perceived national strategic or economic interests.

The aversion to peacekeeping among the American military and policymakers runs deep. American critics of peacekeeping missions, and of conflict prevention programs in general, often chastise the United Nations for its unrealistic planning, weak mandates, and feckless command and control procedures. For these critics the ill-fated UN mission to Somalia (1992–94) confirmed their cynicism and became emblematic of international peacekeeping efforts. Moreover, the death of 18 Army Rangers in the streets of Mogadishu had a profound and traumatic effect on the way American foreign policymakers in general looked at peacekeeping, especially in Africa.

Since the tragedy in Somalia, the trend has been for Western nations to refuse to send troops into Africa's hot spots. Jordan recently underscored this point when it expressed frustration with the West's failure to commit soldiers to the UNAMSIL mission as a reason for the withdrawal of its troops from Sierra Leone.

America's aversion to peacekeeping in Africa also reflects broader U.S. foreign policy on the continent. Africa occupies a marginal role in American foreign policy in general (a point highlighted by conference participants).

Today, the foundation of U.S. policy toward the vast sub-Saharan region (with its 48 states) is being built on relations with South Africa and Nigeria. Secretary of Defense William Cohen stressed the importance of these two relationships earlier this year on a trip to Cape Town when he said: "South Africa and Nigeria will be critical for the stability and the future prosperity of African nations, . . . and we estimate that their participation in maneuvers and joint training programs, seminars, exchanges in military personnel and also academic exercises aimed at military/civilian relations will strengthen ties between these nations" (*Armed Forces Journal International* 138:2, September 2000, p. 30).

Despite the apparently fruitful cooperation between the United States, South Africa, and Nigeria, the road ahead for broader U.S.-Africa relations is unclear.

The future for much of Africa looks bleak. As war and humanitarian disasters continue to unfold across the continent, they are accompanied by growing numbers of refugees, spreading instability, and in some places anarchy. The rise of lawlessness and stateless societies in Africa brings the risk of the development of new terrorist and drug networks. Weak economic growth, the AIDS pandemic, the degradation of Africa's physical environment, and the spread of humanitarian crises in sub-Saharan Africa combine to create a depressing regional portrait.

Each of these realities poses a unique threat to peace everywhere on the continent. Thus, conference participants agreed: Given the menacing socioeconomic setting in Africa today, the United States must be encouraged to re-engage in both the United Nations and African affairs.

Conclusion

Conference participants were unanimous in their conviction that the Brahimi Report is a landmark document on the American foreign policy scene. Not as a source of seminal theory or original analysis of peacekeeping operations—indeed, much of what is contained in the report has been known and talked about for years—but rather for its straightforward simplicity, candor, and ability to synthesize timely and urgent issues. The report should thus be seen as more than a plan for improving the technical capacity of the Department of Peacekeeping Operations; it is also a project around which the multitude of concerned actors can coalesce to construct a unifying vision and effect change. In the atomized and unharmonious world of international policy-making, one must seize upon the rare opportunities to work together and concentrate resources in pursuit of a common goal.

While conference participants were unable to reach a consensus on what next steps should be taken by U.S. and international policymakers in support of Brahimi, numerous recommendations were put forward. One former government official argued for a direct link between poverty and conflict in Africa and advocated a redoubling of aid and development efforts on the continent by Western governments. Others from the academic community suggested that the United States adopt a policy of selective engagement in Africa that focuses on vital interests and achievable goals. Several participants recommended that U.S. policymakers should continue to strengthen key African allies (such as Nigeria and South Africa), support regional organizations (like ECOWAS and SADC, the Southern African Development Community, strengthen the American embassies and diplomatic corps, collect better intelligence on the continent, and bring economic and other pressures to bear on warlord governments. Although none of these proposals received unconditional support from the group, consensus was reached over the continued importance of the democratization process in Africa.

The group also agreed that the agenda put forth by the Brahimi Report offers numerous points of entry for members of the international community. As the report states, "Peacekeeping and peacebuilding are inseparable partners" (p. ix). The U.S. Institute of Peace and other concerned organizations have a longstanding record and ongoing programs that have taken concrete steps toward conflict prevention on the continent. The Brahimi Report both confirms the importance of this work and illuminates new areas of need.

NO ↩

William Reno

The Failure of Peacekeeping
in Sierra Leone

[In May 2000,] Revolutionary United Front (RUF) fighters detained and disarmed a Zambian battalion of the United Nations Mission in Sierra Leone (UNAMSIL) that had been sent to break an RUF siege of Kenyan UN peacekeepers in the town of Makeni. This incident effectively ended a peace agreement between the government of Sierra Leone and the RUF that had been signed in July 1999 after more than eight years of war.

Fighting has continued since. UN Secretary General Kofi Annan recommended in August 2000 an increase in the UN mission's strength from 7,500 to 20,500 troops. Britain, Sierra Leone's former colonial power, unilaterally sent warships and a commando battalion to Sierra Leone. Diplomats in other countries began to pressure Charles Taylor, president of neighboring Liberia, for allegedly aiding RUF forces.

The breakdown of the peace agreement illustrates the difficulties facing conflict resolution when state institutions have collapsed after decades of corrupt misrule. And the RUF exemplifies the kind of insurgency that can develop that neither mobilizes mass followings nor attempts to administer "liberated zones" under the guidance of new political ideas that are an alternative to the corrupt government the insurgency fights. This development poses a significant dilemma for conventional approaches to conflict resolution that owe much more to experiences with classic civil wars in which there are clear ideological or programmatic opponents and in which negotiated settlements to share control of state institutions are stressed. Sierra Leone shows the failure of conventional diplomatic strategies while providing hints of a more radical approach by the British government that draws from British imperial experience in ruling stateless societies and carrying out counterinsurgency efforts.

Insurgency and State Collapse

Sierra Leone's war began in March 1991 when a small force of RUF fighters led by Foday Sankoh, a former Sierra Leone army corporal, crossed from Liberia into Sierra Leone. Initially the RUF was lightly armed, but Sierra

Leone's army was small, with fewer than 3,000 soldiers, and was unable to defeat it.

The RUF received backing from Charles Taylor, whose rebel group, the National Patriotic Front of Liberia (NPFL), had invaded Liberia in December 1989 to overthrow President Samuel Doe. Taylor used support for the RUF to expand his influence beyond Liberia; it is also alleged that he personally benefited from the RUF's control over diamonds in eastern Sierra Leone.

Taylor used the RUF in 1991 to weaken the Economic Community of West African States Monitoring Group (ECOMOG), a multilateral West African peacekeeping force that was blocking Taylor's attempt to install himself as Liberia's president. At the same time, Sierra Leone President Joseph Momoh allowed an anti-Taylor coalition of Liberian dissidents to use Sierra Leone as a base, and ECOMOG used Freetown's Lungi International Airport to launch attacks against the NPFL in Liberia.

Junior military officers overthrew Momoh in April 1992. They complained that corrupt senior officers prevented supplies from reaching front lines and that some politicians were secretly collaborating with the RUF for personal gain. The coup leaders installed themselves as the National Provisional Ruling Council (NPRC) under the leadership of Captain Valentine Strasser, who promised that the army would defeat the RUF.

By 1994 the NPRC had increased the army's strength to 14,000 soldiers, recruiting unemployed youth and members of armed gangs associated with politicians. But the strengthened army could not end the war. A former NPRC minister identified the cause: "There developed an extraordinary identity of interests between [the] NPRC and [the] RUF. This was responsible for the *sobel* phenomenon, i.e., government soldiers by day became rebels by night."

Unable to fight the RUF effectively, in 1995 the NPRC hired Executive Outcomes (EO), a South African mercenary firm. The NPRC also armed progovernment militias, known as Kamajors, which were later organized as the Civil Defense Force (CDF). The South African firm secured most of the country's towns and alluvial diamond-mining areas, which the RUF had captured in late 1994 and early 1995.

EO's intervention, while militarily effective, created serious long-term political complications. Greater security gave societal groups the chance to pressure the NPRC to hold multiparty elections promised by Momoh before he was overthrown. International organizations and foreign diplomats also pressured NPRC officials to hold elections in February 1996. But elements within the army feared that the CDF would replace them. This encouraged some soldiers to collaborate more closely with the RUF. In addition, EO's offensive against the RUF forced fighters to force closer ties with Charles Taylor for aid.

The March 1996 elections brought Ahmed Tejan Kabbah to power. President Kabbah inherited these political dilemmas. Unsure of army loyalty (and the target of at least two coup attempts between March 1996 and May 1997), Kabbah relied on CDF fighters for his security and to battle the RUF. Government reliance on CDF forces intensified when EO left Sierra Leone in January 1997 after disputes over payment of EO's fees. The company's departure and the government's response aggravated tensions between the army and Kabbah. On May 25, 1997 the army overthrew Kabbah's government. The RUF welcomed the coup and formed an alliance, the Armed Forces Revolutionary Council (AFRC), with the army's Major Johnny Paul Koroma at its head. Koroma named RUF leader Sankoh his deputy (even though Sankoh had been detained in Nigeria in March 1997, where he had traveled to discuss the peace process) and appointed RUF members to cabinet positions.

Most West African governments refused to recognize the AFRC, pitting ECOMOG (about 4,000 soldiers, most of whom were Nigerian and who remained in western parts of Freetown and at the international airport) against the AFRC regime. Nigeria and Guinea boosted ECOMOG's troop levels to about 10,000 men and finally reinstalled Kabbah in February 1998. ECOMOG became even more central to the Kabbah government's security after the restoration, underscored by Kabbah's appointment in mid-April 1998 of Nigerian Brigadier Maxwell Khobe as chief of national security.

Human rights abuses, already considerable before the 1997 coup, intensified. While in power the RUF and the AFRC singled out suspected Kabbah supporters and men of voting and fighting age for mutilation, including cutting off fingers, hands, feet, and arms. Victims also included women and children. Eyewitnesses and victims reported that amputees often were instructed to deliver messages that the AFRC and RUF would resist international pressure to relinquish power and that they wanted Sankoh released from Nigerian custody. Mutilations by the RUF and AFRC continued after Kabbah's return, reportedly to discourage citizens from giving political or military help to the restored government.

The Lomé Agreement

Kabbah again negotiated with the RUF when it became clear that ECOMOG troops would leave Sierra Leone following elections in Nigeria in 1999. This decision left Sierra Leone's government more dependent on a small UN mission in Sierra Leone for future diplomatic and military protection. The mission initially consisted of 70 military observers, but its importance lay in bringing some international attention to the issue of Liberian support for the RUF since part of the mission's mandate was to help enforce an embargo on arms supplies to Sierra Leone. This did not solve the government's security problem, however. The RUF forced ECOMOG from the Kono diamond fields in December 1998. Elements of the AFRC regime and the RUF even occupied Freetown for a few days in January 1999 and forced Kabbah to flee once again until an ECOMOG counter-offensive dislodged the invaders.

Nigeria's new civilian government recognized that it lacked resources to defeat the RUF, especially while states in the region covertly supported it. Its pragmatic solution was to hold talks. Negotiations took place under the auspices of the Economic Community of West African States, and included Liberia's and Burkina Faso's presidents, both of whom had supported the RUF. Sankoh was released from Nigerian custody on April 18, 1999 and flown to Lomé, the capital of Togo, to begin negotiations with Kabbah's government.

On July 7 the Sierra Leone government and the RUF signed the Lomé peace agreement. In October 1999 the UN expanded its observer mission to 6,000 troops to assist in implementing the agreement (2,000 Nigerian troops were incorporated into this enlarged UN force in November 1999). The agreement required the disarming of all warring groups, appointment of RUF members to cabinet positions, conversion of the RUF into a political party, and Sankoh's installation as vice president and director of the Commission for the Management of Strategic Resources, National Reconstruction, and Development, which was to regulate the diamond-mining industry. Most controversial to many Sierra Leoneans was the provision in the agreement that Sankoh be granted a pardon so that he could make his conversion from a war leader to a civilian politician. Sankoh himself mistrusted the Sierra Leone government, and did not return to Freetown until October 1999, when the UN established its expanded peacekeeping mission.

Recognizing that the RUF could prevail militarily, United States officials allegedly pressured Kabbah to negotiate with the RUF. Sierra Leone would also become a test case for how much diplomatic and military support non-African states would provide in conflicts involving so-called collapsed states.

Explanations of the United States role vary. One interpretation holds that the Clinton administration valued the appearance of order, regardless of who ruled Sierra Leone. A United States–sponsored peace agreement would thus allow it to appear that the United States had addressed a crisis in Africa while ensuring that it would not have to make a commitment of resources and soldiers to an African problem. This would explain why the US government was interested in Sierra Leone in the first place, since the country is of no strategic interest to the United States. A more optimistic interpretation explaining American interest held that officials believed that the RUF and Kabbah's government would abide by the terms of the Lomé agreement, and that the RUF would evolve into something more like a real political party as its leaders discovered that success in a democratic coalition government required gaining public support and confidence.

The Freetown newspapers stressed American coercion, and even claimed that Kabbah had been "kidnapped" by the Reverend Jesse Jackson (who acted as a facilitator in negotiations) and other American officials and forced to sign the Lomé agreement. Some press commentators said that the agreement was largely written by officials of the United States Agency for International Development. Another interpretation, among many analysts and journalists, focuses on Liberian President Charles Taylor's relationship with the RUF and asserts that the RUF and Taylor have exploited the collapse of Sierra Leone as a state. They manipulate international agencies into believing that the RUF will transform itself into a political party. Their objective, however, is to solidify control over diamond-mining areas for their own profit and to increase Taylor's regional political influence.

Some UN and foreign officials tolerate this deception because they recognize that financial and military backing for large-scale peace enforcement is unlikely. But conflict in collapsed states is fundamentally different from wars between ideological rivals who mobilize mass followings and build "liberated zones" to practice their ideas of governance. Instead, rebel groups use the willingness of outsiders to recognize them as potential government rulers as an opportunity to acquire recognition of sovereignty in peace agreements, which they use as a cover to continue their predatory acquisition of wealth and to shield their transactions with international business partners.

Many Sierra Leoneans regarded positions taken by UN and foreign diplomats who stressed reconciliation as offensive. They pointed out that United States diplomats branded RUF leader Sankoh as a violator of human rights and had made statements that stressed rebel violations of international law. They noted that a year earlier the UN Security Council condemned "as gross violations of international humanitarian law the recent atrocities carried out against the civilian population . . . of Sierra Leone by members of the Revolutionary United Front and the deposed junta." The Lomé agreement included a provision for a Truth and Reconciliation Commission (which has never been never implemented). This provision highlighted inconsistencies in international approaches to Sierra Leone's war, since it marked a shift from foreign backing for the Sierra Leone government to fight and to prosecute heads of an insurgency noted for human rights abuses, then recognized those same individuals as legitimate political leaders and included them in a coalition government to rule the country.

The Failure of Lomé

The Lomé agreement did not bring an end to war in Sierra Leone and may have contributed to its continuation. Lomé's primary shortcoming was the inability of UNAMSIL peacekeepers to enforce the terms of the agreement in the face of RUF noncompliance. UNAMSIL soldiers began to surrender their weapons to RUF fighters soon after the first contingent, a Kenyan unit, arrived on November 29, 1999. Guinea's UNAMSIL contingent was forced to turn over approximately 500 AK-47 rifles, other weapons, and several tons of ammunition in January 2000. Kenyan units were relieved of their weapons on two occasions in January 2000. Later incidents also involved weapons taken by members of the former Sierra Leone army. The largest loss of weapons occurred in conjunction with RUF attacks on UNAMSIL units, beginning in May 2000, as the last Nigerian ECOMOG troops left Sierra Leone. The RUF also took weapons from a remaining Nigerian contingent attached to UNAMSIL, and a loss occurred when the Zambian battalion sent to relieve the Kenyans under siege was detained by RUF forces.

The May 2000 crisis highlighted the role that Liberian President Taylor played in providing weapons to the RUF. This reflected a longer-term relationship in which Taylor served as a commercial channel for RUF-supplied diamonds mined in Sierra Leone. RUF attacks on and the detention of UNAMSIL peacekeepers raised the level of diplomatic attention to this connection. The resultant diplomatic pressure on Taylor, and earlier decreases in financial aid to Liberia from abroad, likely increased Taylor's reliance on this source of income, estimated at upward of $125 million annually from Sierra Leone. Taylor's failure to attract large foreign investors to the country's mining industry also likely increased his reliance on deals with the RUF to gain access to income and resources. As part of the bargain, Taylor harbored RUF commander Sam "Maskita" Bockarie in Liberia, where Bockarie allegedly recruited fighters for the RUF.

The RUF's relationship with Taylor underscored the importance that control over diamonds plays in the RUF's overall strategy. Assistance from its Liberian patron is tied to the RUF's occupation of diamond-mining areas. The long-term political implications of this reliance have been considerable for the RUF. Instead of attracting and mobilizing a popular following in Sierra Leone to overthrow the country's corrupt and inept government, RUF commanders have fought the government with guns bought with diamonds, brought from Liberia, or captured from their enemies. They do not have to rely on the goodwill of local inhabitants or the contributions of their energies and wealth, and they do not have to engage in the arduous political and organizational task of building a mass movement to fight their way to power. The RUF bases its political power on control over diamonds, much as had the corrupt Sierra Leone politicians that the RUF criticized.

The RUF's failure to build grassroots support increased its reliance on diamonds and assistance from Liberia. This meant that the RUF could never realistically satisfy the key provision of the Lomé agreement that it allow UNAMSIL peacekeepers to control diamond-mining areas, nor could it disarm without losing its primary basis of power. The May 2000 crisis occurred in the wake of UNAMSIL attempts to unilaterally occupy areas in the Kono and Kambia districts outside the limited territory under government control. And the disarmament figures themselves reflected RUF noncompliance with the terms of the Lomé agreement. By the start of hostilities on May 2, the UN reported that 24,042 former combatants (out of a rough total of 45,000) had been disarmed, but had surrendered only 10,840 weapons. (The Freetown press, suspicious of these figures, echoed widespread popular suspicions that the RUF manipulated the disarmament process to its own advantage and intimidated UNAMSIL officials, and predicted that violent confrontation with UNAMSIL would occur.) Some fighters reported unilaterally to collect $300 bounties. UN officials noted that, although all factions tried to prevent their fighters from disarming and punished those who did, the RUF was the most systematic and violent. . . .

The Return to War

The RUF's attack on and seizure of 500 UNAMSIL peacekeepers in May 2000 marked the end of the Lomé agreement. RUF leader Foday Sankoh reiterated in a letter to foreign and Sierra Leone officials that the RUF had not received all the state offices provided under the conditions of the Lomé agreement. Critics speculated that RUF officials hoped to use these posts to sell diamonds overseas under cover of diplomatic immunity. A more apparent interest may have been an expansion of participation in government as much as possible to buffer international qualms about the grant of amnesty in the Lomé agreement. This reflected Sankoh's deep suspicion about the motives of the Sierra Leone government and fears that the amnesty agreement would not protect him, given the government's reluctance to provide Sankoh with a written protection from prosecution.

Sankoh himself went into hiding on May 8 after a crowd of several thousand people attacked his Freetown residence, and was shot, seized, and paraded naked through Freetown by progovernment troops 10 days later. He remains in the custody of the Sierra Leone government and could be prosecuted under the terms of a proposed international war crimes tribunal (which remains unimplemented in early 2001). Plans for the tribunal reversed the Lomé agreement's amnesty and left open the possibility that defendants such as Sankoh who would have been exempted under the terms of the Lomé agreement would be prosecuted. This has probably reinforced RUF perceptions that the Sierra Leone government and its backers will jettison bargains when they find the resources and political will to fight, and seek agreements when resources and will are lacking.

With the breakdown of Lomé, Britain added about 650 military personnel to the 15 British military observers assigned to UNAMSIL. Operating under British command, these paratroopers and marines were operationally separate from the UNAMSIL force and aided the Sierra Leone army and progovernment militias in defending Freetown against RUF fighters. The British have also begun a training program for the new Sierra Leone army. By early 2001 an estimated 4,500 Sierra Leone soldiers had completed the program.

Meanwhile, UN Secretary General Kofi Annan's proposal to increase UNAMSIL's strength to 20,500 became wedged inside a bitter dispute within UNAMSIL. In mid-October the Indian and Jordanian UNAMSIL contingents, together numbering almost 5,000 troops, signaled their intentions to depart by February 2001 (in mid-December 2000, even before Indian and Jordanian withdrawals, UNAMSIL had 12,455 soldiers). India's decision followed the leaking of a document written by UNAMSIL's Indian commander, Major General Vijay Jetley, in which he charged that the "Nigerian Army was interested in staying in Sierra Leone due to the massive benefits [it was] getting from the illegal diamond mining" through arrangements with the RUF. He also charged that former ECOMOG commander Brigadier General Maxwell Khobe had accepted $10 million from the RUF to permit mining activities without interference.

Waging Peace

The February departure of the Indian contingent highlighted a key limitation of multilateral peacekeeping in contexts such as Sierra Leone: the inability of the UN bureaucracy in New York and the UNAMSIL commander in Sierra Leone to use military force to preempt RUF attacks or to launch operations against the RUF once UN soldiers had been kidnapped. Jordanian officials announced that their contingent too would depart, reflecting similar concerns that peacekeepers were vulnerable in a context like Sierra Leone where armed groups continued to fight each other and to target foreign soldiers. The peacekeeping mandate of UNAMSIL and the militaries that contributed soldiers to UNAMSIL did not envision combat of this sort, and UNAMSIL personnel were not equipped or given logistical support to engage in sustained combat.

The British approach involved considerably greater use of violence against antigovernment forces than UNAMSIL was able to marshal militarily or diplomatically. British forces attacked West Side Boys groups in Okra Hills on August 30 and September 10 to rescue the remaining 6 of 11 British personnel who had been kidnapped in late August by the former soldiers.[1] On November 13 British marines staged military exercises around Freetown; these followed the signing three days earlier of a UNAMSIL-brokered one-month cease-fire between the RUF and Sierra Leone government officials that was to allow UNAMSIL to travel throughout Sierra Leone. The military exercise was to "remind the leadership of RUF of the need to honor that agreement," the British commander said. But the RUF did not let UNAMSIL enter areas it held (except for occasional visits of small groups), and the result was to create tensions between the British forces and UNAMSIL.

As of March 2001, UNAMSIL peacekeepers were still not deployed in RUF-held areas. This continued to generate tension between UN and British military officers. "It is as if the UN leadership has learned nothing from previous experiences," said a British officer in reference to UNAMSIL unwillingness to deploy. A senior UN officer replied that "if the British want war, they can have it and we will leave."

UNAMSIL's presence, like British support for the Sierra Leone government, helps multiply rebel factions. The RUF has failed to disarm and continues its attacks on UNAMSIL, an intransigence that Sankoh had backed with his words. This, along with international pressure that he be tried for crimes against humanity, has disqualified him from future negotiations on behalf of the RUF.

UN officials sought a new interlocutor, despite the continuing loyalty of many RUF fighters to Sankoh. Issa Sesay emerged as the RUF's putative new head as UN officials signaled that they would talk to him. The spokesman for one RUF faction, Gibril Massaquoi, stated that "90 percent were taking orders from Maurice Kallon," a commander in northern Sierra Leone loyal to Sankoh. Yet an RUF commander stated that "General Issa has betrayed them [the fighters] and they now have nothing to do with him as they will continue the struggle." Fighting later broke out among RUF factions, drawing in rebels loyal to Sam Bockarie, the RUF commander from eastern Sierra Leone with close ties to Liberian President Charles Taylor.

Taylor allegedly maintains close connections with the Bockarie and Kallon factions to pursue an offensive against Guinea, signaling a major regional expansion of this war, even after Bockarie left Liberia in early 2001. Regional disorder would keep Taylor's fighters busy and less likely to challenge him, and would give him and his associates more access to commercial opportunities connected with providing weapons and exploiting local resources. War would also destabilize Taylor's neighbors and allow him to capitalize on internal political divisions besetting the political establishments of neighboring rulers toward whom Taylor harbors personal animosity.

Beginning in October 2000, RUF attacks into Guinea intensified. RUF strategy again apparently focused on forcing the UN and the Sierra Leone government to negotiate with the RUF, but with the RUF left in control of significant territory. In the event of a postagreement election, the RUF would be in a position to intimidate citizens into voting for it, much as Taylor had done in Liberia in 1997. The international community could then consider Sierra Leone "stable."

The Future of Intervention

In trying to bring an end to conflict in Sierra Leone, both the UN and British forces have found it difficult to respond to and influence autonomous militias, whether pro- or antigovernment. These groups shift allegiances and may simultaneously fight against and profess alliance to the same organization. As British officers discovered after the August kidnapping of British personnel by the West Side Boys, when force is used against multiplying decentralized opponents there is no "army" that can surrender. Military victory against irregular forces requires physical occupation and administration. In addition, the defeat of multiple factions of the RUF, the CDF, and the West Side Boys by military means alone would also require attacks on the families and homes of fighters and the use of force at levels that are prohibited by the conventions of warfare and international agreements.

The British solution to this dilemma involves a lengthy commitment. Jonathan Riley, the British force commander in Sierra Leone, has said that "We will leave when the war is either won or resolved on favorable terms." Heir to the institutional legacy of British rule of the hinterland of Sierra Leone from 1898 to 1961, British Prime Minster Tony Blair's administration appears to have clearer ideas than the UN or the United States about political and military strategy in what has essentially become a stateless society. Indeed, former colonial officers have participated in government discussions concerning British strategies in Sierra Leone. And a former colonial district commissioner returned to Sierra Leone to engage in chieftaincy consultations to gain an understanding of the multiple grievances that lead members of communities to take up arms. The effort was also designed to build support for Kabbah's regime among local notables by showing that the government could intervene in local conflicts to their benefit.

This contrasts with the more bureaucratic approaches of the UN and United States, which are seriously out of sync with the reality of conflict in collapsed states. The Americans especially tend to search for general solutions to disorder (to the extent of trying to create computer models to predict conflicts). Some local observers complain that international agencies such as the UN Commission for Refugees, which draw attention to refugees in Guinea where the RUF and other groups battle one another, offer rebel groups the opportunity to use organized refugee movements as human shields to shift fighters and loot supplies.

The UN approach of engaging factions in ceasefires and peace negotiations reflects explicit recognition of the limits to the use of force. This strategy recognizes that UN peacekeepers are constrained in the use of force against local groups and that officers of foreign military contingents or their governments are unwilling to commit their troops to combat. This limited mandate constrains UNAMSIL's use of intelligence and analysis—much to the annoyance of British military officers and many Sierra Leoneans. . . .

Both approaches face serious constraints. It is uncertain whether a post-Blair administration will possess the political will to remain engaged in Sierra Leone for many years. It is not clear if British voters will countenance a long engagement. Yet the UN's preference for negotiations tends to accredit armed groups that prey on society, leading as in Liberia to the installation of a predatory warlord as head of state. This approach creates the high probability of a Sierra Leone left in the control of groups known for grave human rights abuses. Departure on these terms would humiliate UN officials and seriously undermine the credibility of future peacekeeping missions. This contradiction is likely to remain, since it does not appear that the RUF can be beaten on the battlefield. Yet negotiating with the RUF when the United States and other Western powers insist that rulers such as Yugoslav President Slobodan Milosevic face a war crimes tribunal leaves the appearance that Sierra Leone suffers from a double standard in the global application of human rights principles.

Note

1. The kidnapping episode also exposed a factional split among the former soldiers. The kidnappers were loyal to Foday Kallay, who claimed to lead the former Sierra Leone army after Johnny Paul Koroma left to take a government position as head of a Commission for Consolidation of Peace in Freetown.

POSTSCRIPT

Are International Peacekeeping Missions Critical to Resolving Ethnic Conflicts in African Countries?

Neither of these authors, even Reno, is strictly against peacekeeping missions in Africa. The problem is that given the general marginality of Africa to U.S. security interests, peacekeeping initiatives may always be modestly funded and staffed. If U.S. efforts are so meager, then Reno questions their effectiveness. Docking obviously would like to see a greater investment in African peacekeeping efforts.

Since the writing of the articles in this issue, the geography of African conflicts has changed, as well as global conditions more generally. At the global level, the terrorist attacks of September 11, 2001 set in motion a series of events that impact (directly and indirectly) peacekeeping efforts in Africa. While U.S. anti-terrorism initiatives could arguably lead to a renewed interest in peacekeeping, the now three-year-old war in Iraq has left the American public extremely leery of further foreign entanglements. As a result, the United States has increasingly pushed for the deployment of African (as opposed to UN or American) peacekeeping forces. The United States has also progressively narrowed its interests in Africa to a few oil-producing states and South Africa.

Two separate, but inter-related, African conflicts that have changed significantly in the past 5 years are those in Sierra Leone and Liberia. In early 2002, the decade-long civil war in Sierra Leone was declared over by the government and rebel leaders. This conflict resulted in the deaths of tens of thousands of people and the displacement of more than 2 million civilians (roughly a third of the country). The British government in particular committed to help the country rebuild. Ahmed Kabbah was elected president in a landslide victory in May 2002. Foday Sankoh, the rebel leader of the United Revolutionary Front, was indicted for war crimes, but died of natural causes in prison in July 2003 while awaiting his trial. In June 2004, UN-sponsored war crimes trials began. The last of the UN peacekeeping troops left the country in December 2005.

Former Liberian President Charles Taylor was indicted for war crimes in Sierra Leone. After 4 years of civil war in Liberia (closely related to the war in Sierra Leone), Taylor left the country in August 2003, eventually finding refuge in Nigeria. U.S. troops arrived shortly thereafter, and a peace accord was signed in the fall of that year. The UN took over peacekeeping in 2004, and Ellen Johnson-Sirleaf became president of the country on November 23, 2005 (the first woman to be elected as an African head of state). A truth and reconciliation commission was set up in early 2006 to investigate human rights abuses.

For those interested in further reading on conflict, another important circumstance to understand is the war in the Democratic Republic of the Congo, a situation that some have referred to as Africa's first world war given the number of countries involved. A good article on the Congo war is one by Ottaway in the May 1999 issue of *Current History* entitled "Post-Imperial Africa at War." Two good books on U.S. intervention in Somalia include *The Road to Hell* by Michael Maren (The Free Press, 2002) and *Deliver Us From Evil* by William Shawcross (Touchstone, 2001). A good article on the Rwandan genocide and the failure of outside powers to intervene is by Christopher Clapham in the March 1998 issue of the *Journal of Peace Research* entitled "Rwanda: the Perils of Peacemaking."

Contributors to This Volume

WILLIAM G. MOSELEY is an assistant professor of geography, and former coordinator of the African studies program, at Macalester College in Saint Paul, Minnesota, where he teaches courses on Africa, environment, and development. He received a B.A. in history from Carleton College, an M.S. in environmental policy and an M.P.P in international public policy from the University of Michigan, and a Ph.D. in geography from the University of Georgia. He has worked for the U.S. Peace Corps, the Save the Children Fund (UK), the U.S. Agency for International Development, the World Bank Environment Department, and the U.S. State Department. His research and work experiences have led to extended stays in Mali, Zimbabwe, Malawi, Niger, Lesotho, and South Africa. He is the author of over 25 peer-reviewed articles and book chapters that have appeared in such outlets as *Ecological Economics*, the *Geographical Journal*, *Applied Geography*, and *Geoforum*. He also has written pieces for the popular press that have been published in the *International Herald Tribune*, the *Christian Science Monitor*, the *Chicago Sun Times*, and *Dollars & Sense*, and is co-editor of *African Environment and Development: Rhetoric, Programs, Realities* (Ashgate, 2004).

STAFF

Larry Loeppke	Managing Editor
Jill Peter	Senior Developmental Editor
Susan Brusch	Senior Developmental Editor
Beth Kundert	Production Manager
Jane Mohr	Project Manager
Tara McDermott	Design Specialist
Nancy Meissner	Editorial Assistant
Julie Keck	Senior Marketing Manager
Mary Klein	Marketing Communications Specialist
Alice Link	Marketing Coordinator
Tracie Kammerude	Senior Marketing Assistant
Lori Church	Pemissions Coordinator

AUTHORS

FUAMBAI AHMADOU is an anthropologist at the London School of Economics and Political Science. Dr. Ahmadou studies male and female initiation rites in Africa and has published numerous book chapters on the subject.

JOEL BARKAN is a professor of political science at the University of Iowa and senior consultant on governance at the World Bank. His research interests include democratization, macro-economic reform in developing countries, and electoral processes.

THOMAS J. BASSETT is a professor of Geography and affiliate of the Center for African Studies at the University of Illinois, Urbana-Champaign. His research interests include Third World development, African agrarian systems, political ecology, and the history of cartography. He is the author of *The Peasant Cotton Revolution in West Africa: Côte d'Ivoire, 1880–1995* (Cambridge University Press, 2001) and co-editor (with D. Crummey) of *African Savannas: Global Narratives and Local Knowledge of Environmental Change in Africa* (James Curry and Heinemann, 2003), as well as the author of numerous journal articles and book chapters that have appeared in such outlets as the *Annals of the Association of American Geographers*, *Africa* and the *Review of African Political Economy*.

MICHAEL BRATTON is a professor of political science at Michigan State University. His research interests include comparative politics, public administration, and African politics. He is the author or co-author of *The Local Politics of Rural Development: Peasant and Party-State in Zambia* (University Press of New England, 1980), *Governance and Politics in Africa* (Lynne Rienner Press, 1992), and *Democratic Experiments in Africa: Regime Transitions in Comparative Perspective* (Cambridge University Press, 1997).

JUDITH CARNEY is a professor of geography at the University of California in Los Angeles. She is the author of numerous peer-reviewed articles that have appeared in such outlets as the *Journal of Ethnobiology*, *Progress in Human Geography*, and *Human Ecology*. Her book, *Black Rice: The African Origins of Rice Cultivation in the Americas* (Harvard University Press, 2001), won the African Studies Association's Herskovits Award in 2002.

KEVIN M. CLEAVER is director of Agriculture & Rural Development of the World Bank and heads the World Bank Board of Rural Sector Managers. His interests include environmental issues, agricultural policy and adjustment, forestry, and natural resource management. His publications include *A Strategy to Develop Agriculture in Sub-Saharan Africa and a Focus for the World Bank* (1993), *An Agricultural Growth and Rural Environment Strategy for the Coastal and Central African Francophone Countries* (1992), and *Conservation of West and Coastal African Rainforests* (1992).

MARCUS COLCHESTER is the director of the Forest Peoples Programme of the World Rainforest Movement. His primary work has involved securing the rights to land and livelihood of indigenous peoples. He has been a fellow in the Pew Fellows Program in Conservation and the Environment, an associate editor for *The Ecologist* magazine, and an honorary advisor on development in the Amazon to the Venezuelan government.

LIZ CREEL is a population specialist and senior policy analyst at the Population Reference Bureau.

SUNDAY DARE is a Nigerian journalist and a former Nieman Fellow at Harvard University. Dare's career has focused on investigative reporting of political corruption, military dictatorships, and human rights violations. He is a member of the Washington-based International Consortium of Investigative Journalists, an organization composed of leading investigative journalists from around the world.

TIM DOCKING is an African Affairs Specialist with the United States Institute of Peace. Docking is a political scientist who has provided congressional testimony. He also has published numerous book chapters and articles on peace and governance.

MARC EPPRECHT is an associate professor of history and development studies at Queen's University in Kingston, Ontario, Canada. His research focuses on the history of gender and sexuality in southern Africa. His books include *Hungochani: The History of a Dissident Sexuality in Southern Africa* (McGill-Queen's University Press, 2004) and *'This Matter of Women is Getting Very Bad': Gender, Development and Politics in Colonial Lesotho, 1870–1965* (University of Natal Press, 2000).

ARTHUR A. GOLDSMITH is professor of management at the University of Massachusetts Boston. He is the author of *Building Agricultural Institutions: Transferring the Land-Grant Model to India and Nigeria* (Westview, 1990).

ROBIN M. GRIER is an associate professor of economics and area coordinator for Latin American studies at the University of Oklahoma. She has published numerous articles in journals such as *Economic Inquiry* and *Public Choice*. Her areas of specialization include international finance, development, and Latin American economics.

BRIAN HALWEIL is a senior research associate at the Worldwatch Institute in Washington, D.C. where he has published extensively on food, agriculture, organic farming, and biotechnology. He has traveled in Mexico, Central America, the Caribbean, and Africa, learning indigenous farming techniques and promoting sustainable food production. He holds degrees in earth systems and biology from Stanford University. He also has completed research, fieldwork, and coursework at the College of Agricultural and Environmental Sciences at the University of California at Davis.

JULIE HEARN teaches in the Department of Politics and International Relations at Lancaster University. She has undertaken research in Uganda, Ghana, and South Africa on a collaborative DFID-funded research project, "Foreign Political Aid, Democratisation and Civil Society in Africa." She has published numerous articles in such outlets as the *Review of African Political Economy, Third World Quarterly,* and *Africa World Review.*

DUNCAN C. HEYWARD was a Carolina rice planter during the early twentieth century and also served as the governor of South Carolina for four years from 1903 to 1906.

JOHN L. HOUGH is the global environment facility coordinator for biodiversity and international waters for the United Nations Development Programme—Global Environment Facility, Africa Bureau. He has worked on African conservation projects and programs for more than twenty years.

HUMAN RIGHTS WATCH is a nonprofit organization supported by contributions from private individuals and foundations worldwide. The organization is the largest of its kind based in the United States. Human Rights Watch researchers conduct fact-finding investigations into human rights abuses in all regions of the world. They then publish these findings in dozens of books and reports every year. The aim is to generate extensive coverage in local and international media that will help to embarrass abusive governments in the eyes of their citizens and the world.

AKIN JIMOH is a Knight Science Journalism Fellow at the Massachusetts Institute of Technology and program director of Development Communications, a non-governmental organization (NGO) based in Lagos, Nigeria. He holds masters degrees in both medical physiology and public health, and has worked on development and HIV/AIDS issues for over ten years.

GAVIN KITCHING is a professor of political science at the University of New South Wales, Sydney, Australia. His research areas include post-communist agrarian reform in Russia, globalization and Third World development, and Wittgensteinian philosophy and social theory. He is author of the 1980 award-winning *Class and Economic Change in Kenya: The Making of an African Petite Bourgeoisie 1905–1970.*

EZEKIEL KALIPENI, originally from Malawi, is an associate professor of geography at the University of Illinois at Urbana-Champaign. His research interests include medical geography, population studies, environmental issues, and Africa. He is the co-editor of *AIDS, Health Care Systems and Culture in Sub-Saharan Africa: Rethinking and Re-appraisal* (Michigan State University Press, 1996). He has written numerous book chapters and published in such journals as *Geographical Review, African Rural and Urban Studies,* and the *Social Science and Medicine.*

ANIRUDH KRISHNA is an assistant professor of public policy studies and political science at Duke University. His research interests include democracy, community development, social capital, and poverty. His most recent book is *Active Social Capital: Tracing the Roots of Development and Democracy* (Columbia University Press, 2002).

BERNARD J. LECOMPTE is now retired and living in France. He is the co-founder of Six-S. He spent several years working for development agencies in West Africa.

DOROTHY LOGIE is a general practitioner and active member of Medact (a health professionals organization challenging barriers to health).

PAUL E. LOVEJOY is a distinguished research professor of history at York University in Toronto, Ontario, Canada. His research interests include the trans-Atlantic slave trade, diaspora studies, and slavery in Africa. He has published more than twenty books on these topics, including *Transformations in Slavery: A History of Slavery in Africa* (Cambridge University Press, 2000).

JESSE MACHUKA is a Kenyan scientist in the department of biochemistry and biotechnology at Kenyatta University. He also has worked for the International Institute of Tropical Agriculture in Nigeria. Dr. Machuka is molecular biologist who has published in numerous journals, including *Plant Physiology, Phytochemistry, The Journal of Agricultural and Food Chemistry, The Journal of Tropical Microbiology and Biotechnology,* and *Nature.*

OLIVER MAPONGA is the Economic Affairs Officer at the United Nations Economic Commission for Africa. His recent research interests have been in small-scale mining, mining investment regulations, regional mineral economics, and environmental management in the minerals industry.

ROBERT MATTES is an associate professor of political studies and director of the democracy in Africa Research Unit in the Centre for Social Science Research at the University of Cape Town. He is also co-founder and co-director of Afrobarometer (a survey of Africans' attitudes towards issues including democracy and markets) and an associate with the Institute for Democracy in South Africa. His research interests include the development of democracy/democratic political culture in Africa and the impact of race and identity on politics in South Africa. He is the author of *The Election Book: Judgment and Choice in the 1994 South African Election* (Idasa, 1996).

PHILIP MAXWELL is professor and head of the Department of Mineral Economics and Mine Management at the Western Australian School of Mines at Curtin University of Technology. His recent research interests include the regional economic impacts of mining and mineral commodity markets. He is the co-author of three textbooks and has authored or co-authored more than seventy articles, book chapters, discussion papers, or monographs.

THANDIKA MKANDAWIRE, originally from Malawi, is the director of the UN Research Institute for Social Development. From 1986 through 1996, he was executive secretary of the Council for the Development of Social Science Research in Africa (CODESRIA), headquartered in Dakar. He is an economist who has published extensively on structural adjustment, democratization, and social sciences in Africa.

GILES MOHAN is a lecturer in development studies at The Open University. He has published or co-published over ten articles in journals such as the *Review of African Political Economy* and *Political Geography*. He is a board member of Village Aid, a UK-based NGO working in West Africa, and serves on the editorial boards of the *Review of African Political Economy* and the *International Development Planning Review*.

MICHAEL MORTIMORE is a geographer who taught at Nigerian universities between 1962 and 1986, and subsequently was a research associate at Cambridge University and the Overseas Development Institute. He currently is with Drylands Research. He has performed research and published numerous books on the topic of environmental management by small holders in the dry lands of Africa. He is the author of *Roots in the African Dust: Sustaining the Dry Lands* (1998) and the co-author of *Working the Sahel: Environment & Society in Northern Nigeria* (1999) and *More People, Less Erosion: Environmental Recovery in Kenya* (1994).

JOHN MURTON is with the Foreign and Commonwealth Office of the British government, currently serving as first secretary of energy and environment at the British Embassy in Japan.

SIDDHARTHA MUKHERJEE is a senior resident in internal medicine at Massachusetts General Hospital and a clinical fellow in medicine at Harvard Medical School. He has written articles for *The New Republic* and has been a guest on WBUR, Boston's NPR affiliate.

RODERICK P. NEUMANN is an associate professor and director of graduate studies in the Department of International Relations at Florida International University. His interests include social theory, human-environment relations, African studies, and political ecology. His work has been published in *Antipode, Society and Space* and *Development and Change.* He is also the author of *Imposing Wilderness: Struggles over Livelihood and Nature Preservation in Africa* (1998).

WILLIAM D. NEWMARK is research curator at the Utah Museum of Natural History, University of Utah. He is involved in conservation projects in East Africa, and his research has appeared in *Science, Nature, The New York Times,* and *The Washington Post.* His research focuses on the patterns of extinction of vertebrate species, conservation, and development.

JOSEPH R. OPPONG, originally from Ghana, is an associate professor of geography at The University of North Texas. His research interests include medical geography, development, and Africa. He is the co-editor of *AIDS, Health Care Systems and Culture in Sub-Saharan Africa: Rethinking and Re-appraisal* (Michigan State University Press, 1996). He has written several book chapters and published in numerous journals including *The Professional Geographer, African Rural and Urban Studies,* and *Social Science and Medicine.*

WILLIAM RENO is an associate professor of political science at Northwestern University. He specializes in African politics and the politics of failing states. He is the author of *Warlord Politics and African States* (Lynne Renner Publishers, 1998).

ROBERT I. ROTBERG is director of the Program on Intrastate Conflict and Conflict Resolution at Harvard University's John F. Kennedy School of Government. He is also president of the World Peace Foundation, and has taught political science and history at both Harvard and the Massachusetts Institute of Technology. His research focuses on political and economic issues of developing countries, especially Africa and Southeast Asia. He has authored *The Founder: Cecil Rhodes and the Pursuit of Power* (Oxford University Press, 1988) and *The Rise of Nationalism in Central Africa* (Harvard University Press, 1965).

MICHAEL ROWSON is the assistant director of Medact (a health professionals organization challenging barriers to health) and co-author of *Do No Harm: Assessing the Impact of Adjustment Policies on Health* (2002).

WILLIAM A. RUSHING was a professor of sociology at Vanderbilt University before his death in 2001. He published numerous articles in major journals and authored or edited eight books.

GÖTZ A. SCHREIBER was the principal economist in the World Bank's West Central Africa Department. More recently he has worked on Central Asian issues for the World Bank. His areas of interest include macroeconomic policy, human resources, agricultural and rural development, and natural resource management.

RICHARD A. SCHROEDER is an associate professor of geography, and former chair of African studies, at Rutgers University. He is the author of *Shady Practices: Agroforestry and Gender Politics in the Gambia* (1999) and *Producing Nature and Poverty in Africa* (co-editor) (2000). He has published numerous articles in outlets such as the *Annals of the Association of American Geographers*, *Economic Geography* and *Africa*.

GERALD E. SCOTT is an associate professor of economics at Florida Atlantic University. His research interests include debt, development, and structural adjustment in sub-Saharan Africa. He has published articles in journals such as the *Atlantic Economic Journal* and *American Economist*.

ROBERT SNYDER is an associate professor of biology at Greenville College. He has worked with environmental programs in Illinois, consulted for the Environmental Protection Agency, and spent six years in Rwanda engaged in agricultural development related to natural resources. His research interests include food production, sustainable resource use, and international development

MARY TIFFEN is a historian and socioeconomist at Drylands Research. She is interested in long-term change and development, interdisciplinary research, and social and economic interactions with technology. She authored *The Environmental Impact of the 1991-92 Drought on Zambia: Report* (1994) and *The Enterprising Peasant: Economic Development in Gombe Emirate, North East Nigeria* (1976). She co-authored *More People, Less Erosion: Environmental Recovery in Kenya* (1994).

JOHN THORNTON is a professor of history at Boston University. His research and teaching have focused on Africa and the Middle East. His books include: *The Kingdom of Kongo: Civil War and Transition, 1641-1718* (University of Wisconsin Press, 1983); *Africa and Africans in the Formation of the Atlantic World, 1400-1680* (Cambridge University Press, 1992, second expanded edition, 1998); and *The Kongolese Saint Anthony, Dona Beatriz Kimpa Vita and the Antonian Movement, 1684-1706* (Cambridge University Press, 1998).

KOLI B. ZUELI is an associate professor at the Institute of Tropical Geography, University of Cocody in Abidjan, Ivory Coast. His interests include West Africa, development, the environment, and cultural and political ecology.

Index

DATE DUE
